REX APPEAL

REX APPEAL

The Amazing Story of Sue,
the Dinosaur That Changed
Science, the Law, and My Life

PETER LARSON

KRISTIN DONNAN

INVISIBLE CITIES PRESS
MONTPELIER, VERMONT

Invisible Cities Press
50 State Street
Montpelier, VT 05602
www.invisiblecitiespress.com

Library of Congress Cataloging-in-Publication Data

Larson, Peter L.
Rex appeal : the amazing story of Sue, the dinosaur that
changed science, the law, and my life /
by Peter Larson, Kristin Donnan.
p. cm.
Includes bibliographical references and index.
ISBN 1-931229-07-4 (cloth : alk. paper)
1. *Tyrannosaurus rex*—South Dakota. 2. Larson, Peter L. 3. Paleontologists—United
States—Biography. 4. Paleontology—United States—History—20th century.
I. Donnan, Kristin. II. Title.

QE862.S3 L39 2002
560'.92—dc21
[B]
2002024207

Book design by Peter Holm, Sterling Hill Productions

FIRST EDITION

for

JUNE ZEITNER

*who generously shares her love
of fossils and of life*

CONTENTS

FOREWORD

The most famous, most successful animals ever to live on the surface of the earth are the dinosaurs, and the most famous of all dinosaurs is *Tyrannosaurus rex*. And the most successful of all the people who have hunted *T. rex* are Peter Larson and his crew from the Black Hills Institute of South Dakota. *Rex Appeal* takes you inside this small band of fossil sleuths who have crossed over into Deep Time to catch glimpses of the mighty Tyrant Lizard and her family.

In the fall of 1999 I was honored to be one of the guests invited to the Smithsonian Institution to celebrate the opening of its new *Triceratops* exhibit, a remounting of the skeleton of the huge three-horned veggi-saurus who confronted *T. rex* on the tropical lowlands that spread over what is now the Dakotas and Wyoming. The Smithsonian event marked a new age of dino-studies. Computerized manipulation of three-dimensional X-rays, plus laser scans of bone surfaces, let the researchers see every skeletal component as it existed in the living animal, swiveling and flexing at each joint. Bones that had been damaged and distorted could be "healed" inside the computer and then sculpted by rapid-prototype machines to produce a perfect reconstruction. The Smithsonian team resurrected a marching *Triceratops* not seen for 67 million years. Computer animation showed us how the great elbows and hips hurled the five-ton body forward. We all had a sense of what a *Tyrannosaurus rex* faced when an angry three-horn charged.

Only a half-dozen paleontologists were guests. The leader of Canadian dinosaur studies, Phil Currie, was there, as well as representatives from new and vigorous museums in Utah. I represented Wyoming, the state from which the original *Triceratops*

fossils came. All of us there—guests and Smithsonian staff—
were delighted to see Pete Larson among the special invitees.
Triceratops can't be studied without *T. rex*—they're the ultimate
dino pair, predator and prey, who shaped each other through
coevolution. And no one knows *rex*es better than Pete; we needed
his expertise.

There was also a sense that honoring the contributions of Pete
and his coworkers at the Black Hills Institute was long overdue.
His successes have been achieved at great personal cost that would
have discouraged a lesser man.

Why did he bother to do it? Why didn't his talented crew just
give up and go into a more lucrative field where the politics
seemed less vicious and the jealousy less hostile? As he mentions
in this book, Pete could have been a highly paid scientist in the
energy business. There's a simple explanation: Peter Larson has
heard the call to explore the past. When he was a kid, he and his
brother knew that *Tyrannosaurus* and *Triceratops* were out there,
alive in the ancient world. To see the dinosaurs, they had to make
a journey—not across thousands of miles, but across an ocean of
time. Becoming a dinosaur hunter is a lot like responding to join
a religious order. The decision is not only intellectual; it goes
deeper.

This book is, among many exciting things, a manual for time-
travel. Journalists often ask us bone diggers, "Wouldn't you love
to have someone give you a machine that would take you back to
the Late Cretaceous, so you could see a living, breathing *T. rex*?"
I always answer, "No thanks—we already have one." Everyone
has a built-in time machine. It's between our ears. It's our scientific imagination. When Pete's crew digs fossilized carapaces of
soft-shelled turtles and tiny jaws of eel-like salamanders, the
sound of sluggish Cretaceous streams is heard. Lowly reptiles and
amphibians record the temperature of ancient waters and the
speed of rivers. The very grains of the rock map out the geographic pattern of water flow and where the mountains were
when *T. rex*es attacked *Triceratops*. If you know how to listen to
the sediments and to the fossils, they'll play back to you the
parameters of habitat and landscape.

The *Tyrannosaurus* bones themselves tell multiple stories. Almost every adult skeleton displays its personal history of combat. Ribs have been broken and healed, leg bones have been scarred by infection, and sections of backbone have grown together because of compression injuries. The evidence is eloquent and compelling: Life was hard at the top of the Cretaceous food chain.

The Black Hills Institute pioneered the use of veterinary medicine to study *T. rex*, and when they began their analyses hardly anyone talked about *T. rex* bone pathologies. Now everybody does. Thanks to discoveries by the Black Hills Institute, we can begin to understand the exquisite machine that is the *T. rex* head. Pete's finest *rex* skull wasn't Sue's; it belongs to the male specimen dubbed Stan. As I write these words, each bone of Stan's skull is being laser scanned to create a digital *rex* head, a perfect cranium and jaws inside the computer. We'll be able to make the jaw muscles contract and the teeth chomp. And we'll be able to demonstrate the truth of one of Pete's theories—that *T. rex* had a double-jointed face that could swallow chunks of meat wider than its head (I was wrong about this hypothesis; Pete was right).

Everybody who's into meat-eating dinosaurs right now talks about sex. When my crew at Como Bluff dug the tail from a big brontosaur, they asked, "Boy or girl? What does the chevron say?" A chevron is a spike of bone that sticks down from the tail. Pete's researches into the rump of *rex*es led him to discover a sex-linked difference in chevrons. If you find the first chevrons right behind the hips, you should be able to decipher gender roles. Was the female *rex* bigger than the male, a disparity that holds true for eagles and hawks? Was *T. rex* more like a giant lizard or a twelve-thousand-pound roadrunner? Read on and find out.

Long before I met the Black Hills crew in person, some of my older friends called them "Latter Day Sternbergs." The Sternberg family of Kansas are three generations of independent fossil hunters who were held to be saints by my professors at Yale in the 1960s. The Sternbergs eschewed the cap-and-gown trappings of university training and instead learned to find and dig dinosaurs the only way it can be done—by going out to the badlands and doing it. For ninety years, beginning in the 1870s, the Sternbergs extricated lovely skeletons that filled the exhibit halls and research labs of museums all over the world. Their reward: paltry fees, but immense and vocal thanks from scientists and museum visitors.

The Black Hills crew followed the hallowed Sternberg path, supporting their researches by sale of specimens—the most important bones going to public museums. Pete and his coworkers proved to have unusual scientific generosity, always ready to contribute their hard-won specimens to joint projects, and my old professors at Yale and senior scientists at the Smithsonian worked closely with institute people. But there was another element in the community of fossil scholars, a generation of Ph.D.s who had a caste mentality, a belief that only university scholars were entitled to dig precious fossils. I heard rumors and gossip long before I actually met the Black Hills folks, innuendos that they were "poachers and market-hunters." I went out of my way to check the stories out, sitting in on some of the court sessions about Sue. What I saw and heard was shocking and depressing. Professors I knew well made sworn statements that were totally untrue. And yet this campaign of slander was carried out under the pious banner of "Save Our Fossils From Rustlers."

Those terrible days are over now, thank God. But Pete did go through an ordeal that should have driven him and the institute out of the *T. rex* business. He should have dumped his childhood dreams of a *T. rex* museum and gone into a more mainstream vocation. I'm very glad he didn't. The Black Hills Institute has rebounded and is more vibrant and productive than before; beautifully accurate cast replicas of Stan grace exhibit halls over the globe—including the Smithsonian. We are learning *rex* facts faster than ever, thanks to Stan and his kid brother, Bucky, a teenage *rex* being cleaned of his encrusting rock at the moment. All dinosaur science is getting better. The technical methods invented by institute personnel are recognized as the standard for bone labs everywhere. My own crew in Wyoming owes a lot of its success in digging Jurassic monsters to the tricks we've learned watching the institute excavate the Cretaceous maxi-fauna.

Read this book if you love adventure and tales of exploration.

You'll hear the call from the Deep Past, the rumblings from multi-ton beasts who ruled the Golden Age of Dinosaur Giants. You'll look over the shoulder of the world's best, most experienced tyrannosaur hunters, and your scientific imagination will grow powerful.

ROBERT T. BAKKER, Ph.D.
Curator, Wyoming Dinosaur International Society

AUTHORS' NOTE

The Scientist

We never really arrive at the Absolute Truth in science. We may come to a consensus on a subject for a while, but that consensus is always in danger of being overturned by some piece of extraordinary new evidence. For example, for a long time everyone "knew" the sun—indeed, the entire universe—revolved around Earth. Whoops. Now most people think Earth simply orbits the sun—but that's not the whole truth, either. It's more like a solar system of figure skaters spinning around their common center of mass.

In paleontology, we spend a good deal of time arguing over bones. Is this a wishbone or a gastralia fragment? Is this scar where the triceps humeralis or the teres major attached? Does this perfectly preserved front *Triceratops* leg prove the animal walked like a lizard or like a rhino? It's hard to believe, but after a hundred years we're still arguing over which way *Tyrannosaurus rex*'s dewclaw pointed; forget about a consensus on extinct dinosaur behavior. The more elusive the debated habit or characteristic, the more fun and protracted the arguments. At a recent dinosaur-bird conference, people were screaming, pounding the table, and calling each other names. I loved it.

I've been accused of making hypotheses, climbing out on limbs, arriving at conclusions too quickly. I've been told there will never be enough specimens to prove some of my theories. That doesn't stop me, because coming up with new theories and then testing them is one of the things that makes science such fun. In this book, some of the scientific material has been agreed upon by many scientists, some is still under discussion, some is highly debated, and some is an expression solely of my own ideas. To sort this all out,

I began writing a book in 1990, soon after I became acquainted with Sue. Even with my long history in paleontology, my largest girlfriend introduced me to a herd of animals the likes of which I had never before encountered. She and her ilk showed me evidence of family life, accidents, and titanic fights to the death. Don't worry. Throughout my gathering of all this material, not only did Sue bring her fallen comrades to our paleo-shelter for convalescence, but also I remained a stalwart extinct animal rights activist. No *T. rex* was harmed in the preparation of this manuscript.

PETER LARSON

The Writer

We never really arrive at the Absolute Truth in human nature, either. There are *at least* two sides to every story, and tricky time bombs like intentions, opinions, and impressions add confusion to the facts. This book takes Peter's science and positions it in a most unlikely spot: next to politics, the law, and history.

As a paleontologist who simply wanted to play in the dirt, Peter instead found himself embroiled in a monumental legal case much more complex—and scary—than a pile of *T. rex* bones. Imagine yourself waking up one day to FBI seizures, accusations of conspiracy, on the brink of losing everything you've ever worked for—all the while fighting to save authentic, irreplaceable treasures.

This tale caught my attention because I'd dug at Peter's duck-bill quarry and met Sue while she was being prepared. When she became big news, I was working at NBC's *Unsolved Mysteries,* and someone on the institute staff thought I might have an "in" at the newsroom of South Dakota native Tom Brokaw. I checked out the story. I got hooked. Before I knew it, I had quit my job, headed back to my hometown of Hill City, and began writing a book. That was 1993.

I read books on paleontology and Indian law, pumped lawyers for explanations, visited scientific meetings and museums, listened to perspectives from all sides of the story. I learned more about dinosaurs than I ever wanted to, measuring, recording, photographing, mapping, digging, organizing details streaming in from distant corners of the world. I followed Phil Currie around Alberta's

Dinosaur Provincial Park; I tagged after Bob Bakker at Como Bluff; I stood in Ulan Bataar's natural history museum, Tokyo's exhibitions, Italy, Germany, Los Angeles, New York, Washington, Chicago, and more desolate excavation sites than I can count.

I complicated my journalistic job by falling in love with my subject and marrying him, a man who held on tight as he was dragged through devastation. I became adept at pocketing my personal life and listening to the opinions of those who did not agree with Peter. Even when it hurt, I did my job the best I could. As the adventure wore on, after I'd found a workable coexistence between living and reporting, our personal relationship changed again. My final challenge, nine years after I began, was merging what I had written with the science of my by-then ex-husband.

True to form, we never signed a contract allowing me to write about Peter. The result of a handshake, while dodging pieces of falling sky, this book represents the evolution of our intentions.

KRISTIN DONNAN

The Story

Lewis Carroll wrote this story in 1864. It may have been before any of us was born—except for the dinosaurs, of course—but we recognized ourselves, and have let his words help us tell our story. Peter Larson fell down a hole, tumbling, screeching, playing absurd games, and going on trial amid a collection of animals that could exist only in someone's imagination. Kristin Donnan dove in after him, hauling her notebook through tiny doors and wild forests, writing everything down.

Once we landed, we struck out on our own paths, treading lightly through Wonderland. What we didn't realize until our trails kept crossing was that our goals were entangled. We actually had the same story to tell; we decided that two heads *are* better than one.

Our main character is Peter, who led a troop of *T. rex*es through his life at the same time his legal world came crashing down. The book is in his voice. As the text proceeds, it tells the tale of his important *T. rex* finds and resulting legal battles, all of which changed the world of paleontology forever. Interspersed with the main story thread you'll find three types of boxes: "Rex Files" expand on scientific or technical information of particular importance, "Lex Files" provide glimpses into the legal labyrinth that took us years to navigate, and "Ex Files" come straight from Kristin, providing her perspective on what it was like to be a reporter who got yanked into her subject and never quite came back out.

A truly collaborative effort, this book could not have evolved without both halves, both authors. It is filled with fact and recollection, opinion and conjecture. It reflects the flow of life and the method of science. It is our best account of what happened, a record of Pete's relationship with *Tyrannosaurus rex*—and *Homo sapiens*.

The White Rabbit put on his spectacles. "Where shall I begin, please your Majesty?" he asked.

"Begin at the beginning," the King said gravely, "and go on till you come to the end: then stop." [1]

Once upon a time, a paleontologist was busy poking at bones when politics began poking at paleontology . . .

Kristin and Peter at a dig. Photo by Marcia Mitchell.

REX APPEAL

Prologue

The male put his nose in the air. His keen sense of smell picked up a faint scent from across the river. His huge eyes surveyed the dense forest, watching for movement among the lush blend of ginkgo and sequoia trees.

Suddenly they were upon him.

One grabbed him from behind with huge jaws that closed upon his throat—cutting off a horrible scream before he could alert the others. A second set of vicelike jaws snapped one of his lower legs with a loud crack.

Nearby, that sound jerked the dozing, towering matriarch to her feet, where she stood frozen in midstride. Through her scarred eye, she gauged the battle scene, the latest in a lifetime of them. Her mate lay dying. She could smell that. She counted four of them, two with blood dripping from their gaping jaws. Two mating pairs, younger than she, smaller, each individual weighing only around six tons. The queen considered her strategy and released an ear-splitting roar that would have frightened to death any single attacker.

She had lived more than a hundred years, had won—or at least survived—countless of these face-offs. But today she was outnumbered.

One went for her throat. Two charged her flank, hitting her with 24,000 pounds of force. Thrown off balance, she fell on her right side. Into the river. Water flooded her senses, and she violently thrust her face out of the flow, thrashing with powerful legs against slippery mud and soaked, battered fern leaves. No foothold. She roared again, this time to the frightened young. Run! Run!

The largest female of the attackers went for the queen's throat but caught instead her shuddering left jaw. She felt the stab of six-inch teeth as they pierced her thick hide and tore flesh and bone away. The last thing she saw was the baby, swept into midair by one of the males, then unceremoniously beheaded. As her face sunk under water, she still had hope for her older child.

She would not see the teenager as he bolted for freedom. As two adult legs easily outran him. As the fatal bite was delivered to the back of his neck.

She had been deposed, the victim of a coup common to her species. Her reign was over.

(1)

A Dinosaur Named Sue

> Alice started to her feet, for it flashed across her mind that
> she had never before seen a rabbit with either a waistcoat-
> pocket, or a watch to take out of it, and burning with curiosity,
> she ran across the field after it, and fortunately was just in time
> to see it pop down a large rabbit-hole under the hedge.[1]

urassic Park is a lie. It tells us that paleontologists live in well-
equipped motor homes that circle a perfectly articulated, 100
percent complete fossil. Flat and sandy sediment *blows* away
with a quick puff by an eager actor with shiny hair and a bright
smile. Then the pretend scientists use their state-of-the-art imaging
devices and high-tech gadgets to ascertain something new and
incredible about the fossil in the ground. Maybe it spoke
Babylonian, or possibly its unusual front limb joints will reveal
that it could pat its head and rub its belly at the same time.

For those of us who have spent a lifetime in the field, we know
a different art, a different science, altogether. And a different life.
Most of all it demands a commitment of time, of hours and days
of walking, climbing, and jumping—along the prairie, up and
down unforgiving exposures, and across gaping crevasses. If a
fossil is discovered, more than a puff of breath is needed to expose
it; sometimes it takes jackhammers and earthmovers and even
dynamite. Ours is a life of sturdy boots, knees caked with dirt,
nostrils dense with dust. Our hair is rarely shiny. Our tool belts
are stocked with brushes and X-acto knives and picks. For days
and weeks and months we live in tents and sheep wagons, pep-
pered with mosquitoes, black flies, and ravenous no-see-ums. I've

Less glamorous than a movie set, "Rexburg" might remain for months at a time in the Hell Creek badlands, where dedicated diggers battle wind, rain, hail, tornadoes, snow. Photo by Peter Larson.

found that in order to work in the past, to transcend the discomfort, you have to love it.

The fossils to which we surrender our lives are never perfect, are always broken, and rely on our care and feeding to teach us what they know. Like the mysteries of a black hole, sometimes what a fossil has to say is in code, difficult to nail down, a work in progress for our minds. However, unlike a black hole, a fossil is tangible. Hard evidence. Just waiting. Paleontology may not be a walk in the park, but the dinosaurs themselves can be quite friendly. If you overlook their sharp teeth, they are happy to whisper their secrets to anyone with a strong back, enthusiasm, good shoes, a long attention span, and a wild imagination. Anyone—a young child, a rocket scientist, an average Joe— anyone can get to know a fossil.

Hell Creek sounds like an exclamation or a white-water rafting spot, but it's a particularly mean stretch of rock that was deposited at the end of the age of dinosaurs. A layer sandwiched between the Fox Hills and Fort Union Formations, the Hell Creek Formation is *T. rex* country. *Tyrannosaurus rex* has been found in other equivalently aged deposits with names like Lance and Scollard and Willow Creek, but all the *T. rex*es I've had a hand in collecting came from harsh Hell Creek sediments, where 65 million years ago, in what is now South Dakota, Earth's undertaker was moving slowly. Most dead things were eaten or scavenged thoroughly—or the weather scattered them around—before the picked apart and dispersed skeletons were finally buried. We see evidence of this when we dig up fossils, as most specimens are incomplete and broken to bits. Usually their bones long ago fell away from one another, becoming what paleontologists call "disarticulated."

At the end of the 1990 collecting season, we felt as disarticulated as the *Triceratops* skull my son Matthew had just found. The prairie grass had dried to a crisp wheat color, all the moisture sucked out of it by the burning sun and relentless wind. At that time none of us had even seen a *T. rex* in the ground, or sifted through the evidence left at the scene of one of their ancient battles to the death. We had been out all summer, our annual stint at the duckbill dinosaur quarry was complete, and a few miscellaneous excavations were nearing their end. Almost all the staff had hauled home their own tired skeletons and loads of plaster-covered bones; the visiting scientists had left with their data; the volunteers had

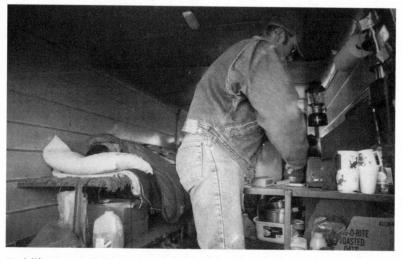

Real life at camp inside a converted delivery truck—kitchen, bunkhouse, and rain hut. Photo by Peter Larson.

Matthew Larson, right, and Susan Hendrickson work on the *Triceratops* Matthew discovered. Photo by Peter Larson.

packed their memories and cameras and gone back to their own formations.

All except Susan Hendrickson. For several years a regular visitor during our summer sessions, Susan had put in her time. She made her living from the earth and its residents, and she was always willing to learn something new, whether it was salvage diving for sunken treasure ships, studying Dominican fossil amber, or, here, digging dinosaurs. This year she stayed after we closed the duckbill quarry for the season in order to scout some pristine neighboring territory with us. She had never found any particularly significant fossils before, but she was game for the hunt.

It didn't look like a day that would change our lives. We were down to our last trickle of energy and our last specimen from the neighbor's ranch. The juvenile *Triceratops* skull was scientifically significant because of its youth, and poetically significant because its discoverer was only ten years old. Already the most instinctive field collector I had ever seen in action, Matthew had challenged Susan to a *T. rex* tooth "duel." He held the world record for *T. rex* tooth discoveries, and he held it over her head. (Because *T. rex* teeth were shed regularly, they are often found by themselves.) This *Triceratops* skull was the latest in his string of finds, and it was a good representative of the three-horned monster. Adults probably weighed up to five tons[2] and possessed the heaviest skulls of any land animal before or since—skulls so massive that they apparently were preserved even when the rest of the animal was eaten and scattered.

It was August 12, 1990, and we were past the chain-gang pick-swinging part of every excavation, where a section of hillside is removed above the bone layer. We had just completed tedious and joint-numbing X-acto-blade detail and had finally sat back on our haunches, brushing the dirt from faces recently pushed into rocky earth. Terry Wentz, our chief preparator and one of the most gifted and careful excavators alive, was on autopilot. We were both elbow-deep in plaster of paris, working on part of the frill and one horn of the *Triceratops* skull. Matthew and his sixteen-year-old cousin, Jason, were carefully preparing other bones for casting. Susan was out scouting. It was just a typical day in the middle of nowhere in the noonday sun, after a lunch of warm soda pop and stale chips.

Suddenly I looked up in the one-hundred-degree heat to see Susan, reappeared from the shimmering distance and stopped in front of us, a curious half-smile on her face. She opened her hand to expose two fragments of fossil bone, each not much larger than a matchbook.

My first clue— the diagnostic honeycombed "camellate" structure that told me Susan had discovered a *T. rex*.
Photo by Peter Larson.

I could not speak. I couldn't believe my eyes, and I couldn't trust my voice. I could do nothing but look at them, cradled in her palm.

Finally I picked them up.

They were portions of a larger bone, and each had a curved external surface on one side. The other surfaces looked like a honeycomb, with quarter-inch compartments—obviously from the bone's interior. The fragments were light and hollow. I had never seen the inside of a *T. rex* vertebra, but I knew instantly that was what I was seeing. The honeycomb texture is called camellate structure, and it occurs in the vertebrae of both birds and theropods—the group of dinosaurs that ate meat. The external curve of the bone indicated vertebrae too large to be from anything but *Tyrannosaurus rex,* the king of the Cretaceous, the baddest beast that ever walked the earth.

I wanted to transport myself immediately to the spot from which Susan had come and *be there,* to blink my eyes and open them at the magical place on the planet where the rest of these bones waited. *"Where?"* I finally whispered. "Where did you get these?"

"There's more. Come on, it's only about two miles away."

I grabbed my camera.

My fatigue only a vague memory, we ran. Every step of the way.

Finally we came to a flat-topped cliff rising to the left. What I saw was impossible. The earth went up fifty-five feet, but my eyes were on my worn boots. Surrounding my toes were thousands of pieces of bone, in all sizes, from tiny, quarter-inch chips to six-inch chunks. In rust-colored profusion, pieces of vertebrae and ribs and unidentified fragments coated the ground in front of the cliff. My eyes then instinctively raised to higher ground, following the trail of bones to the cliff base, then up farther, to the source of those fragments.

Impossible.

About seven feet above the base of the cliff, bony cross-sections — of not one bone, but at least a dozen—protruded from the ancient sandy sediment. This first view told me everything. At one time this fossil had been buried a thousand feet below the surface. Atop the cliff of Cretaceous rock I saw before me, there once was at least another two hundred feet of Hell Creek Formation, and probably an additional seven hundred and fifty feet of early Cenozoic-age sediment, all of which was deposited over this plain and then washed away by millions of years of erosion. The weight of this sediment would have caused the fossil to break; tiny fractures were sure to have appeared in nearly every bone as the years brought the beast closer to the surface and the pressure of the entombing sediment was relieved. Eventually, the insulating escarpment was weathered back to the point where every drop of rain, every gust of wind, every freezing and expanding bit of ground moisture tore the bones apart. As they finally reached the surface, their fractures became larger until pieces fell off, thousands of them, and tumbled down the last seven feet of the wall.

I carefully avoided treading on the fragments as I crawled up the face of the cliff to get a better look. I could see that a small shelf had developed at the top of the bone horizon, indicating that the bones were harder than the surrounding sandy sediment. On top of this shelf, I saw, among other bones, three vertebrae, *articulated—still connected—in their original relative positions!*

Although these bones tantalizingly disappeared into the hillside, there was no guarantee that the rest of the backbone, or an entire

Three of Sue's articulated, dumbbell-shaped vertebrae. The two vertical slots once held cartilage discs. Photo by Susan Hendrickson.

animal, would be attached to them. In the Hell Creek Formation, finding even a few articulated dinosaur bones is unusual, an articulated dinosaur rare indeed, and an articulated *T. rex?* Never. For no logical reason, however, *I knew* the rest of the dinosaur—all of it—remained buried just beyond where I crouched. These joined body vertebrae told me that history would be made in this place. From this moment, I *knew* this would be The Find of Our Lifetimes. This *T. rex* had been safely tucked away for sixty-five million years, waiting patiently. Waiting until Susan stopped by.

In a choked voice I told Susan what I believed she had found.

"It's yours," she said, grinning. As one of our team, she lay no personal claim to the specimen. Black Hills Institute financed the digs, and any finds went to the institute. We both paused, drinking in this most precious moment, a "megafind moment" all scientists live for. I was afraid I'd suddenly wake up and find this cliff had vanished. So I put my hands on the bones and leaned against the tangible mountain that held them. I wanted to see more, to look through the ground to see what it held. I wanted to dig a little and identify a large bone I could see in an erosional cut. My eyes moved systematically across what I could see, my mind racing. I bent closer. *Are all of these rib-looking bones actually ribs? This one looks different—could it be from the hand? Do the articulated vertebrae continue to be articulated? No evidence of the skull, either in the bones protruding from the wall, or in the thousands of fragments on the ground. Good sign.* There were plenty of scientific indications pointing to the *chance* for the skull to be sheltered intact underground, but, again, there was no guarantee.

I remembered I was not alone. I wiped my forehead and grinned back at Susan. "Thanks," I said. "I'm naming it after you. I'm calling it Sue."

During our walk away from Sue's grave and back to Matthew's *Triceratops,* I had already decided what to do, and I told Susan all about it. The challenges of the sudden excavation before us—like exhaustion, the lateness in the season, and low finances—evaporated in the face of the possibility of having a *T. rex* as the centerpiece of our not-for-profit museum. I was thinking big, and I would not take "wait" for an answer.

I have been called an absentminded professor, a single-minded enthusiast—and, in less flattering terms, stubborn. It's all true. My single-mindedness during graduate school resulted in the creation of a new breed of fossil and mineral company, the first to fill an empty niche in the scientific and museum community. My stubbornness insisted on out-on-a-limb business ventures—like taking the risk to add dinosaurs to our fossil inventory when we were struggling to make ends meet. My absentmindedness has sometimes rendered me blind to others and has resulted in ridiculous squabbles with my equally headstrong brother and business partner, Neal. We both love being right, and tenaciously push for what we believe in. This has its good side, too. We mow down obstacles, work extra hours, and give up almost everything in the frenzy of realizing a concept. And right then, the only concept in my head was getting that dinosaur out of the ground.

Walking back to camp with Susan, I remembered that the Day That Changed My Life had not begun quite normally after all. That morning, we'd awakened to an unusual prairie ground fog. South Dakota is not San Francisco or the Scottish moors. This is not a place where the mist drips from your billed cap in the morning, where the afternoon sun is tempered by a sea breeze. Here, the baking, shimmering heat of the day is forecast early, and if a fluffy cloud passes overhead it barely makes a shadow. But when we rolled out of our sleeping bags, it was so foggy we could not see the duckbill bonebed from our tents. In all my years working these deposits, I had never seen anything exactly like it.

Susan's fate for the day was set while I ate my breakfast, a peanut butter and mayonnaise sandwich. I noticed that the right front tire of our faithful 1975 Chevrolet Suburban—the only vehicle remaining in camp after the mass exodus of staff—was nearly flat. About an inch of soft rubber suspended the rim above the prairie floor. I pulled out the spare—a *really* flat tire with no pressure whatsoever. Unbelievably, the pump underneath had a severed air line.

Faith, South Dakota, is only about eighteen miles away, but rough tracks leading into graveled county roads make the trip about forty-five minutes—an uncomfortable forty-five minutes for most quarry workers, who usually drew straws for necessary trips to town. However, after three straight months of uncompromising labor, our pared-down crew was enthusiastic for any semblance of civilization. Everyone except Susan opted to brave the trip to Faith before what little remaining air escaped from the tire. Susan instead gathered some gear and set her sites on a closer objective. A couple of miles away, an outcrop had been nagging at her for weeks. Although that morning it was completely obscured, this would be her only chance to scout out whatever might be hiding there.

A "walk" for a fossil enthusiast is never a stroll or a bird-watching excursion, or even an opportunity to clear one's mind—although all of those might occur. A walk is a melding of geology and gut instinct. It is a search for fossils—even when exhausted, with blistered and cut hands, with bunions on our feet, with sunburn, pulled muscles, holes in our socks, mosquitoes in our ears. Or fog. That fog lends some mysticism to the discovery of Sue. Susan told me that she actually walked in a complete circle—back to camp—before she found her way north across the Moreau River, to Maurice Williams's ranch. Finding Sue would launch Susan into the stratosphere in the minds of paleontology fans around the world. Here she was, an amateur enthusiast, and she had found the fossil jackpot of the century. Popular mythology about the discovery would describe Susan as someone who never lost her way, who leaped from continent to continent with ease, who jumped into sailing ships and propeller planes and battered Jeeps to each crevice of the world—and who walked through the mists to find her namesake.

By nightfall, we all had driven back into town, made obligatory phone calls, and eaten a celebratory dinner. I had adjusted my previously exhausted internal clock and geared myself to tack an addendum onto our already extended excavation season. Most museums would dedicate an entire summer, or even two, to the excavation we were about to attempt to pull off at the end of a season. My mind swam as I tried to anticipate every possibility involved in laying hands on one of the most incredible pieces of history ever unearthed.

What I didn't anticipate—what I could not possibly have imagined—was what actually happened. On one hand, happily, my hunch would prove correct: Sue would end up as the largest, most complete *T. rex* ever found. Preserved in that hillside was nearly all of an animal that stretched as long as three pickup trucks and could have looked in a second-story window. Her skull was in fabulous condition, and at one time could have swallowed my kids as if they were multivitamins. *T. rex* royalty, she took her place as the latest and most majestic scientific media darling. She increased the data bank compiled on her species astronomically. She breathed even more life into the public's dinosaur love affair. She jump-started our company and our scientific agendas, and she launched a successful family venture into the spotlight.

On the other hand, Sue's unparalleled magnificence caught the attention of people with dollar signs in their eyes, and a few challenges and ugly innuendoes floated around—par for the course in the grand slam of paleontology. Most unnerving, though, Sue also caught the attention of government investigators. Many observers likened the next chapter in Sue's saga with horror stories of government investigations gone out of control. During ensuing FBI seizures, years of subpoenas, indictments, the longest trial in South Dakota history, and a prison sentence, a couple of characteristics kept Neal and me alive. Our sense of fair play. Our tenacity. We both believed a friendly discussion could have solved the whole mess before it had started, but once it got too late for that, we were not about to give in.

Beware the Jabberwock, my son!
The jaws that bite, the claws that catch.[3]

I would do it again. I would do it better, and more carefully, but I would reach out my hand to Sue through eternity, even if I knew it meant tumbling down Alice's rabbit hole into Hell. Sue enriched my life. She taught me more about the scientific process than I'd ever before experienced firsthand. She led me into a new specialty area in paleontology. My family's naive enthusiasm coupled with our stubbornness may have prevented us from charming those FBI agents into seeing our side of things, or convincing the U.S. attorney that we were the good guys. Instead, they would call us liars and "bumpkins," thieves of time—and we would fight back. We would not do it alone. With a lot of help, we clamped crampons onto our boots and climbed out of the rabbit hole—back into the right-side-up world.

Sue took us on a wild ride, but honestly, who could ask for a better tour guide? We walked with the Queen of the Tyrant Lizards.

(2)

Past Finders and Three-Piece Suits

Sputnik changed my life. Not in the general sense of expanding all Earth-dwellers' horizons into space. Not even in the sense that it thrust me into becoming a scientist. *Sputnik* actually set a course for my life. It also set the stage for the first debutante dinosaur. If it hadn't been for *Sputnik,* Sue's coming-out party would have rocked the world in a very different way. This revolutionary idea was recently proposed to me by Robert Bakker, Ph.D.—fossil-junkie genius, the Galileo of paleontology, and the most well known of our profession. One of Bob's greatest gifts is his ability to translate paleontology into a lively language anyone can understand, but his insights often spill over into all manner of subjects. Characteristically, the *Sputnik*-Pete-Sue connection was not patently obvious until Bob put his unique spin on it.

Bakker's logic about *Sputnik* goes like this: late–1950s Russians had been beating us. They shot up the first space satellite. They launched the first man to orbit Earth. In the human race for superiority, the United States was behind schedule, so America created NASA and funneled money into the sciences. "The real sciences," Bakker hastened to add, because everyone knows putting old bones together is a very different process than serious endeavors such as finding a cure for cancer or landing on the moon. Rocket science, in particular, was well funded, but the trickle-down theory applied to other scientific endeavors as well. Americans wanted to see their scientists finding things and digging things up and building things, and doing all of this before anyone in Russia did. If the inhabitants of various cavelike paleontology offices simply crawled out of their rock- and bone-filled basements,

The heretical Bob Bakker draws as he lectures to a group of well-informed children—his favorite audience. Photo by Ed Gerken.

shaved the fur from their arms, filed down their canines, and sniffed their way into the administration offices of American halls of science, they might get a field season funded, or enough money to hire a preparator, or maybe even a new rock hammer.

It didn't take long for paleontologists to realize that if they wanted to get funded like other scientists, they had to start looking like other scientists. "They had to wear white lab coats," Bakker explains, "they had to make proposals and marketing plans, and move around boardrooms as if they knew what they were doing." Bakker's idea of a black-tie ensemble is to wear a fringed leather jacket over his usual get-up: boots, jeans, cotton shirt, and collecting vest (his wife, Constance Clark, bets that even Bob doesn't know what stuffs all those pockets). His ponytail trails down his back, beard down his front. I think I remember once seeing him wear a "dress" hat instead of his everyday crumpled straw hat that looks as if it fell from his head during a buffalo stampede. I have work pants and "dress pants" —work pants that haven't been used for work yet. My "dress boots" are safe in their box, to be used in the event of a pick or welding disaster. Philip Currie, the smartest meat-eating-dinosaur man in the world and the curator at the Royal Tyrrell Museum of Paleontology in Drumheller, Alberta, gives guest-of-honor speeches in a tee shirt, blue jeans, and sneakers. I would never have noticed any of this if it weren't for some women in my life who pointed it out.

But Bob noticed. And, as Bob is wont to do, he put forth a new hypothesis. "The craving for scientific funding was so intense," he said, "that a new era dawned. Let's call it the Three-Piece-Suitification of Paleontologists."

Up until then paleontologists had enjoyed a particular exemption from fashion; even the most elite of us experienced our best days in dust bowls or laboratories piled up to our eyebrows in rocks and dental tools. But competition for funding changed all that. Defining more than how paleontologists looked, this fever sought to change who we were. Or who we ought to be.

By the time Sue was discovered, the paradigm shift of Three-Piece-Suitification was well under way. But because Sue was one of the most impressive and scientifically significant fossils ever known, trends that had been hazy suddenly became crystal clear. The paradigm shift surrounded her, surrounded me, and held us to the heavens as Exhibit A. Timing is everything.

In the Beginning

When Sue was discovered, most of the information we had about *Tyrannosaurus rex* came from scientific publications on three specimens. All of them were collected between 1900 and 1906 by Barnum Brown, a skillful, productive, professional freelance collector. The first (BM-R7995) came from eastern Wyoming's Lance Creek beds and consisted of parts of the lower jaws, the pelvis, and vertebrae of the neck, body, and tail. Brown's preliminary report stated that the "vertebrae of the lumbar-dorsal region are deeply excavated [and] . . . hollow,"[1] thus calling attention to the honeycombed backbone I had noticed in Sue.

In 1902 he found 10 percent of a *T. rex* (CM-9380) in the

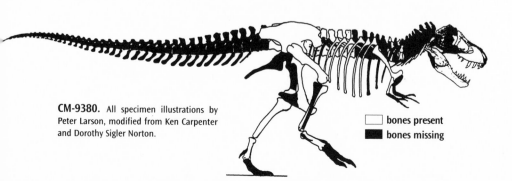

CM-9380. All specimen illustrations by Peter Larson, modified from Ken Carpenter and Dorothy Sigler Norton.

☐ bones present
■ bones missing

Montana section of the Hell Creek badlands—a large portion of the lower jaws, a few skull bones, parts of both legs, partial feet, most of the pelvis, a handful of vertebrae and ribs, a shoulder blade, and one upper arm bone. The arm bone was so tiny in comparison to the rest of the skeleton that when it was described by Henry Fairfield Osborn, chief paleontologist at the American Museum of Natural History, he mistakenly noted, "The association of the small forearm is probably incorrect."[2] Later he reversed his opinion and claimed the undersized arm did indeed belong to this gigantic beast—but plenty of today's paleontologists still fret about what *T. rex* was able to do with it.

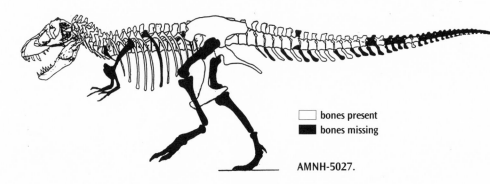

bones present
bones missing

AMNH-5027.

Then in 1906 Brown made his most spectacular discovery (AMNH-5027), again in the Hell Creek beds. This new specimen consisted of a nearly complete vertebral column, pelvis, and rib cage.[3] But the crowning glory, which Brown would forever consider his "favorite child,"[4] was the exquisitely preserved skull and jaws of the true king of beasts. Anyone who has been to the American Museum of Natural History could not have missed this magnificent skull, which, because of its weight and scientific value, has been on display at ground level next to the mounted skeleton. The way the entire specimen was mounted set the precedent for how science and the public viewed *T. rex* for generations: its body was posed upright, its tail propped on the floor. (Recently this superb fossil has been remounted to incorporate the latest science on *T. rex*'s biomechanics—neck and tail working like a giant teeter-totter balanced on the fulcrum of the powerful legs.)

The reason we knew about all of these specimens is not only because they were found, but also because they were "described": cleaned, analyzed, documented, drawn, compared to other specimens, identified, and named. For the huge *Tyrannosaurus rex,* the naming process was beastly. Osborn named two of Brown's *T. rex*es in the same scientific paper, but at the time he did not realize they represented the same type of creature. Brown's *T. rex* number two was discussed first in the paper and was named *Tyrannosaurus rex,* or "tyrant lizard king." Brown's first specimen was listed next, and because bony

The old face of *T. rex,* an upright, tail-dragging reptile. After Osborn, 1916.

armor (probably belonging to a spiky ankylosaur) was found with it, Osborn assumed this beast's body had been covered with plates. He named it *Dynamosaurus imperiosus,* which means "imperial power lizard." Later, when he realized his mistake, all of Brown's *T. rex*es were gathered together under the name *Tyrannosaurus rex,* simply because the rules of nomenclature dictate that the first published name wins.[5] This caused Brown's second discovery to become the "type specimen," or the fossil that sets the definitional standard against which all future *T. rex*es would be measured. In the 1940s it was sold to the Carnegie Museum in Pittsburgh, Pennsylvania.[6] Later, number one (*"Dynamosaurus"*) was sold to the British Museum in London.[7]

To add to the naming confusion, neither of Brown's *T. rex* specimens was the first! One of paleontology's most prolific researchers,

The first *T. rex* bone put on the record was found by E.D. Cope in 1892. Its cross-section shows the honeycombed structure that instantly identifies carnivorous dinosaur bone.
Photo by Peter Larson.

Edward Drinker Cope, first described one of two damaged neck vertebrae found in South Dakota. His intention was to ascribe a new species to this one bone (the other has since disappeared), dubbing it the unglamorous *Manospondylus gigas*, "giant air-filled vertebra."[8] This name did not stick, thanks again to those rules of nomenclature; one vertebra is insufficient to stand as the type specimen for a new species. On a trip to the American Museum of Natural History in 1992, I held in my hand Cope's *T. rex* vertebra, which had been found in the same general region as Sue, and which looked remarkably similar to her bones.

Aside from Brown's three big specimens, he also collected two less complete ones that were described: a braincase, which was cut in half longitudinally to provide a view of the brain cavity (AMNH-5029), and leg bones (AMNH-5881).[9] No one knows how many other *undescribed* specimens of *T. rex* may populate any number of institutions. I have run across some of these fragmentary individuals, including a nice leg and partial pelvis at the Smithsonian Institution in Washington, D.C.—ascribed to *Ornithomimus grandis* by Marsh and collected by John Bell Hatcher long before Brown found his first *T. rex*.[10]

Once *T. rex* was basically understood, a good fifty years would pass before new significant *T. rex* material was discovered—and eighty-six years before new documentation was published! So much for the beginnings of *T. rex* science. However, history is made of more than science. It's made of people. That's where things get hairy.

The term *Dinosauria* was coined by pioneer paleontologist Richard Owen in 1842, but the world's first love affair with these real-life monsters—let's call it the Dinosaur Nascence—flourished from the last quarter of the 1800s to the first quarter of the 1900s. Barnum Brown's *T. rex*es were found then, adding to specimens of other famous dinosaurs, including the favorite *Triceratops* with its enormous three-horned skull and long-necked sauropods with tree-trunk legs. Discoveries of these creatures sparked controversy in nineteenth-century minds, most fundamentally because creationism taught that extinct monsters simply could not have existed. Impossibly, tons of giant bones matching no known creature had been discovered, and Charles Darwin's *The Origin of the Species* tossed out a few possible explanations that could only send the public into a quandary. Thus began the original paleontology debate, a controversy that would ripen and evolve in its own right—bursting forth at Sue's debut generations later.

Museums that still boast some of the world's greatest dinosaur collections acquired mind-boggling quantities of science's newest question marks—often by the trainload. (So much material was gathered that, 150 years later, some of the original field jackets *still* have not been opened!) As fast as rails could be laid, bone-laden trains rumbled eastward out of the unsettled western territory—the stomping grounds of rugged collectors who were as much adventurers as scientists.

In those days fossil-bearing formations were sought after and shared by a healthy mix of museum curators and unaffiliated lone rangers, all of whom developed expertise in a brand-new field of study. Most independent fossil specialists either worked "on speculation," selling what they found after the fact, or collected on behalf of one or more sponsoring institutions. They made their livings—and their reputations—by getting their hands dirty and becoming some of the best and most prolific field paleontologists ever known. The relationship between independents and museums was symbiotic: science needed specimens; collectors needed museums. This legacy would become my role model.

Throughout this history, no one questioned the part that money played in such a relationship. It was simple. Collections were being born, so museums bought and sold specimens as a matter of course, from each other or from enthusiasts or from freelance collectors. Fossils, and the mavericks who collected them, became a permanent part of our lexicon: Mary Anning, who specialized in marine reptiles, including fishlike ichthyosaurs and flippered plesiosaurs with long necks and tails, became the inspiration for the well-known tongue-twister, "She sells seashells by the sea shore."

Of these early professionals, especially well respected was the Sternberg family, a multigenerational collecting crew headed by the famous Charles H. Sternberg. The senior Sternberg began his fossil-collecting career in Kansas in the 1870s. Over a period spanning more than sixty years, he collected, prepared, and sold fossils to museums all over the world. He and his sons, George, Levy, and Charles M., were responsible for much of the early work in the Lance Creek beds of Wyoming, which are the same age as South Dakota's Hell Creek Formation. They also opened up the famous Red Deer River dinosaur beds in Alberta, Canada, an area which is now Dinosaur Provincial Park.[11] Having a Sternberg on board at a field site was one of the best coups a funded paleontologist could imagine.

Field specialists like the Sternbergs, or the prolific lone ranger John Bell Hatcher—who single-handedly collected almost all the important *Triceratops* material available for generations—played a significant role in the foundation of paleontology as we know it today. They delivered the goods, and their stories interwove with legends of great minds and great antics. In fact, when some of the more colorful museum curators were detained at home with administrative duties, they relied heavily upon this cadre of lone rangers—and secret, coded messages that detailed quarry production or sought-after bonebed locations. As more and more exciting *Dinosauria* discoveries occurred, fossil hunting became more and more competitive, and human nature added an inevitable little twist. It threw in a dose of one-upsmanship, a pinch of tempestuous blindness, and a generous helping of jealousy. For some, ethics were skimmed off the top like butterfat. The Bone Wars had begun.

Two champion skimmers were a couple of curmudgeons who made such a fuss that their story has been told and retold, even outside the field of paleontology. Raised to the stature of Galileo asserting that the universe revolves around the sun, Darwin arguing evolution, the anthropological debate over the "missing link," and nature versus nurture, the curmudgeons Othniel Charles Marsh and Edward Drinker Cope were included in Hal Hellman's *Great Feuds in Science.*

Just after the Civil War, Marsh and Cope started out as friends. As time went on, competition consumed them. Marsh was lucky enough to be born the nephew of George Peabody, a millionaire banker who provided Yale with an endowment for a new museum— as long as Marsh was made a professor of paleontology there. Through Peabody's continued funding of Marsh's expeditions, Yale accumulated an amazing collection of fossils. Cope, who preferred to work independently (without official university affiliation), funded his studies through his father's estate. He dedicated his life to travels in the field, and while he taught for a period at the University of Pennsylvania, Cope's extensive fossil collection was eventually bought by New York's American Museum of Natural History.[12] Throughout his lifetime, Cope published more than one thousand scientific papers and described hundreds of new species, including that failed attempt at naming *T. rex.*

Marsh and Cope fueled their friendship-searing rivalry by both personally undertaking numerous collecting expeditions and using teams of collectors to send specimens back to their laboratories. Contractors, including the Sternbergs and Hatcher, were hired to run quarry sites, some of which yielded hundreds of tons of bones and still produce today. Both men were fiercely protective of their finds and equally curious about the competition's. Each sought the inside scoop by hiring spies to infiltrate the enemy camp. At times they even managed to steal bones from each other's quarries or staff. A quintessential escapade is alleged to have taken place in 1872 at Bridger Basin, Wyoming, where the two worked competing digs for the same elephant-sized, tusked, horned creatures that would eventually be called uintatheres. Robert West Howard tells this Bone War tale in *The Dawnseekers*:

> Cope spent hours each day on a hilltop spying on the Marsh dig. This encouraged Marsh's crew to assemble a skull from the jaw-bones, teeth, eye sockets, and horns of a dozen species. They buried "Old What-you-may-call-it" just before Cope showed up for his daily spell at the telescope. When he did arrive, they put on an elaborate pantomime of arduous shoveling and great excitement. Cope sneaked over that dusk, dug up "What-you-may-call-it" and wrote a paper about its "significance."[13]

Slanderous stories from both Marsh and Cope passed among their friends and were printed by the press. It became an all-out, drag-down media slap-fight alleging theft, falsehood, mental instability, and unethical scientific reporting. Unintended side effects of the feud were increased newspaper readership and heightened public interest in paleontology—the Dinosaur Nascence. Unintended *future* ramifications were an unfortunate precedent of mistrust among fellow scientists and a tendency to designate—and fight over—which participants were most deserving of the fossil bounty. As in all lore, it remains unclear as to which details were true and which were fabrications designed to discredit and defame. Despite the controversy, Cope remains one of the heroes of paleontology. In fact, when *National Geographic* photographer Louie Psihoyos embarked upon an interview tour to gather information for his book *Hunting Dinosaurs*, he lured bone diggers to his project by promising an introduction to the real E.D. Cope. (Cope's skeleton had become part of the collections of the Museum of Archaeology and Anthropology at the University of Pennsylvania.) Psihoyos gained permission to tuck Cope's actual skull into his baggage.

Meanwhile, in Cope's day, all remained quiet on the western fossil front while America fried bigger fish than ichthyosaurs: wars, depressions, and the Twist. During that half century, the planet's poster child for carnivores stood silent, posing politely in New York, Pittsburgh, and London. Practicing baring its teeth. Sharpening its claws. Balancing on its tail. Just a giant reptile with puny arms.

Let There Be Light

Then, blast off! *Sputnik* went up, funding trickled down, Three-Piece-Suitification flushed paleontologists out of their closets, and excavations opened. Dinosaurs experienced their next public relations growth spurt, launching a Dinosaur Renaissance that still hasn't splashed down.

Behind the scenes, it was all about money, the well-heeled flurry over funding. In the public eye, however—reminiscent of the Bone Wars side effect—the scrapping produced something else entirely. Dinosaurs were everywhere, and it was exciting. Yale's venerable John Ostrum found *Deinonychus,* an "in-between" fossil that led him to believe that birds were direct descendants of dinosaurs, affirming and resurrecting an idea first presented around 1870 by Thomas Huxley and Charles Darwin— based on the famous, primitive, "transition" dinosaur-to-bird ancestor *Archaeopteryx.* Ostrum's concept that dinosaurs and birds were related sparked the public's interest, but Bob Bakker, who was then at the University of Colorado, and who had studied under Ostrum, fanned the flames.

Bakker built on the bird idea and turned paleontology on its head

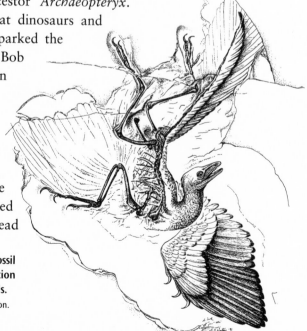

The first "missing link" fossil that suggested a connection between dinosaurs and birds.
Illustration by Dorothy Sigler Norton.

by claiming that dinosaurs had been warm-blooded. A collector, scientist, and philosopher, his elastic mind questioned almost all of the accepted "facts" about dinosaurs. He enthusiastically proclaimed a new life for these extinct creatures and represented them in his excellent drawings as lively, vivacious, leaping runners instead of slow reptilian plodders. He calculated their speeds using footprints and physics, he gave thrilling lectures, he used living animals as instant templates ("Let me duct-tape you to the belly of a rhino and you'll see how *Triceratops*'s front legs worked!"). Paleontology as a field was revitalized in the heat of Bakker's zeal and was greeted by the public with everything from increased museum attendance to, eventually, a purple dinosaur named Barney and *Jurassic Park*.

Early in the Dinosaur Renaissance, the Los Angeles County Museum of Natural History wanted a *T. rex* for a new dinosaur hall. It was 1965. With a special twelve-month endowment earmarked specifically for this purpose, the museum sent Harley Garbani to Barnum Brown's old stomping grounds around Hell Creek, Montana.[14] After finding several other fossils, including the skull and partial skeleton of a *Triceratops,* on July 27 Garbani found *T. rex* foot bones weathering from an exposure.[15] Afraid the field budget would be withdrawn now that he had been successful in his task, Garbani collected and reported only the surface material, covering, marking, and concealing from the museum board the rest of the specimen.[16] It was not until 1969 that he returned to excavate the discovery. The specimen (LACM-23844) included a large but incomplete skull, lower jaws, a shoulder girdle, a few ribs, scraps of pelvis and leg bones, a nearly complete foot, and some rather badly damaged vertebrae. The skull and one foot were put on display at the Los Angeles County Museum in 1973; in the fall of 1996, this fragmentary skeleton would be combined with a Tyrrell Museum replica, mounted and put on exhibit in Los Angeles.[17]

While inspecting this specimen in the collections of the museum in 1991, I noticed the fragmented remains of a small theropod labeled *Gorgosaurus lancensis* (LACM-23845) collected in the same excavation with the *T. rex*. Something was wrong, I knew. I couldn't believe what I was seeing as I gently picked up piece after piece: several skull and lower jaw bones, a nearly complete foot, a shoulder blade, a complete forearm ulna, and some miscellaneous scraps, including a broken tooth. The characteristically diagnostic upper jaw's maxilla still held another tooth firmly in place—I had no doubt. This was a misidentified juvenile *Tyrannosaurus rex* skeleton! Although as badly damaged as the larger specimen, this youngster was exceedingly more important. Here was our first clue to the ontogeny, or developmental growth, of *T. rex*.

Montana came through again in 1967, when an archaeologist with Montana State University at Bozeman, Dr. William MacMannis, collected most of an adult skull from an unknown locality. That specimen (MOR-008) is now at the Museum of the Rockies (MOR) in Bozeman. MOR's second specimen was found in 1981 by Mick Hager, the museum's former director. Although this is the only *T. rex* specimen found by a trained paleontologist, the discovery had little to do with science and everything to do with Hager's call of nature. While the bone surface was quite weathered, eventually he was able to collect a good portion of the tail and pelvis, the right leg, and incomplete left foot of a small *T. rex*.[18] Hager tells me it is very likely that more of the specimen remains in the ground.

Around the same time, South Dakota's first *T. rex* skeleton was found (Cope's partial vertebra was, up to then, the only documented *T. rex* bone from the state). In 1980, rancher Jennings Floden came upon fragments of large bones at the base of a butte in western South Dakota's Perkins County. Excited by his discovery, he contacted Phil Bjork of the South Dakota School of Mines and Technology's Museum of Geology. According to Floden, Bjork investigated the site, made the identification, and, with the aid of student diggers, collected what he believed was the entire specimen. At first, SDSM-12047 included a partial femur, partial sacrum, a few ribs, and eighteen articulated tail vertebrae. However, Floden harbored doubts that the excavation was complete. Acting on a hunch, he enlisted the aid of neighboring ranchers to pick and shovel some twenty feet of forbidding overburden from above the bone-producing horizon.[19] Eventually a nearly complete skull was recovered with much fanfare and celebration.

Canada's first *T. rex* skeleton actually was located in 1946 by Charles M. Sternberg, one of the fossil-collecting sons of the famous freelance collector. Near the town of Huxley, Alberta, Sternberg collected some bone fragments from a rather inaccessible portion of a steep bluff in the Scollard Formation.[20] Thirty-five years would pass before Alberta's Tyrrell Museum of Paleontology collected the specimen.

For better and for worse, TMP 81.12.1 was embedded in a very hard ironstone concretion. While the ironstone protected the fossil from weather, it also formed a tough barrier for the fossil's rescuers. With great difficulty, Phil Currie's crew was able to collect a reasonably complete pelvis, the hind limbs, much of the tail and body vertebrae, an isolated skull bone, and a portion of the neck, which still reached into the back wall of the quarry. Although he believed the rest of the skull remained underground, Currie reluctantly had to quit the excavation—the quarry's back wall had reached ninety feet in height and was in danger of caving in. (In 1993 the cliff did collapse, burying what might remain of the specimen under tons and tons of rock.)[21] Museum staff would later mount this headless specimen with a replica skull from the American Museum of Natural History, and exhibit it in time for the grand opening of the Tyrrell Museum in 1985—the first *T. rex* skeleton to be mounted in seventy years.

On a roll in 1981, having barely finished his first *T. rex* excavation, Currie saw the bones of yet another skeleton, one that had been located the previous summer by a high school student on a fishing trip. Walking along the Crows Nest River near Crows Nest Pass in southwestern Alberta, Jeff Baker found some black objects eroding out of the bank's Willow Creek Formation and contacted Currie. While the fragments were readily recognized as a theropod, Currie's fellow Tyrrell paleontologist Jeff Doran visited the site to make the identification. As soon as he saw the size of the bones, he knew it must be *Tyrannosaurus rex,* and a 1982 excavation was scheduled. The jet-black color of the bones, a product of man-

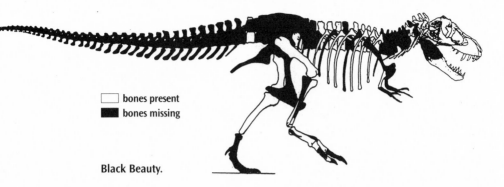

bones present
bones missing

Black Beauty.

ganese deposited by local groundwater, invited the name Black Beauty (TMP 81.6.1), but the excavation was ugly. The bones were encased in extremely hard rock, which would cause challenging digging and preparation to continue until 1993. Part of the specimen would go on display long before preparation was completed, as a 1990 "in-progress" traveling exhibit in Japan. Then, the finished subadult specimen—which includes a nearly complete skull, partial lower jaws, pelvis, many body and neck vertebrae, ten ribs, the right upper arm bone, one finger bone, and many hind-limb elements—went on tour again, first in Canada, then in 1994 back to Japan.[22] Black Beauty started the trend of the traveling dinosaur show; it has the distinction of being the most widely traveled of all *T. rex* skeletons.

The most widely traveled *T. rex* animal, however, was excavated in 1986—in New Mexico! It occurred so far south of the known range of *T. rex* that I was reluctant to include it in my list of known specimens before I could take a look. I was wary because misidentified "*T. rex*" specimens have cropped up in Utah and Texas. This one was a resident of the New Mexico State Museum in Albuquerque, and the specimen consisted of a jaw, several vertebrae, and ribs.[23] For years it spawned a good, old-fashion debate. Was it or wasn't it a *Tyrannosaurus rex*? The question still had not been resolved to my satisfaction years later. In 1998 the museum's curator Tom Williamson, along with Canadian student Tom Carr, asked for my two cents. Once I saw this southwestern specimen, I was convinced it was a *T. rex* who had moved out of town, in one fell swoop expanding the territory of the Tyrant Lizard King.

In 1992 Denver Museum's Ken Carpenter provided further proof of *T. rex*'s expanded range with an excavation within the city limits of greater metropolitan Denver. Discovered by Charlie Fickle, a construction worker who was walking his dog at a housing construction site, the specimen consisted of most of a leg and a partial pelvis.[24] Aside from the anomalous New Mexico specimen, and before the Colorado find, the southernmost discovery of *T. rex* had been in Niobrara County, Wyoming—Barnum Brown's first find, in 1900, the misnamed *Dynamosaurus*. Denver lies a full 250 miles south of Niobrara County and helped fill in that almost unbelievable gap to New Mexico. It also confirmed that *T. rex*'s range had been pushed a total of 750 miles south of our previous assumptions, nearly doubling what I had believed was its confirmed territory.

Roaring monsters were being pulled out of the ground, and with each one came more excitement. New information. Fresh clues. There is something in human nature that compels us to put ourselves face-to-face with a *T. rex*. In fact, it was what scientists did first when *T. rex* was officially identified, described, and drawn . . . next to a human at an equivalent scale. H.F. Osborn, the man who published *T. rex*'s description, noted, "When placed together . . . the enormous proportions of this animal become very evident as compared with

The first reconstruction of the skeleton of *Tyrannosaurus rex*, based upon the "type" specimen. Illustration by Osborn, 1905.

the skeleton of a man, the total length being estimated at 39 feet and the height of the skull above the ground at 19 feet."[25] Standing next to this real monster is the stuff of fiction, a thrill worthy of the *Lost World* television series or *Jurassic Park*. That is the irresistible pull of dinosaurs, and it is reinforced each time a small child stands agape, arms at his sides, head tilted as far back as bones will allow, eyes locked on the silent roaring jaws of a deadly creature towering over him.

That is what science fights for, and that is what funds it. Big kids with big allowances stand exactly like that, too.

The Forbidden Fruit

Bob Bakker approaches his excavations with a Big Question, and he has seen other scientists do the same. "It might be, 'What happened to turn the Jurassic into the Cretaceous?' or 'How did humans evolve from apes?' But nearly all museums have some sort of Big Question to answer," he says. Institutions outline a particular topic, perhaps even form a hypothesis, and then solicit funds for suitable, illustrative projects. Likewise, Black Hills Institute has a Big Question, but ours has two sides. The theoretical side focuses on the K-T Boundary—the geological line between the Cretaceous and Tertiary periods that marks dinosaur extinction. We search for new species and as much information as possible about already familiar creatures of that crucial time. Our Big Question might be phrased, "What was alive at the end of the age of dinosaurs?"

The other side depends upon the marketplace, our funding source. For example, K-T Boundary research could take many forms, and the museum marketplace can suggest specific targets. Recently we focused on *Triceratops* because while there are composite *Triceratops* skeletons in museums, to date no complete, single specimen has yet been uncovered. A complete specimen could help settle some ongoing debates about *Triceratops*'s front leg action; it also would be an excellent display piece to sell to a museum, funding our next project.

For over a decade, my partners and I explored our Big Question, developed our game plan, and then followed in the footsteps of the Sternbergs and other independent collectors. We looked at our paleontology business as a way to kill two birds with one stone: by funding our own scientific projects with sales, we were paid to have the time of our lives. We believed in the paleontology of the old days, where you could spot a fossil enthusiast by the look on his face, where the most fun you could have was to debate how bones went together or from what animal they had come. It was a fraternity, a brotherhood, an instant camaraderie built from shared passions about ancient life. The only calling card you needed was an unusual chunk of bone. Then times began to change.

To the uninitiated, there appears to be only one group of paleontologists: a noble band whose credo is to protect and save fossils. These white knights undertake the admirable and necessary tasks of collecting, preserving, and displaying fossils where the public can view them. When discussing his passion, every fossil lover stands ready to answer the call to arms. We all do. But within the profession, as Three-Piece-Suitification evolved, someone started noticing that maverick collectors tended to resemble Indiana Jones more than Prince Charming. And that the prince usually resided in museums and universities while Jones was out in the field or selling at a fossil fair. Even though museums had been built with purchases made from Indiana Jones's predecessors, an unexpected mutation began to divide paleontologists into groups based generally on whether or not they were independents, and especially on whether or not they sold the fossils they were finding.

What had changed? *Sputnik*. With the Dinosaur Renaissance's money came new exhibits, renewed fascination in science—and a higher demand for fossils. Their value, both intrinsic and monetary, ballooned.

Recalling paleontology's last race for specimens, money fueled this process. It paid for digging materials, wages, preparation supplies, and landowner fees. The Renaissance was a bull market for whoever got there first. It also began to look more and more like the Bone Wars. In the updated version, however, Three-Piece-Suitification adopted a new, politically correct attitude that frowned upon treating fossils as commodities. Such behavior was called unseemly, even poisonous, and the act of selling bones to museums gradually became anathema. In some circles, commercial paleontologists themselves became anathema. After nearly 150 years of buying and selling fossils, commercialism in paleontology was . . . immoral. It started with a little finger pointing and escalated into accusations of the worst kind.

When the prince reminisces about the old days, he conjures stories about how he would travel to a fossil locality, identify himself to its owners, dig to his heart's content, and return to his museum a hero. The fossils were priceless, scientific treasures offered to his institution for free, and the prince was honored as the earth's trustworthy custodian. Nowadays, he tells stories about his sites being plundered by rogue fossil hunters who lack ethics—who hop fences into forbidden territory, who lie about localities, who keep no field records, who sell to the highest bidder. He says sometimes landowners don't welcome him unless he pays. Even worse, Charming says this whole process has made fossils something worth stealing. He blames paleontology's slide into immorality on Indiana Jones and has suggested banning him from public lands.

"No room! No room!" they cried out when they saw Alice coming.

"There's plenty of room!" said Alice indignantly, and she sat down in a large arm-chair at the end of the table.[26]

But there are two sides to everything. For every tale of misdeeds by a commercial collector, there is another about a university crew or a museum curator. Nearly identical stories, different main characters. Some of these are even told by ranchers, or by academics about other academics—or about themselves. In a perfect example of history's repeating itself, while professional paleontologists of all affiliations are slinging mud, the public sits at its collective breakfast table, opens the newspaper, and asks for the headline. Is Indiana Jones's pursuit of a dinosaur like Sue really the problem? Who are paleontology's bad guys?

"Weekend rockhounds, vandals, and the dino pot hunters do far more damage than those trying to steal an intact skeleton," Bob Bakker answers. "If you're going to do it right and carefully, excavation takes time, it takes weeks. Trenching, plaster jackets, you're out there exposed." He's right. The whole process of collecting large, scientifically important, financially valuable specimens—the lifeblood of a company like ours—is a very visible process. On the other hand, fossil removal or damage in other categories is less obtrusive. It also can't sustain a business.

"I'm sorry to say it," Bakker says, "but there is a category of rockhounds, little old ladies who travel to a fossil locality and pick up a piece or two, just for a souvenir. It might be just a little piece, but multiply that by ten thousand, and you have the situation at Como Bluff: it's vacuumed by 'people erosion,' day by day, one chunk at a time." The next problem is vandalism. "I don't know why people travel around smashing plaster jackets in the field," Bakker laments. "When I'm digging in Wyoming, I spread the word through local cowboys, asking that if they see any people doing it, to shoot their tires out. That seems to work."

While finding the truth in mudslinging contests is always difficult, I believe Bakker's third category gave birth to the horror stories—and the damage to the reputation of commercial independents. Bakker calls them "smash-and-grab artists," who specialize in "chunk-o-bone." "Some used to go across whole swaths of Utah smashing stuff, probably selling the chunks to rock shops. They have barrels of junk bones, a buck a piece," he says. "Others are guys who cut bones with a rock saw, looking for crystals that have grown inside. They polish them into bolo ties. These people do most of the damage—they can smash thirty to fifty specimens in the time it takes a good field collector, including legitimate commercial companies, to collect one."

Beyond compelling stories of everything from theft in the field to bad manners, paleontology definitely has been suffering from financial fallout. But far from playing the blame game, solving the problem may lie in better understanding its origins.

Where companies like ours work to fund themselves—and can decide where to dig and when—Prince Charming still has to beg his bankroll and his schedule from the king. Even considering the influx of money allocated to science since *Sputnik,* the fate of public institutions is to scramble over funding. The fate of the academic paleontologist is to subsist in a survival mode that assumes he will receive resources inadequate to fulfill his dreams. He will always have to make do.

Indiana Jones's constraints are self-imposed. How well does he excavate, prepare, mount, and market the fossils he finds? In the world of capitalism, a bull market favors him, if he can deliver the goods. As fossil values increased, Prince Charming began to feel elbowed out of his own game. To compete, he had to convince the king to raise his allowance, again and again. Great museum-funded expeditions were undertaken, new benchmarks were established, and money was raised. But where will it end? Will museums overextend themselves into extinction? Will they go the way of major-league baseball, with its ever-increasing ticket prices, new stadiums, and skyrocketing payrolls?

When Bob Bakker first began trumpeting "leaping lizards," I was an undergraduate geology student who spent his free time nurturing his new company, then called Black Hills Minerals. My partners and I never thought twice about starting what was at first a warehouse providing teaching specimens to university and museum scientists, and, frankly, we hadn't noticed Three-Piece-Suitification. That sort of thing was outside our line of sight. As the Bone Wars heated up, however, what happened next threw the world's newest, fanciest dinosaurs into a different light. It also clued in anyone who hadn't yet chosen sides. This is where I made my first mistake. I didn't buy a sport coat.

What happened next was government. At the time, land management agencies did not lean one way or the other with regard to issues of commercialism or wardrobe. (Their staff wore uniforms, so the argument was lost on them.) Agencies such as the Bureau of Land Management (BLM) and the Forest Service had two primary jobs: to oversee the public's real estate, and to make money doing it. Land managers were in support of processes by which natural resources could be preserved—and marketed. In 1982 the BLM published proposed rules for the collection of fossils on lands under its control, a proposal that included selling excavation rights to the highest bidder. While such a process would have been great for commercial entities who were paid for their labor, it was not supportive of amateurs or fund-hunting scientists. Perhaps naively, our company believed fossils were best protected by collection, and collection was best guaranteed when the highest number of people were out looking for bones. We wanted regulations that would support *everyone's* ability to search, ours and three-piece-suiters and kids on 4-H outings. Black Hills Institute—along with an association of companies like ours, the American Association of Paleontological Suppliers (AAPS)—became political.

AAPS solicited more than 1,700 public comments against the BLM proposal, enough to put it on hold. Next, we urged our state's senator, Republican Larry Pressler (together with Democrat Paul Tsongas of Massachusetts), to introduce a more appropriate and far-reaching Senate bill, one that would provide standardized guidelines for land management agencies to issue permits for fossil collection. The permitting system would regulate access to public lands along with providing revenues—and permits would be accessible to *all* collectors. Special provisions would ensure that important new specimens went to public institutions, and partial proceeds of any sales would go to the land management agencies.

Once the bill hit the Senate, fossils were noticed like never before. The hoopla still was about money, with public institutions claiming that the bill did not solve the funding problem we had identified with the BLM proposal. Any permit costs—any money attached to the procurement of fossils—opened a door they wanted nailed shut. In short, the prince feared that Indiana Jones would beat a hasty path to fossil hot spots before competitive grants could be raised.

Commercial collectors who raised their hands against the original BLM proposal would later slap themselves silly. The new-and-improved bill was buried while the Senate committee did what all big organizations do when presented with two sides of a story. They went to their science advisory board, the National Academy of Sciences, and asked them to form their own committee to advise Congress on how to handle this dead dinosaur problem. The NAS

Committee on Paleontological Collecting was convened in 1984, and it included academics as well as every land management agency under the sun: the Corps of Engineers, the Park Service, the Bureau of Indian Affairs, the Bureau of Land Management, and the United States Forest Service.

And me. My job was to represent the interests of commercial and amateur paleontologists. The committee evaluated the needs of all members of the paleontological community, reached a consensus, and drafted a report in 1987. Our collective mantra was: "The science of paleontology is best served by unimpeded access to fossil-bearing rocks."[27] The report would have allowed all groups to collect fossils on federal, multiple-use, public lands. The BLM and the Forest Service were directed to draft regulations consistent with this report.

A day late and a dollar short. The narrow window of opportunity represented by the BLM's initial effort at creating regulations closed on everyone's fingers. Some land management agents were unwilling to challenge anticommercial views. Everyone was frozen in place. In my opinion, that change of heart imposed an especially devastating death sentence on fossils awaiting collection on public lands. To make matters worse, a new bill has been introduced into Congress which would criminalize any commercial or amateur collecting of vertebrate fossils on public, multiuse lands. Nearly a half-billion acres.

As of this writing in the spring of 2002, neither the BLM nor the Forest Service has complied with the NAS directives. No overall national fossil regulations exist. Land management agencies do have their own individual, divergent policies, which may or may not directly mention fossils. For example, the BLM has no regulation specifically mentioning fossil collecting. The Forest Service relies on two internal regulations: the "Petrified Wood Law," and a short 1986 regulation that allows limited collecting of invertebrate fossils (those with no backbone, like shells and bugs and plants) and *commercial collecting under permit*. Unfortunately, they have never issued a commercial permit. Both agencies occasionally issue *scientific permits*, but without any standardized method for deciding who may receive one. The result is that precedent is set not by guidelines, but instead by the personality that happens to occupy a land manager's office at any given time.

For its part, South Dakota has been as schizophrenic as the federal government. In the mid-1990s it passed a state law declaring, in essence, that all fossils found on state lands were the property of the South Dakota School of Mines and Technology. However, the commissioner of public lands found the law unworkable, and a new law has been proposed: to issue collecting permits to anyone.

By the time the Dinosaur Renaissance had been in full swing for two decades, the emotional and philosophical state of paleontology had changed radically. The battle over money had lost the irony and humor associated with Three-Piece-Suitification. Nothing was funny. The "funnest" science ever had become serious business.

In some museums, policy began to shift depending on the philosophical bent of the highest-ranked paleontologist on staff. Gradually, a handful moved toward the new politically correct rule of no fossil purchases; instead they preferred to trade specimens among themselves or to undertake whatever excavations they could afford. In these circles, "value" was still exchanged, but it became taboo to buy or sell outright. To be sure, this was not a blanket policy, and many major museums continued to revamp old exhibits or initiate new ones by buying real skeletons, replicas, special teaching exhibits, and many creative, new-technology applications. We stayed in business.

In the process of defending these divergent paths, several issues arose. Were fossils found on American ground part of our national heritage or some more expansive heritage before our time? Should all American fossils belong to the U.S. government? If found on private land, should fossils belong to the landowners? In the case of public lands, should they belong to those who acquired surface exploration rights? Were fossils "renewable" resources like hydroelectric, geothermal, and solar power—because they are "endlessly" prolific throughout layers upon layers of earth—or were they "nonrenewable" resources like oil—because there is a finite number of them? What were the minimum qualifications necessary before adequate skill can be guaranteed in the field, and who should decide them? How would ethical behavior be guaranteed when fossil fruit is harvested in remote locations? Who should be in charge? (See chart in appendix C.)

Further complicating the matter, not all fossils are made alike. Like fine art or diamonds, *T. rex* was precious. But like cows or quartz, duckbilled dinosaurs were a dime a dozen. There were good arguments on both sides of the Bone War debate, but they overlooked an essential fact: the credo. We all wanted one-of-a-kind pieces to be in famous institutions where millions of people could see them. When it boiled down to what was really important, we all wanted the *same things*.

Leave it to fate to underscore a point. In the seven years since Black Beauty had been found, paleontology's focus had been squarely on politics. Then, in the fall of 1988, a ranching family from McCone County, Montana, was out fishing on Fort Peck Reservoir. Kathy Wankel and her kids pulled their boat off the lake to wander along an outcropping of the Hell Creek Formation. Guess what she found? Bone fragments eroding out of the hillside. She began excavating, and in November, Wankel and husband Tom took a trip to the Museum of the Rockies. When duckbill expert Jack Horner saw the bones, he knew instantly he was looking at the arms and shoulder girdle of *Tyrannosaurus rex*. Because winter was on its way, the museum did not send someone to investigate until May of 1989, and September would arrive before an exploratory dig was made.[28] They set a date to complete the excavation: June 1990.

This new *T. rex*, MOR-555, had been found on land controlled by the Army Corps of Engineers, an arm of the government. In addition to securing permission from the government to collect the fossil, Horner's associate Pat Leiggi convinced the Corps to build a road to the site with their big equipment. Barnum Brown's days of horse and wagon were gone forever. This was the age of bulldozers, front-end loaders, semi-trucks, electric jackhammers, and satellite TV. Shelley McKamey, MOR's public relations director, rode herd on the frenzy of television, newspaper and

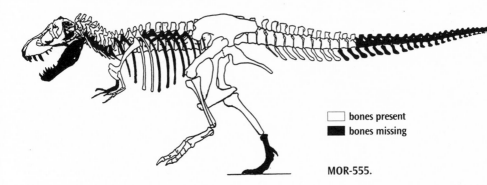

bones present
bones missing

MOR-555.

magazine crews.[29] Jack Horner's picture appeared on the covers of national magazines. Kathy Wankel was flown to Los Angeles to appear on a new version of the old television show *What's My Line*.

After the dust settled, it was evident that Wankel had made a remarkable discovery. Her *T. rex* was 45 percent complete, equal in the number of bones represented to the best specimen found to date, the last of Barnum Brown's discoveries. Although the skull was missing some major bones, and only one tooth-bearing element was present for the lower jaw, it was still an impressive specimen. The vertebral column was complete and articulated from the head to the seventeenth tail vertebra (it was missing about thirty after that) and included spiny attachments called chevrons. Although nearly all of the ribs had been washed away, most of both legs and one complete foot remained.

Most exciting, however, was the presence of both shoulder girdles and one arm and hand—making MOR-555 the only fully armed *T. rex*. Before this, only Barnum Brown's type specimen and Black Beauty had offered up an arm bone, the humerus in both cases, and Black Beauty had added a single finger bone. With this new arm and shoulder material, science suddenly had nearly the complete picture of *T. rex* arms and how they attached to the body.

The only missing piece of the puzzle was the "wishbone," or furcula, the piece that would determine how everything connected. Scientists had debated its existence in *T. rex* for some time: some believed there was none, and that *T. rex* arms were placed wide on the chest; others believed the missing furcula would define a narrow breast region and a closer set to the shoulders. Confirming the position was essential for correct spacing on mounted skeletons.

Ten years later a young paleontologist at the Field Museum, Chris Brochu, would be assigned to write the official "monograph" compilation of science on *T. rex*—using Sue's skeleton as the quintessential specimen. By then Phil Currie and Peter Makovicky already had published on other theropod furculae,[30] and Brochu bravely took sides once and for all, identifying one of Sue's bones as a furcula.

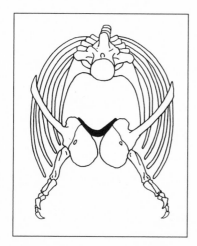

The *T. rex* "wishbone," or furcula, shown in black in the front view of the rib cage, demonstrates the correct positioning of the shoulder girdle and the animal's close relationship to birds.
Illustration by Dorothy Sigler Norton.

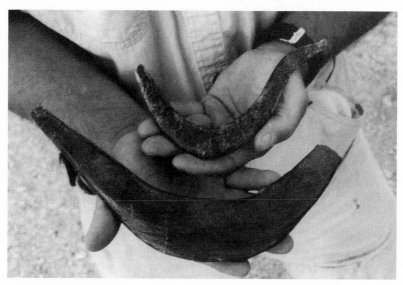

Below, the first confirmed *T. rex* furcula belonging to our newest *T. rex*, Bucky. It is being compared with the furcula of *T. rex*'s relative, *Gorgosaurus*, above.
Photo by Peter Larson.

Unfortunately, the bone in question was dissimilar to other known wishbones, and later was confirmed to be one of the stomach bones called gastralia—briefly reopening the debate. Ironically, what Sue could not confirm, another friend of mine could. In May 2001, I would be the lucky paleontologist to find the first *T. rex* furcula, thanks to Bucky, who saved his.

Cast Out of the Garden

The MOR-555 excavation, while chaotic with media attention, represented the perfect, albeit polygamous, marriage of all facets of paleontology. An amateur collector had found the specimen on government land. A museum staff had excavated with the participation of the discoverer, and with public exposure. The government had assisted the excavation by providing services and equipment. That's it. That's what it's supposed to look like.

Paleontology was just coming down from its most significant *T. rex* high in over eighty years when Susan Hendrickson walked out of a fog and into Sue's life. Sue would become the thirteenth significant *T. rex* specimen to be discovered and collected. She would be the first to blast paleontology sky-high.

Sue came at a time when paleontologists were taking stock— of their bones, of one another, and of their opinions about commercialism. The dinosaur business had never been better. Major tours were envisioned, exhibits revamped, and museum wings designed. Despite Prince Charming's push away from commercialism, the market had spoken; we had become the largest independent fossil preparatory and sales facility in the world. We raised all our own funding. We answered to no one but our customers—which included some of the most prestigious museums and universities in the world. We were the best example of the prince's worst nightmare.

He relied on his strengths in politics. In annual meetings of the largest collection of paleontologists, the Society of Vertebrate Paleontologists (SVP), motions were made to disallow membership to Indiana Jones. When I walked down the hall, conversations ceased. Once Sue hit the fan, the discomfort escalated. There was no turning back. Where MOR-555 and Brown's most complete

T. rex were each approximately 45 percent complete, Sue would be an astonishing 80 percent. Her skull, while ripped open on one side, was complete. She was the tallest and the longest and the beefiest. The queen had arrived. And we had her. Three-piece suits who had cut their lobbying teeth on the shredded Senate bill knotted their ties, shined up their degrees, and unleashed their stationery. This time we were their subject, despite our academic degrees, and despite our own scientific research. We were salesmen, and we were accused of much more than bad taste in clothing.

At first, with our characteristic absorption in what we were doing, we didn't recognize the severity of the problem. Eventually we would be interviewed by media representatives who had been told that institute owners and staff were among the most talented fossil excavators and preparators in the world. On the other hand, they had heard that our collecting habits were shoddy, irresponsible, and harmful to the fossils. We were scientists. We were shifty fossil brokers with no scientific abilities. We were law-abiding, simple ranch boys making a living. We were sophisticated thieves and liars. We saved precious bits of history. We took advantage of history and people to make a buck. The truth? We were sitting ducks with a great, big dinosaur.

Some people take their first look at the Great Plains and see only a dead, brittle sea. They arrive at one of our excavations and focus on the discomfort of our sleeping quarters and the constant, blowing dust. Doubt is written across their faces. After a few days of collecting, however, flies go unnoticed, shampoo lies forgotten, and doubt is replaced with a hearty camaraderie. I love watching everyone from volunteers and visitors to media people and daredevils lose themselves, their eyes drifting across the shimmering slow motion of the tall blond grasses. The only evidence of other people in any form shines at night from a distant, tiny, solitary white light perched on top of a rancher's power pole, miles away.

Since childhood I have gravitated to the peace the prairie has to offer. The treasure hunt for fossils and knowledge has been icing on the cake. During my research missions into vast badlands exposures, I often have felt my own camaraderie with fossil collectors over the decades and centuries, men and women much like me,

Armed and Dangerous

One of my favorite cartoons is a Gary Larson drawing of a *T. rex* family at the dinner table. The momma *T. rex* explains to her youngster, "I'd pass the potatoes if I could, dear, but my arms are as useless as yours!" Kathy Wankel's 1988 discovery of the first complete *T. rex* arm inspired scientists to test the capabilities of those "puny" limbs. A couple of years after MOR-555, Sue would add additional evidence, by providing even more complete shoulder girdles and the second arm ever found. Once Bucky threw in his furcula, the picture was complete.

As in birds, the presence of a wishbone meant that *T. rex*'s arms were connected to shoulder girdles that were tied together in the front by that bone. This gave *T. rex* a narrow breast, and the arms a correspondingly limited range of motion, but that was not enough to make claims about their strength. Just how wimpy was our great carnivore? The first clue was clutched in *T. rex*'s two-fingered hands, tipped with strong, curved, wicked-looking claws. When closed, the fingers came together with the claws angled toward each other and toward the claws of the other hand—making an effective grasping mechanism.[31]

Ken Carpenter of the Denver Museum of Nature and Science and Matt Smith who, at that time, was working on behalf of MOR, demonstrated that in *T. rex* the *strength* of the arm was more important than its length. In fact, they estimated a lifting strength of at least 450 pounds per arm for the relatively delicate MOR-555, and even more for beefier *T. rex*es like Sue.[32]

Other evidence reinforces the idea that the arms were hefting some weight. Sue's humerus bone shows where a ripped tendon apparently reattached itself.[33] Because tremendously high stress would be necessary to tear the tendon in the first place, Sue must have been doing something heavier than hitchhiking at the time. Other injuries to *T. rex* arm specimens, both found since Sue's discovery, echo this conclusion.

In 1906, when Osborn first accepted the tiny humerus

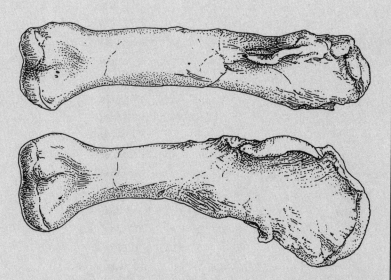

A comparison of gracile (top—MOR-555) and robust (bottom—Sue)
T. rex upper arm bones. Illustration by Dorothy Sigler Norton.

found with the type skeleton as belonging to _Tyrannosaurus rex,_ he theorized, "it served some function, possibly that of a grasping organ in copulation."[34] B.H. Newman, who must have assumed _T. rex_ did not roost like a bird, suggested the arms "could have been used to help _T. rex_ to stand up once it had laid down."[35] After the careful analysis and reconstruction of the arms and their biomechanics, Carpenter and Smith concluded that the arms "were used to hold struggling prey while the teeth dispatched the animal."[36]

Then why were the arms so short? Wouldn't they have been more useful in holding struggling prey if they were larger? I agree with Phil Currie who theorized that as _T. rex_'s head grew bigger through evolution, its body had to compensate for more and more forward weight. To maintain balance, the body and neck shortened and the tail grew heavier. Currie has pointed out that arm size might have been reduced to help compensate—but that doesn't mean that arm function disappeared. If you see a _T. rex_ waving its "wimpy" arm at you, I suggest you run.

people who craved wide-open spaces and a little adventure. Their presence in history has inspired me, informed me, and educated me. Their ghosts encouraged me in my passion and challenged me in my job. But they also set a bittersweet precedent of lifelong arguments, friendship-infecting disputes, and blistering differences of opinion. No matter how I might have imagined my own life in paleontology, the fact is that Black Hills Institute and Sue added a new chapter to history that included this kind of discord.

As time progressed, paleontology's grapevine rumors grew more and more caustic. Familiar colleagues began to turn away from each other, too busy for coffee. Evolution was in progress, fight or flight the order of the day. I preferred to abandon the categories of affiliation, financing, and wardrobe in favor of grouping both Indiana Jones and Prince Charming under the title "professional." However, before that trend could take hold, the prince redefined the good-old scientific scrap. He raised his white glove and slapped my cheek. Our duel had just begun.

(3)

Free at Last

In another moment down went Alice after it, never once considering how in the world she was to get out again.[1]

ome back up here tomorrow," I said without preamble. "And bring along an extra thousand pounds of plaster."

Neal was exhausted from the interminable season, and I could sense his objections sticking in his throat. A thousand pounds of plaster? For what? I didn't tell. I wanted him to experience that same moment of incredulous amazement I had felt.

Sue was trapped in a tall, steep badlands exposure. In order to avoid our own version of Phil Currie's collapsed cliff face, our only option was to cut a thirty-foot-tall shelf into the hill, its back wall twenty-five feet in from the edge, thirty-five feet across. Maurice Williams had no objection to us slicing such a scar into his landscape, since the terrain was not suitable for grazing cattle. "There's no grass up there, anyway," he said. His only caveat was that we were not allowed to drive to the site, which would damage the grass, except for when the excavation was completed and we'd have to bring in a truck to get Sue out of there.

In truth there were several other caveats we wouldn't know about until it was too late. Eventually every conversation we had with Williams would be picked apart by dozens of people. Everything both parties said or did—or didn't say or do—would be placed under a microscope. We would replay each word and deed, explaining ourselves, thinking it would matter. In the end, in an incredible turn of legal phrasing, everything about our exchange would become moot. Moot to the tune of over eight million dollars.

Without any of us realizing the import of the moments we were living, I began my usual pre-excavation process. My telephone calls from Faith on the afternoon of August 12, 1990—a couple of hours after I first saw Sue's bones—began with a request to our new administrative assistant to double-check land ownership with the Dewey County courthouse. Marion Zenker, equal parts iron will and soft heart, used our map coordinates to verify that Williams owned the land. This was what our lawyers would later call "standard practice," and for us it wiped out any doubt caused by the enormous expanses of ground in the Great Plains. Here, fences can be off or boundaries sometimes not marked at all. In practice, a rancher might sweep his arm across a horizon in response to our question, "Which is your land?" but in fact an invisible boundary line might intrude. Marion's research would show that while Williams's actual deed was on file with the Bureau of Indian Affairs—his ranch lay within the borders of the Cheyenne River Sioux Indian Reservation—the land indeed belonged to him and he had leased oil-exploration rights to a major oil company over the years.

My next call was to Williams. I told him what I thought lay buried under his hill, and the mess we would have to make in order to retrieve it. After receiving his go-ahead, I called my brother Neal. Last, I invited Phil Currie to join us, and I did tell him about Sue. After his back-to-back *T. rex*es, I could think of no better expert with whom to share our sandbox. Unfortunately, he was already tied up—we would have to put this puzzle together ourselves. I scheduled one day to clean up Matthew's *Triceratops* dig and to get organized for Sue's, and the next day . . . that would be the day. August 14.

An Engraved Invitation

Maurice Williams was the latest in a long line of ranchers from Kansas to Montana who had welcomed us onto their property to hunt for fossils. Formations on their land eroded to expose turtles, horses, oreodonts (prehistoric "sheep"), saber-toothed cats, and ancient shells of ammonites—creatures related to the chambered nautilus. Once we knew a rancher personally, we would call on the telephone about once a year, stop by the ranch house, and then walk through the outcrops. When we met someone new, often it seemed as if he or she already was known to us. Was one of us.

I found my first fossil at the age of four. Neal, our siblings, and I started our own "museum" well before I was ten. It was an old shack, an outbuilding on our parents' ranch, and our museum sign was topped with the skull of a cow. In our imaginations, this museum was patterned after the Zeitner Geological Museum in nearby Mission, South Dakota. June and Albert Zeitner spent thirty years on the road, rushing to each new mineral quarry that opened in North America and fetching home specimens to thrill us locals. In many ways June Zeitner would be my White Rabbit, the inspired, busy creature whom I followed down into the earth and into my career. With her encouragement I canvassed our family ranch, nestled within the bosom of the Rosebud Sioux Indian Reservation, hunting fossils, doing ranching chores, and watching our father lease grazing lands from our Indian neighbors. Unlike some visiting white folks who felt awkward in South Dakota's mixed heritage, Neal and I felt as indigenous as all the people around us, regardless of culture or race. We belonged here, and we knew the language of the countryside.

Our first museum, 1960. From left, Pete at age 8; Neal, age 5; sister Jill, 2; big brother Mark, 11. Photo by Erwin Ploetz.

The language is slow, relaxed, and respectful. Great Plains business meetings meander and flow, sifting business with pleasure, and often are conducted over coffee—sometimes out of a thermos while leaning against a fence post, sometimes out of a

Teaching fossil hunting the only way we know how: walking and walking and walking. Often young eyes—close to the ground—find the most! BHI file photo.

china cup in the ranch house. Our arrangements always followed a simple, standard pattern: we said who we were and
what we did; we described the geologic formations on the land
and asked if anyone had seen bones sprouting out; we asked for
permission to look; we agreed on terms if fossils worth excavating were found.

Once granted permission to look, we followed directions to
washed-out tracks along fences or through gullies, we bumped
across grasslands, around cattle and sheep herds, through gates
that we shut behind us. The outcrop we sought might rise naked
from the surrounding plains, its telltale geologic signposts visible
for miles away. In other cases, the wavy, rolling prairie suddenly
came to a dangerously camouflaged halt, a nearly invisible edge,
a sheer cliff opening down to a gaping wonderland of giant,
striped sand castles below. *Mauvaises Terres. Mako Sica.* The
badlands. Prairie legend claims that this name was coined by
French explorers who came upon desolate ravines that were
impossible to cross with wagons. The name seems to have stuck,

whether in French, Lakota, or English. In *T. rex* country, this is where the bones are.

I have seen fossils in all shapes and sizes, from microscopic forminifera to stories-tall sauropods. They are found on every continent and on many islands—in virtually every sedimentary rock on earth—because life has been very busy colonizing nearly every square foot of this planet's surface. As the millennia marched forward, rain, ice, streams, lakes, oceans, and wind filled in the low spots. Sedimentary deposits in the form of grains of sand, silt, precipitate, and ash buried at least a little bit of everything that once lived. Somewhere. Then, through either geologic uplift or erosion of surrounding sediments, what was once lowland became highland. Those same elements of nature wash, drag, or blow away the sediments until fragments of ancient life are exposed . . . and then washed into oblivion.

Sometimes life's evidence is a set of footprints on the once soft, limy edge of an ancient lake. Sometimes it is a complete skeleton, neck, back, and tail death-arched in the shape of a G, head thrown against the center of the spine, jaws open in a final scream, preserved down to the very last tiny vertebra of the tail. Most often, however, what we find of an extinct animal or plant is only a small portion of the original organism, an isolated bone, a leaf, the imprint of a patch of skin.

Knowing where to look begins with research and ends with experience. Libraries catalog the history of fossil-producing horizons, sometimes huge areas suitable for the hunt. Those of us for whom geology is second nature can't help but call out the names and ages of sediments wherever we are. I have been teased for providing an unsolicited travelogue: "And right over there? That green color sandwiched between the beige and brown is Morrison, where the sauropods are found. Earlier we saw the Eocene, and as this road descends, you can see the cut changing into . . ." I have been known to swerve slightly off the road, catching one tire on the shoulder, pointing across some unsuspecting passenger at a beautiful example of crossbedding or a spectacular hoodoo. I can't help it. I've learned to surrender the wheel soon after I shout, "Geology!"

REX FILE

Looking Back

Earth is 4.5 billion years old, and life left its first records 3.8 billion years ago. More complex life can be traced back about 540 million years. Scientists have used radioactive isotopes to confirm these dates, but they cannot date fossils directly—at least those older than a few tens of thousands of years. That's why sediment samples are crucial in assigning dates to fossil specimens. Volcanic ash found in sedimentary rocks, where fossils are usually found, often contain a radioactive isotope of potassium and its daughter product, argon. The potassium isotope binds to minerals as volcanic rock cools and crystallizes, and it begins to decay immediately upon crystallization. Because potassium decays at a known rate, its half-life being 1.2×10^9 years, volcanic ash may be analyzed to determine the ratio of the isotopes of potassium to argon, and thus the age of the sample.

If a fossil has been found within a volcanic ash bed, scientists assume the dinosaur died at the same time, or shortly before, the ash bed was deposited. Thus we are able to date the fossil *indirectly*. It's a two-way street, too. If, thanks to analyzing ash beds, we know the age of a species, we can assume that anywhere else we find that species dates to approximately the same time, because a species generally is thought to exist for about one million years.[2] For example, using volcanic ash bed analysis, we know that *T. rex* in Montana is 65–67 million years old, so *T. rex* in South Dakota (and other species found with it) must be the same age.

The striped colors and textures in the badlands' sand castles delineate occasions of sedimentary deposition, particularly rapidly changing ones—perhaps fierce rainstorms or floods—that might have buried carcasses quickly. Their pastel greens, pinks, reds, yellows, and beiges eventually look like road signs to the trained eye.

While luck plays a part in finding fossils, experience puts a paleontologist in the right place to get lucky. Time in the field is the
best dinosaur divining rod there is.

At first that time is spent walking. Usually ten miles or more at
a stretch in the hot sun, looking in gullies, clambering up and
down hills, scaling cliffs, crossing ravines. I love this part of being
a paleontologist. Prospecting may tire the body, but for me it does
wonderful, relaxing things for the mind and spirit. I can meander
along quite joyfully, thinking about almost anything. The origin of
a specific scrap of bone, the mating behavior of *Tyrannosaurus
rex,* the beauty of a flowering cactus, the probability of life on
Mars, the loss of compression in the number-seven cylinder of my
4x4's 350. Meanwhile, my eyes flash back and forth, back and
forth, noting color and texture changes, identifying fragments of
bone, and watching for rattlesnakes. Sometimes, I admit, I focus
so intently on the fragments that I forget the snakes. Not a great
habit, but so far I've been lucky.

At Ruth Mason's ranch, anyone would have gotten lucky.
Anyone would have found dinosaurs, and it was there we dug our
first one. I first met Ruth in her little home on the Moreau River,
a slowly flowing oasis slicing through the plains. Cottonwoods
and native elms furnished uncommon prairie shade over Ruth's
flower beds, which were decoratively bordered with dinosaur
bones and petrified wood. I was a graduate student at the time,
sharing a glass of lemonade with someone who had four times my
exposure to the world.

Ruth grew up working cattle, and later sheep, on horseback
alongside her father on their ranch on the Cheyenne River
Reservation. As a turn-of-the-century white child among the
Indian population, she witnessed all sorts of hard times, economic, patriotic, racial, and social. Despite everything, she never
questioned her life on the prairie, simply put her head down and
worked—alone after her parents and husband passed away. She
knew the territory like the back of her hand, knew exactly where
the big bones always pierced through the Cretaceous siltstone. In
the 1960s and 1970s Ruth repeatedly invited various academic
scientists to come identify what she figured were dinosaurs, but no

one was interested in making the desolate drive, 150 miles from the South Dakota School of Mines, the nearest university. No one wanted to face the potted, rutted road, the dangling barbed wire gates, the dust storms. By the time I met Ruth in 1979, she was in her eighties, a white-haired woman wrapped in baggy bib overalls, a solitary being who had created her life from scratch. "I want to know what kind of dinosaurs they were," she said. "Go on out and take a look."

At that time Black Hills Institute was in the market for a dinosaur. The fledgling business, begun six years earlier when I was twenty-one, recently incorporated with Neal and friend Bob Farrar, was holding on by a thread. To make ends meet, I had worked as an analytical chemist, cleaned the pool at the YMCA, pressed cheddar at the cheese plant, and dug graves at the cemetery. Not long before, a museum curator had asked whether Black Hills Institute could find a display dinosaur for his facility, and I answered "of course" without pausing. We had never found a dinosaur, not a single one.

At Ruth's, I stood looking at more than a half-kilometer of ground where hundreds of bones had bubbled out of the surface. And there were more, a knife-blade under. Within a month, Ruth signed a contract with us for the bonebed, a graveyard of thousands, maybe tens of thousands, of duckbill dinosaurs who apparently had met with some sort of catastrophe. A flash flood, perhaps. We would dig the quarry from 1979 to 1991. Year after year, our trucks arrived, university volunteers camped, children dug their first bone, I undertook my first dinosaur research, and Ruth felt that her history with the ranch had come full-circle. The earth had sustained her, and now, by saving these bones, she was giving something back.

During the thirteen field seasons that the Ruth Mason Quarry operated without incident, Black Hills Institute enjoyed a previously unequaled success. Six tall *Edmontosaurus annectens* skeletons, compiled from disarticulated, mass-deposited bones, were pieced together and mounted for museums in Japan, Wales, Ireland, and the United States. By the time Sue was discovered in August of 1990, two more duckbills had been slated for display in

Japan and the Netherlands. The quarry was a training ground, a guaranteed back-breaking seminar in field technique that produced pristine specimens. It also pumped the lifeblood of Black Hills Institute, increasing the collection for our future museum and injecting funds for research and other projects like Matthew's *Triceratops*, fossil whale recovery in Peru, and eventually *T. rex*. Thanks to Ruth, we knew a wonderful transition from near-bankruptcy to success.

Our experience with Ruth was typical of most of the relationships we've developed with landowners. Great Plains ranchers are a self-reliant bunch. They have survived droughts, wars, depressions, Red Scares, locusts, irrigation technologies, and farm subsidies.

Left: These disarticulated duckbill bones were found piled underground, with parts of various individuals mixed together.

Below: Full swing at the Ruth Mason Quarry, a gravesite of tens of thousands of duckbilled dinosaurs.

Photos by Peter Larson.

They are environmentalists, doctors, veterinarians, mechanics, mathematicians, meteorologists. They are agronomists, gamblers, and philosophers. They make their decisions on instinct and experience, whether in buying a used baler or judging someone's character. Sometimes I have watched them fall in love with paleontology. They have learned to dig, scouted their own outcrops, invited busloads of school children to our remote excavation sites on their property. The Niemis have buzzed out some evenings with a phone message or a casserole on the handlebars of their four-wheelers. The Zerbsts dished up magnificent feasts fit for a king. The Lickings would drive three hours each way to sit behind us in court.

While nothing could replace these relationships, they have become even more vital since the legislative lobbying began over access to public lands. As permitting details are scrapped over, we have done our best to stick to private acreages, those scientific study halls that double as someone's back forty. The ranchers have seen parades of plaster-covered bones march from their fields into their garages, or if it's cold, into their mud rooms. They have visited specimens, pieced together from their soil, now standing on museum display at the Smithsonian, the Field Museum in Chicago, or the Houston Museum of Natural Science. Our rancher–business partners can look back with us on successful projects. Good times, with very few exceptions.

The exceptions were the ones prosecuting attorneys eventually would bring forward as charges against us. Our friendships and our intentions would comprise the most basic ingredients in the prosecution's case against Black Hills Institute. Suddenly our fence-and-kitchen conversations were called opportunities for misrepresentation. The ranchers were cast as victims, unwitting partners in shady excavation deals—and the only people who could testify as to how Black Hills Institute presented itself in the field. To those of us from the prairie, our handshakes are contracts, as good as gold. The poetry of our land, our culture. To the prosecution, poetry would appear unprofessional.

Now our handshakes often include paperwork and an apology for asking for a signature.

Maurice Williams didn't want a contract. Our conversation was held in the great outdoors, in the presence of Susan Hendrickson and Terry Wentz. By that time, Sue lay exposed on her deathbed, and I made an offer of $5,000 for the skeleton, knowing how much we'd already spent on excavation, would have to spend on removal and preparation and mounting for our hometown museum, and could borrow from the bank. If forced, I thought I could go to $10,000. The contract sat quietly folded in my pocket. He said yes to $5,000. He said no to signing. "We don't need to do that," he said. I handed him the check, on which was written, "Theropod Skeleton Sue 8.14.90.MW." That day, out in the wind, our hands connected in a firm handshake. As good as gold. Poetry. I wasn't about to insult him by forcing him to sign a piece of paper.

Our First Date

Pick, shovel, throw. All day. Pick, shovel, throw. The top of Sue's hillside was inaccessible by vehicle. In order to create our gigantic shelf, we had to dig it by hand. No bulldozers. No earth movers. Not even a Bobcat skidsteer loader.

Pick, shovel, throw. Another day, and another.

An entire week.

At first only Neal and I could fit on the shelf. Soon Terry and Susan could join us. Each night we returned to our Mason quarry camp completely exhausted, our skin caked with dirt, our muscles drained.

We already had accomplished the first steps in fossil excavation. On August 14 we started by stabilizing fractured vertebrae; elliptical cross-sections of more than a half-dozen ribs; what appeared to be a rectangular, four-inch-diameter cross-section of two paired bones that had fused while the animal was alive; and the rounded end, or condyle, of a large bone, perhaps from a foot or leg. Including some additional "rib-sized" bones a little to the east of the main mass, we measured the skeleton's initial exposure at nine feet long and eighteen inches thick. These were our first glimpses into the mystery that was Sue.

Drawing roughly parallel lines in the silty dust of the valley floor, perpendicular to the cliff face, we delineated rectangles linking Sue's exposed bones with the closest litter of fragments sprinkled beneath them. In a line from west to east, on our hands and knees, adults and children gently pried up the thousands of pieces, filled sandwich bags, and placed them in their delineated regions until they could be numbered and mapped. After collecting everything we could see, we shoveled dirt from the divisions into garbage bags for future screening. As weird as it might seem, we all would entertain ourselves later in the laboratory with the three-dimensional puzzle of reuniting bones with weathered-off edges. As unlikely as it might seem, a good percentage of matches would be made.

We carefully foiled and padded the fragile, exposed bones of Sue's skeleton, drove anchoring spikes into the wall above and below them, and applied a plaster jacket that covered the bones and held fast to the anchors. After sheltering the mass with a tarp, we thought we had done our best to shield the delicate bones from any rocks that might accidentally fall on, or roll across, the specimen as we picked and shoveled away the overburden.

Pick, shovel, throw. Matthew and Jason said a reluctant goodbye, diminishing our crew by a third. Catching a ride homeward

Neal and Susan stabilizing Sue's bones with foil, plaster, and glue before removing the sediment above them. Photo by Peter Larson.

with Terry—who deserved a hot shower and a few nights in a bed—the boys set off from our field school to return to mathematics and grammar and history. I had no such commitments waiting for me, but it wouldn't have mattered if I had—nothing could have torn me away at that time. From the first moment I had laid eyes on Sue, I had fallen into the Zone. It is magical enough to stand on the very earth, the same grains of sand, on which a dinosaur once stood. But to watch it emerge, to guess what corner

of which bone is next, to have studied the curves and connections and joints and surfaces of a creature and instantly recognize the quadratojugal or the scapula-coracoid from one glimpse—that is what I lived for. With Sue, we were meeting our first *T. rex* personally, and we had so much to learn about those intimate surfaces, bones kept secret for 65 million years. To experience the rush of recognition when a new friend lay within a quarter-inch of the surface was my drug of choice.

One moment for the pick-shovel tag team. Pete, left, and Terry Wentz, right, removing overburden. Sue's tail vertebrae can be seen peeking from the earth at bottom.
Photo by Susan Hendrickson.

Later we would experience another kind of rush—the rush of dread, the weight of foreboding, the fear of powerlessness—and I would discover another puzzle, another reason to live. While in prison, and upon my return to the depleted Black Hills Institute, five years after Sue was seized, I found my family. Like those grains of sand heavy with the ancient memory of a dinosaur, my family had been there all along. Like a man granted a second chance at life, I could finally see them. My children had grown up on the windswept, powerful prairie, trailing after me on long days of prospecting, training their own eyes and fingers. They dug dinosaurs like most kids played Nintendo. Experts in a skill shared by only a handful of eccentrics in the world, they learned my language as a survival mechanism. Their hands worked carefully, quickly, instinctively sensing the all-important seam between earth and bone. They knew I loved them and was proud of them, but they also recognized the Zone, and knew that when my eyes were focused on the ground, I might not see them.

I am thankful for those endless months we drove and hiked and dug together, for every precious moment Sarah, Matthew, and Tim spent sleeping in tents close by. I am lucky that they could recognize my addiction and forgive me for it. In my new life, I am forging a different relationship between the Zone and the Family. New baby Ella will know a new father, whose Zone includes her.

With Sue in the ground, more than thirty feet below me, and the Zone wrapping all around us, I used geometry and my senses to figure the shelf dimensions. Brother Neal and I fell into a rhythm developed over a lifetime of working together in the field. Not too fast, not too slow. Pick, shovel, throw. We used natural fissures in the rock to help us pry large chunks of sandstone and silty material from the face, and, conscious that we easily could bury the object of our desire, we threw the pieces as far as possible, on either side of the tarp covering the skeleton. After a week, we had moved so much earth that we had to throw the overburden over the tops of two huge cones of debris to the east and west of the cut. By then the front of the quarry was open, and Terry and Susan had begun with digging knives and geology picks, working away the few inches of matrix we had left covering the bones.

Susan was working to the east of the main mass, uncovering a lot of small bones, mostly ribs, which seemed to have washed away from the rib cage. Terry, working just north of the center of the initial exposure, dazzled us by finding the ilium, a five-foot-long and nearly three-foot-wide undulating pelvic bone. He also began uncovering the articulated dorsal vertebrae, Sue's backbone, that Susan had first seen poking from the cliff. These vertebrae curved gently along the cliff face and appeared to be in place,

Maurice Williams, on motorcycle, and neighbors come to visit Sue's site as excavators finally reach the bones. Photo by Peter Larson.

still connected to the sacrum, a bone enclosed within the pelvis. I began digging in earnest above and to the side of the pelvis, four feet back from the original cliff face. In making my choice, I used a combination of instinct, logic, experience, and wild hair. I wanted the first bone I dug to be Sue's skull.

With a mixture of anxiety and certainty, I stood over the rock I wanted to remove and peeled off layers of sand by horizontally swinging the head of my medium-sized Estwing excavating pick. Thinking I had plenty of room to work, I fell into the rhythm of the Zone, when suddenly I heard a faint "clunk" and felt a vibration through the pick handle. The other diggers heard it, too, that particular sound that comes only from a pick striking bone. A sound that breaks the most fundamental rule of fossil excavation—never touch the fossil with a tool.

"Must be the skull," I joked.

Carefully, I held the pick steady, in place, as I crouched down, placed one hand over the loosened sandstone, and carefully slid the point of the pick out of the impact hole. As I removed the sharp point, I pushed the fragmented sand back into place and dribbled fast-drying cyanoacrylate "super" glue over the disturbed sand. I probed with my X-acto knife, and in a matter of minutes I uncovered a skull all right—the palate side of a four-inch-long turtle skull. The pick had struck it at the opening of the right ear, but after my repair, there was virtually no damage to the small specimen. My ego had been hit a little harder, but I repaired that by pontificating on how Sue's large skeleton must have trapped the turtle skeleton as it tumbled along in the current of the stream. Somehow this science lesson did not stem the teasing from my crewmates.

After recording the position and carefully wrapping and labeling the turtle skull, I got back to work with the pick. In a half-hour or so I was back in the swing of things, striking with the pick, turning over loose rock, brushing the surface, throwing the debris. Then we heard another clunk, louder than the first. I cringed.

"Must be the S word," I said, afraid now to tempt fate, wanting to believe I still had room to spare. I was working at least a foot above Sue's bone layer and assumed that this, too, was an interloper of the turtle variety.

"Sure, Pete," answered Terry.

I pushed the sandstone back down with my hand as I once again withdrew the pick, then glued the material. While waiting for the glue to dry, I moved one foot to the west and swung the pick again. Yet another clunk.

"This is it!" I said. Only two bones could be this thick, could protrude this high above their ground layer. We'd already identified the pelvis; this had to be the skull. My colleagues just laughed. Debris, they thought. Maybe concretion, just a hard ball of rock.

Again I got down on my hands and knees with glue. I retired the small pick and pulled out my X-acto knife. I worked contentedly the rest of the day on my discovery, with each bit of bone I uncovered bolstering the accuracy of my divining rod. It was not debris. Not a turtle. No concretion. By the end of the day, I could see enough bone to believe I'd found the prize—even if I had done so with a pick instead of a knife blade. Twice.

By noon the following day, I was no longer alone in my fantasy. The right side of the magnificent skull looked up at us from its long-empty eye socket. The head stretched more than four feet long, was nearly three feet wide, and its nose dove under the pelvis. It appeared uncrushed, and was highly ornamented with

The Doctor's Kit

The overall approach to excavating an average fossil has been in place for more than a century: stabilize, protect, remove. While most techniques commonly used by paleontologists are as old as the hills, a few have improved over time. One significant improvement is the use of cyanoacrylate glue, which has several distinct advantages over any other form of readily obtainable adhesive. Commonly called "super" glues, the thinnest varieties have a nearly complete absence of viscosity, or surface tension, and will follow and fill cracks invisible to the naked eye. These also act as consolidants, filling pore spaces and hardening bone. Thicker, more viscous glues are better for adhering larger pieces of bone together, since their flow can be controlled.

Once in contact with bone, superglues polymerize with the water found in all fossils, thereby creating an extremely strong bond. Best of all, they work in a matter of seconds and they last a lifetime—maybe into the thousands of years. Although superglues are available from a number of sources, only a brand called Paleobond has withstood our rigorous testing.

Some scientists prefer not to use superglues because, once cured, cyanoacrylates have the disadvantage of being difficult, although not impossible, to remove. Acetone and commercial cyanoacrylate solvents work quite well to remove the glue and to "unglue" pieces, but they are time-consuming. It's a tall task, for example, when working with superglued sandstone matrix that has become a *very* solid mass, or with a porous matrix that suddenly has all its pore spaces filled.

Other sealers are easier to remove in the laboratory, and also can be applied in large quantities in the field. Especially good is acetone-thinned polyvinyl acetate (PVA) the consistency of water. PVA's only downside is drying time, which can be several hours. Which product to use at which moment depends on personal preference, matrix condition, and how much time is available on any given day.

Aside from hardeners, and the advent of four-wheel-drive vehicles, perhaps the most noteworthy technique in the field collector's bag of tricks has to do with supporting the bones. Independent field collector Charles Sternberg has been credited as the first to dip burlap strips into a gooey paste of rice to create a hard "jacket" for especially fragile pieces. Later one of Marsh's crew modified the process by using plaster of paris, which is what we still use today.

My preference? Superglue as a starter, foil and tape as the salad course, followed by a nice helping of plaster-covered bandages. If necessary, supportive wooden splints, boards, and planks can be added for large bones or blocks, with a final layer of liquid plaster. A brandy for dessert.

ridges and textured areas. It was, quite simply, the coolest thing I'd ever seen. I asked Terry, one of the most careful collectors in the world, to take over while I went to work with the pick behind the skull. As the day drew to a close, Terry had uncovered a number of teeth, in place, in the upper jaw's tooth-bearing maxilla. The lower jaw was tucked up under the maxilla, in its natural closed position. As those two days unfolded, revealing what once was the window to Sue's soul, I was so immersed in the Zone that I sometimes forgot the magnitude of what was happening.

As the sun made its rounds, more and more of the skeleton came to light. Sue lay in the quintessential dinosaur death pose, her gigantic frame circling around us, tail articulated to the pelvis and gracefully arched backward, its tip nearly touching the back of her skull. With each new element we exposed, we delicately sought the layer between bone and earth. We angled our X-acto blades toward the bone surface, dislodging the sediment and nudging it to fall cleanly away from the bone, without touching the bone itself with metal. Lying on our sides on the rocky ground, or balanced on our knees and elbows for entire days, faces within inches of the earth, we watched for telltale flakes of bone. Our hands moved automatically, extensions of our thoughts, our thoughts mere shadows of our instincts. We shot the thin super glue into hairline cracks, knowing it would instantly slither down the tiniest tunnels, bonding splinters back into place. The softest brushes swept away dusty debris so we could check for color, texture, minuscule bits of some-

thing important threatening to masquerade forever as a crumb of sandstone. Hours would pass and we would only know it from the spasming of cramped muscles. In the mass of bone, one piled atop another, each motion of our hands revealed something new. It was impossible to stop, inconceivable to slow down, insulting to have to eat and sleep.

The only process I didn't mind stopping for was scientific. Our record keeping had begun before I set foot next to Sue's skeleton, when I paused on that initial approach to shoot my first photos. Susan even obliged me by reenacting her discovery for our video camera and audiotaping a descrip-

Recording scientific information is one of the most important aspects of fossil collection. Photo by Layne Kennedy.

tion of her find. Throughout excavation we took photographs galore, making sure to include a scale within the frame when focusing on individual bones or groups of bones. We shot panoramas and video footage to help future generations relocate the discovery site and the geologic horizon.

For the Record

Field scientists keep regular records of their work not only at excavations, but also at potential excavations, or even at interesting bits of geology. Generally, I draw a map of the section, measure vertical dimensions with a Jacob's staff, and describe changing lithologies as to type, color, texture, hardness, grain size, and inclusions. Using topographic and land ownership maps, I mark the location to the nearest quarter-quarter-section and ascertain ownership (final confirmation comes from the courthouse). Once we reach a specimen's bone layer, I draw a sketch map of the fossil, orienting it with a north arrow established from my Brunton pocket transit. I add its measurements, and for research purposes note associated fossils.

Ironically, these and other field notes—which we keep religiously—later would form the basis of the government's investigation into our business. Our maps would come in handy, too. At Sue's site, my field notebook carried my standard record:

SPECIMEN NUMBER: SUE.8-14-90.MW. (BHI-2033)

SPECIMEN DESCRIPTION: (Initially) Large theropod skeleton, some articulation in vertebral column. (Later) Left scapula-corocoid, humerus, cervical ribs, prox. end tibia, 2 femurs, pelvis, sacrum, 11 dorsal vert., skull + lowers, ribs, metatarsal, 35 caudals (8 w/o chevrons).

PRESERVATION: Good to excellent, some ironstone concretions, some siltstone—mostly sand—comes away from bone well.

FORMATION: Approx. 10 feet above base of Lower Hell Creek Formation.

LOCATION: SE1/4, SW1/4, NW1/4, Sec. 32, T15N, R18E, Maurice Williams ranch, north east of Ruth Mason Quarry, Ziebach Co., South Dakota.

COLLECTOR: SUSAN HENDRICKSON, with Terry, Neal, Pete, Matthew, Jason.

Every excavation is unique, and before we remove even one fossil, we must record bone placement. A bone map is crucial in reconstructing the series of events that led to the preservation of a particular fossil and is consulted during bone reassembly. After many years of mapping trial and error that explored everything from coordinate systems to one-to-one tracings, I developed a simple and effective method that utilizes a collapsible, portable frame constructed from four pieces of 1-inch angle iron. A tough, colored fishing line is strung through drilled holes, forming 1-foot-square "windows" that correspond to designated pages of grid paper. Using corner stakes, the grid may be moved to the right or left, forward or backward. It only needs to be in place while maps are drawn and can be removed or replaced easily as digging progresses. Each

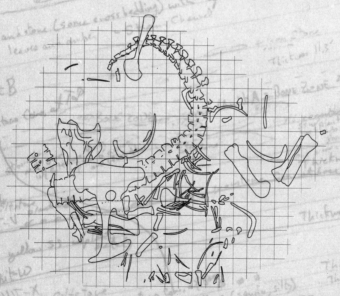

Sue's completed bone map, in miniature with grid markings. Each square represents one square foot. Illustration by Peter Larson and Terry Wentz.

bone is identified and numbered, both on its package and on the map.

By the end of excavation, the material associated with Sue's gravesite had grown considerably and was carefully included in our records. In addition to leaves and snails, we discovered a colony of perhaps a dozen freshwater clams. Sue's body had come to rest on these unfortunates, and whatever had caused her death also had caused theirs. Aside from the infamous turtle skull, we collected other turtle bones from at least two different species, and assorted bones and teeth of crocodiles, lizards, and fish. We also found evidence of other dinosaurs: the pelvis and vertebrae of the hypsilophodon called *Thescelosaurus;* a skull bone and tail vertebrae from *Edmontosaurus;* teeth of *Nanotyrannus, Dromaeosaurus,* and a *coelurosaur;* the lower jaw of an *oviraptor;* and some *T. rex* parts that didn't quite fit with the skeleton we were excavating. Food for thought.

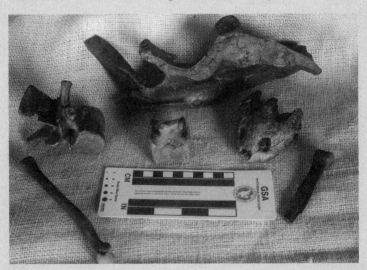

A selection of bones from other creatures found with Sue. Bottom row, foot bones from a toothless meat-eater, an Oviraptorid. Middle row, from left: vertebra from primitive plant-eater, *Thescelosaurus;* tail vertebra from the duckbilled *Edmontosaurus;* the infamous turtle skull. At top, *Thescelosaurus* pelvic bone. Photo by Ed Gerken.

Even though many of Sue's bones were still out of sight in a large mass of bone and rock, we could see that most of this magnificent beast was preserved. She would become the standard-bearer for *T. rex*, the species cover girl—and not just because she was nearly complete. Our preliminary measurements showed that Sue led the pack, her legs stretching a little longer, her skull winning the size contest by a nose. Susan loved it. She had found the biggest, beefiest *Tyrannosaurus rex* ever, and it was a she. Or so we suspected, for reasons I'll explain in the next chapter. Maurice Williams had assumed Sue was a boy, asking on a visit to the dig site, "You going to mount *him* in Hill City?" I could tell already how much fun we would have with this, the world's scariest monster wearing a dress. I liked the smile it brought to people's faces. Plus, the whole thing gave me an idea for a research project.

During the excavation itself and soon after, when bones were examined in the laboratory, we began to catch a glimpse of the new science written all over Sue's face. Her gender took a momentary backseat while we took stock of what was looking out at us from the matrix. Sue had been bitten and battered and broken. We would find when the skull was isolated in the laboratory that one side of her jaw had been pulled away at the hinge; one bone behind her eye dangled by a thread, and another had been crushed—all evidence of what I identify as the injury that killed her.

Early on, we found the first of Sue's fifty-four-inch-long shoulder blades draped over the rear of the tail. Eventually we would uncover both of Sue's shoulder girdles, two pairs of two bones each—and more complete than MOR-555's. Under and around the tail and downstream to the east and south we discovered a plethora of ribs, gastralia, and smaller bones—along with that important *T. rex* arm and hand from Sue's right side.

And that wasn't all. Articulated together but removed from its socket in the pelvis, the left leg had drifted downstream a few feet. Neal noticed it first: at least two-thirds of the shaft of the fibula, the smaller of the two lower leg bones, was encased by an unusual, huge, injury-repairing growth of bone. The "exostosis" formed a thick callus which would have made the healed bone stronger than it had been before it was hurt, although there may have been some

Extra bone growth on Sue's left leg's fibula, where an injury resulted in massive infection. Photo by Peter Larson.

muscle impairment because of the rough texture and expansion of the healed bone. It appeared that Sue, a creature that walked on two legs, survived a major injury to one of those legs.

During her lifetime, Sue sustained multiple injuries that left scars on her bones as they healed. Called pathologies, these scars indicate not only that Sue was hurt, but also that she survived each accident marked on her skeleton; otherwise, the injuries would show no repair. At one time or other, Sue suffered from multiple broken and sometimes infected ribs, crushed tail vertebrae, a badly broken lower leg, a torn tendon on the right upper arm, and multiple injuries to the head.[3] Certainly Sue could not have obtained all these injuries at once and lived. This seems to point to significant time passing between traumatic events, which in turn also suggests that Sue lived a long, difficult life. Likely the Tyrant Queen lived to a ripe old age of perhaps one hundred years before she finally went down for the count.

Pathologies whisper even more to us, in the form of hints that cause scientists to tread lightly out on their own limbs. For example, the lower leg is comprised of two bones, the larger tibia and smaller fibula. To me, it appears as if Sue's fibula was shattered over one-half of its total length, which would have incapacitated her. The healing was further complicated by a bacterial infection, called osteomyelitis, evidenced by the spongy appearance of some of the exostosis. Other scientists disagree, saying that, although the bone was infected, the exostosis does not necessarily mean the bone was actually broken, and that Sue might have been able to hobble. (Even so, imagine her chasing a *Triceratops*—while leaning on crutches grasped by puny arms?) I learned firsthand when I broke my tibia in 1995 that the muscles of a broken limb cease to function. The brain shuts down nerve impulses to the muscles in order to prevent further, self-inflicted injury. If Sue's leg was broken, or even seriously impaired by infection, she could not have walked, hunted, or defended herself. How could such a beast have survived a long convalescence with one functional leg? Perhaps the same way I survived mine! As I lay helpless and in pain on the couch, I was brought healing sustenance by my caring mate.

Did *T. rex* have a caring mate? Or even an uncaring one? Harley Garbani's reburied LACM *T. rex* offers a clue: two specimens, an adult and a juvenile, were buried together. Sue also was buried with parts of others of her species—fragments of another adult, a juvenile, and a baby. While more evidence and research are necessary, these preliminary findings suggest that *T. rex* did not walk alone.

It was an incredible feeling to stand within the circle of Sue's enormous chain of vertebrae and scan her skeleton for all its parts. While it might appear that everything lay snugly in place, or close to it, we had to consider that Sue had been buried in a streambed, presumably thanks to fast-moving water. What if small bones had been carried away in the flow? Sue's disarticulated leg provided a big clue to the stream's direction, but I looked for corroborating evidence of "crossbedding" in the sandstone stream channel. Crossbedding occurs as water or wind moves sand grains from place to place, redepositing them on the lee side of moving sand dunes or sandbars. If enough grains were moved while Sue was being buried, they would have created thinly bedded sloping surfaces which "crossed" normal horizontal bedding planes—and any loose fragments would have followed that slope.

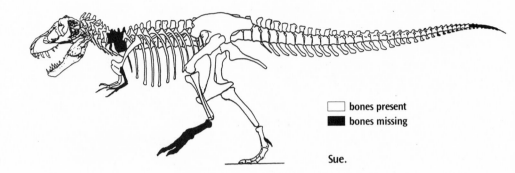

bones present
bones missing

Sue.

After taking several measurements with my handheld transit, I determined that the stream flow was 135 degrees east of north. Looking at the specimen, this seemed consistent with the accumulation of ribs and small bones at the rear of the pelvis. Unfortunately, it also might have meant that some of the smaller elements could have washed farther to the southeast—and perhaps already eroded away as the skeleton was exposed along the cliff face. While that would be disappointing if true, at least we could safely bet that parts of Sue were not still trapped under a very tall hill.

The last phase of large-scale excavation is really a team sport. In this case, with the lack of access for vehicles and the configuration of Sue's bones, it would have to be more like Cirque du Soleil—feats of unbelievable strength, death-defying moments with pulleys and chains, and undeniable magic. We were going to have to pull this one out of a hat.

We began by cutting down the matrix around each specimen's perimeter in order to suspend it four to ten inches above the bottom of the excavation. The larger the bone, the higher the pedestal, whose job it was to elevate and expose the specimen without disturbing its main support. As a bone became more and more vulnerable, we applied super glue or PVA to any newly exposed fractures on its surface. Then came several layers of heavy-duty aluminum foil followed by strapping tape wrapped tightly over both the specimen and the matrix directly under it. Then, buckets of water, plaster of paris, a stick for stirring.

An unruly, untidy chorus line, or perhaps one person with many arms, we repeated our pedestal procedure over and over, hovering over bone after bone. Glue, foil, tape, plaster. We took turns dragging strips of gauze and then burlap through the white, watery paste, creating plaster casts. If the bone was very large, we added splints of wood held in place with more bandages, and ended with a straight layer of plaster mixed with water.

After the casts crystallized and became very rigid, the specimens were turned over, their undersides cleaned and glued, their field number marked with an indelible marker. After all of the single bones and small groups of bones had been removed, we were left with a huge, multiton mass—the result of intertwined body parts difficult to separate in the field. Its contents were precious indeed, consisting of the skull, the pelvis, the right leg and foot, and several groups of vertebrae that created the neck, backbone, and tail. When the bones are so intertwined, we find it safer for the skeleton if we whittle away whatever maneuverable sections can be removed and then work our magic on the rest. We are not alone in finding it most practical to work with large blocks when excavating large skeletons; a number of researchers have used helicopters to remove theirs from difficult locations.

As we undercut and pedestaled the main mass, we looked for fractures that would "naturally" divide it into sections. Gently allowing the pieces to disconnect, and then entombing them in plaster casts, we successfully removed several smaller blocks containing mostly the back and tail vertebrae. Even so, we would have to wrestle a block approximately eight feet wide, eleven feet long, and nearly three feet thick—and which we later would learn weighed approximately nine-thousand pounds. To stabilize it while we prepared our attack, we wrapped a protective coating of foil, held on by strapping tape, and a layer of plastered burlap strips over the top and edges of the block.

Lying on our sides and swinging out in front of us in slow, tedious, arm-cramping motions, we removed rock from the base of the block, until it stood on two columns a foot wide and five feet long. Once we broke through with the tunnel, we shaved sand away from the bottom of the block with old, sharpened car springs. We worked very carefully to avoid exposing the bone, while removing as much weight from the block as possible. As soon as we smoothed the tunnel's surface, we began plastering. There was no time to lose, as the rapidly evaporating ground moisture in the sand grains allowed the plaster to adhere better. We were also worried about the possibility of a collapse of the block under its own weight. Only two days before, a four-hundred-pound plastered section broke away only moments after Terry had crawled out from under it. The fossil broke along a natural fracture, and was essentially unhurt; it would have been a different story for Terry. Keenly aware of the danger of working under the block, we continued to create more support with the plaster, and then chiseled away at the columns—until the block stood on four-foot-wide legs. Plaster, chisel, plaster, chisel. Finally, we had enough room and stability to slide beams through the tunnels, and we built a pallet under the big block.

We had worked sixteen full days. It was the first of September and time for the only gas-guzzling members of our team to come to the rescue. While some of the crew maneuvered trailers and pickups into position and loaded them with casts and bags and bones, the rest finished framing. Thanking our physics and engineering professors, we built wooden triangles for a stabilizing trestle over the block, something that would keep it from flexing and breaking under the strain of driving 130 miles to Hill City. We then fastened the trestle, frame, and underlying pallet to the block's plaster cast, and chipped away the remaining sandstone blocks under it. Everything was ready—for the death-defying, magic part.

At other sites we have used pipes as rollers, or a forklift attachment for our Bobcat skidsteer loader, both of which help in loading most pieces onto trucks and trailers. At the Sue site, there was no place for rollers and we had no Bobcat. What we had were chains, heavy-duty come-alongs, crowbars, and two lowboy trailers—our own and one brought by our younger brother John and his best friend, Bob Tate. These recruits came in the nick of time, three days earlier, adding fresh muscle to the removal of heavy casts we were unable to budge alone. They drew the line, however, when I generously volunteered Neal and Terry to assist Maurice Williams in the bloody job of dehorning young, crabby cattle, and they chose to stay on-site with me. After all, *somebody* had to supervise Sue.

Using chains and come-alongs to load the 9,000-pound block containing Sue's skull, pelvis, right leg, and other bones. Photo by Susan Hendrickson.

The two cones of overburden dirt turned out to be a blessing in disguise. With them we were able to smooth out a ramp and cover it with a trail of plywood sheets leading from the block to the bed of a trailer. Once the bone mass rested on the plywood, we jacked the come-along and levered the crowbars and pulled. And pulled. And pulled. Slowly, the massive block inched down the slope toward the trailer. It seemed to take forever. Inch by inch, Sue was leaving home. By the time the block was chained into place on the trailer, the sun was hovering near the horizon. We had done it.

Every fossil presents its own opportunities, problems, and challenges—roads must be built, hoists must be constructed, consolidants must be tried, new packaging methods must be engineered. Rabbits must be pulled out of hats. These are the problems I love to solve. Throughout our Sue excavation, however, Maurice Williams tossed into the ring a problem I found I would not love solving. He visited from time to time and seemed pleased with our dream that Sue would be the cornerstone of our new Black Hills Museum of Natural History. He marveled that he must have

The beginning of the end: Sue's exposed skull with two of its future custody claimants. From right, Maurice Williams, John Larson, Terry Wentz, Bob Tate, Peter, Neal, and Maurice's son Brady. Photo by Susan Hendrickson.

ridden by this hillside at least a hundred times, never seeing anything out of the ordinary. He cashed our check, and it cleared. So we were surprised when strangely, on his last visit, he joked that we had "taken" him financially. We weren't sure what to make of his humor, and nearly two years would pass before we found out.

Maurice Williams was the last thing on our minds in the fading daylight of one of our more challenging dig sites. With joyous hearts and aching backs, we loaded our tools and tidied up the excavation. We watched as the setting sun backlit an ominous approaching thunderstorm, and the caravan of two pickups, two trailers, three people, and a sixty-five-million-year-old dinosaur trundled off across the darkening prairie toward Sue's new digs. It would not be the last time Sue would be moved in plaster jackets and crates, nor the last time I would watch my colossal girlfriend, the debutante dinosaur of the century, drive away.

(4)

Sex and the Single Rex

MOR-555, AMNH-5027, TMP 81.12.1. Museums have to call their dinosaurs something—usually a number—and often it is preceded with letters denoting the institution: Museum of the Rockies, MOR; American Museum of Natural History, AMNH; Tyrrell Museum of Paleontology, TMP. The specimen numbers reflect membership in accessioned collections, the official registry for an institution. Every place is different; Tyrrell uses the date of collection, while Black Hills Institute, BHI, simply numbers consecutively; Sue was BHI-2033. Usually fossils receive two numbers, an informal one in the field—ours delineates the ranch and date of collection, SUE.8-14-90.MW—and the official accession number.

Marion Zenker, our administrative assistant and the keeper of all loose ends, claims that we handle our dinosaur naming differently than most institutions. "Some ranchers have a herd of anonymous cattle with numbered ear tags while others have two beloved milk cows named Bess and Peg. At BHI, dinosaurs are pets!" We have a tendency to nickname our significant fossils after their discoverers. Sue probably would have been Harold or Tiny Tim if someone other than Susan Hendrickson had found her.

Therein lay our rub.

We recognized the dilemma—and the humor—while digging and preparing Sue. Unlike our duckbill dinosaur "extras," two of whom we named "Doug" and "Bill," Sue was a star. We knew she was a star the second we laid eyes on her, and we knew she would be studied and evaluated and written about. Even at the dig site, the inevitable question came up time and time again. I think Terry asked it first, and, flexing her bicep, Susan answered that her namesake definitely was a girl. Neal started singing the Johnny Cash song about a boy named Sue. Had we given Sue the "right" name?

Someone suggested we look under her tail as if she were a kitten. We could look under her tail all we wanted, but her flesh was long gone. The most obvious clues had disappeared. I wondered while looking at the huge skeleton curled around us whether it was possible to truly, definitively determine gender only from bone differences. I knew various scientists had made postulations, even identifying two *morphotypes* in various species—one robust and one more delicate, called gracile. These morphotypes not only reflected overall size, but also the thickness and sturdiness of the bones themselves. Some scientists had guessed that the differences indicated gender, and that robust specimens like Sue were probably male. But no one had found a definite key. Since Sue was our first *T. rex,* I didn't recognize in the field some gender clues I later would come to know intimately. Therefore, my research began in the laboratory, where I watched the bones emerge under Terry's capable direction of our team of trained technicians.

Like most fossils, and also modern bones, Sue's bones retained their original composition, calcium phosphate. They had not been "petrified," as many people think happens to dinosaur bones. She did have a problem, however. Sometimes chemicals traveling in groundwater invade and fill the empty cell spaces in fossils, a process called permineralization. Some of Sue's cells, and some of her bone surfaces, had been coated by pyrite, "fool's gold." Pyrite can be deadly to fossils; when it interacts with water, bone-decomposing sulfuric acid is produced.

In a heat- and humidity-controlled room, Terry began the time-consuming process of untangling Sue's bones from one another and stabilizing them. Wherever he found pyrite, he either removed it or sealed it so that air and water could not come in contact. To separate bones, or to remove matrix from an individual bone, he focused on the rock surface, not touching the bones themselves with any tools except a soft brush. On a scale of 1 to 10, where 1 is the hardness of talc and 10 the hardness of diamond, bone has a hardness of about 3.5. Steel has a hardness of 5, and will always

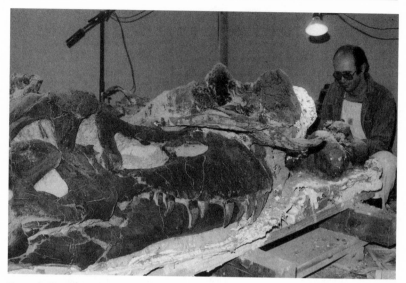

Terry dedicated hundreds of hours working his magic on Sue's main block.
Photo by Ed Gerken.

scratch bone if enough pressure is applied. While every significant
specimen is important, Sue's bones would be removed from their
enclosing matrix and mounted as a standing, show-stopping, Miss
Universe research specimen. Knowing that every move he made
was permanent, and keeping a careful eye out for any scientific
information—something trapped in the earth with Sue, unusual
sediment characteristics, anything—Terry worked cautiously.

Sue's cracks and fissures had been glued in the field, but as
Terry removed more and more sediment, he found new cracks—
and new bones. As preparation proceeded, he faced thick plaster
casts and various types of matrix. He could choose anything from
hammers, chisels, pinchers, and awls, down to scribes, dental picks,
needles, and pin vices. Probably the most useful, however, were
pneumatic, or air-powered, reciprocating air-scribes that acted like
miniature air-driven chisels. Originally developed for inscribing
jewelry, air-scribes can be controlled to within 1 mm of the surface
of a fossil, delivering strong, short strokes to the 8.5-hardness car-
bide tip. This handheld, pencil-like tool worked for Sue's soft,
medium, and hard matrix, chipping off tiny fragments and their
coatings with ease.

Left: "During": Sue's pelvic vertebrae (sacrum), in midpreparation, with most of the matrix removed.

Below: "After": Final cleaning of the pelvic vertebrae with the air-brade brings out their beauty and intricate detail. Photos by Ed Gerken.

Next he chose X-acto knives and nonpowered, needlelike hand scribes to cut away stubborn glue and to expose the actual surface of the bone, followed by a "sponge bath" of acetone and a medium-stiff brush for the last residues of glue and hardeners. Final cleaning of the well-preserved bones, which had maintained their integrity and hardness, was accomplished with the "air-brade," a miniature sandblaster. For this precious specimen, Terry used baking soda, hardness 1.5, as a gentle abrasive. He watched for any soft or chemically degraded areas, and propelled the baking soda at high speeds with variable pressures of compressed air—basically, Sue was getting a cleaning at the dentist's. The result was that Sue's bones gleamed, free of 65 million years' worth of dirt and rock, their undulating surfaces smooth yet untouched despite their journey through time.

In twenty-one months, Terry, Neal, Bob, preparator Sandy Gerken, a couple of volunteers, and I prepared about 7 percent of Sue's skeleton and all of the outside surface of her skull, which had been preserved with the jaws closed. We chose to leave intact the matrix inside her skull, believing that delicate structures never before seen might have been preserved there. In order to take a look inside without disturbing the fossil, we would need to do a CAT

Up Close and Personal

A *T. rex* requires approximately 25,000 dedicated hours of skilled preparation. In fact, when comparing collecting time with preparation time, the difference comes in several orders of magnitude; a fossil that took only one hour to collect may easily take ten, one hundred, or one thousand hours to clean, restore, and ready for exhibit. To make matters even more challenging, depending on fossil delicacy, the size of the pieces a scientist is working with, or just fine bone details—even on a large specimen—a good chunk of preparation time may be spent under magnification.

Binocular microscopic preparation can be very strenuous on eyes and hands; for most of us, microscope work can last only a few hours a day. This type of preparation necessitates the use of very small tools, which I actually fashion and sharpen under the microscope. My chief tools are handheld scribes, with tips formed into two basic shapes: a very sharp point and a flattened, rounded, and sharpened knife rather like a tiny rounded screwdriver tip. The actual removal of the matrix is accomplished by pulling the tools across the matrix next to the bone surface— thereby separating the rock from the bone.

Another way to get into tiny places is with chemicals, especially on bone-containing matrices of limestone, or calcium carbonate. A circulating bath of acetic acid buffered with calcium phosphate will slowly dissolve limestone, but will not harm bone. Careful treatment of fractures in the bone is necessary, because they are sealed with a natural cement of calcite—also calcium carbonate—which is vulnerable to the acid. Repeatedly coating exposed bone surfaces with PVA or glue will protect them from further action by the acid.

No matter how thorough preparation is, cleaning will not bridge gaps, fill cracks, or restore bone when chunks have weathered away or been lost. Although a variety of fillers may be used, I have found that a two-part epoxy putty is the most versatile and durable, as well as being easy to use. When first mixed, the putty has the consistency of clay and can be formed and textured easily or forced into cracks. Epoxy putty hardens in several hours to a very strong and durable restoration medium. It may be easily removed by first raising its temperature with a heat gun or industrial hair dryer to approximately 250 degrees, when it once again becomes pliable. It is also easily removed with baking soda and the air-brade. For large areas or missing bones, other restoration media are effective, such as a water-based plastic called "water-putty." It works similarly to, but is much more durable than, plaster of paris.

Restoration materials are usually neutral in color, and can be mixed with dry pigments—preferably to create a shade slightly darker than the color of the original bones being prepared. The object is for restored parts to be unnoticeable from a distance, but easily detectable upon close inspection. If future researchers have any difficulty recognizing restorations, an ultraviolet light will unveil the fabrications.

scan. But Sue's skull, of course, was much too large to fit in a standard hospital scanner. We began discussions with NASA to use their massive CAT scanner, designed to detect flaws in rocket engines.

After cleaning and restoring bones, we apply a thin, final coat of PVA. This extra protection on the cellular level excludes oxygen, water, and airborne pollutants that could eventually degrade the bone. In addition, this final coat protects the bone from oil and acids found on the probing fingers of curious paleontologists.

Boys and Girls

Throughout the time Sue was under the knife, I was reading about sex. I was pleased to learn there were several factors that could help me determine if Sue was a girl or a boy. The first was something we *Homo sapiens* all take for granted, and I was eager to apply it to dinosaurs. Let me put it this way: if a row of naked humans lined up for inspection, we could easily distinguish the males from the females based on physical characters. Body size, body shape, and genitalia might be the first things we would notice. The fleshy parts of our subjects would draw our eyes to hip and chest areas, and we might notice how the legs angle from the trunk to the feet. Likewise, if we lined up a row of human *skeletons*, we would again notice two morphotypes. We would detect that one group was, in general, larger—and those specimens were built from bones that actually were thicker and more substantial. Upon closer examination, we also would see subtle differences in some of the skull bones, in the elbow, and more dramatic differences in the pelvis. Among other things, the bones of the robust male pelvis fuse with maturity while those of the gracile human female do not. "Thank God," says any woman who has given birth to her rather large-brained offspring. Thus, we would recognize two different types of *Homo sapiens* skeletons based upon sexual differences. This is called *sexual dimorphism*.

Sexual dimorphism is exhibited in creatures of all kinds, living and extinct. While dimorphism takes shape in different ways, humans are most familiar with how it is manifested in mammals. We have more experience with mammals, whether through farm life with its annual cycle of mating, birth, growth, and death, or simply through a litter of kittens or puppies. We can often tell which are boys just by glancing in the cardboard box. We know that the mother is usually smaller than the father, that a bull is "beefier" and more menacing than a cow. Because we are so familiar with mammalian sexual dimorphism, we intuitively take it to be the norm.

This state of affairs has led to some misconceptions in the world of dinosaur science. More than thirty researchers had explored sexual dimorphism in dinosaurs before I began thinking about the topic, with nearly half the subject's published works focusing on duckbilled dinosaurs. Duckbills' impressive upswept headdresses, called cranial crests, were one of the first features to catch the human eye. One of the earliest to publish on this was a German paleontologist by the name of O. Abel, who proposed in 1924 that males and females might have flaunted slightly different

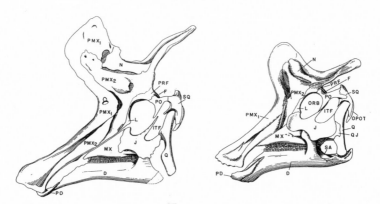

The crest differences in these two *Lambeosaurus lambei* skulls may denote sexual dimorphism. From *Hadrosaurian Dinosaurs of North America*, Lull & Wright, Geological Society of America, 1942.

crests.[1] Ceratopsians, the umbrella group that includes all horned dinosaurs, also attracted a lot of attention because their skeletons exhibited differences in body robustness and horn size.

When Abel was visiting hadrosaur haberdasheries—despite some minor flap about dinosaur similarities to birds—most paleontologists considered dinosaurs reptilian. So did they look to living reptiles for clues as to sexual dimorphism? Of course not. Prejudice firmly in place, initial comparisons were made with mammals! Paleontologists compared *Triceratops* to living horned mammals that were similar in obvious physical characters, like rhinoceroses, and concluded that the more robust individuals with larger horns were males.[2] The situation probably was not improved by the fact that at that time almost all paleontologists were men, only too happy to place the larger, more robust, shall we say "hornier" individuals in the male column.

In looking at the animal kingdom as a whole, however, we see that the situation is more complicated. An important breakthrough came when Jim Grier, ornithologist and herpetologist at North Dakota State University, pointed out that in many bird species, especially raptors, females are decidedly larger than their male counterparts. Early ornithologists even coined a special term for this condition. Displaying their bias, they called it "reversed sexual dimorphism,"[3] implying that these big girls were abnormal.

They were not: Earth's matriarchal ecosystem is filled to the brim with reversed sexual dimorphism. The Black Widow spider, who eats her smaller mate after copulation, is the rule rather than the exception among invertebrates. In these spineless creatures, males of only a very few species ever attain a body size even close to that of their girlfriends'. In most species of fishes and amphibians females also outsplash the males. The same goes for reptiles, with reversed sexual dimorphism common in most turtle and snake species. Only in mammals do males generally outsize females. But even here, there are notable exceptions. Female baleen whales and African hyenas, for instance, are always larger than males of the same species. When counting heads on Noah's Ark, it looks as if the terms *normal* and *reversed* might have been, well, reversed.

The explanation for a larger female as the norm may lie in the very act of procreation. During the breeding season, males daily produce tiny sperm cells by the millions. The female, by contrast, contributes her half of the genes and a very large bundle of nutrients encased in a relatively huge egg. Born with a set number of eggs to release during her lifetime, she only has a finite number of chances to reproduce. Not only does this mandate that she invest more energy in nurturing these "tickets to eternity," but also that the size of her body should necessarily be larger than her man's in order to carry all the extra baggage. If it is therefore *normal* for the female to be the larger of the two sexes, then why are those testy bulls larger than cows? What happened in mammalian evolution that would support this change? Like deer, like lions—like primates—a larger bovine male has a distinct advantage when engaging in physical competition with other males for the right to mate with multiple females. This advantage applies to all herding or gregarious species where a dominant male fights off smaller rivals for top-dog status in a harem of females.[4]

But that doesn't happen in birds of prey, the subject for whom the term *reversed sexual dimorphism* was originated. Raptors, and other species of birds where females are larger than males, are monogamous.[5] Monogamy eliminates physical competition between males for harem rights. Probably because of the absence of this type of macho sexual competition, male birds of prey are smaller than females.[6] And proud of it.

So was that it? No. There was *Syntarsus rhodesiensis*.

Dinosaur Sex

In 1990, South African paleontologist Michael Raath noticed the familiar delineation between robust and gracile skeletons in a bonebed of disarticulated juvenile and adult *Syntarsus rhodesiensis,* a small Jurassic theropod. Because the two morphotypes were present only in the adults, he was sure it was sexual dimorphism at work. Since the sample contained a significant number of juveniles, he reasoned that most of the accompanying adults were females, because they would be more reluctant to leave their young if a dangerous situation presented itself.[7] Females of most species normally have a larger investment in the young, both in the nutrients supplied with the egg and usually in the care of the developing young. The large group might have indicated a situation similar to certain of today's avian rookeries. Raath then went out on a limb and concluded that, because robust individuals outnumbered gracile, the larger *Syntarsus*es must be female.

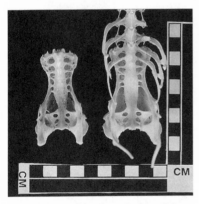

Male (left) and female goshawk pelvises. Disregarding the female's ribs in this photograph, the relative overall pelvic width is the important feature. The female's body is more substantial.

Photo by Peter Larson.

Raath, backed up by Noah's Ark, opened the door to the *possibility* that Sue was female, but to do it, he was extrapolating about social behaviors of an extinct animal. I happened to agree with Raath's logic, but still I needed more. What if *Syntarsus* was just an exception to the rule? Or what if male *Syntarsus*es really loved baby-sitting?

Enter Ken Carpenter, paleontologist at the Denver Museum of Nature and Science, who had done research even closer to my heart, and much closer to Sue's pelvis. In looking at the North American *Tyrannosaurus rex* and its Mongolian cousin *Tyrannosaurus*

(Tarbosaurus) bataar, he identified robust/gracile differences in two bones: the upper arm's humerus, and the ischium, one of the pelvic bones. He also noticed the general dimorphic appearances of other skeletal parts. Carpenter, like Raath, concluded that the robust morphotype was female—but in this case because the robust ischium made for a deeper pelvis, and more room for the passage of eggs.[8]

Bingo. It was still extrapolation, but it was connected to something concrete, something biological that just might become a future fact.

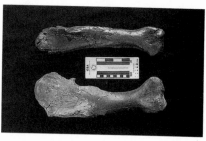

Before launching toward such a tantalizing carrot, however, there was one more possibility to consider. What else could it mean, these two closely related morphotypes of basically the same skeleton? Were these robust and gracile differences due to sexual dimorphism in one species, or were they evidence of *two different*

Gracile and robust *T. rex* upper arm bones. The question was whether Sue's, on the bottom, was evidence that female theropods were larger than males.
Photo by Peter Larson.

species? Specifically, are the skeletal differences that delineate gender the same or different from those that separate one species from another? That answer came care of Bob Bakker, who for some time had been nursing a theory about Barnum Brown's third *T. rex* find— Brown's 1906 "favorite child," the magnificent standard-setter for the species who had stood upright, cleaning its fingerclaws for generations at the American Museum of Natural History. After examining all significant *T. rex* skulls, Bakker narrowed down what appears to be the key interspecies diagnostic clue: Brown's baby, AMNH-5027—and we later would add South Dakota's first *T. rex*, SDSM&T 12047—had a shorter muzzle and proportionately deeper skull than any other *T. rexes,* including the type specimen, CM-9380. Bakker believed these differences were enough to designate a *new* species, which he has referred to as *"Tyrannosaurus X."*[9]

Later, in 1992, we would add yet another *X* to Bakker's list. Near Buffalo, South Dakota, Donald Zimmershied's son Mike found a specimen that had been poked at—and subsequently abandoned—by a local scientist.[10] The specimen, dubbed "Z-rex"

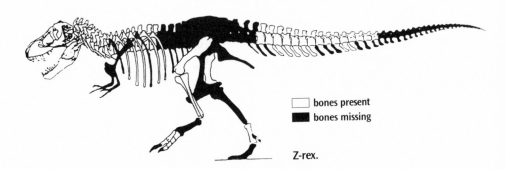

bones present
bones missing

Z-rex.

after the Zimmershieds, was excavated by fossil collectors Fred and Candace Nuss and Allen Dietrich and moved to Kansas, where I examined it. At 45 percent complete, the specimen was a good one. It included most of the vertebral column, limb and foot bones, and most of the ribs. Best of all, however, it contained a nearly complete skull, one of the best yet collected—and its measurements and features matched perfectly with *Tyrannosaurus X*. Even then, with just a few *X*'s to consider, robust and gracile subgroups clearly emerged in that "species," too.

I decided to log some serious miles. In order to acquaint myself personally with the then-twenty significant specimens of *Tyrannosaurus rex*, I went to most of the major, and many minor, natural history museums in North America. I also visited the Natural History Museum in Ulan Bataar, Mongolia, to gather information on *T. rex*'s nearest relative, *Tyrannosaurus bataar*. After careful inspection, I readily recognized adult robust and gracile morphotypes, particularly in those specimens with skulls, which displayed telltale differences in certain individual bones, including the one directly in front of the eye and another near the jaw hinge. In robust specimens, an especially noticeable bone—the angry "eyebrow" called the postorbital—was even more menacing because of an additional, fused, gnarled lump. Ralph Molnar, an Australian paleontologist, also had noticed this bone in his study of *T. rex* skulls, and believed that the presence or absence of the lump could be a sexual difference.[11] The rest of the skeleton, aside from the skull, also showed a general thickening of the bones in the robust morphotypes. I saw Carpenter's curved, heavy humerus—

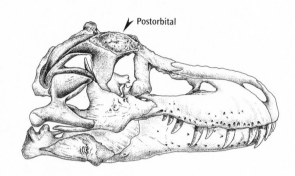

Postorbital

One skull bone in particular that potentially shows gender differences is the postorbital. In Sue's skull, and in other robust specimens, this larger "eyebrow" fused in place. Illustration by Dorothy Sigler Norton.

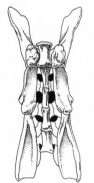
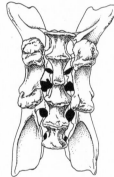

Relative widths of gracile (left — MOR-555) and robust (right — Sue) *T. rex* pelvises, one of the first direct indications that the larger animal might be the female. Illustration by Dorothy Sigler Norton.

which was very distinguishable from the rather straight, gracile arm bone—and the pelvic ischium.[12] I also noticed distinctive differentiations in the sacrum, another pelvic bone. It seemed that finding any one of these diagnostic bones could provide an indication of the characteristics of the entire skeleton.

Of all of the specimens I evaluated, Sue remained the biggest, most robust, and fiercest-looking. She flexed her thick arm, knitted her knobby eyebrows. "Well?" she asked. I looked at her, and she at me. Were female tyrannosaurs and other theropods larger than males, as Raath and Carpenter proposed? Did females have a wider pelvis? If *T. rex* was monogamous, like birds of prey, Sue probably was larger than her mate. But back in the early 1990s, when I began this study, all I knew for sure was that birds of prey were excellent models. Without soft tissue preservation, it's hard to tell boys from girls in *falcons*, let alone dinosaurs.

Family Ties

In political discussions "character" means integrity. In scientific jargon, "character" indicates a physical trait, like fused or unfused pelvic bones, or having five fingers as opposed to two. Some characters are more diagnostic than others—lots of creatures fly, but having wings doesn't necessarily mean everyone is related. When Carolus Linnaeus, a mid-1700s Swedish botanist, developed the most familiar classification system of living things, he began with a basic unit called the species. To be a member of a species meant an organism could breed successfully only with another member of that group. Next came the genus, an umbrella for multiple species intuitively recognized to share characters. For example, domestic dogs, *Canis familiaris,* do not normally interbreed with wolves, *Canis lupis,* and therefore do not share a species name. However, they are very closely related—they share many similar characters—and are placed in the same genus. Broader distinctions collected genera into orders, then orders into families, then classes, phyla, and finally kingdoms in an ascending order of hierarchy.

In recent years, systematists have looked for better ways to quantify their observations. One system, called cladistics, actually counts the number of shared characters among groups and creates a diagram illustrating the rankings. While retaining the basic genus and species, cladistics abandons the standard hierarchy of the classical system and allows the data themselves to determine relationships. The complex, almost limitless system usually necessitates a computer to crunch the numbers. On the political front, paleontology is in the midst of one of its disputes. Partisans either shout *cladistics* from the rooftops or they shout it down. Pro-cladists believe that such a quantitative analysis leads to almost indisputable results; anti-cladists say fallible humans make the initial judgment calls that are placed in the computer.

Perfect or not, cladistics also examines "derived" characters, specializations that depart from more generalized ancestral or "primitive" conditions. For example, *Homo sapiens* did not start out standing upright and walking on two legs. We modified the primate skeleton by rotating the pelvis, shortening the arms, and attaching the skull vertically atop the spine. We share these derived characters with other species and subspecies of the genus *Homo* and with the genus *Australopithecus*, but not with other primates like chimpanzees (genus *Pan*) and gorillas (genus *Gorilla*). They have the primitive condition of being semi-erect or even a more generalized quadripedal posture using all four limbs for ground locomotion. They do not share the derived characters described above with the genus *Homo*.

Further, our being bipedal does not mean we are related to every other bipedal animal. Birds also are bipedal, but they attained their bipedalism through a different, parallel track. Unlike humans, they experienced a shortening of the body, a rotation of the femur so that it is parallel to the ground, and a less-radical 45-degree rotation of the body—all resulting in a shift in the center of gravity, freeing their arms for flight. Different ancestors, and different derived characters, independently yielded bipedalism.

What is the usefulness of classification systems when it comes to gender studies? On one hand, knowing what animals shared characters with *Tyrannosaurus rex* might shed light on what anatomical features to watch for. On the other hand, for me it provided even more essential information via "extant phylogenetic bracketing."[13]

Specifically, "character studies" have concluded that primitive crocodile-like animals called thecodonts were the ancestors of dinosaurs, and also of birds and crocodiles. Important diagnostic similarities in how bones literally form is fundamental in determining ancestry; for example, some crocodile bones, some dinosaur bones, and most bird bones have hollow spaces, illustrating their evolutionary closeness. Thecodonts and today's crocodiles are extremely similar, which means crocodiles provide an excellent "hindsight" model for their extinct elders—and therefore dinosaurs' elders as well. Plus, the Dinosaur Renaissance has stacked up all kinds of evidence suggesting birds are actually descended from dinosaurs, making birds another dinosaur model. This means scientists have a *bracket* of living animals with which to compare *T. rex*—a modern version of *T. rex*'s ancestor and also its descendant. For example, if neither crocodiles nor birds give birth to live young, it is highly unlikely that the creature between them on the evolutionary scale did either. Unless *T. rex* walks again thanks to DNA miracles, this is the closest we will ever get to seeing Sue "alive."

Using extant phylogenetic bracketing, I could safely choose crocodiles and birds as before-and-after models for the "living" *T. rex*. I could not only study their skeletons as possible templates—hunting for at least one skeletal character that definitively tied into gender—but also make some assumptions about *T. rex*'s long-decayed soft body parts, its biological functions, and even its behavior. If these animals all were related, most likely they functioned in similar ways. I believed the first place to start was with the pelvis, the most obvious, functionally gender-cued area of the body. I started rounding up not mammals, but Sue's egg-laying neighbors on the family tree. Gingerly, I would look under their tails.

The Inside Story
Sex. Everyone's favorite topic. I never imagined I would know so much about it—especially in the animal kingdom. Mating for both crocodiles and birds is accomplished through a multipurpose

opening in the body, the cloaca, that handles fertilization, delivery of eggs (for females), and removal of waste. However, because in these groups the possession of a penis is a primitive condition (an assessment many human females would agree with), mating mechanics differ. For the first subgroup, including crocodiles and some primitive birds, such as ostriches, waterfowl, chickens, and turkeys, the male's sperm is delivered through a primitive penis called an "intromittent organ." After copulation, this organ is retracted inside the cloaca by "penis-retractor muscles."[14] In the second, more derived subgroup—including most birds—there is no penis. Mating usually involves only a brief cloacal contact, called a "cloacal kiss," during which the male's cloaca inverts directly into the female's, and thus into her oviduct.[15]

Here's my extrapolation: since both ancestors and descendants of *T. rex* functioned basically the same way, it stood to reason that Sue and her mate did, too. Probably everyone she knew well had a cloaca. Although not everyone had a penis, *T. rex* males probably did, since ancestors and at least *some* descendants had them. It all sounded so logical, but still I needed some bones to back me up.

I wasn't the only one. Eberhard Frey of the Museum fur Naturkunde in Karlsruhe, Germany, coincidentally was trying to gender-type crocodile fossils. In dissecting recently deceased crocodiles, he had paid particular attention to the reproductive organs, and had noticed something critical. In male crocodiles, Frey found that penis-retractor muscles anchored just under the tail, on a bony spine attached to the bottom surface of a tail vertebra. This particular spine is the first in a row of multiple spines called chevrons, or haemal arches. Frey also noted that in males, the first two chevrons were the *same size,* whereas in females, the first chevron is only half the size of the second. He assumed the gals did not need the extra surface area in the absence of penis-retractor muscles.[16] Voilà. Direct skeletal evidence for the presence or absence of a penis. Now I was getting somewhere.

Phil Currie added more testosterone to the fire. For several years he had been carefully preparing and examining specimens of *Saurornithoides* and other small theropods, called troodontids,

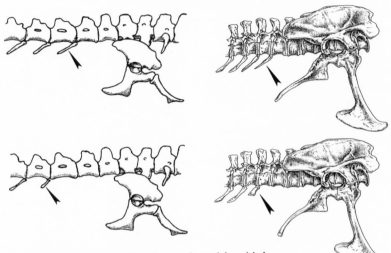

Left: The male crocodile's first chevron bone (above) is longer than the female's (below). Since the bone in males is used to anchor the penis-retractor muscles, its presence is a definite gender indicator. Illustration by Peter Larson.   Right: *T. rex* skeletons mimic the crocodile model, suggesting that the gracile specimens are males. Illustration by Dorothy Sigler Norton.

from China—a group he and others believe is closely related to tyrannosaurs.[17] Intimately familiar with *Saurornithoides,* Currie had prepared well-preserved, undisturbed, articulated robust and gracile specimens. Peeking at their privates, he found the longer "male chevron" on the more delicate, gracile animals, and the shorter "female chevron" on the robust ones.[18] It worked! Those big *Saurornithoides,* with no penis anchor to call their own, appeared to be girls!

Of course, I couldn't wait to apply my new information to *T. rex*es. When I examined both naturally articulated and mounted dinosaur skeletons in various collections, I immediately recognized differently shaped and sized chevrons. Again, they corresponded to gracileness or robustness, and, presumably, to the presence or absence of a penis. MOR-555, a gracile *Tyrannosaurus rex,* was still tantalizingly cocooned, undisturbed in its matrix when I was given permission to have a look. Sure enough, the first and second chevrons were approximately the same size and shape. It looked as if Kathy Wankel was the proud discoverer of a gigantic, bouncing boy.

Fabulous evidence, but it hinged on the presence or absence of one small bone—a chevron attached to its vertebra only by ligaments, which easily decompose. I still believed the pelvis had to be the most sexually diagnostic region of a dinosaur skeleton, and I felt sure there had to be more than one small bone as evidence. Going back to Carpenter's observations about pelvic depth, I wondered how much space actually would be necessary to pass an egg. Logically, the difference between male and female should be much less dramatic in egg-layers than in mammals, where full-blown *babies* exited through a birth canal. However, in my subsequent *T. rex* snooping, I confirmed Carpenter's deeper pelvis observation—and while Sue was in the stirrups, I also noted the increased *width* of the pelvis. In robust individuals, the sacrum, a set of vertebrae located within the pelvis—and thus the pelvic opening—was wider than in the gracile form. Much wider.

The next piece of evidence fell in my lap unexpectedly. Always curious as to what a *T. rex* egg might look like, I often studied whatever dinosaur eggs I could. I found them fascinating to examine, and enjoyed comparing the round herbivore eggs to the oblong theropod variety. Research showed that fossil dinosaur eggshell fragments have been around for a long time. The first ones were discovered in France in 1859 and attributed to the sauropod *Hypselosaurus,* and the first complete dinosaur eggs and nests were found in Mongolia by an American Museum expedition led by Roy Chapman Andrews in 1923.[19] Since then, dinosaur eggs or nests have been recognized in over 130 separate localities worldwide, in North and South America, Europe, Africa, and Asia, with the bulk of new localities sprouting up in China and Mongolia.[20] While some eggs have been attributed to various meat-eating dinosaurs, unfortunately to date scientists have yet to find a nest or a single egg that can be attributed with certainty to tyrannosaurs.

During the early 1990s, however, paleontology was impacted by China's relaxing of its export policies. Dinosaur eggs and nests flooded the rest of the world, and in so doing, revealed some ancient habits of extinct mothers—especially something that made me think of females and their hips. Virtually every cluster

of elongated theropod eggs I examined presented a consistent design: the eggs were arranged in some sort of circular pattern, and they were *paired*.

A big obstacle faced by dinosaur egg researchers is that they are generally studying empty shells. Obviously, the best way to identify the species to which an egg belongs is to have an embryo inside. Unfortunately, most dinosaur hatchlings flew the coop before the eggs or nest were preserved, leaving only the bottom halves of abandoned eggs. Every now and then, though, paleontologists get lucky. I met my

This nest of Chinese theropod eggs shows the typical circular and paired laying pattern.
Photo by Peter Larson

first articulated theropod embryo at the same time the world did. Thanks to a business associate of mine named Charlie Magovern, I was able to work on the earth's first known specimen. It had been included in his purchase of a half-dozen, king-sized, flattened,

This cast replica of bread-loaf shaped, paired eggs called *Macroelongatoolithus xixlanensis* approximate the probable dimensions of *T. rex* eggs, which have yet to be discovered. Photo by Peter Larson.

A cast replica of a theropod embryo preserved just at the moment of hatching. The original specimen is now on display at The Children's Museum in Indianapolis.
Photo by Peter Larson.

paired eggs from Guilin University in China. In their original, inflated state, each would have rivaled a serious loaf of French bread, measuring about four inches in diameter and eighteen inches in length.

Eggs described before their tenants are identified, like dinosaur trackways without known track-makers, are given their own names. Sometime near the end of the Cretaceous, one of Magovern's large eggs, christened *Macroelongatoolithus xixlaensis*[21]—"large, elongate egg-rock"—was caught in the act of hatching. In 1993 this unbelievable specimen became a joint project. Magovern, Denver's Ken Carpenter and preparator Karen Alf, and the institute's David Burnham and I formed a tag-team. With the aid of microscopes, we delicately uncovered the little skeleton, which lay on its left side, curled into a fetal position on top of one of the parallel-lying eggs.

Since this embryo had not run off in the night, I was able to see firsthand the closest thing to a *T. rex* embryo. From this generic theropod template—which eventually would be identified as an oviraptorid—I could extrapolate as to a *T. rex* embryo's position in its egg, its measurements, and its probable form upon hatching. *Macroelongatoolithus* eggs measured up to 5 by 20 inches, rivaling in volume the world's blue ribbon winner: Madagascar's extinct Elephant Bird, *Aepyornis*. So far, *Aepyornis* eggs are the largest ever, measuring 9.5 by 13 inches. A two-gallon omelet![22]

National Geographic magazine published a photograph of Magovern's prepared embryo in May of 1996, along with another photograph that caught my eye. Displayed in the Institute of Cultural Relics in Nanyang, China, twenty-six exposed eggs lay in a circle nearly nine feet in diameter. Each egg's long axis pointed to the center of the circular nest, and they all were arranged in pairs. Magovern's specimen had exhibited pairing, as had another Chinese specimen of a dozen smaller (2 x 5 inches) eggs that lay in a two-tiered circle. MOR's Jack Horner had discovered several nests in Montana with identical theropod *Troodon* embryos encased in 2.5-by-6-inch elongated eggs. Although departing from the radical long-axis arrangement of most such clutches, these, too, were still apparently laid in pairs.[23]

The pairing of eggs was significant not simply because of its consistency, apparently across several species of theropod. It was significant because the eggs were *planted* into the sediment when they were laid; they retained their arrangement over millions of years, which means they had remained planted from laying through hatching, and onward through fossilization. For a theropod dinosaur to have laid her eggs in so specific a fashion, her body had to function in a specific way. For example, I believe she had to lay *all* her eggs in one sitting, moving in increments around the circle; and the fact that two eggs were laid at a time carried revolutionary implications for the animal kingdom, not to mention for *T. rex*. Perhaps because of these implications, some scientists disagreed with my premise, but I soldiered on to see what I would see.

The egg pairing clue spoke volumes about the theropod reproductive tract—a reproductive tract whose closest templates were living crocodiles and birds. However, while these animals provide excellent general models, their reproductive tracts are very different from *T. rex*. I had to discover how these animals functioned in order to extrapolate how in the world a dinosaur could pass two eggs through her system at the same time. If biology supported this possibility, I thought I might have even more evidence to support the wide-hipped female theory.

Since crocodiles were the closest living thing to a dinosaur ancestor, I began with them. In female crocodiles, each ovary releases an egg which then enters the funnel-shaped opening of its corresponding oviduct. Depending on the species, both ovaries may release eggs simultaneously, or they may "fire" alternately. Once within the assembly-line oviduct, the eggs move through stations where they collect egg white, fibrous protein membranes, and finally a calcium carbonate eggshell. Mature eggs stack up inside the oviduct "like a chain of sausages," awaiting fertilization through the shell pores,[24] after which they are laid all in one sitting—usually sixteen to eighty in less than one hour.[25]

While bird eggs follow the same path, and gather the same ingredients, their mothers differ in important ways. Both ovaries exist in birds, but the left one has atrophied so that only the right one functions. Also, while crocodile eggs line up in the reproductive tract, birds process only one at a time. In approximately a day, one egg travels from ovary to nest, and then the process begins again, which means days pass while a bird lays her entire clutch.[26]

In recalling the circular and sometimes multitiered arrangement of theropod nests—filled with from a dozen to nearly one hundred eggs—I believed that in egg laying, theropods were most loyal to their crocodile heritage. Not only did they apparently lay their eggs in one sitting, but also, because they laid them in pairs, theropods could not have shared birds' single-ovary, one-egg-a-day adaptations, which probably evolved to create the weight reduction necessary for flight. Further, since some crocodile species' ovaries initiate the formation of two eggs simultaneously, it stood to reason that a theropod's body could have done this. And if eggs began their trip through the reproductive system in pairs, it certainly was possible that they remained in pairs, and were laid that way.

For this to happen, both oviducts would have to deliver an egg
at the same time into the cloaca. In order to remain paired, and not
to slip into single file during delivery, the eggs must have been forced
out by the following pair of eggs. No living animal, including the
crocodile, is known to lay paired eggs, which contributed to Jack
Horner's speculation that this unusual arrangement could have been
manipulated by the female dinosaur after laying.[27] I found this
improbable, considering the regularity of nest patterns, and extrapolated that theropod dinosaurs exhibited a little self-expression by
being the first, last, and only group to fire eggs from both barrels.
What do paired eggs tell us about Sue's sacrum? All I know is that
if I were a female *T. rex,* and I were delivering two two-gallon eggs
simultaneously, you bet your booty I'd want a wide pelvis.

At this point in my research I was 95 percent sure that
dinosaur gender could be determined from skeletal characters, but

placement, nerve openings, leg length]?" Once he'd put down what he was doing, paced frantically around the room, and waved his arms a lot, a miraculous thing would happen. He would defend *this* paragraph or *that* conclusion—and in so doing not only explain so what, but also make his vision come alive. It would catch an updraft and spiral into the sky, reaching heights not available through the staid confines of a purely scientific presentation. I found I was drawn into Pete's ideas through the colors of his enthusiasm, his tenacity, and his whimsy.

After the tumultuous details of our own lives, and especially the life reflected in this story, we were still able to laugh, hash out dinosaur trivia, and settle on a paragraph or conclusion or even just a fact. Almost always, we would settle because Pete would acknowledge that his version might have been too complex, and I would admit that my interpretation might have missed the point. We would reach a happy medium that passed the test of both the dinosaur man and the skeptic.

it would not be until Sue's debut that my margin of doubt would reduce to almost nothing. I would have to wait until she was prepared. I had come a long way from sorting through robust and gracile skeletons to measuring chevrons and tracing penis-retractor muscles. I'd been around the world examining pelvises and assisting in preparing the world's first nearly complete and articulated theropod embryo. All of this to discover if our dinosaur should be named Sue or Hendrick or Androgyny.

In the quest for that additional 5 percent of gender evidence, I would run smack into the more complex implications of sex: relationships. In the meantime, Sue proved that girls could knock the tar out of boys. I was about to discover that other boys could, too.

(5)

A Body of Evidence

"Contrariwise," continued Tweedledee, "if it was so, it might be; and if it were so, it would be: but as it isn't, it ain't. That's logic."[1]

I didn't sell the fossil to you, I only allowed you to remove it and clean and prepare it for a later sale." So wrote Maurice Williams in a letter about Sue that ironically also suggested we meet to sign a contract. Prior to the letter, a Canadian named Gordon Walker had offered Williams $1 million for Sue if he could get the dinosaur back.[2] That twist made the papers. These intriguing exchanges occurred a few months after Sue's excavation, a few months after I'd fallen in love with an extinct giant Miss Universe, a few months into my research on sexual dimorphism.

Meanwhile, back at the U.S. attorney's office, no one was discussing dinosaur sex. Instead, prosecutors were reading Society of Vertebrate Paleontology (SVP) letters about wealthy individuals and foreign companies decorating their mantels with fossils. They read about lying, cheating, and stealing. At the same time, congressmen read about how much money was being spent on fossils, and were begged to enact legislation that would prohibit fossil commercialization.

In response to our National Academy of Sciences (NAS) pro-collecting report, an SVP committee circulated a position statement warning against "documented cases of unethical practices by commercial collectors, commercial operations masquerading as legitimate academic institutes, the great increase in sales of scientifically important specimens to interior decorators and hobbyists, and the rapidly inflating prices that create profound security problems for institutional collections."

I know the SVP committee did not represent the entire membership in its position; only a small, vocal group wore three-piece suits. I don't know if this contingent of anticommercial lobbyists was unaware of the code of ethics under which legitimate commercial houses like ours operated, or if they simply refused to believe that we would follow them. They scoffed at stories of American Association of Paleontological Suppliers members who had been approached by private collectors to procure or sell something worthy of a museum and had refused, suggesting alternatives—cast replicas, for example, or common originals.

Regardless of our code, the lobbyists grouped all commercial entities—good, bad, and ugly—under the same umbrella. Those in land management agencies who were finally swayed by the lobbyists began to change their own priorities. Unauthorized fossil excavations suddenly topped the list, and some agencies took steps to draft new law enforcement policies aimed at stopping theft from public lands. Unfortunately, since the field of paleontology lacked generalized fossil regulations like those NAS recommended, the policy foundations were based on interpretations of regulations—which were intended for preservation of historic sites or antiquities: human artifacts.

For example, Nebraska's National Forest Service created the July 9, 1990, "Action Plan for the Enforcement of Laws and Regulations Pertaining to Cultural and Paleontological Resources," which reported that "successful prosecution can result in fines and imprisonment for petty offenses or criminal charges which carry the penalty of up to $250,000 and five years in prison." One of the plan's writers, Jay Bradt, appeared with Black Hills Institute co-owner Bob Farrar, along with others, on an August 13, 1991, National Public Radio "Morning Edition" broadcast on "fossil poaching." Citing a rising number of illegal excavation incidents, Bradt said, "Realistically I think it's probably going to take a case in federal court." A whole subgroup of paleontology began to gear up for litigation—the Bone Wars were taking on a whole new look.

While visions of federal court cases danced in the heads of land management agents, the accompanying anticommercialism letter campaign flourished. We received piecemeal samples of the effort either through the grapevine or eventually as evidence—documents spit fitfully through the Freedom of Information Act process, years after Sue's discovery had faded. Alarming paragraphs said fossils were "torn out of the ground by hand without proper collecting techniques," that pieces were left behind in excavations, and that management agencies targeted "potential vandalism sites." Veiled references to our company and prices for our specimens were used as the quintessential example of bad paleo-manners.

Then, hitting even closer to home, the same Nebraska Forest Service office suggested "periodic investigation" of South Dakota's rock shops—shops "informants" said were "procuring and selling artifacts and fossils which have been obtained from the Forest."[3] The South Dakota U.S. attorney's office, dead-center in the mailing loop, eventually took advantage of the willing foot soldiers already on active duty. An official affidavit revealed that a park ranger and "friend" to our company, the late Stanley Robins, had ingratiated himself to the institute for a reason unrelated to friendship: "As part of his duties, Ranger Robins investigates the theft of fossils from public land. Since July of 1990 he has been investigating the Black Hills Institute of Geological Research, Inc."[4] The Bone Wars had become the Spy Wars.

Assistant U.S. Attorney Robert Mandel, a strong bulldog of a man in both build and fortitude, later would draw a line between what interested the prosecutor's office and what did not. He downplayed the hoopla stirred up by the SVP and land managers, asserting that the U.S. attorney's interest in Black Hills Institute was piqued simply because of Sue. "I believe it was just because it was a very prominent fossil," Mandel said. "This was an event of a significantly different magnitude from anything that was being looked at." He claimed the SVP made no impact on him whatsoever.

However, it was through the smear campaign that a troubling rumor began and festered. I believe that the rumor, and its accompanying deluge of letters to Congress and the U.S. attorney's office, probably did turn heads in government offices. Many of those letters claimed that Sue, or at least her skull, was for sale "for $500,000."[5] While this would have been anathema to us— perhaps more so than to anyone else—the government apparently saw it as the last straw, or at least a straw significant enough to support an entire case. The U.S. attorney's office decided a war horse was in order.

By March 1992, the Black Hills Museum of Natural History filed its articles of incorporation. While affiliated with Black Hills Institute, the museum was intended to be a separate organization; its board of directors was elected, and its not-for-profit IRS paperwork was already underway. The still-partially imbedded Sue—all of her, not just her beheaded skeleton—was officially donated to the museum in perpetuity. Skull CAT scan arrangements were being finalized with NASA. We remained stumped about what to do with Maurice Williams's incredible claims, and we were in the dark about how serious the U.S. attorney's office was about choosing its steed and riding into battle.

We distracted ourselves with a different sort of journey altogether.

Two's Company

From a distance it could have been nothing more than a coarse, reddish brown lump of rock. But even from my initial vantage point, nearly twenty feet away, there was no mistaking what I was seeing. The badly weathered right side of a pelvis was exposed at the edge of a long, steep cliff, perched nearly one hundred feet above the valley floor. Pieces of bone lay directly below, caught in the tenuous grasp of irregularities in the cliff face. A yawning black sinkhole opened its hungry mouth only half a dozen feet below the brown mass, swallowing forever any piece of bone unlucky enough to have fallen into it.

Thin and wiry, sun-bleached blond, Stan Sacrison was permanently tanned from years of "kicking around" under the unforgiving South Dakota summer sun. An almost-silent, intelligent, solitary resident of the high plains, Stan was a tradesman who had studied at the South Dakota School of Mines and spent his leisure moments spotting fossils in the dusty Hell Creek area. Having

The honeycomb texture of these iron-stained articulated vertebrae was a dead give-away that Stan was a *T. rex*. Photo by Terry Wentz.

grown up in the small South Dakota town of Buffalo, his path to fossil hunting was a simple walk to a neighbor's ranch. All he had to do was ask, and he had asked John, Betty, and David Niemi.

The Niemis, hearty Finnish stock, and their neighbors, the Clantons, owned fossil-rich badlands outcrops cutting through their ranch lands. The bones on their property were no strangers to the ranchers, but until Stan Sacrison took a look, the fossils simply lived and died in the endless cycle of the prairie. What he had found cut through the sediment in a pasture shared by both families—a patch of ground officially owned by one and grazed by the other. The reticent Sacrison thought it was a line of eight artic-ulated vertebrae.

To take me there, Sacrison followed a circuitous route, first stopping by a nice *Triceratops* shoulder girdle. "What about the string of vertebrae?" I asked anxiously.

"Still a ways off." Sacrison was anything but anxious. First, a microsite with *Nanotyrannus* teeth. As we walked, Sacrison told us briefly that he had found the vertebral exposure five years before, and had been informed by a local scientist that it was "only another *Triceratops*." Discouraged from collecting it, he still had his doubts about the identification and looked forward to knowing once and for all what it was. Still, he did not pick up his pace. We stopped by a second *Triceratops* specimen, this time a nose and beak.

"How far to the vertebrae, Stan?" I asked. He grinned as we wound our way through the badlands. My eyes drifted toward buttes to the north, landmarks we had been moving toward since leaving the Niemis' ranch house several hours before. The color changes between the buttes and the badlands at our feet were not striking, but there was a distinct difference in hues. The upper beds were more sand-colored than those below. Sacrison identified a narrow coal seam, correctly pinpointing the K-T Boundary. We were in *T. rex* country.

Finally Sacrison pointed to a cliff. I stopped breathing.

Shielded by the pelvis, a string of at least eight articulated vertebrae could be seen, arching their way beneath the protective sediments. I had seen the same dead giveaway in Susan's hand, the honeycomb structure of the interior of *T. rex* vertebrae.

Nine times out of ten, when following up a tip on a dinosaur specimen, we come back empty-handed. Nine times out of ten, when we actually collect something, it is just an isolated bone of little or no consequence. In about one chance out of 100, the find turns out to be something really noteworthy. And in most of these cases, the tip comes from someone who lives or works on the prairie. This latest tip came to us thanks to Don Parsons, a fellow bone hunter who knew Sacrison, had seen the site, and suggested we pursue it. Bless you, Don. We already had excavated Sue, woman enough to keep us scientifically happy for years—yet amazingly, I had just seen Number Two. Politics and letters and accusations faded to a tiny silhouette on the horizon.

We named him Stan then and there, long before we peeked under his tail. Later, luck would be with us—at least in sexing *T. rex*es—because this gracile skeleton would in every way appear to be a gentleman.

After checking with the courthouse and confirming the lease arrangement of the particular pasture where Stan lay, we held our official meeting with the Niemi and Clanton families—landowner and lease holder, respectively. Even on that first of what would become dozens of conversations over the years, cookies and tea were laid out across the kitchen table. Gentle laughter and generosity flowed between the families, who decided instantly to share equally in decisions and whatever income might arise from the excavation of Stan. After agreeing on a finder's fee for friend and discoverer Sacrison, we all shook hands. A simple, longhand page was written out and signed—evidence that we had learned at least a little about clarifying the details—but no one wanted or needed anything formal.

Feeling very welcome indeed, we arrived in force at the Niemi ranch on April 14, 1992, to begin the excavation. While crew members set up camp, Stan Sacrison's twin brother, Steve, maneuvered his 800-series Bobcat front-end loader down the steep grade below our prairie campsite. His target was Stan's butte, where the site poked out, suspended between the level of the prairie and the valley floor below. The Bobcat eventually would remove more overburden than all the rest of us put together, but first it set to work building a road up the embankment to the specimen, and

An aerial view showing our Stan campsite and the newly graded road threading down the steep badlands to the site. Photo by Layne Kennedy.

then further on to the level of the plateau. Next we began our standard procedure for all excavations—beginning with careful photo documentation, collecting and labeling loose bone fragments, sketching our preliminary map, gluing visible fractures in the main exposure, and placing our portable map grid. Once that preparatory work was finished, it was time to get to know Stan's unique characteristics, his singular scientific footprint that would determine how we would proceed.

This dinosaur's major challenge: he had retreated beneath a rock-hard, yellow sandstone layer which, in turn, was covered by a thick coat of softer, gray siltstone. To get to the sandstone cap, Steve Sacrison again took center stage. Watching him, I was struck by the realization that there are people who do their jobs with a beauty and grace that catches the eye, even in the middle of the weather-beaten prairie, even in a Bobcat. With precision that made it seem as if he had grown metal arms with a bucket attached, Steve dug and dragged the overburden, systematically stripping away rock with the detail of a paleo-brush and the grace of a dancer. This ballet was an exceptionally beautiful sight for those of us who were able to put away our picks and shovels. For a moment we let ourselves believe it was going to be easy.

That night it rained in the land of "gumbo"—sticky, slimy, gooey, messy, gray siltstone. By the next morning the wet mess was covered with snow, something that can happen at any time of year in South Dakota. Everyone slept in as snow gave way to rain again. While the fossil itself was embedded in sand that allowed the water to wick away quickly—theoretically allowing a quick resumption of digging—we could not traverse the road to reach the specimen without becoming a struggling, unrecognizable blob of mud. Day One of playing cards and reading crime novels. Then another.

When the weather cleared, we learned our job would not be easy. In some places the sand was cemented so thoroughly with dolomite and siderite crystals that a pick simply glanced off the hard rock. Sacrificing silence for 7500 watts, we plugged the Bosch electric jackhammer into our generator. Slicing through the cement behind and to the anterior side of the pelvis allowed us

access to the bones, and with hand tools we began to find tail vertebrae. These provided our first clue as to how much of Stan was
there. The vertebrae had disarticulated and washed away from the
pelvis; if they had not, the tail would have been lost to erosion
years before.

This positioning, along with crossbedding, indicated stream flow direction: the ancient river that entombed
Stan had flowed *into* the hill. A very
good sign; I'd much rather wrestle
dolomite than lament about erosion.
As we continued to chip and peel away
the hill, around the backside of the
pelvis, we encountered bones from the
left leg, all but the first neck vertebrae—and teeth. Rich black-enameled
and chocolate-brown-rooted teeth were
lying loose in the sandstone. After a
final count, we would end up with
more than thirty of them, enabling us
to study tooth development, placement, and replacement. Since they
retained their roots, we knew the teeth
had not broken off during a careless
meal. By definition, teeth with roots

Neal uses an electric jackhammer to cut
through the hard rock layered over
Stan's skeleton. Photo by Peter Larson.

had been preserved safely tucked inside their sockets and had fallen
out of a desiccated skull, loosened by time and the work of Mother
Nature. Stan's skull had to be somewhere nearby.

To find it, we fought with ever-worsening concretions, extremely
hard masses where the sandstone had cemented solidly. If a concretion was not too large, and bone protruded from it, we simply
mapped, cast, numbered, and removed the whole thing for later
disassembly in the lab. If the mass was large, but with areas of no
obvious bone, we carefully broke pieces off the edges. If we found
bone, we reduced the mass to a moveable chunk; if we found no
bone, the concretion became useless rubble. The whole jackhammer marathon earned us aching shoulders, especially when

Internal Investigations

X-rays allow us to look inside a rock containing a fossil without touching it. Internal structures or pathologies of individual bones—or even fossil fish, birds, or bats trapped in thin-bedded lake sediments—are revealed when exposed to X-rays. Exquisite detail is often possible when a standard photographic negative is placed below the specimen and then irradiated from above. Computer Axial Tomography, or CAT scan, has added another dimension to standard X-ray examinations by rotating around the object, making X-ray "slices" at regular intervals. These slices are reassembled in a computer to produce a 3-D image that can be rotated on the viewing screen. This allows us to "cut open" the bones to see what is inside without doing any physical harm to the specimen. It also allows us to look at brain cavities, nerve pathways, inner ear structures, and more features otherwise unexplorable through other nondestructive methods.

We had hoped to follow up Sue's CAT scan with more

Neal and I took turns trying to tackle the largest obstacle, a concrete-like shelf eight feet across and growing.

Meanwhile, Terry Wentz and Dave Burnham were mapping and removing bones. They had discovered parts of the jaw, including a thin, flattened, and elongated bone from inside the mouth that looked like some sort of alien "boomerang." These skull bones, scattered like Hansel and Gretel's crumbs, led directly under the cement shelf we were battling. Although a disarticulated skull is not nearly as dramatic or impressive a sight in the field as an articulated one, I was very, very excited to find that Stan's skull had been preserved in this condition. Unlike mammalian skulls, *T. rex*'s approximately fifty individual skull bones are not locked together by "sutured" joints. Thus, when Stan died, the flesh and ligaments holding the skull together slowly rotted away, allowing detailed testing. We planned to start with physically removing thin sections of bone fragments in order to examine individual cells, molecules, chemical compounds, and elements. These microstudies would reveal details about growth, diet, metabolism, relationships—even the most basic building blocks of life.

Jurassic Park boldly imagined that we could reconstruct dinosaurs by cloning their preserved DNA. While DNA easily decomposes after an animal dies, a quick burial could potentially preserve DNA if it included a rapid dehydration of the tissues in an environment without oxygen.[6] Fossil bones have been found with preserved original proteins that proved to be hemoglobin—which means fragments of DNA might still exist inside! Most likely, however, any hidden *T. rex* DNA has been fragmented.

Considering that we have yet to map the billion or so *human* DNA bases, likely no one will ever be growing tyrannosaurs. However, by examining proteins in DNA molecules, scientists will be able to learn how closely *T. rex* was related to a *Triceratops*, or even to an eagle.

the teeth eventually to slip out of the jaws and the skull to fall to pieces. Stan must have laid unburied on the surface, probably on an exposed sandbar or the sandy bank of a river, long enough for this to happen. We were lucky an ancient something hadn't hauled his bits away.

Because the matrix that filled and surrounded Sue's skull had preserved it in one piece, we had chosen not to risk damaging delicate internal structures through disassembly—NASA would show us what was preserved inside through its scan. Now, with Stan's disarticulated skull, we had the best of both worlds. We would be able to study Stan's individual bones in detail, and retain Sue's "preassembled" version.

Stan Sacrison had never been happier. He had joined the very exclusive club of those fortunate enough to find the skeleton of the

Working around the bone masses of Stan's skeleton, preparing them for removal. Photo by Peter Larson.

monster of all monsters. Seeing Sacrison watch the skeleton and skull slowly emerge from the ancient sediment was a great pleasure to all of us. He good-naturedly weathered the inevitable spring

Stan Sacrison with his discovery: Stan the *T. rex*. Notice the large rooted tooth next to Stan's left hand. Photo by Ed Gerken.

storms, helping to uncover numerous ribs, a right leg bone, more tail vertebrae, those infamous tail chevrons, and always more teeth. Sacrison augmented his self-taught field skills by adding our usual large-scale procedures to his repertoire: gluing, foiling, taping, plastering, mapping, and removing bones and blocks of bones.

He wasn't the only one having fun. We found such an abundance of fossil leaves within the layer of sandstone above the specimen that I immediately contacted Kirk Johnson, paleobotanist and curator at the Denver Museum of Nature and Science. An expert on flora found near the K-T Boundary, he collected over one thousand paleobotanical specimens at the site, and

Left: Preparing to remove one of the large palm fronds found in the layers covering Stan's skeleton. Photo by Peter Larson.

Below: *Bisonia niemii,* the beautifully preserved leaf of one of the many new plant species discovered with Stan. Photo by Peter Larson.

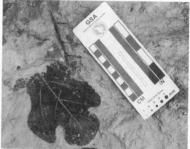

was sure it could yield thousands more. In fact, such excellent data was preserved—both as impressions and as organic films on the bedding plane of the sandstone—that Johnson used actual Stan fossils as templates to cast plastic leaves for ancient "trees" in Denver's museum displays. The variety of fossils included sycamores, metasequoia, sequoia, araucaria, palms, poppies, and a host of forms not living today.[7] Johnson also identified brand-new species from these specimens, and named one of the more prolific and spectacular ones after our favorite landowners. He called it *Bisonia niemii.*[8]

During the course of the dig, virtually every school child in a fifty-mile radius came to the site. We even had a visit from the Sky Ranch for Boys, a juvenile home and working ranch for boys in trouble. We discovered that Terry Wentz is a fantastic public speaker and teacher, with infinite patience and a kidlike sense of humor. We all took turns explaining what had happened to Stan and how the skeleton lay in the ground, breaking up our day with mini science classes. Neighboring ranchers also filtered in, equally interested in the lessons. By the time we finished, probably three-fourths of the population of Harding County had come to greet Stan as he entered the world for the second time. It was great fun for us to see long yellow school buses negotiate the rough terrain to our site, and the Niemi and Clanton families were gracious

School children arrive at "Rexburg," eager to have a look at a real *T. rex*.
Photo by Ed Gerken.

Kids play follow-the-leader on the footpath to the Stan dig site. Photo by Ed Gerken.

to the end, directing visitors to the quarry. Our excavation sites had always been open to visitors, but this was the first time we coordinated with the school system to this degree. Professor Stan may have masqueraded as "just a dinosaur," but he was a science class in disguise.

By the time our crew had removed everything except what was bonded to the hillside by the great cement shelf, our site was much less entertaining. Neal and I had jackhammered, hammered, and chiseled out two masses of the concretion. One seemed to contain the bulk of the skull; the other contained the pelvis, some of the body vertebrae, and the lower leg. Like Sue's site, our location made rescue of the blocks difficult; no suitable trucks or trailers could make the trip up our steep and narrow road, so again, we found ourselves further cutting down the blocks. Now old pros, we undercut and tunneled and plastered and reinforced with wood. One block threatened to collapse, so we piled a soft bed of sand and carefully rolled the 1,500-pound block onto its head. We built pallets and pillars until the Bobcat could once again begin its dance.

Fitting the machine with pallet forks, Steve Sacrison carefully lifted each specimen and carried it away. Some of the blocks were so heavy that we had to supply a human counterbalance to the forward-tipping Bobcat. With crew members clinging to the rear of the machine, Sacrison slowly moved each block over the road he had built three weeks earlier, easing around sharp corners, cresting the steep hill to the level of the prairie. By the time he had filled our trailer with over 60 percent of our 65-million-year-old precious cargo, it was completely dark. We finished our task by the light of Coleman lanterns and Bobcat headlights.

The next morning we policed the quarry, road, and campsite to make certain that we left nothing behind to spoil the spring beauty of the colorful badlands. It was early May. The sun was shining brightly as we loaded into our caravan and began the long, slow trek down the trail to the Niemis', the highway, then home and into our future. For just a moment, I was able to forget everything else and love the life I had chosen. I loved the herds of sheep with their new lambs and how Dave Niemi's border collie, Caesar, sat with him on the seat of his four-wheeler, bracing against his back

Adding people-weight to the rear of the Bobcat helped it to negotiate the difficult trail loaded with a heavy block of Stan's bones. Photo by Dan Counter.

for balance. I loved the simplicity of the round, rolled hay bales I'd always told my young children were Sasquatch bedrolls. In that moment, our future seemed bright enough to hurt our eyes. Two *T. rex*es! But even I could not ignore the facts folded up in the *Rapid City Journal* next to me on the seat. The paper had run a story about the discovery and excavation of Stan, and the day after, April 27, a new story appeared: "Sioux Say Sue Theirs." Apparently our second *T. rex* had fanned a smoldering ember on the reservation.

Seize the Day
Back in October 1990, two months after Sue's excavation, the Cheyenne River Sioux Indian Tribe had passed a resolution claiming ownership of Sue despite Williams's personal ownership of the land on which she was found. Initially, they based their claim upon the history of that land—it used to be theirs. Maurice Williams's ranch was large enough that, for it to remain relatively contiguous, some parcels had to be leased or included under other agreements. According to institute attorney Pat Duffy, the

parcel that contained Sue first had been deeded to the tribe in an 1868 treaty; the tribe later traded it to Williams. Because of notions of tribal sovereignty and how they related to the treaty, and because the fossil had been found on a piece of property the tribe used to own, the tribe said the dinosaur was theirs. Others familiar with Indian culture would say the tribe's claims instead were based on a spiritual unity that binds all Indians. One writer (speaking anonymously) said, "Maurice Williams does not walk alone. He walks with all members of the tribe, and with the thousands of souls of their dead." She said that in the Lakota bands that populate the Great Plains, the individual is not as important as the tribe. That, she said, is why the Cheyenne River Sioux Tribe claimed Sue the dinosaur for its people.

Regardless of its motivation, the tribe's internal resolution raised many issues, but made little impact in our courts. We were now aware of their claim, but as no actual court case had yet sprung from it, Duffy advised no action. Apparently the tribe thought it was the right time to assert itself. They joined Maurice Williams in claiming title over our big girl.

When I first met John Niemi, he'd recounted a snapshot in the history of the plains from a time before his ancestors arrived on this continent. In an Old Country accent with a slow, melodic delivery, he described cave walls a few miles north of his ranch. He had seen etchings there that were attributed to General Custer's troops, records of their final thoughts before they met Sitting Bull for the last time. The Niemi family and the Cheyenne River Sioux all reflected the heritage that lived on in generations of encounters between the first Americans and the Americans who came after them. Before another year was out, I would play my own hand in that legacy.

We had been home about one week. We had unloaded Stan's bones, stored them, and begun the assessment process. We recognized what we would be able to do with the two extraordinary specimens now within our walls. Sue, as the species centerpiece, was undeniably the largest, most complete *T. rex* ever found, and Stan was the second most complete. Closer in size to MOR's famous 555, Stan had a higher bone count and higher percentage

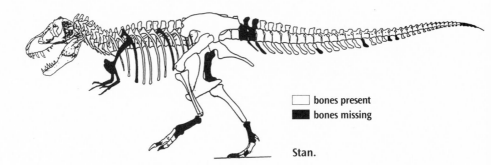

bones present
bones missing

Stan.

of bone mass. Between Sue and Stan, especially considering the significance of Stan's skull in the scientific world, we were almost ready to initiate a monograph—the standard-setting work, the Bible of a species. A *T. rex* monograph had never been done, and this one would be different from any we had seen before: we had organized an unprecedented collaboration of thirty-four scientists from around the world, each of whom would contribute in his or her particular specialty area. We also toyed with ideas of tours and exhibitions, where enthusiasts could visit a matched set, a "mating pair" of *Tyrannosaurus rex*. It was time for us to burst into the mainstream.

We did. But not in a way we ever could have anticipated. At 7:30 A.M. on May 14, 1992, one of my staff pounded on the door as I took a shower in my trailer house across from the main institute. I heard her say "FBI."

> The rabbit-hole went straight on like a tunnel for some way, and then dipped suddenly down, so suddenly that Alice had not a moment to think about stopping herself before she found herself falling down a very deep well.[9]

When I emerged a moment later, I dove into Alice's Pool of Tears. Accustomed to climbing over barbed wire fences in the field, instead I vaulted POLICE LINE—DO NOT CROSS tape. Accustomed to knowing everyone in our hallways, I was met instead by FBI agents and sheriff's officers already searching our building. In our break-room kitchen, two agents handed me the search warrant Neal and

Bob already had seen. Teams had been dispatched; paleontologists from land management agencies oversaw the packing of fossil specimens, while various other agents conducted the main search—which they had interpreted as permission to open each drawer, photograph each room, and videotape every fossil, shelf, box, nook, and cranny. This process seemed crazy; what the warrant asked for was relatively easy to find.

She weighed ten tons.

Upon a closer reading, I realized the search warrant's scope—and its implications—did indeed reach past the skeleton. Citing a violation of the Antiquities Act of 1906, the document said we had *stolen* U.S. Government property and, somehow simultaneously, Cheyenne River Sioux Tribal property. We were to surrender everything that had to do with Sue:

> All the fossil remains of one tyrannosaurus rex dinosaur skeleton (commonly referred to as "Sue") . . . and other fossil specimens . . . taken from an excavation site on the property of Maurice Williams . . . (including) all papers, diaries, notes, photographs . . . or other records relating to the excavation of the tyrannosaurus rex ("Sue").

The questions that poured into my mind were left mostly unanswered in the frenetic momentum of that agonizing instant. Agents were bustling around, asking what this room was or where those fossils were, while my brain was back on square one. *Stolen? Stolen from the government? Stolen from the tribe? How could Sue be everyone's property at the same time, including, as the warrant stated, Maurice Williams's?*

Sue became the newest media phenomenon on the first day of the seizure. Plucked from the very runway of her debutante ball—mere hours before her skull was slated for its NASA trip—she made headlines around the world. This time she was the prize sought by a posse sent up from the big city into the Black Hills to capture a dinosaur. Apparently anticipating spotlights, Acting U.S. Attorney Schieffer, yet to be confirmed to his post, arrived late to the event wearing makeup for television cameras. Some wondered if politics or fossils were his real targets, but his supporters believed he was saving the world's best dinosaur from a questionable fate; it was here I learned that the NASA CAT-scan trip had somehow been twisted by the rumor mill into a "secret sale" to unknown buyers.

Pete, daughter Sarah, and institute employees Lynn Hochstafl and Denise Etzkorn are comforted by Hill City Mayor Drue Vitter. Photo by Louie Psihoyos.

Louie Psihoyos, the *National Geographic* photographer who had been scheduled to accompany Sue to the Marshall Space Flight Center in Huntsville, Alabama, instead found himself covering fast-breaking news alongside local and national media. They all added to the surrealism of what would become three days of occupation, and they captured our darkest moments on film. For years, whenever our case was discussed on the local news, the same selection of footage would accompany the update: children skipping school to parade tearfully and defiantly in front of our building carrying placards; National Guard soldiers loading crates with front-end loaders. "They had the Black Hills Institute surrounded as if a live *T. rex* were loose inside the building," Psihoyos later wrote.[10] I would have preferred that.

No one before had seized a *Tyrannosaurus rex*. It was a complex procedure made more complicated by the number of participants, the emotional distress of our frightened and incredulous crew and families, and the obvious outrage of demonstrating local citizens. Despite FBI Special Agent Asbury's warnings that if the children were not dispersed, they would be arrested, the kids maintained a steady chant, "Don't be cruel! Save Sue!" In fact, their chant grew louder and more anguished, nearly a primal scream, when boxes started emerging from our buildings.

As we took the advice of our attorney, Patrick Duffy, and complied with the order, we nonetheless searched for relief. We first asked what provisions—including a possible chaperone of government representatives—might allow the CAT scan to remain on schedule. FBI agent Charles Draper, the only of our visitors who seemed at all interested in the science of the situation, called his superiors to see if an exception could be made; his efforts failed. Next we tried our best to persuade the government to settle for something less than a seizure. When we were told Sue was considered evidence in a criminal investigation, we asked if she could remain safely in one place, undergoing preparation and study, while legalities continued. Under guard if necessary.

Nothing doing. To the press, Schieffer said something for which I was totally unprepared: "The fossil is property of the United States. Period."[11] I was flabbergasted. If there was one entity that didn't seem to have any conceivable claim to Sue, it was the United States Government.

Not even the passionate, temperamental, and charismatic Pat Duffy could stem the tide. He stormed, he reasoned, he issued curt explanations. His flamboyance and self-assurance flowed through every gesture, every twitch of his eye, every lick of his lips, but still official pictures were shot, boxes packed, paperwork removed. We had two choices—get out of the way or help. We gave up talking and settled on minimizing any damage to Sue. Neal, Terry, and I hustled from room to room, supervising groups and packing fossils. Amidst all the confusion, Bob Farrar, our soft-spoken, analytical partner, tried to keep track of paperwork, lists, and records of seized items.

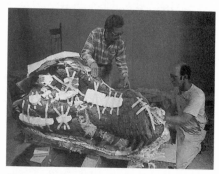

Pete and Terry pad and protect their giant patient against jolts during her transport. Photo by Louie Psihoyos.

We all adopted a new view of our government-hired former colleagues, who now stood in our buildings as crew chiefs. These paleontologists representing Dinosaur National Monument, Fossil Butte National Monument, and the nearby South Dakota School of Mines and Technology circled their prey with Bureau of Indian Affairs officials, sheriff's officers, local police, and National Park

Service and Forest Service rangers. They came ill-prepared, woefully lacking in requisite packing materials and plaster—which we were forced to provide. The camouflage-wearing National Guard arrived later with flatbed trucks when it was time to load up.

National Guard troops load a flatbed truck.
Photo by Louie Psihoyos.

Thankfully everyone was in uniform, or it would have been even more confusing. Hill City's restaurant employees also found the uniforms helpful; they identified the people to be refused service. By the second day of the raid, the FBI brought sack lunches.

At the end of the second day, an official FBI teletype reported, "One load of bones removed via military vehicle on May 15, 1992. During removal, citizens of Hill City, South Dakota, including small children, vocally demonstrated in front of the building. When vehicle loaded and began to depart, the children ran in front of the vehicle. No other incidents occurred." The report also cautioned agents about possible problems for the next day: "Removal of remaining bones including skull to occur on May 16, 1992. Information developed from local authorities that possibility of larger demonstration is to occur May 16, 1992. This may include human chain to block departure of vehicles. . . . Decision to be made . . . whether or not to remove remaining items then or at later date."

The report's final note reflected a concern that would play a major part in future court proceedings. It read, "Above matter receiving heavy media attention both locally and nationally."

On the third day, news cameras and private video captured the throng of people following the last canopied green truck—which carried Sue's skull—as it pulled out of town on its thirty-mile journey. The atmosphere was somber, reminiscent of a funeral, although there was no human chain. It's true that Marv Matkins, the largest and most loyal real estate agent I have ever known, at first laid down on the street in front of the truck. And later, children trotted after it as it gained speed; video footage shows uniformed arms barring their progress, even as the youngsters already had lost the race. The casket floated out of sight to a second burial with no service, in the boiler room of Rapid City's South Dakota School of Mines and Technology. Intended to be her safe haven, this building was fitted with a sea-freight container, unceremoniously filled with boxes of Sue. Arguably the most important fossil of the twentieth century would remain unavailable to science for more than five years.

My relationship with Sue did not end in May of 1992, but the work on the monograph screeched to a halt, as did Sue's preparation and my access to some of the most important sexual dimorphism bones ever collected. But everything did not stop. We learned about legal filings and research, about what to do when our own resources were not in our files. We learned about digging deep. I was once invited to a ceremony in a cabin in the woods, where Lakota medicine man Vincent Black Feather attempted to heal our emotional wounds. Unlike tribal government officials, who were asserting ownership claims, this man said something that would help sustain me for the years of coming legal battles. I no longer recall his exact words, but in essence he said that Sue and I had connected, and that she had come to me because of all people, I loved her the best. He also said she would return. Not as the centerpiece of my entire career, or the realization of my professional dreams, but as something I could feel thirty feet below me in a cliff, as some*one* who had become my friend—and for whom I felt deeply responsible.

A Guardsman attempts to keep young protestors at bay as a loaded truck leaves Black Hills Institute. Photo by Ed Gerken.

Whenever I passed by the School of Mines, I stopped and peeked in the window of Sue's boiler room, gazing with my forehead against the glass at the freight container. Sometimes I told Sue about the latest hearing or court decisions, perhaps an upcoming business trip or what was happening with Stan. Somehow I never

On the seizure's first day, institute owners and employees fashioned armbands of police tape. Here, Terry Wentz, who turned his Checker into a rolling billboard, sets off for a protest parade. BHI file photo.

wondered if I'd gone around the bend. I visited once a week, or once a month. "How is she?" a passerby once asked.

"Not so good today," I answered. "I couldn't hear her very well."

A Civil Action

I have always loved a good legal yarn, a book where I can figure out the details, exercise my logic, guess what's coming. Something by John Grisham or Dashiell Hammett. I read these stories during rainy days at excavations, or at night before going to bed. During our years of legal trouble, I used these books as a means of escape; before that, however, through all my years of playing detective, it was nothing personal. I looked at legal cases linearly, like puzzles or games, as if they were complexities formed of simple parts—club, spade, knife, blood stain, mallet. Mental exercise identified the elements—poker, hit-and-run, croquet, fraud—and put them together to solve the crime. From my analytical point of view, the legal system seemed relatively straightforward.

As our own legal drama unfolded, I began to see that the system didn't always shepherd us as smoothly as fiction would

Protestors march on the state capitol in Pierre, South Dakota. Photo by David Burnham.

have us believe. For us, something basic—whose dinosaur?—was in dispute. Our motives in claiming her were misunderstood: alarmingly, frighteningly, the government painted us as people we didn't recognize. My insight shifted the more personal the legal world became. I suddenly noticed in newspapers that sometimes personal feelings, opinions, or prejudices affected how an entire case was approached. Sometimes witnesses lied, or attorneys tampered, innocents were convicted, or guilty parties got away with murder. Sometimes judges were only mammals, looking at the facts from their own particular viewpoint.

Once the seizure occurred, we seemed caught in every bad metaphor I had ever read about. David and Goliath. The impersonal eye of Big Brother. We were Odysseus and his men clinging to our ship while waves lashed us for daring to defy the gods. One night while lying in bed, unable to sleep, my stomach knotted in anxiety, I named my experience in terms I could feel more viscerally. Behind my closed eyes, I was standing on a hillside in the prairie, the wind buffeting my shirt so it flapped at my shoulders. The hill suddenly exploded, and my brother, our partner Bob, everyone we loved, and I were all clinging to the steep exposure, fingernails in the dirt, steel toes clutching for a foothold high above the valley floor. Dust whipped into my eyes, my fingers bled, but I could not let go. Rightly or wrongly, I felt everyone was on that cliff because of me. I had to keep climbing. We all did. My eyes flew open in the dark.

We sued the government for Sue's return.

"Can you play croquet?"

The soldiers were silent, and looked at Alice, as the question was evidently meant for her.

"Yes!" shouted Alice.

"Come on then!" roared the Queen, and Alice joined the procession, wondering very much what would happen next.[12]

For many months we would remain ignorant of how the government's game was played. We heard reports of their visits to friends, colleagues, ranchers, and clients, but aside from excruciating hints that appeared in the newspaper—an investigation into "ongoing, multistate criminal activity"[13]—the U.S. Attorney did not tip his hand. That nebulousness invaded our lives and at first defined our primary legal case, the Big Mystery in which we were defendants. The second case was ours, a civil dispute we filed almost immediately after the seizure, contesting the ownership of Sue. These two disparate legal actions each engaged an unwilling party. It became a tortuous game of strategy for both players; the institute stood across the queen's croquet grounds against a stacked deck of formidable public resources, but the government suddenly had to divert its attention to a squabble in the stands. Later the institute would become a defendant again, in a *third* case, this time in the tribal court of the Cheyenne River Sioux Indians. Sue was the catalyst for all three of these cases, the prize, the mother lode in dispute, the dynamite that had ignited—but ironically, in the long run, she would become the least of our worries.

In the short run, however, we worked with what we could see. Putting the Big Mystery aside for a moment, we focused on getting Sue back. At the time, I felt completely out of my league, but I was fueled by my idealistic beliefs in justice. We were in the right, after all—surely, when all the cards were on the table, everyone would see that. Right? In hindsight I recognize how unprepared we were, how inexperienced.

Midwesterners watched the case with interest and equal naïveté as it splashed its way across headlines and newscasts. Everyone I met seemed to have an opinion about what legal arguments to make or what lawyer to hire. With the recent increase in the public's conversational literacy due to high-profile, controversial cases across the country, the seizure—and our unprecedented suit of the government—eventually would be described in the same breath in our part of the country as Waco or Ruby Ridge. Suddenly, everyone was a master gamesman. I heard more and more discussion of government overreaching and excess, and I was told more and more about where the government had gone wrong.

I also heard a refrain about the inadequacy of our lawyers. Even in the early stages, while we struggled to gain a legal foothold, the prevailing opinion was that no lawyer in our area could be anything but over his head from the start. What some well-wishers did not realize is how we weighed our choices. We were told that local judges do not receive well the legal equivalent of out-of-town Three-Piece Suits in their courtrooms, and the concomitant assumption that local talent—including the judges themselves—was not quite talented enough. We were home-grown, but we knew where we stacked up against other experts in our field; we had no reason to believe the same wasn't true in other specialties. Plus, the case was unprecedented; *anyone* litigating it would be feeling his way. Our lead attorney, Pat Duffy, had just won a large case in environmental and land use issues that might impact our strategy; later, we would hire another local legend, Bruce Ellison, who was one of the most highly respected Indian law minds anywhere, and a champion for Leonard Peltier, among others. Ellison, a man of integrity, accepted our case because he believed in us.

So, with our partners chosen, we settled down to the game.

Alice thought she had never seen such a curious croquet ground in all her life; it was all ridges and furrows; the balls were live hedgehogs, and mallets live flamingoes, and the soldiers had

> to double themselves up and to stand upon their hands and feet,
> to make the arches.[14]

Our play was simple and straightforward, despite the fact that our government-issued flamingoes would not keep their heads down. We set our sites on the croquet stake and struck a single blow at our hedgehog. "May we please have our dinosaur back? We bought her fair and square." It was an approach that would change very little as the case meandered through months of other issues.

The government's position illuminated its reasoning behind the seizure. The U.S. Attorney's office had entered the match because, in 1969, one-eighth Lakota Sioux Maurice Williams put some of his land—including Sue's parcel—in "trust" with the United States. The trust agreement that exists between American Indians and the federal government originally protected Indians from unfair land deals. This was necessary because when whites first invaded Indian territories, Indians did not relate to the idea of owning real estate and therefore were easily manipulated out of their holdings. This real estate problem was a manifestation of a clashing of two cultures. Not only had the federal government seized Indian property, returning only the least desirable parcels, but they also discounted the complexity of Indian cultural and spiritual tradtion. Today, the Bureau of Indian Affairs (BIA) oversees trust land transactions, and trust holdings are not taxed.

Still, we could not see how trust land status affected Sue. We wrote in our initial claim: "The contract between Williams and the Institute was not to purchase his land, nor for an interest in his land, nor for any option to later purchase his land. The sole purpose of the Williams-Institute contract was to excavate and transport Sue from the site, a purpose unconnected with Williams' land, except to the extent necessary to carry out the excavation."

What happened sent the hedgehogs scurrying off the field. We found ourselves in a thick book called *Federal Indian Law*,[15] in a case that suddenly, inadvertently, took on huge dimensions encompassing generations of confusion in American courts and hundreds of years of conflicting policies.

Being enmeshed in trust law wreaked havoc on our initial

flurry of legal filings. The doubled-over playing-card arches mercilessly changed positions on the croquet field. We didn't even know *where* to aim our hedgehogs, and had to change our initial claim twice after filing, not only deleting parties to the case but even amending what we actually were requesting. What had seemed so simple, the fact that we had bought the dinosaur, was in danger of being lost in the shuffle of the queen's deck.

To make matters worse, Williams's letter about our not having actually purchased Sue threw a wrench into our entire premise. Terry Wentz and Susan Hendrickson had witnessed the $5,000 check change hands, and confirmed what I remembered about the verbal purchase agreement, but nothing was in writing or on videotape. There wasn't a single neutral little bird who could confirm what had happened. In newspapers Maurice Williams was quoted variously as saying either that he didn't know what the check was for, or else that he had been paid the money for "egress" or "mitigation." He always remained consistent in maintaining publicly that he did not sell Sue in August of 1990—regardless of my obvious intention to buy her. I believed he knew that I *thought* a dinosaur sale was occurring that day in the prairie, when I had signed the check and written Sue's specimen number on it. Our public difference of opinion stomped across the press and legal documents, where each of us asserted our disparate positions.

Aside from the check itself, the only evidence we ever had in writing—which occurred long after Sue's disposition had been decided—came in the form of Williams's alleged statements to a tribal representative. These were recounted in a March 4, 1994, affidavit by newly appointed Cheyenne River Sioux Tribal Chairman Gregg Bourland: "At first, Mr. Williams told me that the $5000.00 was payment received for the sale of the fossil, which sale Mr. Williams believed to be voidable under federal law. At other times, Mr. Williams told me that the $5000.00 was a payment received by him to compensate him for the damage to his land caused by Black Hills' exploratory activity." A powerful little bird, but he sang out much too late.

In the initial heat of filing paperwork, even considering

A Matter of Trust

In a legal sense, trust is when Congress has plenary power—absolute and total authority over its beneficiaries. If the formation of reservations was the first shoe's dropping, creating a policy of perpetual government reliance was the second. In Indian Country, trust is a living, breathing entity, something that has been contested, misunderstood, violated, reinvented, terminated, and reinstated for generations.

Indian trust lands held by the U.S. Government still today are fraught with a crucial lack of definition. Literally, the government holds the title, but opinions differ as to whether, strictly speaking, the government actually *owns* the land. Members of the bar from both prosecution and defense perspectives in our case admitted the problem, but came down on opposite sides of the fence. Everyone agrees that lands in trust are managed by the government for the "benefit" of the trust beneficiary, whether a group or individual. But interpretations vary widely as to who actually owns the land.

"If you take a place like the Dakota Territory, this land

Williams's claims, we decided to press on with the assumption that a purchase had occurred. Everything we had done since the excavation underscored our belief in the purchase, and we believed we could successfully tackle the issue with Williams in due course. First we had to play defense. Trust law became our argument du jour.

We began with what we saw as an obvious lack of connection between trust law and a dinosaur skeleton. It escaped us how a real estate agreement between Williams and the United States impacted our transaction. The understanding that Maurice Williams had to work through the BIA to sell his *land* seemed immaterial to our work. We were dealing with a *dinosaur*. Apparently, trust status had had no impact on Williams's oil leases, and presumably would not have impacted gravel or timber was all land of the United States. Title to all this land resided in the United States," Assistant U.S. Attorney Robert Mandel said, representing the government's position. "There are many Indian people who would of course disagree with that. But as a legal reality, once this became part of the United States, the lands were land of the United States . . . if a trust patent is issued, the title remains in the United States, but it's for the benefit of a tribe or an individual Indian."

Pat Duffy disagreed. "The law states that the government *holds* the title insofar as to benefit the land's actual owner. The Indian or Tribe owns equitable title, while the government owns the legal title. It's just like when I hold money in trust for a client; I might own the account, but *he owns the money*."

If the government literally owned someone's trust land, Bruce Ellison laughed, it was "only in this case." He added, "I've never seen a case saying trust land is owned by the government. I've seen cases saying it was managed, supervised and controlled on behalf of the allotees or the tribe. How could you say trust land is government property? There is no treaty, no statute that says that." And there still isn't today.

sales. These are all "severable," personal property items. Like fossils.

There was one additional key—and it seemed to transcend the trust issue altogether. Schieffer would interpret the 1906 Antiquities Act to support his view that Sue absolutely was "property of the United States. Period," and that the "fossil found on Williams' trust land belongs to the US government, not Williams."[16] My research for the NAS committee taught instead that the Antiquities Act in no way directly pertained to paleontological materials. In a nutshell, the act restricts the removal of archaeological objects—not paleontological ones—from public lands; after two court cases in the 1970s, it was declared unconstitutional for being "fatally vague."

From the air, an archaeological excavation looks similar to a paleontological one. Shovels, brushes, knives. Bones. Everyone seems studious and careful while they draw maps and write scientific notes. From the U.S. Capitol, these two disciplines may look enough alike to be regulated similarly—but I fervently believe that is a mistake.

Homo sapiens have walked the planet for about 100,000 years. Our early traces are preserved in only limited areas, in the first few feet of living soil. Relatively few and precious, nearly every archaeological occurrence is important enough to be preserved, carefully logged, and curated. Thus the need for strict regulations.

Conversely, fossilized plants and animals are preserved in virtually every sedimentary rock on earth, hundreds of millions of years worth, often to depths of miles beneath the surface. No matter how much we search for and dig for fossils, there are always more. While each has the potential to add to the book of science, none has the cachet of a human tomb. While each should be handled with care, many are not nearly as scientifically important as we wish. And very few provide the fossil jackpot of Sue. For every Sue, there are billions of fossils that are worth nearly nothing financially and not so much scientifically. Thus, there is a lesser need for legislative rigidity.

Duffy's further research bolstered my understanding. As he explained it, a notification by the Department of Justice specifically addressed a potential legal problem when applying the Act to items recovered from lands held for the benefit of an Indian. The key: those artifacts were property of the Indian landowner, not the government. "This was not just the DOJ's opinion on the Antiquities Act," Duffy explained. "This was the DOJ's opinion on the disposition of things buried in the ground on land held in trust for an Indian."

If this DOJ opinion was true, then Sue had not been government property. Sue had not been tribal property. Sue had been Maurice Williams's property, to sell as he saw fit. As his personal property, she was not land. The trust status of Williams's parcel should not have affected his ability to dispose of the fossil.

In arguing from our different points of view, our filings were understandably polar. I referred back to the government's filings, and never did understand how their arguments led from the concept labeled "trust land" to the one marked "belonging to the United States." "That was the single most imbecilic facet of this case," Duffy would say. For the life of me, I could not understand how the government had decided to seize that dinosaur, or how trust law became twisted into that particular knot. It seemed inconceivable even when it was explained to me. I had the ironic thought that all of this was indeed a fine subject for discussion— instead of seizure.

As we started to understand the government's angle—and realized the complexity of competing ownership claims—we changed our request for "quiet title" into one for "injunctive relief." This set aside the question of whose property Sue was, and instead focused on her simple return to our laboratories during the pendency of the litigation. There is some truth to the adage "possession is nine-tenths of the law," and Duffy hoped that the dinosaur's physical presence at the institute would take the issue out of Judge Battey's hands, along with his ability to steer the whole case. If it worked, any decision about Sue made in civil court could not haunt us in the criminal case.

To contest *ownership* as opposed to *possession* would necessitate the inclusion of the Cheyenne River Tribe and Maurice Williams—and the accompanying string of contradictory legal decisions attached to them because of America's early history. If the Indian Country debate had remained unresolved ever since the federal government displaced the indigenous population, it seemed unlikely that lawyers would solve it in the ownership battle over Sue. Duffy's advice was to narrow our goal. As he and law student Lois Lofgren wrote in their 1994 *Law Review* article, "The complaint instead raised only one issue: whether the Institute's claim to the fossil, based on its purchase from Williams, was superior to the government's need for the fossil as evidence in a criminal action the government had yet to file."[17]

To our request for injunctive relief, Eighth Circuit Court Judge Richard Battey just said no. Quickly, cleanly. No.

We asked the Eighth Circuit Appeals Court to review the decision, and they ordered a hearing as to why we thought Sue should be returned. It was our big chance, and the only major time the Appeals Court would say yes to us.

Bob Bakker attended the hearing, insisting on Sue's behalf that a patient—especially one invaded by pyrite—needed "continuity of care," and that we were the fossil's best doctors. Our witnesses argued that our facility was the best, equipped with temperature and humidity controls—and that the School of Mines boiler room was not only ill-equipped but also stacked with chemicals. We argued that our personnel were the best, some of the most talented in the world and certainly the most intimately knowledgeable about the specimen. We argued that the FBI and the National Guard had bumped and dropped sealed crates, and Sue might have been badly damaged. We argued that those crates had been sealed while the plaster was still wet, possibly introducing water into her pyrite-permineralized bones—and that she might turn to dust in her coffin. We were truly worried about all this—our dinosaur was broken!—and we marched into that room full of righteousness.

Sitting in the witness box with his ponytail, Bob Bakker made a public assessment of our facility that was heart-warming. "Those of us who have Ph.D.s who work for universities regard ourselves as sort of a priestly class, that we have special training, and a special duty to care for these sacred relics of the earth's history." He then admitted to a great bias against commercial collectors, who he called "pot hunters, market hunters, and thieves of time." Specifically, however, he took Black Hills Institute out of that category:

> I still believe that nearly all commercial collectors are pot hunters, but I am forced to change my views about the Black Hills Institute because of the care I saw them lavish on the specimen called Sue and the other specimens found with Sue. . . . I was invited to study the specimens, any and all of them. I have seen many of the fossils of Sue and found with Sue. I have seen Peter Larson give important fossils found with Sue to Phil Currie of the museum in Alberta. I have

seen the Black Hills Institute make Sue more accessible to a greater range of people than is usually the
case in a university museum. And more importantly,
I saw that the Black Hills Institute technicians are
better trained, have more technical skill, and clean
and glue bones better than 98 percent of the university museums that I know. . . . I am very good. They
are better. . . . I remain extremely suspicious of any
commercial collector. I must be persuaded they are
operating for the good of the public and the good of
science, and this is one of those rare cases that I have
been so persuaded.

Bob was great. Unfortunately, however, we were not truly prepared for the game. We had earnest testimony, but we needed figures and humidity readings. We needed measurements and
statistics and suits who toed the line. Government witnesses hammered us. They said all the things we had not prepared to discuss.

Among the arrows in Acting U.S. Attorney Schieffer's quiver
was a statement issued by Michael Woodburne, chairman of
SVP's Government Liaison Committee. The statement, on SVP
letterhead, was drafted on May 20, 1992—the week after the
seizure. Its lead paragraph read, "The Society of Vertebrate
Paleontology firmly supports the action of the US Attorney's
office in Rapid City as regards the seizure of a specimen of
Tyrannosaurus rex that apparently was collected on Federal lands
without proper permitting procedures as required under Federal
statues [sic.]."

On June 8, June 26, and June 27, further statements or letters were released, two of which were addressed to Schieffer
directly. They expressed the Executive Committee's objections to
our wish to return Sue to Hill City. The letters were signed by
Woodburne and others, including Robert Hunt, SVP's secretary-
treasurer—who testified at the hearing, and quoted from the
documents. One of his main points was not only that Sue should
remain at the School of Mines, but also that we were unworthy
to curate her.

In our opinion, there's no compelling reason why scientific study of this dinosaur should proceed in haste
nor should a commercial fossil collector direct such
research as to its course, its timing, or its method. A
responsible research program should proceed from a
consensus of qualified vertebrate paleontologists once
the skeleton is adequately curated in a public repository for fossil material.

The government's coup de grâce was Sally Shelton. Shelton had
a master's degree in museum science with a thesis in vertebrate
paleontology. She described her expertise area, museumology, as
"a program in which people study various aspects of the museum
field in preparation for going into careers in collections management, administration, registrar-type positions, curation." She cited
expertise in "just about every conceivable kind of preservation"
and she masterfully wielded examples of difficult paleontology
preservation issues, construction vibration and its effects on collections, correlates to the proximity of a nearby train track to
Sue's storage site. She catalogued it all using a document called the
"Conservation Assessment."

Shelton recommended a recording hygrothermograph to
measure and graph temperature and humidity over time, humidity
strip indicators, passive pest monitoring in the form of sticky
traps, and sulfite test strips for the presence of sulfur dioxide in
the atmosphere—a by-product of pyrite decay. She had run the
hygrothermograph for twenty-four-hour intervals inside and outside the steel container within Sue's storage room. Citing standards for temperature and humidity in various conservation
situations, she believed the 90-degree-plus temperature in Sue's
tank should be lowered, but otherwise, the environment was suitable for temporary storage of Sue—especially considering the low
levels of pyrite found in the X-ray defraction analysis another government witness had presented. The chemicals stored in the
building with Sue, which we worried would be toxic to her
skeleton, were dispatched by Shelton as causing no risk. She saw
no evidence of rehydration of the fossil, no disturbing cracks in

the plaster covering Sue's bones, no evidence of pyrite oxidation. She found the School of Mines and Black Hills Institute storage facilities "roughly equal," and she believed more risk would come to Sue through moving her again than from leaving her where she was. She also believed the ownership issue should be resolved before anything more was done with Sue.

By the time we lost the hearing, our case was fifty-one days old. The complaint had been amended twice and we had filed in the Eighth Circuit Court of Appeals. Judge Battey ruled that "the Court has been presented with no credible evidence that the fossil is suffering damage. The court, therefore, finds that the best temporary custodian is the School of Mines and Technology at Rapid City." His final word came immediately at the hearing's conclusion and we wondered how he possibly could have written the extensive document *after* testimony concluded. He dictated that curation of Sue was not to commence at the School of Mines, but instead the facility would simply store the specimen. Sue was not going home.

In the institute's subsequent appeal of this decision, known in legal circles as Black Hills II, the Eighth Circuit upheld Judge Battey. Describing the three-day custody hearing as "not unlike the dinosaur in size," the Eighth Circuit found in favor of leaving Sue at the School of Mines until the dispute over her ownership was resolved. In a rap to the knuckles of our attorney, Pat Duffy, the decision concluded: "We are confident that the experienced district judge will exercise firm control over this case so that the case will proceed to determination and that the litigious legal maneuvering that has resulted in several interlocutory matters that we have considered will not recur."

In English that meant, "Quit it."

Our troops—accustomed to the catacombs of the institute, solitarily chipping ancient sediment from bones—did not quit it. Inflamed, they marched up to the fax machine and unleashed an international public-relations campaign. Our legal filings went out over the wire; letters were sent to the Attorney General, U.S. Senators, and the President. The media responded to the compelling story of what looked to them to be a band of ruddy rednecks caught in the crossfire. Duffy would say many times, in his South Dakota drawl, "If it weren't for the press, especially at the beginning, the gov'ment would have come in here and thrown a log chain around the whole building." The elusive case was trapped by the sticky written word, stamped in varying type faces from Hill City to New York to France to Australia to Japan to Los Angeles to Denver.

"Who's going to walk off with a dinosaur?" Jack Horner asked *The New York Times,* when he called the seizure "absolutely ridiculous," affirming that the specimen could have stayed with us until our legal difficulties were sorted out. Bakker and Currie added to what the newspaper called "the protest."[18] Some papers ran humorous headlines: "Federalosaurus Rex Rides Again," and "US Attorney Investigate Thyself."

None of it was lost on the U.S. Attorney, who acknowledged the media hype in a Petition for Rehearing filed in the appeals court on July 6, 1992:

> The popularized perception of this case is that the heavy handed government went overboard with an armed invasion of a well meaning scientific research institute which, at worst committed an isolated technical violation of a minor criminal law or, more likely, was in a good faith property dispute with an individual Indian who reneged on a fair, arms length commercial transaction. . . . Because of the attention this case has generated, these perceptions have been repeated in the national and international media.

He was right. Public perception called the government's seizure out of proportion. All in all, our custody battle and its attendant media buzzed around the government like an annoying gnat. In that same brief, the U.S. Attorney tried to reverse any misunderstanding that he might have unnecessarily seized Sue. "Because of the time constraints, as well as tactical and other considerations," their earlier briefs had not been complete. He was afraid that "prematurely exposing even limited aspects of a criminal case may make successful prosecution more difficult. . . . The scope of the investigation goes beyond the warrant. This is not a simple investigation into the fossils removed from the land held in trust for an individual allottee on the Cheyenne River Sioux Reservation."

It wasn't? Then what could it possibly be? The Big Mystery continued. And so did the custody battle. By the time both parties requested "summary judgment," nine months had passed and the government had abandoned two of its three claims bolstering the seizure: those accusing the institute of stealing government property and tribal property. But still the dinosaur was no closer to us, and Schieffer was falling back upon the trust status of Williams's land and the Antiquities Act.

Again, summary judgment would fall somewhat short of ownership and would prove a stopgap for whoever won—assuring some measure of a court's belief that one party "deserved" the specimen more than the other. Theoretically, then, that decision later would assist in the final disposition of the fossil even when Williams and the tribe were included.

The reason we were requesting summary judgment was yet another example of how strange our case had become. The concept of summary judgment had not dawned on anyone—except the judge. The U.S. Attorney had filed a motion for, among other things, *dismissal* of our case, referring to a legal code called 12(b), a relatively standard response to almost any complaint. Apparently throwing in everything, just in case, the motion also had mentioned that the court did not have jurisdiction, and that the involvement of the tribe, a sovereign nation, confused the issue. In reading the judge's order in response to the dismissal motion, it appeared to me that the judge saw flaws in the government's arguments, but instead of simply denying them, as he did with us, he taught the U.S. Attorney what he *should* say. It was as if he laid down a trail of crumbs leading to the prize. The order read, in part: "[The government] has not designated which subparagraph of Rule 12(b) forms the basis for its relief. By process of elimination . . ." and the judge chose the bit that would solve the government's sticky problem of having wrongly seized the dinosaur. He highlighted the part that mentioned summary judgment. Then, the judge *converted* the dismissal motion to one of summary judgment, ordered the U.S. Attorney to prepare *that* motion, and instructed him which legal cites to use. He even hinted at how he would be "graded": "The trilogy of <u>Celotex</u>, <u>Anderson</u>, and <u>Matsushita</u> provide the Court with the methodology in analyzing defendant's motion."

It was incredible. We had no choice but to prepare our own motion for summary judgment, outlining our own reasons why we deserved to possess the dinosaur more than the government. We sang the same tune: that the seizure was unnecessary, that we had not broken the law, that we had purchased Sue, that she should be returned to us.

Months passed as we awaited the decision. The irony of where we happened to be standing when we heard the outcome of the civil case was exceeded only by the irony of the decision itself. Our crew was on its way to the annual Tucson fossil trade show, in February of 1993, driving in a caravan containing fossils for sale and display. We stopped to check in at a pay phone in none other than Truth or Consequences, New Mexico. Judge Battey had, not surprisingly, voted for the government, but in a way none of us anticipated. We knew he had given them the template for a loophole, but we had not guessed the loophole itself: in a mind-boggling setting of precedent, the judge called Sue, the actual fossil herself, *real estate*. I remember standing there listening to Marion read the decision. I remember my heart dropping a few inches as she explained that if Sue were considered part of the land, Williams would have had to have received permission from the Department of Interior to sell her to us. Without that, our sale was null and void. It was the only way the government's arguments could stand. The dinosaur, the Queen of the Tyrants on whom we had lavished love and nearly a quarter-million dollars, would belong to Maurice Williams once again. She was just a piece of turf.

At this moment the King, who had been for some time busily writing in his note-book, called out "Silence!" and read out from his book, "Rule Forty-two. *All persons more than a mile high to leave the court.*"

Everybody looked at Alice.

"I'm *not* a mile high," said Alice.

"You are," said the King.

"Nearly two miles high," added the Queen.[19]

Later, when I had an opportunity to read the judge's memorandum opinion, I was astounded by what looked to me like a plain contradiction. Battey had written, "The Court has found no case authority specifically holding that a paleontological fossil such as the fossil 'Sue' embedded in the ground is an 'interest in land.'" After explaining how he rationalized his precedent-setting decision calling Sue an interest in land, he concluded that "plaintiffs must assume much of the fault caused by their failure to conform their conduct to the federal laws and regulations." How we could conform to a *lack* of legal authority was beyond me.

On February 10, one week later, we filed a Motion for Reconsideration, which was denied the next day by the same judge. Black Hills III, our third appeal, took that decision to the Eighth Circuit. We said for one last time that we had bought the dinosaur from a man who was fully able to sell it, that there was no history on which to stack the real estate decision. Ironically, and I'm sure unintentionally, the government made us feel better. In their brief, they finally abandoned their third of three claims that initiated the seizure of Sue—the one alleging that we had violated the Antiquities Act. While Mandel claimed their objective was only to "simplify" the issue, to us it seemed they had won on the most unlikely idea—that a dinosaur was actually real estate— and they stuck to it. They repeated that we simply had not followed procedure, that Williams and I had neglected to chat with the BIA before we sealed our deal.

Oral arguments in front of the Eighth Circuit were made for the government by Edward Shawaker from the Department of Justice. When later asked why he thought the U.S. Attorney's office had abandoned all their initial claims, he answered, "It was not my case at that time, but I'm sure that in looking again at the claims, they had to say they didn't have merit." Baseless, just as we had always said. While that didn't get us our dinosaur back, it certainly removed the specter of theft that had sullied our reputations. At least for a moment.

Maurice Williams seemed pleased with his victory. His euphoria may have been dampened momentarily, however, as the Cheyenne River Sioux Tribe once again dealt themselves into the game. Unconcerned that the purchase by the institute of Sue had been moot, the tribe focused on the *attempt* of Williams and our team to make a transaction. On April 13, 1993, the Cheyenne River Sioux Tribe asked for forfeiture of the dinosaur:

> This is a civil action which arises out of the illegal removal of fossils from the Cheyenne River Indian Reservation. The Tribe alleges that defendants engaged in a civil conspiracy to violate Ordinance 1, by doing business on the Reservation without a tribal business license, and to convert tribal property to their own use. Accordingly, any property used in furtherance of this conspiracy was used in violation of tribal law . . . and the property was subject to an action for civil forfeiture.

Our lawyers said tribal business licenses applied to industrial realms, not to a personal case of an individual selling his property, but the tribe calmly asserted that business had occurred illegally. The price for this action was forfeiture of Sue. The price of the neglected business license? One hundred dollars.

It is always challenging when courts from different sovereign nations litigate matters that have to do with each other's citizens. But here, in this corner of rural America, the challenge is unique. The Lakota walk in two different worlds; they are members of one culture who are forced to be fluent in another. From my perspective, it seemed that when it came to legal issues, ours again had overtaken them. Despite my own emotional connection to Sue, our case argued buying and selling. Commerce, not spirituality. Likewise, tribal lawyers filed in legalese.

In tribal court, in the world of litigation, the judge ruled against the tribe. We were dismissed. Two cases down, one to go.

Kevin Schieffer left office in 1993 with the changing of the guard in Washington. The bulk of the criminal case against the institute fell to First Assistant U.S. Attorney Robert Mandel. I credit him with being willing to give an interview, and also with being clear in how he viewed our approach to the business of fossil collecting. His interpretation of our intentions provided the hook on which the government hung its whole "investigation into multistate criminal activity."

Mandel explained it this way:

> You can imagine someone who collected ancient cars, if you will, those rusty old hulks you see out by the roadside, some of which have great value. If [a collector] were to see one on a farmer's land somewhere, why, someone might offer to take that thing away without any charge to the farmer. "I'll just get the scrap out of it, probably worth a couple bucks." Needless to say, that offer would be made when something was an item of great value. You get into the question of whether that's a dishonest practice or an immoral practice. That's a value judgment. Some people would think that's clever; others would think it's crooked.

Mandel believed we absolutely knew there was a real estate problem before removing Sue from Maurice Williams's land, that we guessed the BIA would not allow Sue to be sold for such a small sum. He believed the information initially released to newspapers that announced Sue's discovery, including the description of the site, was carefully crafted to avoid pinpointing the locality. To avoid suspicion. Regardless, after Sue was handed back to Maurice Williams, she no longer had anything to do with our criminal case.

Sue, the specimen that had initiated the entire process, now became the least of our legal worries. The emotional impact of losing her was tremendous, but it paled next to what was in store. As far as we could see, the charges against us regarding

Sue were indeed "baseless," and therefore she had ceased to be a source of illegal activity. We could not be charged with theft of government and tribal property, or with violating the Antiquities Act.

Mandel, of course, saw it differently. He said that the removal of the causes for seizure was "a totally separate issue as to whether or not there was a crime committed. [Dropping Sue from the criminal case] was a strategic decision." Although Sue was "the most valuable specimen" on his list, others were "factually better" for potential prosecution. Whether Sue had been purchased by us or not was a messy "jury issue" that clouded the questions of illegal behavior.

Mandel moved Sue from the top of the evidence list and relegated her to the tip of the iceberg.

The SVP did not wait to watch the proceedings or to hear decisions. On June 8, 1992, less than one month after Sue's seizure, the SVP had adopted a new resolution. To me, an SVP member since 1974, it felt a little personal as it proposed that:

> The collection, preparation, display, and sale of vertebrate fossils taken from federal lands within the United States by commercial interests be prohibited by federal statute; that suitable penalties of consequence be adopted to further discourage such commercial activities; that members of the Society who engage in commercial collection and sale of vertebrate fossils from federal lands be notified that such activity is in conflict with the stated position of the Society; and that continued commercial collection and sale of fossil vertebrates from federal lands following the aforesaid notification shall constitute grounds for consideration of expulsion from the Society.

Dr. Clayton Ray, a well-respected scientist at the Smithsonian Institution, is not a fan of commercial fossil collecting. A gentleman to his core, he at one time shared some joint research projects with me, but eventually backed out of them to avoid any appearance of impropriety or self-interest when arguing commercialism with the SVP. Ironically, despite his own views about fossils and money, he threw in *against* SVP's anticommercial position, citing its "harmful, divisive, negative, exclusionary focus" regarding commercial collectors.

In a memorandum to the SVP Executive Committee on June 30, 1992, Ray regretfully resigned as the vice president of the society. He wrote:

> The discovery of "Sue" was announced widely, quickly, and repeatedly; it has (until recently) been available to the public and profession without restriction; and research plans have moved rapidly, including a planned broadly participatory symposium. All of these facets have been exceptional as compared to common performance among the likes of us with megafinds—the norms are secrecy until it suits our purpose or the restrictions of National Geographic or Science; highly limited access; and sitting on it for years. So what is our problem here? If there is one, it seems to me it is whether the landowner had the right to sell Peter trespass rights for collecting. Ordinarily, it is the seller, not the buyer, of the Brooklyn Bridge who is in trouble with the law.

Holding in one hand a receipt for the Brooklyn Bridge, while struggling to maintain my other hand's tenuous fingerhold on the ledge of that perilous cliff, I took refuge in the idea that this was only a game. A croquet game from someone's imagination, but a game nonetheless. Certainly, it would soon be over and I could get back to my *real* life. As Robert Mandel rode his war horse through Hill City, I clung to my slightly tarnished belief in our legal system and pulled out my maps. There had to be a road out of Wonderland.

BHI file phot

(6)

The Young and the Restless

 *yrannosaurus rex*es were built out of approximately three hundred bones. The number is inexact for several reasons. Some of
us think there are forty-six vertebrae in the tail, but no specimen has been preserved down to its very tip, so there might be
more. Correspondingly, the number of chevrons—which attach to
the underside of the tail—might change with a longer tail, plus
there might be different numbers of chevrons in different individuals. Also, scientists have their own personal opinions about what
counts as a bone. Do you or don't you include the stomach gastralia or those lumps on Sue's eyebrows? I say no; the gastralia are
derived from the skin, like scutes on a crocodile, and the female's
eyebrow lumps are fused onto the postorbital while the male's are
not. It wouldn't be fair for him to have two more bones just
because he didn't fuse. We will be able to eliminate these variables,
except for differences of opinion, when and if we find one—or
even better, several—perfect *T. rex* specimen, laid out in one inter-
connected piece, uneroded, unnibbled, and preferably with skin
and passport intact. With each passing season, we get closer and
closer to that goal; Sue's face has launched a thousand inspired
collectors to pound the prairie for *T. rex*. Thankfully, with all the
concomitant excitement, our story was not the only *T. rex* news-
cast worth airing in the 1990s.

In museums, a skeleton is considered very good if it is 40 percent complete; most mounts commonly displayed are less than
that, with missing bones filled in either by replicas from other
specimens or by artists. Figuring a specimen's "percentage of
completeness" is, unsurprisingly, a bone of contention among

scientists—especially those scientists who have their hands on a cool fossil and want it to be the coolest fossil of them all. "My *T. rex* can beat up your *T. rex*." Completeness can be calculated in two ways: either by counting the *number* of bones present, or by estimating the relative *mass* or *surface area* of bone. I think bone count is the only empirical, reproducible, and fair method, because estimating mass or surface area is too subjective.

By 1992 very few *T. rex*es ranked high on the completeness chart. Sue was approximately 80 percent complete any which way she was measured; using the trusty bone count, Stan was more than 65. Tied for third place at approximately 45 percent were AMNH-5027, MOR-555, and Z-rex. Because of their relative wholeness, all of these triumphed in supplying literally tons of information about their species. Even so, we needed more specimens—not just to get the absolute bone count or to determine sexual dimorphism or to verify how many similar species ran wild at once, but also to get a handle on dinosaur growth.

The problem? All our very complete specimens were adults.

I had been excited about juvenile *T. rex* specimens since I saw my first one, the fragmentary LACM-23845 specimen found together with an adult in 1965. Youngsters were hard to come by; up until 1993, aside from my little LACM friend, only two other subadults were on record, Barnum Brown's nearly grown "type" specimen, CM-9380, and Canada's Black Beauty. But even that record wasn't entirely agreed upon in the scientific community. First, LACM-23845 had been misidentified as *Gorgosaurus lancensis*. Second, some scientists thought a junior-sized species called *Nanotyrannus lancensis*, which was known from one single skull, was really a young *T. rex*. To complicate matters even more, *Nanotyrannus* was first named *Gorgosaurus* and grouped together with that young LACM *T. rex*. It was all so sketchy.

Even so, I had my own ideas about *Nanotyrannus*, which I thought would clear up part of the picture on *T. rex*'s youth. *Nanotyrannus* was a creature with a similar overall shape to *T. rex*, but smaller. Its skull was more lightly built than the beefy *T. rex*, and its tooth count was higher than *T. rex*'s, numbering at least three more in both maxillae. The teeth were bladelike and had smaller and more closely spaced serrations than *T. rex*'s round, punchlike teeth. In short, I believed *Nanotyrannus* was not built for chomping through bone and anything else that got in its way; it was a more delicate eater, stripping meat from bones with a napkin tucked in its collar. This hypothesis was bolstered at a *Triceratops* dig we conducted. The unfortunate victim, named Kelsey, had been munched on by an apparent pack of *Nanotyrannus*es—more than twenty shed teeth littered the area. However, unlike a *T. rex* kill, where *Triceratops* bones are bitten in half or completely missing, all of Kelsey's bones were whole. These dainty diners did not ravage even one bone. With one exception: as in most munched *Triceratops* finds, Kelsey's feet were missing. They must have been a Cretaceous delicacy, perhaps pickled to tempt patrons of the K-T Bar & Grill.

Satisfied that *Nanotyrannus* was out of the juvenile-*T. rex* race, I reviewed what else we knew about *Tyrannosaurus* ontogeny, or growth stages. Nobody grows in one giant leap. For example, Barnum Brown's type specimen was a subadult, which means it was almost full grown, maybe 90 percent. It represented the equivalent of an eighteen-year-old human, still filling out but with the same basic dimensions as a grown-up. However, an eighteen-year-old human looks significantly different from a fifteen-year-old, or a prepubescent kid, or a baby. Nailing down *T. rex*'s ontogeny would be essential to totally understanding the species— how its body changed, how fast it grew, perhaps even how many offspring fledged in one season. Ontogeny also would help sort out the interspecies confusion; a neat row of successively taller skeletons would confirm if we were looking at growth stages in one species or at several members of similar, but different, species.

I started with what we had. The bones of the "eighteen-year-old," robust type specimen, CM-9380, fell just short of the size of a gracile adult's. However, even so close in size, it retained juvenile features, such as a lack of fusion between sections of the two-part vertebrae. Black Beauty was about 75 percent grown, maybe a human fourteen-year-old. Its skull, while not extremely well preserved, was quite complete, and its dimensions made sense when compared with the next-largest CM-9380. Black Beauty also had

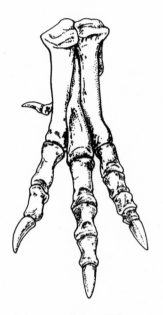

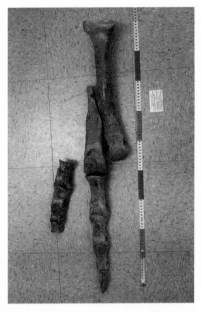

An adult *T. rex* foot, which measures approximately four feet long. Note the birdlike reversed first digit. Illustration by Dorothy Sigler Norton.

LACM's juvenile *T. rex* foot, showing puppylike proportions, measures three feet. Although the foot is ¾ the length of an adult's, it is only half the mass. Photo by Peter Larson.

both upper and lower leg bones—the only juvenile ones found to date aside from a fragmentary specimen at the Smithsonian Institution. This one was collected more than one hundred years ago by John Bell Hatcher, and included only three bones, of which the femur and tibia were two. So far, this still-sketchy leg material suggests that *T. rex* youth, when compared with adults, ran on long, skinny legs. The lower leg, particularly, seems to have started out proportionally longer than the upper leg. LACM-23845's braincase and nasals spelled out the complete length of an "eleven-year-old," two-thirds-grown *T. rex* skull; and its very diminutive arm bone, the ulna, helped put the rest of the body in perspective. However, the most intriguing picture LACM-23845 put in my mind was that of a gawky puppy. Its foot was extra long and extra skinny for its body size. All of these youngsters made me wonder if *T. rex* started out as an enthusiastic, big-footed, adorable, three-foot-long killing machine.

Stan Sacrison with the first evidence of Duffy, his second *T. rex* find. The white bone at bottom center is the ischium, a pelvic bone. Photo by Peter Larson.

A Child of Our Own

It's different when you know someone personally. Aside from my short exposure to the junior LACM specimen, my first significant personal relationship with a juvenile *T. rex* began at the end of June 1993. A year had passed since Stan's excavation and Sue's seizure, and we were still up to our necks in legal proceedings. Desperate to get out of the office, I found myself sitting on a hillside with Stan Sacrison. To the northwest, less than a half mile away, we could still see the large shelf near the top of the ridge where we had jackhammered Stan out of the sandstone. I guessed God was throwing us a bone to keep us from losing our minds over the Big Mystery: I was sitting next to a fractured but beautifully preserved and completely exposed pelvic bone, the ischium. It was just lying there, absolutely uncovered on the surface. Beside it protruded ends of ribs and two broken, honeycombed vertebrae.

Amazingly, Stan Sacrison had just found his second *T. rex*. During last year's Stan excavation, we all had taken walks exploring for bones. I know I had been on and around this very butte. I had walked probably within one hundred feet of this specimen, yet I had not seen it. Others, too, had been here, on their way to a microsite just over the top of the butte's east side. Looking at these fragments, I could see that they obviously had been exposed for several years, but still, no one had recognized them. Except Stan Sacrison, who became the third person ever to have found a matched set of *T. rex*es. He joined Barnum Brown, the *T. rex* champion from the turn of the century, and Harley Garbani, the amateur who found the two LACM skeletons in the same excavation. Since Stan Sacrison already had a namesake, we had to be more creative this time. But what do you name a creature you'd never want coming after you? It only took a moment: Duffy.

John Niemi also was a good sport. "You just go right ahead and dig," he said (the courthouse would confirm that this one was on his property). "We'll worry about the details later." Since almost the entire county—well over 500 people—had arrived for the Stan dig, I asked whether we should keep this one out of the newspapers; we didn't want the Niemis' main memory of us to be one of inconvenience. But no, he said, the more the merrier.

I couldn't wait to get back home. The crew was as far in the doldrums as I had been; I drove home with an Ann Murray song playing in my head, "Sure could use a little good news today." It worked. People piled out of the institute as if it were on fire. On July 12 we pitched camp on the prairie less than a hundred yards from where Duffy lay buried. The Sacrison brothers, Stan and his Bobcat-wielding twin, Steve, were waiting for us. They were not alone. Steve Sacrison already had cut a road up to the specimen, and the first residents of "Rexburg," our camp, were already in residence. Rexburg became quite a little town, populated by amateur diggers who had always loved working at the Ruth Mason duckbill quarry, or who had been bitten by *T. rex* fever at Stan's site. During the excavation, we would number as many as a dozen vehicles and a half-dozen tents. For the first time ever, we even trucked in the incredible luxury of portable toilets.

Everyone was itching to get to work, and I laughed at how different this excavation would be from Sue's. There we had a "skeleton crew." Here, until more bone was exposed, we barely had enough work to go around. Standard procedure, therefore, was completed quickly and easily—photos, maps, fragment col-

Standard procedure begins with collecting and labeling loose bone fragments. The undisturbed ischium is visible in the center of the photo. Photo by Ed Gerken.

lection, and bone stabilization flew by. Some workers then began above the specimen, where they slowly dug into the matrix in search of bones. My shoulders began to rejoice immediately: this time the matrix was soft and pliable, and the jackhammer remained neatly packed away. I never would jinx a project by actually giving voice to my next thought, but I'll admit it flashed through my mind. Could this dig be . . . smooth sailing?

It was child's play even for our smallest helpers. Being a prairie kid myself, I was not surprised when institute children or the families of volunteers were eager to dig fossils. I became familiar with the sight of my son Matthew, early teens, bare-chested, shirt wrapped around his head like a sheik, outwardly bored but excavating smoothly, quickly, cleanly, and much beyond his "age level." Or my son Tim, the kid with a gnat's attention span, on his stomach for hours, spying tiny teeth and bones in a microsite—an area where small, disarticulated remnants collected in an ancient stream eddy. And their older sister, Sarah, the young scientist, who seriously contemplated the physiological implications of each fragment. Perhaps because we were so used to one another, I sometimes forgot how unusual these children were. But when I did notice them solving bone retrieval problems, using physics to lever something out of the ground, or gently guiding an adult volunteer, I was continually surprised at how early their quick eyes, enthusiasm, and unselfconscious directness enriched our work site. Even more, I counted my blessings—my odd job was the perfect place for children, and I was the luckiest dad on Earth. We not only spent summers together, we made history together.

At the Duffy site, all of Rexburg's children pitched in. They had all worked on dinosaur bones before, and knew the feel and sound dinosaur bones provide to alert a digger to their presence. Pleased to be able to quickly turn over one knife blade's sediment at a time, they began with enthusiasm, keeping a keen eye out for anything that resembled bone or bone fragments. So early in the dig, however, not much had popped up. The attention spans were challenged—bones are interesting, but dirt is not. Digging more and more slowly with X-acto knives into areas where there may or may not be bones, the junior staff started to fidget. The four-year-old contingent took frequent breaks for peanut-butter-and-jelly sandwiches; the preteens escaped occasionally to hunt for microsite teeth. They were ready for action. They were starving for bones.

On the second day it rained, as it would frequently on this dig. The showers provided our first lesson in patience with Duffy the dinosaur. Since Duffy's bones were not in sand, the flaky siltstone all around the specimen—and up the road to it—melted into a familiar, greasy gumbo that clings to anything touching it. We couldn't even shovel away the top, gooey layer, because the gumbo would not release from the shovel; if we tried to throw a shovelful of mud, shovel and all would usually go flying. Try camping in mondo mud with pent-up kids. It wasn't pretty.

By covering the site with tarps and working between rain showers, we began to expose the specimen. Slowly but surely, we uncovered, mapped, and removed twenty-five nicely preserved, fractured bones, including at least ten ribs, a half-dozen vertebrae, a strangely broken and scattered portion of the pelvis's ilium, and, remarkably, both fused scapula-coracoids—the double-boned shoulder girdles. The shoulder girdles would have been plenty to celebrate; MOR-555 and Sue were the only others to have them (aside from Barnum Brown's type specimen, which had a single scapula). However, Duffy's shoulder blades were *only thirty-six inches long* compared to Sue's fifty-four-inchers. We had welcomed into our family our first teenager. Approximately 75 percent grown, Duffy represented the equivalent of a fourteen-year-old person. All of our ontogeny questions flooded into our heads. Would this youngster have floppy feet? Long, gangly legs? Like Charlie Brown, would it have a big head?

Our wave of enthusiasm was short-lived. Many of the bones were sunken in the bone layer, and the matrix had been jumbled—especially toward the edge of the exposure where Sacrison had found the first bone. We had taken note of a sinkhole below that original discovery point, which long ago would have gobbled up loose fragments, but now it appeared the sinkhole was bigger than we thought. As the excavation increased in size, so did evidence of the sinkhole, which seemed intent on swallowing our treasure. I knew that Hell Creek sinkholes developed from groundwater flowing into fractures in the sediment of a hill. As rains added more water, the holes expanded, pulling earth and bones and rocks sometimes five feet, sometimes thirty, sometimes hundreds of feet down. How undignified if our first child were sucked under. We had to look—we craved information on this youngster—but our first foray below the bone horizon turned up only scraps. So much for "smooth sailing."

Now on a rescue mission, we pushed outward with our digging tools, expanding the boundaries of our quarry. Bobcat Sacrison removed two, four, and then more than six vertical feet of overburden. He scraped away the covering siltstone to within eighteen inches of the bone horizon. The diggers attacked the inside walls of the crater, searching, searching, learning the site's second lesson in patience. Bone frequency diminished down to a few chevrons, some tail vertebrae, and a couple of teeth. Even though the teeth held onto their roots—which meant Duffy's skull had at one time been close by—the crew's volume sunk five, then thirty, then a hundred decibels. This was maddening—until, quite some distance from the discovery site, we came upon a "pile" of bones

Barry Brown and Peter attack the overburden with picks. Photo by Layne Kennedy.

comprising about 5 percent of the skeleton. It made no sense. Why was *this* over *here?*

Taphonomy is the science of reading the geologic footprint of the moments surrounding the burial of a creature. Through a study like this I had concluded that Sue probably struggled with another *T. rex* who ripped open her face and left her to die in a river—she was found in the sandy "channel" deposits of the actual throughway of the water. Stan appeared to have laid upon a levy, sandbar, or "point bar" out of the main flow, next to a river. It looked as if Duffy had died on a floodplain, on ground not usually under water, and therefore he was not cemented with sand. He had taken pity on us by choosing a dark "over-bank deposit" siltstone for a deathbed, a much more manageable sediment. Just southwest of the site, the matrix turned sandier, which meant the original stream channel was nearby. Judging from that, and the fine silt grains enclosing Duffy's bones, we concluded that this specimen probably was buried by a mud-laden, flood-swollen stream derived from the ancestral Rocky Mountains more than a hundred miles to the west. The current in the streambed was fast, but the waters that overflowed its banks slowed enough on the broad floodplain to dump much of the silt gathered on the water's trip to the sea. With the use of an altimeter, I later found that Duffy was buried only about twenty feet above Stan's elevation. Considering the ancient lay of the land—the difference between the elevation of a sandbar on the edge of a stream and its adjacent floodplain deposit—an exciting idea struck me. These two neighbors, only a half mile apart, could have known each other!

I pulled myself back to the point. Taphonomy wasn't helping me with what I really needed to know—the details of Duffy's demise. In excavations in or near stream channels, I usually could rely on crossbedding to give me direction. Because this unit had been deposited in one event, one slow-moving settling of material, crossbedding evidence was not preserved. I looked at the bone map, searching for some pattern to the bone distribution. Nothing. Except for this new pile, the further we moved away from the original discovery, the fewer the bones. Was the discovery site the primary location of bones? Did this pile indicate water flow? Or perhaps the discovery site was only a remnant, with the bulk of the skeleton long ago eroded away with slices of the butte?

I thought about it. If a great deal of the skeleton had eroded away in the past, I believed a lot more bone fragments would have been sprinkled down the hill—evidence of years of breakage and disintegration. Instead, the only fragments we found were those right next to the bones in the original exposure. Could 90 percent of a *Tyrannosaurus* skeleton just disappear down a sinkhole?

By the end of the second week of dogged digging with almost no reward, people were ready to give up. I wondered what other method could help us find direction in this widening, elusive dig— but I definitely sensed more of this dinosaur somewhere in this hill. I could taste it. Reluctantly, we packed up our children and headed home. Without much of Duffy.

Belly Up to the Bar

We learned no more about young *T. rexes* in 1993 but were kept plenty busy. We were nursing a sinkhole of our own, a legal vacuum that was sucking every dollar we had. We had been hit hard in the blustery winter that year, before Duffy's excavation, by a series of grand jury subpoenas. Several called our employees as witnesses; several required that we provide handwriting samples. The impossible one, however, asked for our business records. Nearly all of them. "Any and all field notes . . . any and all photographs, slides, negatives, videotapes . . . within the possession or control of Black Hills Institute." It asked for fossils, along with all records concerning them. The list of specimens spanned several single-spaced pages—sometimes specimens we had collected more than ten years earlier, specimens buried deep in the catacombs of our storage areas. One of the most troublesome was the entry citing material from "all specimens excavated and removed from Peru." These were large whale fossils that had afforded me some of my most precious memories. Unforgettable summers in the desert, wracked with dysentery, short of tools, ecstatic with the challenge and beauty of it.

The subpoena was served late in the day on January 28. We were to deliver these fossils, and original documents, by 3 P.M. January 29, just shy of one full day later. In a Motion to Quash Subpoenas filed on January 29, we argued:

> The subpoenas are oppressive and burdensome because they literally require the production of all of the Institute's books and records within about 24 hours. . . . Here the government's investigation must be limited to fossils allegedly taken from federal lands. The United States simply has no jurisdiction to investigate the excavation of fossils from private land or state land, let alone fossils collected in Peru pursuant to permits issued by the Peruvian government.

"They wanted everything we could find," Neal told the press. "We rented an extra copier and used one at another business. We had three copiers going, people running back and forth, moving boxes. We worked into the night, because we only had one day to collect every business paper we had. They took everything. Every picture, every contract, everything."

True, the subpoena did not ask for each and every scrap of paper in the building, but in effect emptying our cabinets was the only way we could comply, considering the time restriction. We had no idea how long the government would keep our business papers, and we wanted copies for our records. In my affidavit, I explained, "We are unsure what falls within the scope of the subpoena; and consequently, we fear that any omission might place us in contempt." It was a terrible time, and our first glimpse of the Big Mystery's true scope, though we still didn't know what the government believed we'd done wrong.

Needless to say, our motion was denied. We drove up to the Federal Courthouse with truckloads of institute corporate documents—an estimated 100,000 of them. Just a blink ahead of the deadline. Ironically, later the government would accuse us of "overcompliance."

We appeared at the courthouse other times, too. In May, June, and August, further subpoenas asked for more handwriting samples, a few more specimens, additional documents. By the time spring and then summer arrived, the grand jury had become personal. No longer just a concept, it was alive, with a line of human faces in front of which our own employees were called to testify. In the government's attempt to ferret out evidence of our "ongoing, multistate criminal activity," each morning became another ordeal. In anguish I watched our friends and associates parade by, into a torture room where I was not invited. I could do nothing except sit in a grand jury waiting room. Sometimes ten or more of us were provided with only three hard, plastic chairs. Thankfully, we were used to camping, so we sat on the floor, tensely leaning against beige walls, for hours on end.

As unlike Assistant U.S. Attorney Robert Mandel as a person could be, his partner, David Zuercher, added his own wiry, high-strung agitation to the proceedings. Perhaps he was simply nervous, or trying to be efficient, but to us he seemed unrelentingly officious, brusque, and mean-spirited. Zuercher almost always avoided eye contact and would throw open the door on our nervous crew, call the next witness, and snap, "Let's not keep the grand jury waiting." If the witness wanted a quick, whispered moment with his or her attorney first, Zuercher would warn, "You don't want to obstruct justice." To us, he was a caricature of Barney Fife on steroids, and while his presence added tension, he also made us laugh.

Whatever humor we could scrape from our angst, the grand jury became an unending nightmare. When friends and clients called after having received their own subpoenas, all we could counsel was to answer questions honestly and to get a lawyer. Get a lawyer. We were restricted from talking to some friends and associates, and we left others alone so as to make doubly sure they would not be accused of collaborating with us on their testimony. We heard rumors of offers of immunity, of threats of imprisonment, of coercion, of scare tactics. Even people we hesitated to talk with—for their own protection—would call us in hysterics after lengthy interrogations in their living rooms. I awoke each morning wondering what looking-glass I'd slipped through. The weight in my chest confirmed that this was not a dream. Marion Zenker, a big-hearted person with no malice in her, took the stand for nine days straight, her already spare frame bent with tension and grief. As our primary record-keeper, she was the target of questions dealing with an endless number of details. "They ask the same questions every day," she cried. "They ask as if I'm lying. I've told them everything I know."

June 4, 1993, was déjà vu of the worst kind. Instead of police line tape, officers and agents cordoned off Black Hills Institute with their bodies. Unlike the first visit, people were allowed in and out of our buildings, but the atmosphere was much more invasive—this time around, agents even threatened to kick down doors if their right to access was questioned. This was Seizure II, a sequel, but with all the impact of the original—and it seemed to be carefully timed for a period when both Pat Duffy and I were out of town. While Neal stood by with the support of Duffy's lawyer brother Dan, a female paleontologist admired the fossils in our collection. One of the FBI agents suggested she keep a list of the fossils she would like them to seize next time. That evening, agents who had participated in the seizure celebrated "the raid" at a local watering hole; one took the opportunity to intimidate my first wife, and suggested that she might want to provide damaging testimony.

Apparently having culled out the most useful material from the endless January exercise, Subpoena II listed twenty-two fossils as "evidence of a federal offense." The Big Mystery had become the Narrowed-down Mystery.

Senator Tom Daschle wrote a letter to a constituent about Seizure II on July 9, 1993.

> I understand your frustration. The investigation has lasted a long time with unclear results, and there is no question that many aspects of it have been mishandled. The initial raid . . . was unfortunate and unnecessary. . . . I had been assured that the government's involvement in the case would take a more constructive approach. However, the latest seizure of evidence has understandably reawakened concerns that the government could be returning to the strong-arm tactics of the past.[1]

Daschle's words made us feel better, but he could not engage in the legalities of our case. Between our lawyers and the U.S. Attorney's office, there followed a flurry of official letters and motions, postures and conjectures. We wanted to know the basis of the government's choice: what had caused it to believe these particular fossils had been "removed without appropriate government approval"? It all came down to FBI agent Bill Asbury, whose thirty-eight-page affidavit apparently had convinced the U.S. Attorney's office that we had committed crimes.

We asked to see the affidavit. The government said no. The judge concurred. "The affidavit formed the basis of a search warrant. . . . To reveal the information now would be premature and would serve no useful purpose. Upon later motion by [the institute] showing some definite and particularized need for the information sought, the Court may reconsider unsealing this affidavit." We thought that having our necks on the chopping block was "particularized need" enough, and that the affidavit would spell out what we had supposedly done wrong. Eventually we saw the document, but it was long-winded and less than illuminating, laboriously stating that we held in our possession the fossils in question. What we'd hoped to see was an explanation of *why* the government thought our possessing them was illegal. The unsealing of Asbury's affidavit did nothing to shed light on the Narrowed-down Mystery.

None of us was sure exactly when it happened, but the first grand jury to hear our case retired without indicting us. Or so we heard. It was more like a rumor than a fact, a ghost instead of a person. There was no sign-up sheet where we could look at the schedule, no regular procedure to confirm or deny. Our lawyers, in and out of the courthouse frequently, in conversation with the administrators of the offices, filing papers and picking up papers and checking on the status of this or that—they had heard about it. The grand jury had been dismissed.

Could it be over? Could we all finally breathe?

We knew grand jury proceedings were secret, and that nobody outside the prosecutor's office knew all the ins and outs, but rumor had it that the grand jury had sat for some twenty months without an indictment. We interpreted that to mean "they chose not to" indict us, and we quietly rejoiced. Later, Mandel would say that although he could not reveal grand jury details, we were not to assume that what we had heard about timing was "factually correct." He also said it is commonplace for one jury to serve its usual eighteen months, which can be extended, and then retire while a case is "midstream." "There's certainly been more than one occasion where a complex case has been through two panels," he said. "I even think we might have had one that went to a third panel because of the expiration."

But we didn't know that. Tentatively, ever so cautiously, we laid a path of eggshells between our main building and Rex Hall. We figured if we walked on them, from our offices to our dinosaur mounting projects, maybe the sky would not fall on our heads. If we were very quiet and bothered no one, maybe we could just build our dinosaurs. Amazingly, despite the almost total collapse of our bank account, we still were in business. Even more amazingly, we had a customer.

The Japanese have a mixed record in the United States when it comes to business and economics. Americans tend to feel a little upstaged by Japan's pursuit of perfection, a little jealous of its ranks of disciplined students and workers, a little in awe of its cultural legacy. At Black Hills Institute, however, all we knew was Japan's insatiable exuberance for dinosaurs. Sue might have been more famous and beloved in Japan than anywhere else, and our subsequent dig sites had welcomed television and print crews, along with annual tours of Japanese enthusiasts—teenagers to octogenarians who happily donned rain gear for long trips in foul weather, or sun hats for grueling days in 100-degree heat. All to dig fossils, to learn about fossils, and to take millions of photographs.

Even considering the black cloud that followed us throughout the first half of the 1990s, even considering the sound business question, "Should we risk throwing in with someone under federal investigation?" Tokyo Broadcasting Systems saved our bacon. TBS, the country's largest private broadcasting company, wanted to sponsor a tour of Stan. Always aiming high, they wanted the biggest, best, fastest, strongest available specimen to stroll through various exhibit halls in Japan for a year; Sue would have been their first choice, but she was a little tied up. Such an event would complement the new theme parks sprouting like mushrooms since the Dinosaur Renaissance. We told TBS about our situation, with the invaluable aid of Yoshio Ito, an anatomy professor and amateur paleontologist with incomparable international relations skills. As an ambassador for TBS and an interpreter of Japanese custom for us, Ito told the truth about our case *and* about the benefits of a joint project. In truth, however, project director Mitsuo Shirooka did not waver. Their injection of funds into our facilities paid for our staff to retain their jobs, paid for the preparation of Stan, kept our hands and minds busy, and kept our business afloat. Their injection of faith and trust did wonders for our hearts.

The *T. rex* World Exposition design was magnificent, chronicling all the science we had by then gathered about *Tyrannosaurus rex*. It examined what life was like in the Cretaceous via a reproduced environment with fossils and models of other contemporaneous dinosaurs. It explained fossilization and extrapolated ancient biology from bones, through sexual dimorphism to an evaluation of *T. rex*'s brain. TBS signed with Aurora Oval, a design firm, which envisioned the largest dinosaur exhibition ever staged, including cutting-edge graphics and displays, and incredible three-dimensional projections and film clips. This was a high-tech project planned by a group that knew exactly what it wanted. TBS and Aurora Oval wrote the book on research, on detail, on structured meeting plans. After negotiations, revisions to the plan, and endless design specifics, we signed the life-saving con-tract that spelled the survival of Black Hills Institute. At least for a moment.

We started a full-court press, taking parts of Stan into every preparation laboratory we had, building self-contained air-scribe chambers in our more spacious garages for the big blocks. Every free hand held a tool, whether a design pencil or a chisel, and our staff grew to its largest ever as we set to work to release Stan from the rock and to preserve the only lifestyle we had ever known. It was excellent therapy.

Comfortable on our eggshells, focusing on some of the most artistically challenging and scientifically concise work we had ever done, we grew accustomed to receiving long-distance phone calls from exotic locations. We learned to recognize the voices of our perky Japanese interpreters who carefully ticked through lists of questions. Ostriches with our heads firmly planted in legal sand, we were unprepared for the sky's falling. But even from our muf-fled position we heard the first cables snap, sending the whole fir-mament careering toward our backsides.

Our Japanese partners politely welcomed investigators into their offices, and wondered please what could we tell them about this process? Like pine bark beetles, federal agents swarmed all over Japan, and then Peru. European investigators interviewed Italian, Swiss, and German colleagues. The phone rang off the hook, and we never knew what accent might be on the other end. Our fossil collecting sites, collecting partners, and clients were being investigated. The companies and museums were furnished with a scathing document delivered to foreign governments by American officials. The letter said, "Fossils, which are protected under the law as cultural objects, were stolen from America and Peru," and that our sales to other countries were therefore tainted; it did not say there was an investigation, it said we were *thieves*. Period.

"That's a lie," stormed Pat Duffy to the *Rapid City Journal*. "It is a wicked fabrication. If that isn't defamation, I don't know what is." There was more: the document also said we had misrepresented ourselves and forged permits and smuggled fossils. "Robert Ludlum couldn't keep up with this conspiracy," Duffy added. "There isn't a criminal mind short of Lex Luthor who could keep up with this."[2]

It also meant another grand jury, a fresh one. Duffy asked our local paper, the *Pennington County Prevailer News*, "How can you counter this? This investigation is out of control. On the one hand, the first grand jury could find nothing wrong. The prosecutors apparently couldn't get them to bend. On the other hand, now my clients will be forced to go through the painstaking and expensive process all over again with the new grand jury. This, now, is just intimidation and an attempt to ruin reputations." Realistically, grand juries are vehicles for the government to present its most damning view of things, in order to judge whether a case is worthy of pursuit—with defendants having no voice in the proceedings. Therefore, the second grand jury was provided with a synopsis of earlier testimony, the new drama of the international forays, and only the U.S. Attorney's word on the subject.

What seemed impossible to endure suddenly worsened. In late November, 1993, after the new grand jury's being impaneled for less than a month, we were indicted. Finally, we assumed we could wring from the document the logic and secrets behind the investigation, but the Narrowed-down Mystery remained opaque. It could have been written in Japanese for all the sense it made to us, as the paragraphs simply named various localities or actual charges, but not the circumstances. All we knew was that we had been officially charged with: 36 counts each against the institute, partner Bob Farrar, and me; 38 against my brother Neal; 5 against Terry Wentz; 4 against Jun Shimizu, a Japanese company representative who had bought fossils from us; 2 against Ed Cole, a commercial collecting friend who had worked in the field with us; and 1 each against Ed's wife Ava and son Ed Jr. Later, Shimizu, Ava Cole, and Ed Cole Jr. all would be dropped from the case in exchange for their testimony. The charges? Conspiracy, theft of government property, interstate transportation of stolen goods, money laundering, wire fraud, obstruction of justice. My potential prison time? 353 years—in the same ballpark as Jeffrey Dahmer and Charles Manson.

The *Rapid City Journal* wrote a story called "Sue unnamed in T. rex indictment." Shocking, since most people assumed Sue was the whole problem. The story, written by Bill Harlan, concluded, "The case of Sue is complicated, but with a canceled check for $5,000, the Larsons are unlikely to face criminal charges for collecting Sue. . . . The fate of Sue likely will be settled in civil court."[3] The story reminded us that nearly a year had passed since Judge Battey first called Sue real estate. The appeals court still remained silent.

It would take months of legal instruction to understand the charges against us. It would take hiring more than Pat Duffy, who had been accused of conflict of interest in representing us all—the government contended that as individuals, we might have disparate priorities. In paranoia, we translated that to mean it was assumed (or hoped?) that we would turn against one another, but logic told us it was standard procedure. So did Duffy. Finding enough lawyers from separate firms in our small community would have been amusing if it weren't so tragic and cripplingly expensive. "It was the low point for the whole camp," Duffy would say later. "I was running around trying to get more defense attorneys, asking them to defend people who had no visible means to pay, in a case that, in our worst moments, looked like a forfeiture. And I was giving them my word that it was going to work."

In mid-December, 1993, we marched into our arraignment. We pleaded not guilty.

By the time we were finished, the appeals court's decision had arrived by fax. If we hadn't been so numb already, we would have felt all sorts of things. Amazement at the panel's agreement that Sue had been part of Maurice Williams's land. Incredulousness at its blindness to how that decision stripped Indians of even more power, overstepped from real estate into personal property, sneaked the cool stuff into the hands of government agents instead of landowners. Anger at what looked like a conspiracy among law-enforcers for some ends much beyond our small endeavors.

We couldn't even wrap our minds around it, but Pat Duffy summed things up nicely to the *Journal:* "What a vicious bit of irony that this decision comes on the day they are arraigned on 39 counts."[4] Undaunted, we tried to climb higher, but the Supreme Court declined to hear our case. Even Sue was not big enough for them.

We had never seen a more tumultuous or difficult year than 1993. As 1994 turned the corner, we were almost afraid to look. Still clutching our naïveté to our fluttering chests, we hoped against hope that the indictment could be sorted and organized and understood and explained away. Plenty of cases ended before disaster struck. I wanted to have one of those.

Gadgets and Gizmos

I divided my time between meeting with attorneys, sketching out our case, overseeing Stan's preparation, organizing the Japanese exhibition—which, thankfully, was not canceled once we were officially called criminals—and pondering that troublesome Duffy site. My stubbornness was working overtime. I was not about to roll over for the government, because I knew we had run our business with integrity. I was not about to let the case drag Stan behind schedule and scuttle the tour, slated for the summer of 1995. And I certainly was not going to allow some teenage dinosaur to hide from me.

Thinking that technology might come to our rescue, we tried to smoke out Duffy with Ground Probing Radar, or GPR, a tool that pulses electromagnetic radar waves from a transmitter through a few meters of earth. As the waves pass through sediment layers of differing densities, an antenna picks up a portion of the wave when it is reflected back at each density interface. The transmitter and antenna, pulled at a regular pace across the

From right, John Carter, with the assistance of Sam Farrar and Matthew Larson, pulls a Ground Probing Radar sled over the Duffy site in hopes of locating hidden bones.
Photo by Ed Gerken.

ground, communicate with a computer that translates what is "seen" into cross-sections on a television monitor. We knew the technology had been very successful at locating buried tanks and ancient graves, so why not dinosaurs? It was a worthy experiment, but after failing at the Duffy site and two others, we concluded that GPR wasn't finely tuned enough to pick up individual bones.

With the new school term barreling down at us, and teachers soon to be herding their classes to the site, we had to get organized. The only thing missing? A bunch of bones in the ground. One evening, while discussing our poor success rate for the season so far, Neal suggested we try something new. Like me, he was not willing to give up on Duffy, and he asked: why not simply move more sediment away with the Bobcat? We had nothing to lose.

Steve Sacrison thought about it. "You know," he replied, "I bet I can shave down the matrix a quarter-inch at a time."

For a moment there was silence. We all were thinking about those teeth with roots on them.

Technology finally triumphs as our "Ground Probing Bobcat" locates widely scattered bones by scraping the surface away a fraction of an inch at a time.
Photo by Ed Gerken.

"It sure beats digging for days between bone scraps," Terry said.

The next morning, I watched as Steve Sacrison accomplished the impossible. Who needed GPR? We had stumbled upon a tool unknown in the annals of paleontology: the Ground Probing Bobcat. It was uncanny, really, the way the machine responded to Steve's delicate, precise direction. He simply touched the edge of the Bobcat's bucket to the earth and shaved away the crackled siltstone surface. Entranced, most of us followed in his wake, behind the machine, looking for signs of bone as he scraped parallel swaths until he had covered 12 by 30 feet on the west side of the specimen. And then again, over the same area, slowly removing the siltstone a fraction of an inch at a time. After about an hour, Steve was approaching what I believed to be the level of the bones. And then Leon Theisen, a former employee and longtime collecting companion, shouted "Bone!"

Everything stopped while Leon, a careful and precise collector, crouched next to a brown mark about one-eighth inch wide and an inch long. "Turtle shell." We all exhaled.

After several more hours and a few more turtle scraps, we began hitting the concretion layer below the bone horizon, which meant we could eliminate the west side of the site. On the east side,

The Space Age

Despite the failure of GPR to help us, technology is definitely revolutionizing the art of bone hunting. GPS, or Global Positioning System, devices have become indispensable to paleontologists. The handheld electronic instrument communicates by trading signals with twenty-four orbiting GPS satellites, thereby monitoring almost the entire Earth's surface. When reading a given location, four satellites triangulate to pinpoint latitude and longitude within thirty feet or better.

Before GPS can be put to work, of course, someone must discover something. For years fossil collectors have dreamed of a "bone detector" that would allow them to find fossils buried beneath the surface. Various "magic machines" have given it a shot. GPR technology isn't quite there yet, but a second remote-sensing technique, called seismic sensing or acoustic diffraction tomography, has been used on the New Mexican sauropod *Seismosaurus,* with slightly better success. Very expensive and much more invasive, some believe the results may not justify the means. A gridded series of seven-inch-diameter holes was drilled through layers of rock thought to contain bones. Hydrophones were lowered into the holes to disseminate a sound wave, in this case set off by a small explosion. The waves change speed as they travel through materials of different densities, resulting in a three-dimensional display. The researchers identified a number of targets, but upon

the GPB hit paydirt right away. One tooth, then another, then an odd skull bone that eventually took shape as the unmistakable *T. rex* quadrate. In dinosaurs, the ball portion of the ball-and-socket jaw hinge is on the skull and the socket is on the jaw, the opposite of the human skeleton. We had found one of Duffy's.

With a modified mapping technique—measuring from each

excavation, only one of these—perhaps a coincidence?—proved to be bone.[5]

A third method, used by bone-prospecting amateurs for decades, has met with greater success—but it only works if dinosaur bones are radioactive, as in the case of the Jurassic Age Morrison Formation. Uranium and thorium, transplanted by the movement of groundwater, often settle in the open cell spaces of fossils. These radioactive elements eject atomic particles, or radiation, as they decay, which may be detected by a Geiger counter or the more sensitive scintillation counter. Radon gas, a daughter product of the process, is also detectable by the scintillation counter, which absorbs radiation and re-emits it as measurable light. Amateurs have found uraniferous bone buried more than a foot underground by passing a scintillation counter over the surface of the earth in a series of passes.

This method was finally "discovered" by professionals in the summer of 1996. Workers from the University of Utah and Dinosaur National Monument teamed up to locate the skull of a Jurassic Age *Allosaurus,* displaced from its skeleton. Excavators had nearly given up on the possibility of finding the skull, after three years of work. With a scintillation counter, the skull was located beneath a thin covering of rock in only minutes.[6] Although this is a startling success, it is unlikely that this method will work on bone buried more than three feet beneath the surface, and it will not work at all on nonradioactive bone typical of the Hell Creek Formation.

bone to two permanent stakes—we watched our excavation grow little by little. We took turns walking in front of and behind the Bobcat, checking immediately as each bone was uncovered, often without so much as a scratch. Sometimes the Bobcat would penetrate only one millimeter at a time, sometimes nearly ten. Ideally, we wanted a penetration of less than five millimeters, but more

Pete and Terry hunker over a Bobcat-uncovered Duffy tooth, carefully excavating with X-acto knives. Photo by Ed Gerken.

than two. I knew no one in paleontology would believe that a piece of heavy equipment could be used as delicately as a hand tool. I wanted to patent something. I felt as if Steve had just invented sliced bread.

With the discovery of a quadrate, which was more than ten feet from the edge of last year's excavation, we realized we had much more to find. Steve Sacrison kept driving, sometimes yanking away even more overburden from the back of our quarry, and sometimes delicately scraping. By the time we ran out of money for the season, we had found a substantial portion of the left side of the skull, plus large tooth-bearing bones from both sides of the upper and lower jaws—along with a rib, some more tail bones, lots of teeth, and many unidentified fragments.

The next season, in the summer of 1995, Steve and his dance partner leveled off most of what was left of the top of that portion of the butte before we started again. The first thing he scraped clean was another tooth. Eventually we would find more than forty. That year, the skull would gradually fill out even more: some of its right side, most of the lower jaw, and what appeared to be the braincase. Again short of money due to legal costs, we stopped

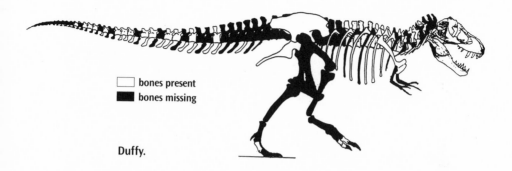

bones present
bones missing

Duffy.

long before we wanted to. In 1996 more skull materialized. Our exercise in patience was paying off, piece by piece, year by year.

Duffy proved to be one of our most challenging excavations. With very few geologic cues, it was literally a crap shoot as to where his bones may have settled when the slow-moving flood waters shuffled his bones. The only way to find them was to keep digging—some of the bones were found fully sixty feet away from our original site! To date, approximately 25 percent of this juvenile has been found—typical teenage behavior, never around, and no cooperation.

Duffy's last laugh is another mystery we haven't solved. It started with the massive tooth-bearing bones, some of the strongest bones in the skeleton. They were badly damaged, broken apart into more than a dozen pieces each. Other bones, particularly some very fragile ones, were completely untouched, including the pterygoid, a long, thin, folded palate bone that rarely turns up unbroken. It was pristine. An ectopterygoid, a second palate bone, was still articulated—impossible in this distorted, mish-mash site. None of these bones could have remained on the surface for very long before burial, because there was none of the typical "weather checking" that etches the surface of bone after even a short stay in the sun and rain. Perhaps when the flood had abated, other dinosaurs had trampled Duffy's carcass. Say, a wandering herd of several thousand thirsty duckbills?

Duffy has turned out to be crucial to our understanding of *T. rex*

Missing Children

Why are so few juvenile *T. rex*es discovered? Several possibilities pop to mind. While they were small, most likely they were tasty morsels for bigger beasts. Another idea to keep in mind: fratricide. Even in birds of prey, parents often can care for only one or two young; sometimes the strongest fledglings will kill—and even eat—their weaker siblings. When it comes to diminutive *T. rex* bones, there simply might not have been much left over for us to find.

On the other hand, young *T. rex*es may not have remained small for long—again decreasing our chances of finding small specimens. This puts paleontology in a catch-22: with so few specimens, it is difficult to measure how fast they grew, which keeps us in the dark about crucial elements of physiology, metabolism, and even relationships. Here's what we do know.

First, on a microscopic level, bones simply look different if they belong to creatures that grow fast or slowly. In fast-growing bone of birds and mammals, for example, the "matrix" of the bone is randomly organized and is infused with many canals that house nutrient-supplying blood vessels. In reptiles, the opposite is true.[7] Theropods like *Tyrannosaurus rex* had bones that resemble those of mammals and birds, which is the first piece of evidence suggesting that they grew quickly.

Second, because bone grows, it is constantly being remodeled. Old bone is resorbed and new bone deposited. In endotherms the result is a special type of bone called "haversian bone."[8] *T. rex* femurs have dense haversian canals. One

growth stages. Like Black Beauty, Duffy was about 75 percent grown, a middle teenager in human terms. With no decent foot bones, he could not confirm the puppy-paw theory I'd formed after examining LACM-23845. However, Duffy had the best skull, and it fit in with the puppy model: Duffy had a very large mouth and very large teeth. What's more, for the first time we explanation for this is rapid growth, but another may be strain.[9] The shear bulk of *T. rex* would have kept limb bones under constant stress, and thus constant remodeling—which means that the presence of haversian bone only suggests but does not prove rapid growth.

Third, unlike reptiles, mammal, bird, and theropod bones show closely spaced "rest-lines" near the outside edges of the long bone shafts. These indicate that, after maturity, the bone growth rate slowed or stopped.[10] Whereas reptiles continue to grow way past sexual maturity, albeit more slowly, theropod skeletons seem to demonstrate a rapid spurt of growth to maturity followed by an adulthood of nongrowth, just like mammals and birds.

Even though our evidence is sketchy, this research demonstrates that a reptile growth model is less appropriate for *T. rex* than one derived from mammals and/or birds. Mammals can reach full size from a minimum of a few weeks (mice) to a maximum of twenty years (elephants), and nearly all species of bird accomplish this in less than a year.

Using those templates, we can then interpret the only evidence we have of *T. rex* growth rates—Sue's excavation site. With Sue's remains, we found parts of two smaller skulls; in life they would have measured ten and eighteen inches long. If these progeny represented two successive broods in two successive years, *T. rex* young would reach full adult size in about three or four years. However, if *T. rex* raised multiple broods in one year—as some birds do—they could have reached forty-foot lengths in less than twelve months. No wonder we don't see babies in the fossil record.

were able to see that the back of the skull was truncated compared to that enormous snout. A puppy he was, or perhaps a foal, with a nose disproportionately longer than an adult's.

After Duffy's discovery, two more juvenile specimens joined the ranks, bringing with them a few more tantalizing morsels about the ontogeny of *T. rex*. Joining LACM-23845 as another

Duffy's juvenile skull sports disproportionately large jaws with adult-sized teeth.
Photo by Ed Gerken.

"11-year-old" would be Tinker, a South Dakota native. Found in 1997 and announced in 1999, this fossil initially was excavated by Mark Eatman, a commercial fossil collector. He removed a partial lower jaw and some other bones from a still-undisclosed site and then sold his discovery to a triad of businessmen based in Texas.

The new owners contacted Bob Bakker, who went to their laboratory to see the specimen. Recognizing instantly that Tinker was young, Bakker was beside himself when he called me from Texas. "You *have* to see this!" he hollered, which I was more than happy to do. I saw tables covered by bones in and out of plaster casts: vertebrae, ribs, and a complete humerus—curved, like a female's. No legs or feet, but Tinker had a number of skull bones.

Unlike a *Nanotyrannus*, Tinker's skull was noticeably beefy, with eyes that looked disproportionately large—typical in youthful faces. The LACM skull, the closest in size, was quite beaten up, so Tinker's confirmed not only overall measurements, but also Duffy's big mouth and teeth—and the relatively diminutive nature of the back of the skull. Even this small creature seems to have made its living with its mouth. I believed then and there that *T. rex* was built to get that powerful, flesh-biting head into use as soon as possible. I pulled out my tape measure. A dentary, the tooth-bearing element of the lower jaw, was almost exactly two-thirds the size of Stan's. The ischium, from the pelvis, also was clearly diminutive. Putting that mouth on this little girl scout—it sounded more like Stephen King than Michael Crichton. I counted sixty bones in all, and was assured that there was more still in the ground. Go back and collect it!" I said. Go back, go back, take a Bobcat if you have to.

Last but hopefully not least is Bucky, yet another South Dakotan. Found by Bucky Derflinger in 1999, Bucky began as one toe bone and one unidentified fragment. Then one tail vertebra turned up, then the pelvis's ilium weathering out about 100 feet away. Soon Derflinger added another toe bone to the count. He invited us up to excavate the specimen in the spring of 2001. At first, in looking at the size of the toe bones, I believed we were looking at two specimens—those feet looked way too big to belong to someone with such a small ilium!

We started digging between the two excavations in an effort to bring them together. Sure enough, we found bones throughout the 300-by-50-foot area. As of this writing, bones still are being excavated, using a bulldozer to cut away the prairie and reach the bone layer thirty-five feet below. While more of Bucky no doubt will come to light, at the moment the specimen includes no skull and no legs. Its significant youthful information: nearly tied with Duffy and Black Beauty in size at 80 percent grown, Bucky's ulna is outsized—85 percent the size of Sue's! Perhaps this suggests that like Black

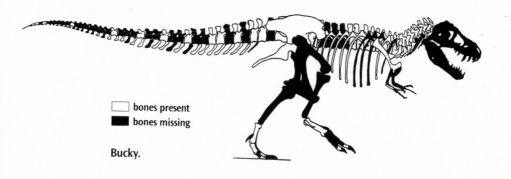

☐ bones present
■ bones missing

Bucky.

The Bucky site shows great promise. Photo by Neal Larson.

Beauty's long legs, Bucky's big toes and LACM-23845's puppy feet, arms grew to full size quickly. Running animals experience fast leg growth; for example, deer and horses have disproportionately long legs in their youth so they can run early. Even if *T. rex*'s arms were not used for running, they may have grown at a fast initial rate, along with the legs. When compared with the younger LACM-23845's *very* diminutive ulna, we can guess that limbs experienced a growth spurt somewhere between the ages of "11" and "16."

I was especially pleased to notice Bucky's two shoulder blades, which are significantly more robust than Duffy's. I was reminded of Tinker's robust humerus. Once I get more acquainted with gender differences in *T. rex* minors, we may have to rethink some names.

With the half-dozen juvenile *T. rex* specimens known to date, we can almost assemble piecemeal a composite subadult. We can also work backward to envision a brand-new baby *rex*.

Paleontologist Dale Russell used a growth series of six skeletons of *Albertosaurus liberatus*, a very close relative of *Tyrannosaurus rex*, to establish a pattern of skeletal development. As this dinosaur grew up, it had to "grow into its big feet." He found that for *Albertosaurus*'s childlike proportions to shift into adultlike ones, different parts of its body grew at different rates. The body, neck, shoulder blade, and hips picked up their pace against the upper leg; the head and arms grew at the same rate; and the tail,

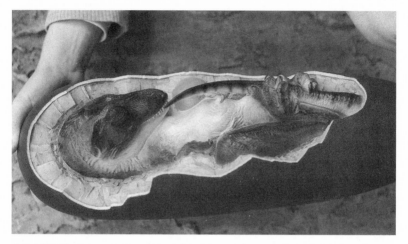

Artist Bill Monteleone's conception of a *T. rex* embryo ready to hatch, based upon measurements extrapolated by the author. Photo by Peter Larson.

hand, lower leg, and feet grew more slowly. Using these data, Russell was able to extrapolate backward to approximate the dimensions of a hatchling *Albertosaurus*.[11]

Using Russell's extrapolations, I was able to estimate the dimensions of a hatchling *T. rex* that would fit inside the largest of all theropod eggs. Beginning with Sue's length measurements as the adult, the hatchling dimensions came out as follows:

Component	Adult		Hatchling	
	Feet	Metric	Inches	Metric
Skull	5.0	1,530 mm	3.7	94 mm
Neck & body	14.2	4,280 mm	11.8	299 mm
Tail	21.2	6,380 mm	20.0	510 mm
Arm & hand	3.0	926 mm	11.0	276 mm
Leg height	10.9	3,290 mm	11.0	276 mm
Foot	2.5	750 mm	2.4	61 mm
Hip height	13.0	3,900 mm	13.0	330 mm
Total length	41.6	12,500 mm	36.0	921 mm

Imagine a *T. rex* a yard long and a little over a foot tall. That's what a hatchling would look like. Cute? Maybe, but not for long.

(7)

Worlds Apart

$\int$ enator Tom Daschle was curious about a few things. In a June 1, 1992, letter to Attorney General William Barr, he asked,

> Were the extraordinary means used (e.g., the surprise raid by FBI agents, the use of the National Guard, etc.) to seize the skeleton necessary? . . . Although the media has reported that the Department of Defense authorized activation of the Guard, my understanding is that the authority to activate Guard troops is reserved for the Governor unless the troops are federalized and that such action is warranted only when there is a compelling national interest (e.g., war or other national emergency).

Before his tragic death, South Dakota Governor George Mickelson said, "I knew nothing about the activation of the National Guard, it makes me mad as hell that I was not advised, I deem it underhanded, and I do not agree with the federal officials that undertook this whole process."[1]

By July of 1994, two years had passed since Sue's seizure. Perhaps her disposition was decided, but the propriety of using military force was by no means dead. The seizure still stood as the initial whack of the hedgehog that provided the government with Sue and paperwork and notebooks and God knows what else. Our lawyers, fired up by Neal's attorney, Bruce Ellison, were certain the participation of the National Guard had been improper, for at least two reasons. First: although at the time its significance escaped us, the legality of using soldiers to help pack and load boxes and crates was questionable. (The only thing we knew about the National Guard's involvement was that one forklift operator was crying as she worked.) Second: through the pendency of the custody battle, the government had abandoned its *reasons* behind the seizure, the actual "cause" for the action. While Schieffer would say the seizure causes had not been abandoned as baseless, and instead that he had simply used an "alternative argument" in the civil case,[2] to us the change of tack revealed that the seizure had been wrong. Our motions said that the government "knew or should have known" that Sue should not have been seized—and that she *never had been evidence* of criminal behavior. In 1994 we brought our own mallets—real ones without beaks.

"Fruits of a poisonous tree," *"posse comitatus,"* "the appearance of impartiality." We filed two briefs requesting suppression of evidence, the easiest way to end this debacle. One brief argued a lack of probable cause, the other that the military had been improperly used while executing the May 1992 seizure. As a civil state, and not a military one, we are protected by 18 U.S. Code 1385 from *posse comitatus*, the use of the military against civilians in all but drastic situations. The law allows for military personnel and equipment to *facilitate* law enforcement actions, but prohibits their *active involvement*. Therefore, the deployment and management of the Guard in Hill City became a fine line that was fought in a spirited legal volley. If the seizure had been illegal, it was "a poisonous tree." Whatever "fruits" had been seized, and whatever subsequent actions sprang from the action, such as the following seizures and subpoenas, would then be "tainted." On that basis, we asked for hearings and claimed that the materials should not be used in our case.

Judge Battey, the same judge who had crafted the counterintuitive real estate decision, simply said no. No, even though the governor had been boxed out of the National Guard decision. He said the Guard had only added muscle to the FBI's action. No poisonous tree. No tainted fruit. No suppression of evidence.

We thought the judge was getting a trifle tedious. Earlier in the year we had requested he step down, or "recuse" himself, from our case. In state court, it is thought so essential that a defendant receive a fair hearing that if a judge is believed to be biased—or if it might *appear* he is biased, even if he is not—he will immediately remove himself from a case if asked. The defendant has one "free" chance to knock a judge off the bench. In federal court, the judge himself decides if he is biased, or if such an appearance exists. Again, this would be amusing if it weren't so important.

We thought Judge Battey was not simply ruling against us, but ruling in such a way as to restrain us and to allow unwarranted latitude to the government. We gave examples, such as when we were reprimanded for speaking out to the press, but the Acting U.S. Attorney was not criticized even for doing the unthinkable: calling a press conference at the seizure and writing an unprecedented op-ed piece to "explain" his action. We believed the judge showed his bias when, in deciding the results of our disastrous custody hearing, he had written that we "may indeed" have obstructed justice, and that we were "completely rob[bed] of any credibility."

Neal and I filed affidavits supporting our motion for recusal. Mine asserted that before signing the seizure warrant, the judge "could have known, with minimal research, what the government now freely concedes: that 'Sue' was not, and is not, evidence in a criminal case." I also commented on Battey's converting the government's motion to dismiss into summary judgment, and in paving the way for his real estate decision: "It seems to me that every strategic step *en route* to the government's taking of my property was authored, not by the prosecution, but by Judge Battey himself." Neal's affidavit added a personal note:

> It also appeared to me during the civil proceedings that the Trial Judge had a bias in favor of the government and against the Institute. For example, whenever the government wanted documents, it simply took them from the Institute. When the Institute wanted documents . . . it was considered 'fishing' by the Judge. . . .
>
> I therefore believe these facts show Judge Battey has a bias in favor of the government and against

me. I do not believe that he can fairly sit in judgment
of my case. I face a 38 count Indictment. I face hundreds of years of imprisonment, millions of dollars
in fines, and the destruction of my business which I
have worked hard to build. I want a Judge who
without question will be fair in the determination of
any issue in this case, both before and during trial,
which affects my freedom, including whether my
wife has a husband, whether my children have a
father, and whether we have a business left when this
is all done.

When denying our request, Judge Battey wrote, "A judge is not
to be disqualified because of a state of mind acquired from the evidence and prior rulings." He said we merely exhibited "subjective
feeling," and that "the fact that the Court made credibility deter-
minations in a separate civil case by stating that a defendant 'may'
have obstructed justice is insufficient to show a 'pervasive bias.'"

I don't know what other people's legal files look like, but ours
were not pretty. In addition to reflecting the number of losses we
had sustained, and reminding us of how much money we had
spent, they revealed a Cold War in the letters zinging back and
forth between Pat Duffy and the government. Tempers were
short, protocol corners were cut, corrosive "jokes" were preva-
lent. Legitimately worried that the Cold War hindered our
chances of winning, family members hog-tied me and flew me to
Washington, D.C., where we met with lawyers in pinstripes and
very shiny shoes. The three experts in white-collar trials—a firm
partner, a specialist, and an associate—gazed from floor-to-
ceiling windows overlooking downtown as they explained their
strategy. They could help us win our case and Pat Duffy could be
their homeboy point man. They did this all the time, they knew
all the legal cites, they had a game plan that worked. They would
send the associate ahead of the team to comb the files and
acquaint himself with the details; the chiefs would follow later,
closer to trial, to prepare witnesses and to tailor their expertise to

paleontology. Interim documents would be written from the main office by the specialist while the lead man was in Japan on a huge corporate case. All this—and it sounded impressive—for a mere $500,000 retainer.

I have another tendency, an offshoot of my stubbornness. When afraid, when in doubt, or simply when weighing options, I make one decision and stick to it. Even with the sky falling on my head, I don't like to rehash. Most likely there is more than one way to arrive somewhere, and instead of pulling out my hair weighing the possibilities, I pick one—usually by gut instinct— and stop comparing. Those D.C. lawyers obviously knew a great deal about white-collar law, and they very well may have made a positive impact on our case. They also may have made no difference; we'll never know. I had put my money on Pat Duffy, and that was where my faith would stay. He was an impressive specimen, a feisty, impetuous specialist who knew our local system like the back of his hand. I couldn't imagine raising $500,000 up front in any event, but even if I could have, I would not walk away from Duffy. I could not turn my back on him after all he had tried—and was still trying—to do.

Yes, so far we had lost nearly every decision. Yes, the heat from the words in written exchanges between our lead lawyer and our prosecutors could be felt through the envelopes. Probably Judge Battey was angry with Duffy, too. No matter. Yes, I said to my family members, it was good to meet those lawyers, but I'm just fine where I am. Thank you. I stopped thinking about it, although the family gnashed its teeth for a long time.

Meanwhile, our game was to be played both on paper and in the Great Plains. First, Bob Farrar set to work with documents, digging up records and reconstructing past negotiations with buyers of fossils on the list. Next, because the government claimed we had been on public lands and improperly collected fossils there, we bought a Global Positioning System unit. Neal and I grabbed the indictment and whatever field notes we could locate in our subpoena-exploded files. We folded 6'1" Pat Duffy and his 6'4" lawyer brother, Dan, next to Bruce Ellison in the backseats

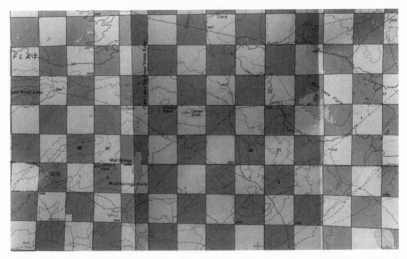

In much of the west, the landscape is nearly flat, fences are nonexistent, and land ownership is "checkerboarded" (this map reflects an area in Wyoming, in which the federal government holds title to the shaded areas and private citizens own the white sections), making location of sites difficult without a Global Positioning System. Bureau of Land Management 1:100,000 topographic map for Rawlins, Wyoming, 1991.

of a rented Suburban and headed off. We were going to show these boys how and where we hunted for fossils. At the same time, we were going to check our field notes and records against the disputed locations themselves, and against a more precise reading with the GPS.

We drove to Wyoming, we located roads we had been on years before, and discovered roads we had never been on—but which seemed to take us to localities we had written down. We hunted for remnants of excavations, and sometimes found some—but not always our own. Often Neal and I would recognize peaks and valleys, recall that we had been exactly on this spot, but the weather had long ago erased any evidence of our presence. Usually our locality information was correct, but sometimes it wasn't. Once we had written a 4 instead of a 5, just one number off—but in the prairie that puts you in the wrong square. No wonder the government thought that particular fossil had come from the wrong land. Pat looked across the prairie. "You may as well mark your spot on the ocean as get through the plains without a GPS unit and a fenceline."

We reviewed how we had received permission from one person or another, and how a parcel of National Grasslands property had been mistaken for a landowner's pasture. We reviewed how policies in the National Forests allowed one type of collection but disallowed others. We retraced our steps as best we could, working on understanding first *if* we had been in the wrong place, and then, if so, *why*. It wasn't torture, because we were outside. We could talk about fossils and teach our interested legal team about life in the field. They were great students, enthusiastic hikers, tireless assessors. And messy eaters. The Suburban was a sea of candy wrappers and fast food bags by the time we returned home. The Duffy brothers were just two of four; I would have hated to pay their parents' grocery bills.

The Art of Science

In 1994, the third Canadian *T. rex* was found by school teacher and paleo-volunteer Robert Gebhardt, who was working with Tim Tokaryk, paleontologist from Saskatchewan's Eastend Fossil Research Station. Many of the collected bones were excavated in a large block, and further erosion at the site exposed more bones. While Tokaryk and his crew would have more work to do in the laboratory and in the field,[3] the specimen quickly revealed two tantalizing facts. The skull was not only disarticulated, promising new detailed information, but also it compared very well with *"Tyrannosaurus X."*

That same year, the first fragments of a Sue-sized skull were found in Montana by Craig Pfister, a student at the University of Wisconsin, Madison, who was volunteering with a group from the Museum of Geology. Other volunteer students continued screening the site's material, successfully shaking out more significant portions.[4]

We would not see these specimens right away, because we had our own scientific research project—the biggest display challenge we had ever faced. It was the culmination of all the science collected on *Tyrannosaurus rex* up to then, and it would conclude with our most challenging mounting project. Stan had come home from the field in May 1992. From that time through the spring of

Cloning through the Ages

Humans have been making casts replicas for at least four thousand years to produce everything from jewelry to ceremonial objects to weapons to dinosaurs. Early casting techniques relied upon soft materials, such as beeswax, which were formed into the shape of the desired object. Clay formed around the wax would then be baked, melting the wax in the process. The clay mold, filled with molten metals, such as copper or bronze, would be broken away once the metal cooled into a replica of the original beeswax object. These early casts were one of a kind, because both the original wax object and the mold were lost in the process. Eventually, techniques were developed that enabled craftsmen to reuse molds and therefore create multiple reproductions; however, these molds could not produce the kind of exquisite detail possible with the "lost-wax" method.

Today, fossil casting techniques focus on two priorities: safety of the original; and reproducing as much detail as possible. In paleontology, replicas are especially desirable for rare or one-of-a-kind items. Quite frequently, the most important fossils—those showing unique features or which are important for the study of evolution—exist only as one-of-a-kind specimens or perhaps as members of a handful of examples.

Most modern, high-quality reproductions are made from a small selection of durable yet malleable materials. For producing molds, either liquid latex rubber or liquid silicone is popular. More elastic and less adherent than latex, silicone is perhaps more desirable for fragile fossils. Silicone also reproduces detail even more faithfully than latex, and it is more versatile and nonreactive to a wider variety of casting materials.

Block molds are especially useful for small fossils. These are self-contained blocks of material that are poured in halves and can be pulled apart to reveal the cast inside. Large or relatively complex fossils necessitate shell molds, where the silicone is formed into a ¾-inch-thick shell, rather than a solid block. This makes it easier to remove and safer for the massive bone. Shell molds cannot hold their shape, and therefore are supported by a second shell. These outside shells, called "mother molds," are formed from a ridged material like plaster of paris reinforced with gauze, cloth, or fiberglass fibers; or, better yet, resin reinforced with fiberglass cloth. Even a high-density polyurethane foam may be used to create a mother.

In very particular circumstances, alginate can create quick, temporary, one-time molds for smaller fossils. A derivative of seaweed used by dentists to make quick molds of teeth, powdered alginate is mixed with water and poured into a cardboard box in which the fossil is suspended. Within a few minutes, the fossil, which was not completely submerged, may then be carefully pulled free of the alginate. The mold will survive only for a few hours, but it can be used repeatedly, although quality decreases with each successive use.

The casts themselves—the actual objects being produced—are made by filling the mold and then peeling it away. Casts of poor durability may be made from either high-grade plasters, or, in the case of the alginate molds, dental plaster or water-based casting compound. We prefer a variety of hardening resins, such as polyurethane or high-density polyurethane foam. Alternately, for large, flat objects, marine resin and fiberglass cloth may be brushed into the mold for a thin, lightweight cast. In all of these applications, many technicians use coloring agents and fillers when the liquid resins are mixed, in order to duplicate the color of the original fossil. These agents also add strength to the product and can decrease the cost of the casting materials.

1995, preparation revealed bone after bone; it was time to put him together.

Before we sent our best ambassador to Japan for a year, we wanted to make molds of his bones. Not only could we use them to replicate Stan, but also the molds would act as insurance if, Heaven forbid, some part of the specimen were irreparably damaged. We were fortunate in the skill of our preparators; the bones emerged from the preparation stage as clean as a fossil can be—microscopic detail had been preserved on bone surfaces, but virtually all dirt and residue had been carefully lifted away. Stan was a perfect candidate for replicating. We could produce molds that would retain so much of his minute detail that a visiting scientist would be able to use the copies, called "casts," for research. In addition, casts could be sold to museums or other display areas, so Stan could be available for viewing across the country—and the world.

We had been experimenting with casting techniques for years, and had developed our own method that seemed to work best for both retaining detail and not harming the fossil. However, we were certainly not the only ones to replicate fossils. The process enjoyed a long history, one that had placed *T. rex* in museums from the United States to Europe to Asia. In fact, when considering the relatively small number of real *Tyrannosaurus rex* specimens available—only a handful of originals are on display worldwide—most displays *must* be of replicas. And most of those displayed replicas were made from Barnum Brown's favorite, his 1906 specimen at home in the American Museum of Natural History since 1915.

To prepare Stan for molding and casting, we made sure all bone surfaces were free of any debris and protected only with the thinnest application of polyvinyl acetate. We chose polyurethane foam for the mothers and also for the largest cast pieces, silicone for the molds, and liquid polyurethane for most of the cast bones. The casting process was a feat of engineering for us, especially when it came to the five-foot-long pelvis. That mother mold, fabricated in three pieces, was reinforced with wood and measured approximately 3 x 4 x 6 feet. A mold of that size is difficult to manage, and can easily damage the original fossil. Thanks to one of our most particular and detail-oriented craftsmen, Larry Shaffer, the challenging design worked flawlessly.

Stan also did wonders for the bottom line of the Lego corporation. When casting the bones smaller than twelve inches, we made "block molds" using clay and a box of Legos, which easily assembled to form walls to hold and form the silicone mold material while it hardened. Half of a mold was poured at one time, with the unexposed half of the fossil embedded and protected in clay. Once the mold's first half was cured, the fossil was turned over, the silicone treated with a mold-releasing agent, and the process repeated. Since the Legos were much more easily disassembled and reassembled than wooden boxes, the mold-making chore was streamlined and relatively painless. We just had to ensure that detail-obscuring air bubbles were eliminated from the silicone through the use of a vacuum chamber before pouring, and by vibrating the mold during and after pouring. The results were great, and our sturdy, reusable Lego blocks were lifesavers—we needed tubs and tubs of them!

Tammy Mahoney prepares to pour silicone in the second half of a block mold made with Lego blocks. Photo by Terry Wentz.

We also found the unique shape of the blocks perfect for making interlocking "keys." In both the two-piece block molds and the more complex "shell molds," the silicone fit exactly together, time and time again.

Our large shell molds were more elaborate clay affairs than the boxes we built for the small blocks. The object was a ¾-inch layer of silicone that could create the replica, but also could be peeled off safely, like a *Mission Impossible* mask. Since these are so flexible and delicate, they must be protected by an outside covering, a hard shell—and in making the molds, we began with that outside layer. We first protected and covered a fossil with a sheet of clay where the "mask" would eventually be, then applied the outside layer, the polyurethane foam mother—again, half at one time. Once both

Hadley Little removes the top of a mold, revealing a freshly cast theropod jaw replica.
Photo by Terry Wentz.

sides of the mother were cured, we removed the interior clay, repositioned the mother, and poured the thin silicone mold. Once *that* cured, we could remove the original and pour the cast inside. We constructed all our molds in such a way as to allow the cast's liquid plastic to be poured in through pour spouts; air escaped through bleeder holes, allowing the plastic to flow into all portions of the mold.

As cast replicas of Stan's bones emerged from their molds, they were trimmed of any seam or pour spout remnants and repaired with epoxy putty if an air bubble or tool happened to mar a surface. We had included coloring agents so the replicas approached Stan's actual bone color, but we did not want them to match exactly; scientists must be able to easily distinguish real from fabricated bones. One final step: as we mounted sections of Stan's *cast* skull—the original bones of which had been completely disarticulated and reproduced individually—we then *recast* it. This time, the cast skull was copied in sections so that future cast replicas would be much easier to assemble. We wanted to leave Stan's original skull bones unmounted and easily accessible to scientists, but we also felt the public would want to see his mounted head. Therefore, we created a separate exhibit, affixing original bones from the left side to a cast of Stan's skull; the right skull bones remained loose. Once we cleaned and stored our molds, I began one of my favorite projects ever: designing and fabricating the world's first original *Tyrannosaurus rex* skull and skeleton mount in more than thirty years.

I was well aware of the legacy behind me. The first dinosaur skeleton ever to be mounted was the duckbill *Hadrosaurus foulkii*. It was found in New Jersey in 1858, and described by Joseph Leidy. In 1878, a mass accumulation of *Iguanodon* was excavated in Belgium, and over a period of years, several of these skeletons were mounted in a single striking exhibit there. Also before the turn of the century, Bone War champion Othniel Marsh made sure a number of Cretaceous and Jurassic dinosaur skeletons appeared in the Yale Peabody Museum. Then, finally, in 1915, Henry Fairfield Osborn unveiled the first mounted *Tyrannosaurus rex* skeleton, with a cast skull, at the American Museum of Natural History.

For the next eighty years, skeletons of many species of dinosaurs were mounted for museums all over the world. The American Museum's *Tyrannosaurus rex* casts were sprinkled everywhere, as were casts of a huge long-necked sauropod: *Diplodocus*. Andrew Carnegie, whose crews excavated and mounted this skeleton for his museum in Pittsburgh in the 1920s, was so proud of this achievement that he delivered casts to museums in the United States, Europe, and South America. After that, other real dinosaurs, and more *T. rex* casts, made the rounds, including a cloned MOR-555. However, after the 1915 specimen, *original* bones of *T. rex* would not be mounted again until the 1960s. Then the type skeleton, which had been sold by the American Museum to the Carnegie Museum, finally was displayed.

In the years following the formation of our company in 1975, we had mounted numerous fossil skeletons, many of which were dinosaurs, all of them smaller than Stan. I also visited museums in eighteen countries on four continents, and viewed thousands of mounted dinosaurs, both cast and original bone. Each one renewed my fascination with the artistry that returned a measure of life to a pile of bones—and fueled my desire to specialize in that particular part of paleontology. Now it was time to mount Stan. I was excited and a bit apprehensive: Stan would be the standard-bearer for modern paleontology, and the legacy-holder for paleo-artisans in the twenty-first century.

We faced a unique challenge in mounting original, scientifically significant, absolutely irreplaceable bones. It would be a very different process than when we worked either with cast replicas or with original, but very common, bones. With casts, the plastic could easily be drilled or cut in order to attach or implant steel supports, and channels could be cut to hide as much as possible of the framework. With common originals, such as duckbills, drilling some parts for easy assembly was fine. However, with one-of-a-kind or significant skeletons like Stan's, aesthetics became less important than scientific considerations—where each and every bone should remain unharmed and individually removable for study. Few mounting methods satisfied these criteria. In most mounted original skeletons, the bones not only were trapped by the mounting framework, but also drilled! We needed to devise a new method of mounting original skeletons, and we needed it right away.

From an artistic standpoint, we wanted Stan to look "alive" and "in motion." In order to accomplish this, we focused on two resources; first, the bones themselves. The fact that Stan had been bipedal—his living weight was supported by the hind legs—would determine his overall posture. In addition, no two *T. rex*es were exactly alike, and many of their bones were crushed or broken when they died or after they were buried, dictating mounting restrictions. To create the best representation of how Stan stood, our crew would have to allow the bones to determine their own positions—unless something drastic had occurred that we needed to repair. The second resource was a scale model of *Tyrannosaurus rex* based almost entirely on actual bones. Artist Joe Tippmann created a special edition of his one-eighth-scale model of Sue's skeleton, with a movable spine, jaws, and limbs. Experimenting with posing the model helped enormously and also prevented our

Mounts are modular for easy transportation and set-up. This *Albertosaurus,* a smaller relative of *T. rex,* has had its head and tail sections removed, ready for crating. BHI file photo.

falling into common reconstruction traps. For example, artists' renditions of "living" theropods almost always show the "hands" as drooping, with the palm downward. Although most theropod hands can do this, the most natural position for these hands is as if the palms were holding a basketball—or someone's head— between them. With Tippmann's wonderful creation, we could transfer realistic placement, angles, and curves from the model to the full-scale mount.

The last consideration before we started building was transport of the finished product. Stan was going to be shipped, set up, and disassembled at several locations in Japan. Unlike early skeletal mounts, which were simply welded in place, Stan would have to be modular, like our previous skeletons. As the U.S. Attorney would attest, many of our mounts already had been shipped for thousands of miles—and they had to fit through normal "people doors" when they arrived at their destinations. We sketched out where Stan's framework would come apart, and outlined the modules: platform and support poles, legs, pelvis, several tail and body vertebral sections, ribs, shoulder girdles, arms, skull, and jaws. Even considering Stan's weight and dimensions, we wanted his assembly and disassembly to be possible in a matter of only a few hours by a small crew.

Because of the tremendous weight of Stan's original bones, whose open spaces had been filled with ironstone by moving groundwater, and because his multistop tour made suspending cables impractical, we decided to use vertical pipes to support the weight of the skeleton. This rigid construction also would allow the use of smaller-gauge, and thus more-easily-hidden, steel to support the individual bones. Our plan called for three vertical posts: one at the pelvis, one near the front of the chest, and one near the middle of the tail.

The main support of most dinosaur mounts is directed from the pelvis, down through the legs, to the floor. The pelvis becomes the fulcrum, or balance point of the mount, transferring gravitational stress from the front and rear of the dinosaur. Because of the extreme weight and great size of Stan's pelvis, we were concerned about the constant movement necessary with the Japanese tour schedule. Lifting this fragile component into position also would be very risky. Electing to use a cast pelvis not only removed the danger to the original fossil, but also allowed us to hide a substantial amount of support steel within a very large component.

We cut channels in the cast pelvis, laid pipes inside, and closed the seams. The now relatively lightweight centerpiece, attached to the middle support pole, could be levered up by a few people, like the flag at Iwo Jima, and bolted into place. Extending outward from where the vertebrae lined up to the pelvis, we welded rectangular tubing and straps. A solid and rigid truss was formed as the metal was heated and bent to accommodate the curves of the spine and varying dimensions of the vertebrae. For each vertebra, we fabricated an individual, custom-made "basket" from which a researcher could easily pluck it for a close-up look.

Stan's legs received personal treatment, much as each vertebra had. Steel was placed on the interior surfaces and carefully heated and bent so that it "flowed" with the undulations of the bones and supported the weight of each bone from the bottom. Other components, such as ribs and chevrons, were glued to narrow-gauge steel and attached to the framework. Cast transplants from other specimens for Stan's missing arms, shoulder blades, and a few toes were easily attached. Real toes were bracketed in place, but cast claws were used so that they could be drilled and bolted down, holding the other toe bones in place.

As always, the last thing to mount was the skull. Because of the weight, fragility and rarity of this specimen, we did not mount the original skull on the skeleton—which was already occupied in its own separate display that could be viewed more closely by the public. A cast was fitted on the skeleton by drilling a pipe into the occipital condyle, the "ball" on the back of the skull upon which the head swivels on the neck.

Later, in Japan, I would collect a favorite memory. Our Japanese assembly crew quickly bolted together Stan's framework, stood up the pelvis, and Neal and I arranged the bones in order.

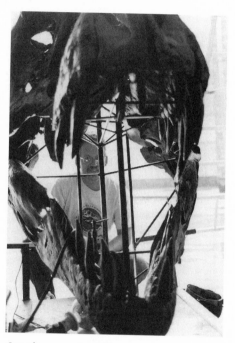

Complex armature is necessary to support Stan's real skull bones. BHI file photo.

Sitting high atop a very tall step-ladder, I received vertebra after vertebra from a line of enthusiastic worker ants, and we all watched as Stan's skeleton seemed to develop like claymation before our eyes. By the time his lower jaws were hung onto the skull, and his head placed "just so," applause erupted. One hour and 55 minutes had elapsed.

The Lost World

Stan was slated to be the centerpiece of the largest and most comprehensive *T. rex* exhibition ever. To prepare for the great bulk of the display, we needed more than Stan. We started by compiling a

A crew of Japanese Expo workers brings Stan's real vertebrae to be placed within the steel armature especially constructed for the skeleton. BHI file photo.

chorus line of *T. rex*es. For this production, we purchased and mounted a cast of MOR-555, while Aurora Oval found an ancient reproduction of the original mount of AMNH-5027—the famous one who used to stand upright.

T. rex was the headliner, but we wanted more. We wanted to show the world of *Tyrannosaurus rex,* a slice of its environment, a taste of its experience. Therefore, we set to designing a theater production from the past, cast with long-dead players backed by the most comprehensive, cutting-edge research available on the Cretaceous world. Aurora Oval's design team was ready to adapt anything we could present into a display, whether interactive, video, or traditional.

The exhibit started with the basics: Pangaea, the original continent. A beautiful video display showed how the earth's land-masses had developed and moved through time, leading to the period where *T. rex* populated at least 500,000 square miles along the eastern flank of today's Rocky Mountains. Sites of known *T. rex* specimens were highlighted in an inverted triangle on the map, a giant slice of North America starting from southern Alberta and Saskatchewan and angling south to one point—the single New Mexico specimen. We explained that the formations in which these fossils were found have different names, but they were deposited at roughly the same time: at the close of the Mesozoic era, uppermost Cretaceous period, upper Maestrictian stage. That translates to approximately 65 million years ago, during the last 1.5 to 2 million years of the age of dinosaurs.

These particular rocks would provide the raw materials, the props, for our display, because they document much of what we know about terrestrial life at a critical time in the history of Earth.

Even so, the record of the ancient ecosystem is missing chunks of time; ten feet of sediment may represent 100,000 years or one minute. The fossils embedded in these irregular chunks of Cretaceous sediments—which might seem like dry, crumbly, and unrelated details in the field—reveal the only clues we have, exquisite snapshots of the environment, climate, animals, and plants of the lost world of *Tyrannosaurus rex*. From these glimpses of geography, geology, and paleontology, we pieced together a story of a world that came to an abrupt end 650 thousand centuries before *Homo sapiens* appeared.

Mr. Fukuhara, an integral part of the Aurora Oval design team, drew dozens of diagrams for the Expo display. BHI file photo.

In order to replicate its features and transport visitors into that ecosystem, I closed my eyes and pictured Stan, alive: when awakening from his afternoon siesta, what did he see? To present an accurate picture of his landscape, we decorated the stage with the help of soil specialist Greg Retallack of the University of Oregon and K-T Boundary plant specialist Kirk Johnson of Denver's Museum of Nature and Science. Their research showed that a sparse forest was sprinkled with rare and relatively small trees that grew no more than one foot in diameter and 60 feet high.[5] This forest joined a flat coastal plain with an annual rainfall of 35 to 45 inches.[6] Cretaceous ground cover included moss, ferns, ginkgo, cycad, sequoias, palms—and an overwhelming abundance of modern flowering plants, including relatives of the bay laurels, sycamores, magnolias, palms, and berry-bearing shrubs. But absolutely no oaks, maples, willows, or grasses grew around or under *T. rex* feet.[7] The look of the environment also was inferred from the presence of particular "actors" in the fossil record. Today's soft-shelled *Trionyx* turtle, for instance, is completely aquatic; its presence in *T. rex* country suggested the existence of permanent bodies of water in the Cretaceous, such as year-round running streams and rivers.[8] Similarly, the presence of narrow-snouted crocodiles and broad-snouted alligators implied a tropical or subtropical climate.

Our prop list complete, we needed to cast our extras. Aside from some dinosaurs, most animal life in the Cretaceous was relatively small. Half of the mammals scurrying through the brush were marsupials, relatives of the opossum. The other half was a combination of rat-sized creatures with unusual multiconed teeth, and tiny insect eaters the size of mice. Thanks to the work of the late Richard Estes, a longtime researcher of the fossiliferous areas of Lance Creek, Wyoming, we also could provide an overview of Cretaceous lower vertebrates. We auditioned thirteen different species of lizard, including one monitor; the oldest known North American snake, *Coniophis precendens;* and amphibians including salamanders, aquatic or semiaquatic frogs, and turtles.

When it came to underwater actors, a cattle call produced fourteen species of fish and four shark relatives; freshwater clams, snails, bivalves, and mollusks; and brackish-water oysters. Estes believed this particular array of underwater species indicated the presence of a delta, because it brought to mind the "primitive fish fauna of the Mississippi River drainage, especially in its lower reaches near the Gulf coast."[9] Just off the delta, in neighboring sea waters, lived an amazing variety of ammonites, extinct relatives of the chambered nautilus. The ammonites were our Esther

Williams, starring in their own underwater stage number intended to show off their beautiful, iridescent shells, the study of which comprised Neal's favorite area of expertise.

While ancient water teemed with life, either the air was very quiet or evidence of flight is elusive. Bones of pterosaurs, or "flying reptiles," have been found,[10] but they are so rare that specimens have yet to be referred to genus or species. Bird bones also are rare; although we collected a number of specimens from at least three species at the Ruth Mason Quarry, only a few specimens of any kind have been referred to families. Of course the story of birds, and how they carried *T. rex*'s banner out of the Cretaceous, provided the finale.

All of these bit players would be displayed in the exhibition as under-glass specimens or fragments—or in "real life" models, as someone running for the bushes, a bit of color. Top billing for this show, however, was given to *T. rex* and *T. rex*'s dinner. We staged a revival of an ancient feast, with selections from the Cretaceous menu.

"Ornithischian" translates to the scientific designation "bird-hipped," but in the list of main dishes, it means "tastes like chicken." These herbivores naturally made up the bulk of the Cretaceous dinosaur population, and by far the two most abundant forms were duckbilled hadrosaurs and horned ceratopsians. Of Hell Creek duckbills, *Edmontosaurus annectens* took the stage at over thirty feet long and nine feet tall at the hips. The star of tremendous bonebeds like Ruth Mason's, this species must have traveled in huge herds, since we find its remains in quantities of perhaps as many as ten or twenty thousand individuals. In the displays, we used real, cast, and fleshed-on model adult and juvenile duckbill skeletons—frozen in an eternal run for their lives.

Next on the abundance menu were two of *T. rex*'s favorite dishes, the three-horned *Triceratops horridus,* and the similar *Torosaurus.* While both are known for their huge frills, the *Torosaurus*'s perforated variety was even larger than *Triceratops*'s solid model. Having collected more than a dozen *Triceratops* skulls from Hell Creek siltstones and sandstones, we chose an eight-foot-long skull named Billy and a partial skeleton, fresh

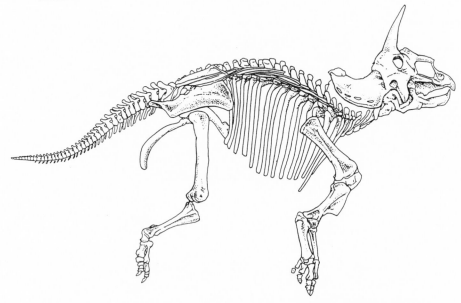

Triceratops was one of the main foods for *Tyrannosaurus rex*. This skeleton, known as Raymond, is the only articulated specimen collected to date; usually they were eaten and their remains are only fragmentary. Illustration by Dorothy Sigler Norton.

from an excavation in opened field jackets, as good examples. The Japanese art team ordered sets of our actual field clothes—jeans, work boots, crumpled hats—for a digging display peopled with mannequins "working" on the field specimen.

Once their bony bits were stripped off, armored dinosaurs were also tasty. *Ankylosaurus* was a tank-bodied, club-tailed creature with armorlike scutes to protect it from predators. Another dinosaur that used bone as a weapon was the jester *Pachycephalosaurus*. Fun to pronounce—pack-ee-sef-ah-low-SORE-us—these unusual creatures apparently bashed heads, like today's male bighorn sheep, with thick skulls covered by more than six inches of solid bone. Scientists have postulated that the bony heads also could have been used to decline unwelcome dinner invitations.

Other meat-eating dinosaurs are usually known only from fragments, single bones or teeth, but we included them in our show. *Nanotyrannus lancensis* made a special appearance as isolated teeth and in a reproduction of the only known skull. We were fortunate to include our spectacular, original, articulated skeleton, patched with cast head, neck, and tail, of *Struthiomimus,* the "ostrich-mimic" dinosaur. This species already had starred in a memorable scene of *Jurassic Park,* where *T. rex* chased a group of them. The movie's raptors were represented by a cast skeleton of *Dromaeosaurus*—in life armed with superb eyesight, large brains, and wicked claws on the hands and feet. Especially beautiful in our production were three life-sized figures based on the skeleton. These nasty killers hunted in groups to bring down prey, and the models were created each in a different pose, in a different leap, at a different phase in the fifty-yard dash. Placed in a row, they became one creature in motion.

Next came applications of science, such as the sexual dimorphism exhibit, where the cast *T. rex* pelvises illustrated what we knew at that time about the "male" chevron and its relationship to living crocodiles. People would be able to crank a lever, applying torque to a *T. rex* cast arm. Participants would see how the muscles worked in the "puny" limb, and its surprising weight-bearing strength. They would view fossil dinosaur eggs, and life-sized and small-scale models of how *T. rex* may have grown, and how it may have interacted with its own kind.

And finally, the show-stopper that would make their mouths drop: five casts and one artist's model of the most amazing and significant *Tyrannosaurus* skulls backed up Duffy's and Stan's original heads—the best of all *T. rex* skulls. The business-end of *T. rex* is one of the most sophisticated and awesome pieces of biological equipment that has ever evolved, and this unmatched lineup would illustrate, as nothing else could, the magnificence of the king of beasts. A *T. rex* skull design is architecturally pure, and was constructed to efficiently procure, dispatch, dismember, and consume prey. We wanted to prove this to our audience, and, with the help of the Japanese design team, we launched into the latest science on the Tyrant Lizards.

The Art of Eating Things Bigger Than Your Head

Snakes are able to dislocate the bones of their upper and lower jaws—from the braincase and from each other. This allows them to

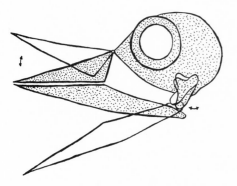

A bird's kinetic skull allows it to open both jaws to their greatest extent. Illustration by Peter Larson, modified from Welty and Baptista, 1988.

expand their skulls and mouths, giving them the ability to engulf and swallow objects from which they theoretically should be slithering away.[11] This characteristic of the skull bones moving independently is called "cranial kinesis." Some lizards also accomplish a form of kinesis, where the lower jaw not only hinges, but moves forward and backward in relation to the upper. Called "streptostyly," this movement pulls the prey toward the throat. Gulp. Birds, too, are able to open their mouths overly wide, and kinesis is probably the only reason woodpeckers are not completely brain-damaged: the braincase pulls away from the upper jaw at the moment of impact.[12]

Most cranial-kinesis dinosaur literature generally purports that there was little or no movement possible in the skull of

Stan's skull was found disarticulated, as shown by these individual bone casts, and provided much more scientific information than it would have otherwise. Photo by Ed Gerken.

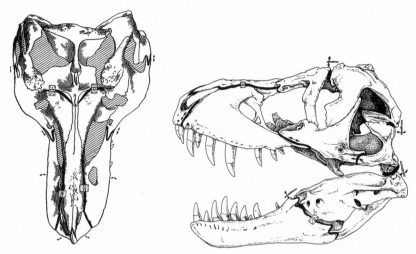

Movement between skull elements is indicated with arrows and "hinges." This movement allowed for shock absorption and swallowing large chunks of flesh and bones.
Illustrations by Peter Larson after Osborn (top view) and Dorothy Sigler Norton (side view).

Tyrannosaurus rex.[13] While he would later change his mind, even the radical Bob Bakker was among the skeptics. He recognized the importance of kinesis in other theropods like *Allosaurus,* but at first believed that "tyrannosaur's skull was one unified whole, very solidly constructed, with no moving parts except at the joint of the jaw."[14] Ralph Molnar, who spent hundreds of hours examining LACM-23844, MOR-555, and another Museum of the Rockies incomplete and partially articulated skull, MOR-008, concluded that "streptostyly may have been present, but provides no good evidence for cranial kinesis."[15]

Stan presented us with an unparalleled opportunity. Never before had such a complete skull been disarticulated and still remained in wonderful shape. Like a model airplane, or a puzzle, or a father's worst nightmare—playground equipment with no assembly instructions—Stan's bones were just lying there, waiting for me to see how they fit together—and moved, or didn't move. Of course, I played with casts, not the real McCoy.

The first thing I noticed: two ball-and-socket joints on each quadrate—the bones at the back of the upper jaws, one on each side. With a double joint built into the bone, it hinged above, onto the rest of the skull, and below, where it hooked to the lower jaw. This meant that both the left and right sections of the lower jaw could independently move backward and forward in relation to the upper jaw. While Bob Bakker at first did not think the upper skull had movement, he did recognize that the front and rear halves of the lower jaws were able to move independently. "The prong and groove joint would let the front half with teeth slide, swivel and twist."[16] Inside the mouth, the palate also was free to move in relation to the braincase, although the braincase itself was tightly fused and rigid. Most important, one other ball-and-socket joint, on top of the snout, allowed the nose to raise independently of the back of the skull. Taken together with hinges or flat articulations between bones of the upper "lip" area, I believe this means *T. rex*'s mouth could raise and flatten out like a lizard's or a bird's.

The final blow for an unsuspecting duckbill: when *T. rex*'s jaws closed, the teeth of the lower jaw passed inside those of the upper jaw. Together, the jaws formed a pair of gigantic shears fitted with recurved teeth the shape of armor-piercing bullets. Independent movement of skull bones would have allowed fine-tuned direction of huge jaw muscles. With tremendous force, those muscles could have bitten down hard, even through bone, with the assurance of shock-absorption. We had seen evidence of just that in Sue's excavation, where the serrated marks of *T. rex* teeth remained on the matchstick remains of leg bones. With this skull configuration, *T. rex* could bite off big chunks of, well, whatever, and then maneuver them into its throat. A little give here and there would have gone a long way in preventing headaches, broken skull bones, and even broken teeth.

Greg Erickson, then a graduate student at the University of California, Berkeley, has been studying *T. rex* teeth and the bite force they were capable of delivering and withstanding. He and a group of biomedical engineers from Stanford University studied a *Triceratops* pelvis with fifty-eight *Tyrannosaurus rex* bite marks. Comparisons of these with marks artificially induced with a known force into the pelvic bone of a cow showed that 1,430 pounds of force were necessary. Extrapolating for the point of a single rear tooth, Erickson found that *T. rex* jaws were capable of

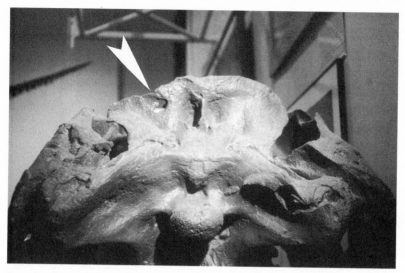

It took a force of 3,000 pounds per square inch for a *T. rex* jaw to punch this hole through the top of Stan's braincase. That bite also removed a portion of the supraorbital crest, a very important muscle attachment point that used to be above where the arrow is pointing. Photo by Peter Larson.

supplying a *minimum* force of 3,000 pounds. That's worth running from, considering that today's king of the jungle, the African lion, can bite with a *maximum* force of only 946 pounds.[17]

While all of this skull movement and biting power was impressive, we were sure it took brains to know how to use them. In outlining material for interactive displays, we also outlined yet another bone to pick with other scientists about *T. rex*'s head. Compared to the skull of a mammal, one of the most striking features in *T. rex*'s skull is the presence of huge holes called *fenestrae*, which means "windows." These windows were pathways for all kinds of internal structures, such as sinuses and nerves, but exactly how much sensory fire power was inside has been debated for many years.

"The brain proper was extremely small in comparison with the enormous size of the body."[18] When first describing *Tyrannosaurus rex* with these words in 1912, Henry Fairfield Osborn relegated the Tyrant King to the ranks of pea-brained dinosaurs. Thankfully, more recent research has redeemed my favorite monster. In making his evaluations, Osborn had been referring to the braincase from AMNH-5029, which had been

A section through *T. rex*'s braincase showing the opening for the brain and various nerve and sinus passages. After Osborn, 1912.

cut in half and exposed the brain cavity. A cast of the brain cavity had displaced 32 cubic inches of water, about half the size of an adult human brain. Osborn, however, realized that brains of most reptiles do not fill the brain cavity completely, and so he estimated that the actual size of the brain itself was 15 cubic inches.[19] More recent estimates have put the size of the brain enclosed within the braincase at 24 cubic inches.[20]

However, CAT scans of *Nanotyrannus* have shown cartilaginous coverings in the skull that were still preserved—and housed olfactory bulbs *outside* the brain cavity.[21] Neither *T. rex* brain-size estimate included the possibility of "extra" olfactory bulbs. In *Nanotyrannus,* they were huge, adding perhaps another one-third to the volume of the brain. Most recently, Chris Brochu of the Chicago Field Museum performed the long-awaited CAT scan of Sue's skull. What he found was even more surprising: the olfactory lobe more than doubled the size of the brain cavity, giving *T. rex* a human-sized brain.[22] Even when we *discount* the olfactory lobe, *T. rex* still had a larger brain than any other dinosaur, and a much larger brain than any reptile, living or extinct. Perhaps more surprising, *T. rex* even had a larger brain than any bird and most mammals.[23]

When it comes to brains, does size matter? Certainly, bigger brains are generally more intelligent; however, regardless of intelligence, brain size generally increases as body size does. But the increase is not linear. A human's brain accounts for 2.1 percent of its body weight, whereas a shrew's is 4.3 percent, a cat's is only 0.9 percent, and a whale's is a measly 0.01 percent.[24] We believe that a cat is more intelligent than a shrew and a human is more intelligent than both. Some people believe that a whale's intelligence surpasses that of a human's. While it is safe to say *T. rex* wasn't a pea-brain, it isn't possible to give it intelligence tests. We can, however, make educated guesses about its strengths and weaknesses from looking at the various parts of the brain cavity, the nerve pathways, and the sites of the sensory organs.

Let's get back to those huge olfactory lobes, the largest of any animal, living or extinct. To understand their ancient function, we can look at some related ones in living animals. Together with the cerebral hemispheres, in reptiles the lobes make up the part of the brain that is used for smell, and for instinctive behaviors of attack, defense, and territoriality.[25] In birds, this large section also houses complex instinctual behavior, sensory integration, and *learned intelligence*.[26] Using these models, especially birds, we can guess that the presence of large lobes is initial evidence of a very high-functioning and intelligent *T. rex*. In addition, because the king of any food chain must be agile on its feet, it is no surprise to learn that the most spacious portion of *T. rex*'s brain cavity would have held the cerebellum—responsible for precision movement and equilibrium in living animals. This large relative size also occurs in birds, where the cerebellum is one of the most highly developed parts of its brain.

Osborn added to the overall idea that *T. rex* was no slouch by identifying well-developed optic lobes,[27] used for eyesight. Birds have the most highly developed sight of any living animal, thanks to color oil droplets that filter and enhance color images.[28] Crocodiles and birds have both rods and cones, light receptors sensitive to color and shades of gray. Since its closest living relatives both have color vision, I would bet that *Tyrannosaurus rex* did, too. There certainly was plenty of room in the retina for both rods and cones because there was space for a *T. rex* eyeball the size of a softball, five inches in diameter. That is four times the diameter of an ostrich's, the largest eye of any living land vertebrate.[29] The enormous diameter of the opening for the optic nerve, more than half an inch, indicates that *T. rex* had not just an optic nerve, but a cable—the animal equivalent to a transatlantic fiberoptic line.

T. rex's eyes faced forward, which allowed for stereoscopic, or binocular, vision—similar to humans'. Stereoscopic vision is important in depth perception and gauging distance, both vital to a predator. Given what we know about vision in birds, it is probable that *T. rex* had the ability to judge distance, size, shape, color, depth, and motion with a precision greater than any animal alive today. This reveals one howler in *Jurassic Park: T. rex* most certainly would have seen that kid in the dark. And clearly, with the largest olfactory lobes of all time sniffing him, movement or no movement, the boy would have been dead meat.

For our exhibit, Aurora Oval created an excellent interactive display, where visitors could walk up behind life-sized, "fleshed-on" models of a *T. rex* and a *Triceratops* skull—to peer through their eyes. Since *Triceratops*, like today's bison, was a prey animal, its eyes were placed on the side of its head. This might eliminate binocular vision, but would enhance peripheral vision—giving a wider field of view to spot the first sign of trouble. When looking through cameras positioned in the models, people would "see" what it was like to be both dinner and diner.

Many of the bones of the braincase are hollow in birds and *T. rex*.[30] These hollows are connected, via airway openings, to the respiratory system and the inner ear. Phil Currie believes one function of the open spaces in a *T. rex* braincase was to produce "a damping effect of the air cushion for better detection of low-frequency sound."[31] While crocodiles have a good sense of hearing,[32] most birds are unable to hear high frequencies. However, birds are able to discriminate between rapid shifts in tone with much greater accuracy than humans,[33] which is not surprising given the complexity of some of their songs. In all probability, *T. rex* was able to hear well, with particular sensitivity to low-frequency sounds—such as the heavy footfalls of an approaching meal.

Tyrannosaurus rex had other nerve passages, even more fenestrae and brain cavities; in short, *T. rex* was wired. It was the gold-medal winner of the Cretaceous Olympics. Its senses were well developed and some, like sight and smell, probably were incomparable. So then what? What did *T. rex do* all day?

To Kill or Not to Kill? That Is the Question

Despite what Osborn thought was its smallish brain, *T. rex* was "undoubtedly the chief enemy of the *Ceratopsia* and *Iguanodontia*." So he wrote in 1906, asserting *T. rex*'s reputation as the Tyrant Lizard King. In 1916 he added, "*Tyrannosaurus* is the most superb carnivorous mechanism among the terrestrial vertebrata, in which raptorial destructive power and speed are combined; it represents the climax in evolution of a series."

Things started to get ugly for *T. rex* in 1917, when Lawrence Lamb first slandered the beast by proposing that tyrannosaurs were overgrown garbage disposals. Lamb, who was reporting on a relative of *T. rex, Albertosaurus liberatus,* noticed the lack of wear on the teeth. He assumed this must indicate a lack of hard use (instead of frequent replacement—we now know each tooth was replaced with a fresh one every two or three years[34]). Much more recently, MOR's Jack Horner went so far as to say that the world's favorite monster had beady little eyes, useless arms, and a nose good only for sniffing carrion. He even said that *T. rex* couldn't run fast and had no way to catch its prey.[35] While Horner has waffled a bit more recently, and scientific evidence has pointed away from beady eyes and useless arms, there is still plenty to argue about.

"But do cats eat bats, I wonder?" And here Alice began to get rather sleepy, and went on saying to herself, in a dreamy sort of way, "Do cats eat bats? Do cats eat bats?"[36]

We know *T. rex*'s punchlike teeth could neither strip leaves from trees nor crush and process fruits and berries. They had only one use, and that was to cut through flesh and bone. We know what happened to Sue's dinner after she ate because we found the acid-etched tail vertebrae of an *Edmontosaurus* in her stomach contents, along with other digestive tract material.[37] We can even compare the digestive tracts of birds and crocodiles in an effort to reconstruct *T. rex* innards, and ponder whether it had two stomachs or one, but really, none of that tells us whether that unfortunate duckbill was dead or alive first. Those teeth and stomach acids would have worked perfectly well on the already deceased. We know *T. rex* had biting and swallowing and digesting down pat, but what happened before it sat down to dine?

The first point to dispatch is the business about an undiscriminating nose. Horner asserted that those oversized olfactory lobes would have been much more useful in scavenging than in preying — because turkey vultures also have them. So do albatrosses, storm petrels, and kiwis, although Horner did not mention them. While sniffing out dead things is a noble use for olfactory lobes, sniffing out living things is, too. Most scavengers, and most birds, do not share the olfactory lobe trait, but dogs—the best living trackers in the world—do. And many other mammalian and reptilian predators rely upon their sense of smell to identify, track, and locate prey.

Now, what about those troubling issues of running and catching? Ecologist P. Colinvaux was entranced with the fact that there are no terrestrial predators anywhere near the size of *Tyrannosaurus rex* alive today or anytime during the Cenozoic, the "Age of Mammals." He wrote in 1978, "The tyrannosaur was not a ferociously active predator . . . most of its days were spent on its belly, a prostration that conserved energy. . . . Nothing like it has been seen since, because the true active predators of the age of mammals were able to clean up the meat supplies before a sluggish beast such as a tyrannosaur could get to them." Although Colinvaux did not say that *T. rex* was strictly a scavenger, he certainly believed that its size made it a misfit incapable of normal predation.

Both evolution and biology tend to negate the idea that *T. rex* was simply, or even primarily, a huge, lazy creature that did not make its living thinning *Edmontosaurus* herds. Greg Paul, an independent paleontological artist and researcher has pointed out that "the idea that animals as big as most theropods were true scavengers is ecologically unfeasible." I agree with him that vultures and condors are the "only true living scavengers. In fact, pure scavengers must be soaring fliers, because they alone can rapidly look over and cover the great distances needed to find and reach the occasional carcass."[38] (And even vultures have been filmed killing and eating hatchling turtles scrambling toward the ocean.[39]) Evolution bears Paul out: there are no large-bodied, ground-dwelling, strict scavengers in today's ecosystems. Probably there never were. For example, when we think of scavengers, we think of hyenas and jackals. However, less than 20 percent of a jackal's diet is scavenged,[40] and hyenas, long looked upon with repugnance because of their giggly, scavenging habits, obtain only 30–50 percent of their food from scavenged carcasses.[41]

Colinvaux's assertion that *T. rex* needed Geritol begins to fall by the wayside when certain bone characteristics are taken into account. First, the tremendous bone remodeling that made discerning growth lines difficult in rear limb bones indicated stress on the legs.[42] To achieve such a level of remodeling, *T. rex* couldn't have spent all day on its belly, snoozing or eating bonbons. I think Colinvaux, when using Cenozoic *mammals* as a model, failed to note that Mesozoic *dinosaur* herbivores were simply larger than their later prey counterparts. Consequently, large carnivores were an evolutionary trend that culminated with *T. rex*, and *T. rex*'s size alone did not mean it was sluggish by nature. In fact, its overwhelming similarity to birds indicates an active, warm-blooded creature capable of sustained activity.

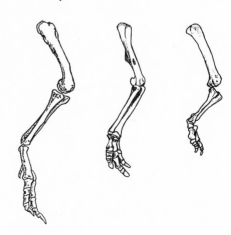

Because the length of adult right femurs (upper leg bones)— of *T. rex* on left, *Edmontosaurus* duckbill in center, and *Triceratops* on right—often were very close in size, the remainder of the leg made the difference for generating stride and speed. Because *T. rex* stood on tiptoe, even its oversized foot bones added length, making *T. rex* faster whether walking, running, or skipping rope.

Illustration by Peter Larson after Dorothy Sigler Norton; after Lull and Wright, 1942.

Second, on the ground, *T. rex*'s legs were substantially longer than those of all its potential prey, and the lower legs (tibia and metatarsals) were much longer than the upper legs (femurs)—the mark of a sprinter. Whatever its speed, it was certainly faster than anything it might choose to run down. By measuring trackways and leg bone ratios, scientists have estimated *T. rex*'s cruising speed to range from 15 to 45 miles per hour.[43] While Jim Farlow, a researcher from Purdue University, worries that a *T. rex* traveling at that great a rate of speed would be extremely susceptible to injury—should a beast of its size stumble and fall—even he and his coauthors agree that speeds of 30 miles per hour are not out of the question.[44]

The last running wrinkle is that using models to project speed is an inexact business. For example, looking at a crocodile trackway, a crocodile skeleton, or even a crocodile in repose, there is nothing to indicate the animal is capable of speeds up to ten miles per hour.[45] A crocodile generally meanders, but if it needs to sprint, it raises its body up on its usually-bowed legs and puts the pedal to the metal.

To tie up Horner's arguments, we can all agree that what he calls *T. rex*'s "tiny little arms" could not have been much use in *catching* prey. However, Horner also wrote, "I don't think *Tyrannosaurus rex* could catch a *Triceratops,* certainly not with its mouth."[46] Why not? He uses the analogy of big cats, who are heavily dependent upon the front limbs for the capture of prey.[47] I would counter with the example of dogs, hyenas, crocodiles, lizards, birds—well, in fact, most mammals and virtually all reptiles and birds—all of whom don't capture large prey with their forelimbs. They use their jaws. *T. rex* did not *need* its arms for prey capture, although it may have used them to grab onto captured prey in order to reposition its mouth[48] or play "God Save the Queen" on someone's ribcage.

"How cheerfully he seems to grin,
How neatly spread his claws,
And welcomes little fishes in
With gently smiling jaws!"[49]

One last bit of evidence? Ken Carpenter noticed the incredible remnants of a little game of cat-and-mouse. A duckbill specimen, which has been on display at the Denver Museum for decades, suffered an unusual trauma to five vertebrae near the base of the tail. Four of the spines that protrude from the vertebrae were kinked from being broken, while about one-third of the fifth spine was actually missing. Carpenter concluded that since the animal's injuries had *healed,* and the pattern of damage fit the mouth of a large theropod, the pathology was evidence of an attack—one that got away.[50] Who was the only concurrent theropod with a big mouth and enough height to reach the relatively tall *Edmontosaurus*'s spine? *Tyrannosaurus rex.* Hardly the sluggish scavenger.

"I'm not convinced *T. rex* was only a scavenger, though I will say so sometimes just to be contrary and get my colleagues arguing," Jack Horner now writes. "To my mind, *T. rex* was simply the greatest opportunist of them all."[51] He has come around to agreeing with nearly all other current researchers of *T. rex,* who believe that, like any predator, *T. rex* would be very interested in conserving energy. When it happened upon a free meal, it would have run off interlopers and sharpened its teeth. If the majestic bald eagle may be seen picking at flattened morsels along the highway, a *T. rex* certainly could snatch a rack of ribs off a downed *Triceratops.*

With every new fossil we dig, we find something new. Maybe one tiny bit of eggshell, or the first *T. rex* wishbone. Year after year, we collect more evidence about this king of the Cretaceous food web, and more evidence that the only threat to the Tyrant Lizard was a little matter of an astral body zinging toward Earth. When the curtain closed on the end of the Cretaceous, nothing like *T. rex* would ever live again. We hoped like crazy that we would be able to continue watching the show.

(8)

A Mad Tea Party

I put the kibosh on our first round of plea negotiations. In my mind, in mid-1993, before we were indicted, during grand jury shenanigans and handwriting samples, to accept a plea would imply we had done something wrong. Not only did I believe we had done nothing wrong, but also at that point we weren't even sure what the Big Mystery was really about. I was a mule, all four legs locked, head down. I could hold my tongue when government representatives suggested potential prison time, fines, restitution. But I kicked, bellowed, and turned my back when the government said we would have to surrender our claim to Sue. This was, of course, months before we were forced to do that very thing.

Even without my stubbornness, successful negotiations between Duffy and Mandel would have been difficult. The letter exchange reflected the tension. Duffy: "Our telephone conversation this morning did not reveal the even-tempered Bob Mandel I have come to know and love over the last few years." Mandel: "I can tell you that we are a long way apart if that is the best that you can come up with." Duffy: "I don't want to fight with you over this, but my last plea suggestion was infinitely more realistic than the 'chamber of horrors' you conveyed to me during our session together."

The chamber of horrors fell silent for more than a year, but the game of croquet heated up. We were indicted, we prepared our defense, we built our *T. rex* exhibit. Our trial was scheduled for January 1995. In the summer of 1994, over a year after the first go-round, the idea of a plea arose once again. My mule logic had changed to this: facing such a massive case, even if we were innocent of each and every charge against us, it was possible that a few might slip through the cracks. We might be convicted of something. Duffy put the fear of God in me. "With the state of the law today, sentencing is a breathtakingly high-stakes game," he said. I remember my brother, a devoted family man with small children—and, at that time, a pregnant wife—saying that fighting for principle was not worth an idealistic prison sentence. We started to have "real life" conversations that weighed idealism— and finances—against pain.

Eventually pain won. After any remaining ego of ours took a backseat to practicality, Duffy played point man in serious negotiations with the U.S. Attorney's office. "It was two lawyers dancing like a couple of sumo wrestlers," Duffy recalled. "But our side certainly was open to ending it." It looked to me like two sumo wrestlers vying for some new real estate: forceful offers and counteroffers. The government's first proposal went like this: I go to jail, we pay fines, they keep the fossils they had seized, and Sue disappears, once and for all. Even then, Sue was not dead for us. We knew we had lost her, but we also had spent over $200,000 on her excavation and preparation. We had filed a lien against Maurice Williams after the dinosaur was returned to him; it provided for our reimbursement if and when he sold the fossil.

We insisted upon one particular non-negotiable: none of us would go to prison. Discussions began in July 1994 and proceeded through mid-September. Duffy was in fine form, pointing out serious weaknesses in the government's case and shredding the indictment. Finally, an agreement was tentatively reached—I still have my handwritten notes that outlined its points. We would choose for the institute one or perhaps two "white collar" charges from a list of felonies, or, alternatively, one "fossil" misdemeanor. In this way, the corporation would plead guilty to something and pay a fine—capped at $100,000. No individual would face prison. We would surrender the already seized fossils, return one whale to Peru, and drop the lien action. We agreed to pay the ransom and free our families.

On Monday, September 19, 1994, we defendants and our pack of lawyers were sitting in Pat Duffy's conference room. We all

Headlines in the *Rapid City Journal* altered the course of our criminal trial.

agreed that the negotiation was satisfactory, and our lawyers prepared it for submission to Bob Mandel. Thursday, September 22 looked to be the probable day of signing and presentation to the judge. It was dizzying. I felt as if I had to freeze in place, to stand still until the document was signed. Everything I knew, everything I believed, everything I had worked toward hung on one set of signatures. Again, I was a mule. Everybody was. We told no one. Neal didn't even tell his wife. No employees, no friends, no risk. We wanted to be done with this more than we'd wanted anything.

Late in the business day, near closing time, a telephone call was transferred into the conference room. Duffy took it, listened, and put the phone on hold. The *Rapid City Journal* was running a story on the plea bargain. Hugh O'Gara wanted to know if Duffy had any comment.

We just sat there for a moment, stunned. Plea bargains were supposed to be secret. Weren't they?

Duffy got back on the phone and said, "We're preparing for trial, and lawyers always are open to negotiations." After he hung up, the lawyers discussed the ramifications of the story; we all were so used to publicity by now, we weren't sure what it would mean. I remember walking out of there in a fog, living through yet another moment I had no control over—and no hope of controlling. I wondered if calling O'Gara would help, but I imagined that begging him not to run his story would simply put my desperate quote in it.

Tuesday morning, "Fossil Case Won't Go to Trial" appeared in the paper shortly before the defense team met with the U.S. Attorney's office to present our agreement.[1] The article not only told many of the exact details of our plea bargain, but also set a very particular tone. "Hit by several recent setbacks in the cele-brated 'Sue' fossil prosecution, the federal government is virtually giving up the case," it began. After crediting "sources connected with the case" and listing various details of the Narrowed-down Mystery, O'Gara administered the coup de grâce. "The sudden turnaround by the government came from several serious blows to the government's case, some of them unpublicized." It listed the judge's recent decision not to move the case from Rapid City to another South Dakota town, the sealing of the list of prospective jurors, the trial schedule, and the death of the ranger who had "befriended" the institute and acted as what O'Gara called "the chief government witness."

The last paragraph was just one sentence: "The plea agree-ment under negotiation calls for no publicity by either side in the settlement."

We all were alarmed at how detailed the article was. Its level of detail seemed to indicate "publicity by either side in the settle-ment"—but whom? The fear that had gripped my stomach since first light loosened a bit when Duffy reported that the plea meeting had gone well. So far, the deal was still on, regardless of the article. On the street, everyone called out congratulations.

Wednesday morning, the sky fell on our heads.

The judge called the pack into his chambers at 8 A.M. He was concerned that the article had irreparably tainted the jury pool, should the plea fail and a jury become necessary. He also was con-cerned about the ethics behind leaking the story—and the identity of the source. Battey questioned each lawyer as to his knowledge of the article's origination. Every one said on the record that he had not known of the article until he was either asked to com-ment by O'Gara, notified by another attorney who had been approached by O'Gara, or read it in the paper.

While Judge Battey said he would accept their word as officers of the court, he had a definite opinion as to the identity of O'Gara's Deep Throat. "Given the strong inference of these types of news reports, based upon the previous history in this case, the very strong inference is that the source of the case was one or more of the defendants in the case." Another straw on the camel's back.

Finally, the most important objection Battey had to the article was its subject matter. Blustering with disapproval, he criticized not only the article's anti-government slant and its detailed revelations, but especially the *negotiation's substance*. He was so adamant in his disapproval that he violated a rule called 11(e), which prohibits a judge from engaging in dialogue about in-progress plea bargains. Since the judge's job is simply to review what the prosecutors present, the rule reads: "The court shall not participate in any such discussions." Instead, he participated, and in so doing, he expressed some of his personal opinions about us.

> A plea agreement, if reached between the parties, has to pass muster with the Court. From what I saw in the paper, if that's the plea agreement, it's not a plea agreement, it's a capitulation by the government. I am going to look very closely at whether or not in any plea agreement of your client, principal officers of a closed corporation, can escape by putting the fault over on the corporation. . . . It looks to me from what I see in filings that there are relative degrees of fault, even among the conspiracy members. . . . But I will wait. I don't want to affect that plea agreement.[2]

Somehow it seemed clear that what he said definitely would "affect that plea agreement." To his credit, he acknowledged stepping over the line in a letter the next day. He mentioned Rule 11(e) and urged attorneys from both sides to "proceed or not proceed by disregarding my remarks." With that lukewarm encouragement, we were sure the government was not about to saunter into chambers and present the ridiculed "capitulation." While Mandel later denied being bullied, he did admit that the article did nothing to move the plea agreement forward. As Duffy put it, "If Hugh [O'Gara] hadn't pronounced winners and losers like a carnival barker, the public perception would not have been of government capitulation. The public would have thought it was a wise use of government resources." Predictably, talks stalled. What had previously been an acceptable agreement no longer was on the table. We had been so close.

The issue of Hugh O'Gara's Deep Throat would nag at us for years. At one time or another, Mandel, Duffy, Neal, Neal's wife Brenda, Kristin, and Kristin's mother—Marcia Mitchell, a former *Journal* writer herself, and known to O'Gara—all asked O'Gara whodunit. Citing professional ethics, and apologizing for the trouble his story had caused, O'Gara nonetheless refused to identify his source. However, he absolved several people: to Mandel, he said no government employee had spoken; to Duffy and Brenda, he ruled out any defense attorney and anyone from Duffy's law firm; to Kristin he assured it was "no one in the family," meaning the Larson clan; to Marcia, and also Neal and Brenda, he answered, "You don't want to know." Who else could it have been? We were able to rule out one more suspect: Mary Garrigan, Duffy's wife. "I know the judge painted me with that brush," she later said. She was right. Plenty of people assumed Garrigan, who worked in the newsroom alongside O'Gara, had leaked the story. But she hadn't been privy to those details.

Later, Kristin asked O'Gara if he would conduct an anonymous interview of the secret source on her behalf. She asked simply for Deep Throat's motivation. Was it to scuttle the plea negotiation? Was it somehow intended to help someone? If so, whom? "You'll get no more help from me!" O'Gara snapped. Although his story would cost the defendants money, grief, anxiety—and eventually much more than that—O'Gara tucked his journalistic ethics into his pocket and hung up the phone. Mandel, who believed O'Gara's story had been "inappropriate" in revealing a private issue, later said, "Part of the freedom of the press is the freedom to do a crappy job."

Meanwhile, back at the law office, Duffy and Ellison prepared more documents, asking once again that the judge recuse himself based on the plea bargain tirade. We thought for sure his statements illustrated that his "impartiality might reasonably be questioned." After the government argued that the judge had shown no *personal* bias, Duffy wrote: "The government has elected not to discuss the Court's admitted violation [of Rule 11(e)], or the import of the Court's pointed statements finding that a conspiracy exists; that varying degrees of culpability exist within that conspiracy; and that Peter Larson cannot 'escape' responsibility for his conduct."

"How do you like the Queen?" said the Cat in a low voice.

"Not at all," said Alice: "she's so extremely—" Just then she noticed that the Queen was close behind her listening: so she went on, "—likely to win, that it's hardly worth while finishing the game."

The Queen smiled and passed on.[3]

The judge denied the recusal motions as "frivolous." Duffy made the familiar trip to the Eighth Circuit Court of Appeals on October 10, 1994, the day after Neal's youngest child, Elisha, was born. On December 29, less than two weeks before trial would begin, the appeals court upheld Battey. In a nutshell, it said that our judge had earned his opinions through "living with" our case for two years, and that his comments did not indicate his inability to be fair. Apparently, just because he thought we were guilty did not mean he couldn't be a good judge.

We all believed our arguments were sound, and that something aside from the law had to be influencing the string of rejections we had received throughout our long case. Our supporters flirted with ideas of a good-old-boy network, and we heard more than once the tongue-in-cheek "Just because you're paranoid doesn't mean someone's not after you." Duffy later put this dynamic in simple terms. "The vortex of the case was going to pull everybody into it. Not to the waist, not to the nostrils, but clear under. Personalities had taken over. Battey's, mine, Peter's; we tried to squeeze our personalities out of that case, but, well, it had gotten personal."

Taking Stock

Terry Wentz has always looked great in a suit. Unlike me, he actually owned a suit, probably more than one. Before I could go to court, Kristin took me shopping. "I can't wear a suit," I said. "I have to be comfortable if I'm going to get through this." She nodded in that way that meant I did not understand what was happening, and she steered me and my crutches through the door of Seeley's. Seeley's had lots of suits; with my broken leg, I couldn't even run away. She grabbed my elbow, saying soothing things as I blanched at the rows of pinstripes, and kept my momentum going until we got to the racks of khaki dress slacks. I didn't know there was such a thing. Pleats! I chose a few colors I could live with, along with dress shirts that matched, and a plaid jacket with leather elbow patches. "Like a professor," she said. "It doesn't count as a suit." At the eyeglass store, she showed me how scratched my lenses were, and I retired the frames I had worn since high school. She even gave me a haircut.

We didn't buy seven weeks' worth of outfits. I had to mix and match for what repeatedly has been called South Dakota's longest trial, although I don't know if anyone checked the history books to be sure. After that, the jury would deliberate for two and a half weeks. While this was a big event for the bar in South Dakota, and a monumental event in our personal lives, all of the maneuvering, the documents, the motions and replies and appeals—all of it also put paleontology to the test. As I saw it, the fate of fossils hung in the balance.

The Sue-as-real-estate decision changed the face of paleo-law and set a precedent in a field devoid of consistent regulations, let alone specific laws. The Dinosaur Renaissance, *Sputnik*'s funding, the Bone War dance between commercialism and academia, all of that came to a head in the fossil world's largest single legal undertaking. Everything we believed about public land management, how fossils should be dealt with, and who should deal with them would be discussed. Interpretations of policy, customs, fees, standards, values—everything would be laid out in one place for the first time. What was said about us—the largest independent fossil company in the world—would reflect on how our branch of paleontology fit onto the tree. Were we just gold diggers? Did we contribute to science? Was there really a place for us? Could museums collect all the fossils that need to be collected? Were fossils "safer" in the hands of academics? Or, were we specialists ready, willing, able—and allowed, even encouraged—to bring science to the public?

I believed there had to be a way, a proactive arrangement between independent collectors and three-piece suits. Our company already had spent decades attempting to bridge the gap. I wanted not only to prove our innocence, but also to establish the value of what we did for a living. Dale Russell, head of North Carolina State University's Department of Marine, Earth and Atmospheric Sciences, reinforced my thinking. "It seems to me we have to play to each other's strengths. Academics have a need, obviously, and the Institute has something that it can provide," he said. "I think [academics] also can help the non-academic side. We both have different breadths of experience to share with each other." He said everyone wins when we have "knowledge of our position in the universe in our various specialties." That sounded like self-awareness, and it needed mutual respect, not hostility, to flourish.

To earn respect, first we had to succeed in court. Our only experience so far, the embarrassing custody hearing, really was croquet compared with what would come. Despite the fact that the government earlier had been willing to "capitulate," Mandel laid out marching orders for a full-scale trial. In the federal courtroom, maneuvers that seemed stilted, disconnected, and strangely indirect were stepping-stones intended to send us directly to jail. We had to learn, and learn fast, the language of what FBI Special Agent William Asbury called "the rules of engagement." As a chief government witness, and coordinator of much of the field effort, he lined up his weapons: a couple of anticommercial generals bolstered by land management foot soldiers, ambiguous laws and policies, volumes of seized documents, and evidence from reconnaissance missions. Ready or not, we were at war.

Our main bunker was Pat Duffy's office, where many nights after court our defense team gathered. We discussed the day's events, changes in our approach, surprises in testimony, cross-examination techniques. We reviewed charts that kept track of the unwieldy brigades, and from which we organized our defense strategy—beginning with linking series of related counts with their primary fossils, locations, or subjects: "Sharkey," "White Collar," "Red Buttes," "Tiny."

No matter how organized or strong your case, however, having the wrong jury can sink you, and we paid a lot of attention to jury selection. One attractive, accessorized, well-spoken woman in the jury pool became the focus of a major disagreement on our side. Neal's attorney, Bruce Ellison, thought she was out of our social league and wouldn't relate to us. Bob and Terry's lawyers voted to oust her as well; but Duffy and I thought her husband's shipping business would provide perspective on how difficult it is to perfectly manage overseas shipping, a source of several counts against us. "Besides," Duffy added flatly, "she's a fox. I figure it's between me and those government lawyers, and if I can't charm her, they certainly can't." Duffy is an attractive man, a witty, intense man. I encouraged everyone to bend to his instinct. We both were very wrong. The "Fox" became the jury foreperson, and eventually would prove to be the most important person in our entire case.

Our next set of maneuvers involved preparing for witnesses, who fell into several categories. Ranchers, of course, provided the foundation of how we handled our affairs in the field. Over the years, we had forged handshake relationships with more than one hundred of them. Only a few played a role in the case, testifying either about property boundary confusions or misunderstandings about what kind of company we had. When all was said and done, of all our ranchers, only two testified with *complaints*. And these, we believed, had been poisoned by the prosecution's interrogation techniques.

More numerous were government agents, whose job was to validate evidence by stating, for example, that they had seized the material, or had located a fossil site and taken photographs. Other expert witnesses used their skills to examine fossils or fossil excavations, or represented customs agencies, airlines, Indian tribes, or other entities. Forensic witnesses had collected handwriting samples, or had tested bits of plaster or DNA from cigarette butts left at excavation sites (none of our field workers smoked, and Ed Cole admitted that certain cigarettes had been his; agents tested them anyway). The last category included those with whom we had collected fossils, or from whom we had bought them. Because they wouldn't have been called if the localities were not in question, some of these people were given immunity to testify against us. One of these people was billed as the bombshell witness, the big kahuna: Sue's discoverer, Susan Hendrickson.

The *Rapid City Journal* covered the trial with kid gloves, seemingly avoiding moments that elicited gasps from the gallery. Nevertheless, observers, and the jurors, as they would later say, were keenly aware of what appeared to be the judge's next exhibition of unfair play.[4] "[The defense] couldn't use anything on their behalf," juror Lucinda Fortin said. The number of sustained objections for the prosecution versus the defense became so lopsided that defense attorneys began to keep score. The entry of evidence was likewise unequal. The judge allowed Special Agent Asbury to introduce more than six hundred exhibits in one fell swoop, simply saying he could vouch for them. In fact, even *before* these exhibits were entered, jurors were provided with binders filled with anything the government wanted to put inside. Yet almost every time we attempted to enter something into evidence, it was rejected. Everything from maps proving localities to a witness's own report to our own scientific research—rejected.

Here one of the guinea-pigs cheered, and was immediately suppressed by the officers of the court. (As that is rather a hard word, I will just explain to you how it was done. They had a large canvas bag which tied up at the mouth with strings: into this they slipped the guinea-pig, head first, and then sat upon it.)[5]

Randy Connelly, Bob's attorney, called it the Houdini Case: we were to be tried in a straitjacket, upside-down, in a tank of water. In one brilliant, tempestuous moment of attempting to loosen our bonds, Pat Duffy swept up a large stack of unadmitted research and tucked it under his arm, pacing the floor. By the time the judge asked him to put the material down, the jurors were smiling. They got the point.

We knew that Sue had not been included in our indictment, but we believed she would play her own role in the trial. We hoped her story could help illuminate the pitfalls in negotiating land use issues and how the government handled our case. Instead, the judge instructed our attorneys not only that Sue had no place in our case, but also that she could not be mentioned in court at all.

To the prosecution, Sue had nothing to do with the Mystery-cum-war. The case boiled down to one concept: intent. Mandel believed external circumstances would show the jury that our motivation was as old as the hills: greed. Getting something for nothing, making a bigger profit margin, maximizing the deal—all regardless of morality or ethics or the law. To accomplish this goal—to get access to fossils and public lands and influential people—the indictment charged us with donning a "cloak of scientific legitimacy," an attitude that would ingratiate us to museums and other "legitimate" scientific entities.

The indictment further charged that everything we did was part of a conspiracy to "maximize [our] commercial benefit . . . regardless of legality." Creating a business, learning to read maps, and even donating fossils to other institutions all were evidence of our intent to defraud others. In the prosecution's mind, everything was suspect—and there was no room in a professional's life for a mistake.

Starting from the ground up, the indictment assumed that collecting or retaining fossils formed the foundation for most of the other charges. To this foundation, the government added drug-trafficking "RICO" laws. If we drove a "stolen item" from its site to our laboratories, that was called interstate transportation of stolen goods. If we used the fax machine to transmit a letter about that fossil, that was considered wire fraud. After a sale, if we used the money to pay a loan installment, that was considered money laundering—we faced $6.6 million in laundering fines, according to Duffy. These "white collar" charges also included structuring financial transactions, giving false information on customs forms, and obstruction of justice—failing to produce particular fossils and documents during and after seizures.

This Land Is Your Land, This Land Is My Land

In opening arguments, Duffy made a crucial point about the foundation of the case: "Out of perhaps a million fossils my client and his partners exhumed and restored, out of a million, they imported or exported close to 100,000. Of all of these, questions have been raised about *fourteen* fossils. Fourteen, and we have responses to each and every question."

In fact, it was even simpler than that. These fourteen fossils had come from only seven sites. Seven times, either we had been in the wrong place or the government had.

In researching these sites, both the defense and prosecution would point to the same pile of evidence as its primary weapon: my field notes. While the government argued that the notes paved the way to our illegal activities, we countered the opposite, both theoretically and literally. The theoretical argument had two prongs, both of which went to our intent. First, it was counterintuitive that I would have kept such copious notations of known illegal activities—and then openly surrendered them to the authorities. Second, some of the contested sites fell on public lands, a morass of politics and confusing policies. Usually we were above the morass; ironically, our standard practice was to stay away from public parcels until land managers either complied with the NAS recommendations or paleontology settled on some other compromise. Even so, in a few special instances we had tried to navigate the seemingly endless variations of pamphlets and statements from the Forest Service or the Bureau of Land Management. We were willing to defend our decisions, because we believed we were well within their guidelines.

When it came to my field note information itself—the actual locations of the disputed fossils, the discussion often focused on how exactly, how correctly, I had plotted our position. In general, we agreed with Mandel when he said, "If the question is how good a grade do they get on map-reading, hey, they get their merit badge for that." The truth about infallible map reading, however, would be graphically illustrated in court, when lawyers and witnesses pulled out maps of different colors and from different years. BLM maps, topographical maps, copies of maps, highlighted maps, maps with notations, overlays of maps.

It became obvious that pinpointing localities on huge prairie expanses, especially before we owned a Global Positioning System unit, was not an exact science. Often miles on end gently rolled out to the horizon, with no roads or fences within sight. Compounding that, the unmarked land included "checkerboarding" of properties—where parcels owned by different entities were intermixed. It is common for public and private lands to actually invade each other's space; in some cases, an unmarked square of public land is completely surrounded by private land.

Even considering checkerboarding, the differences among maps, and the personalities of controlling entities, more than 99 percent of the time we knew where we were—and we believed we could be there at the time. It was that other fraction of a percent that was tricky.

Our contested locations fell within Indian reservations or on public lands controlled by the BLM or the Forest Service. In almost all of these cases, we had received permission to collect from ranchers on what we understood to be their private property. On the reservations, we did not argue whether we had been there, or the accuracy of the questioned sites. The problem here was the checkerboard, which mixed parcels owned by our ranchers with tribally owned parcels—and sometimes the ranchers *leased* parcels from the tribes. In these cases, the technicalities were almost identical to the situation with Sue, because the lands were held in trust. As it would turn out, the fossiliferous localities on Sharkey Williams's land fell into this category, and Matthew's *Triceratops* was one of several fossils that had been seized.

Public land issues fell into "invertebrate" and "vertebrate" subcategories. Creatures with no backbone generally are paleontology's best peacemakers. During my legislative stint, I became well aware that land management agencies have long *encouraged* people to collect these abundant specimens. Public offices across the country always have, and still do, direct visitors to localities where they can find invertebrates, dig them up with earthmovers if they like, and keep them. At one locality, officials told our lawyers and us that we could collect as many as would fit in our pickup bed. In 1986 policies changed to include the caveat that if the specimens were collected *for sale,* a permit was necessary— although to my knowledge they were never issued when requested. Before that, and for fossils collected before that, no regulation existed. For these reasons, we were ready to argue that our collections had not broken the law.

When it came to vertebrates, policies were more restrictive; these were the ones we had really tried to avoid. Despite our care, the indictment alleged a few such collecting instances, and we believed that someone had made a mistake—either us or the government agents. Sometimes we knew the United States had indicted us for removing fossils with backbones from localities we had never visited.

With 6 defendants, 5 lawyers—Terry Wentz and Ed Cole shared one—153 collective charges, 10 different offense categories, 92 government witnesses, 9 defense witnesses, and more than 600 pieces of evidence, the case was unwieldy even for those who understood it. To help the jurors—and the judge, and the other lawyers, for that matter—keep track of the significance of the testimony, the government used a big magnetic board that listed all the charges. When each witness was called, Mandel or Zuercher would move an arrow on the board to indicate the corresponding charge. Because of this complexity, a handful of illustrative counts can serve as examples of the problems that brought us into court, and the methods we used to fight them.

Red Buttes

Tim Monnens owned a private ranch within the boundaries of the Standing Rock Sioux Indian Reservation. We had a permit to collect on tribal lands, and we had Monnens's permission to collect on his ranch. Pleased to receive payment for fossils, Monnens even brought his family to picnic while they watched our *Triceratops* excavation on a couple of occasions. The site's pasture lay in a $5\frac{1}{2}$-square-mile region that was undivided by fences—although it contained a square of leased Indian land. The rancher believed we were well away from the Indian parcel until the government surveyed the area three times as part of the investigation—and found that the tribal line reached 170 *feet* beyond the fossil. The nearest fence was a mile away.

The government charged us with theft of "goods and property of the United States held in trust for the Standing Rock Sioux Tribe." The fact that we held a valid permit from the tribe was discounted for the same reason that Maurice Williams had not had the right to sell Sue to us.

The jury did not convict us of any of the charges related to our collecting on tribal lands.

Buffalo Gap and BLM

Two similar charges of collecting on public lands would have very different outcomes. On the first, what turned out to be a Buffalo Gap National Grasslands locality, Neal received permission from a rancher to collect. The rancher told him that the entire pasture was part of a grazing association of private ranchers, and when Neal checked his 1989 map, it showed the pasture in a different color from government lands. We had never met this rancher before, and as he had been out working cattle, we had not gone to his house—and therefore could not locate it later. The fossils we found there were scraps—worthless both scientifically and commercially. We just picked them up because we were there and they were there. In court, the government entered into evidence a 1994 map that showed the same land in a different color—a color we would have recognized instantly as government land. After the judge refused to allow entrance of our own map, the jury found that we could have been more careful. Government evidence showed the value of these fossils at four dollars per pound, putting the government's loss at about ten dollars. The company, Neal, and I each were convicted of one collecting misdemeanor at this locality.

The government's BLM paleontologist, Laurie Bryant, searched some sections I had identified in field notes as sites where we had collected fossil turtles. What I had written clearly indicated BLM land, but Bryant could find no excavations that definitely could be connected to us. Since the sediments were similar for hundreds of square miles around that area, in fact locating any years-old disturbances would have been a tall order; similar fossils could have been collected from anywhere. That meant there was no way to show that any particular spot had spawned a particular turtle fragment. Nonetheless, based on my notes, she believed we had been there, period. We explained that I simply had made a mistake by writing the wrong number in my field notes—I was a section off. While Bryant admitted that she, too, had made errors in her own field notes, apparently she did not believe us.

Thankfully, our witness, the landowner from whom we had permission to collect, Lyle Heath, knew exactly where we had been. He had taken us there. Heath could accurately locate himself via regularly spaced oil rigs and section markers among a tremendously checkerboarded region. He was so familiar with his territory that he knew where each road crossed each boundary—and he distinguished between my mistake and our location. Duffy asked, "Did any of those government paleontologists, or any of those federal agents who came to talk to you, did any of them say, 'Lyle, could you take us out, show us where those fossils came from?'" "Definitely not," Heath answered. "They had the wrong map. They had a BLM map for a different area. That's not where we were." We would be convicted of no wrongdoing in this locality.

Crinoids

In 1993, when we were younger and stronger, after clawing our way up a thousand-foot cliff, after Neal literally saved my life by grabbing my arm when I lost my balance, after roping off to keep from plunging to our deaths, we had collected a slab of wonderful fossils called crinoids. They look like delicate plants, but in fact are invertebrate animals. Although we sell fossils and casts, we also collect spectacular fossils for permanent display at the Black Hills Museum of Natural History and for scientific study. In this case, we made many pertinent arguments: invertebrate collection on Forest Service land has always been and is still allowed; the collection occurred before the commercial-permit amendment to policy; the fossils were not collected for commercial use; and I had lectured on them as objects of scientific study.

We did not argue the validity of the site identification, even though the reconnaissance team in charge of scouting and verifying this site did not retrace our nearly vertical steps—a titter echoed through court when an overweight agent at first said he had been there. Despite the lack of clear-cut policy, the government claimed that our collection violated regulation, and that our company's work dictated the fossils would be used commercially. We thought we had this count won because the fossils had been collected well before the commercial stipulation, and because we had held them without offering them for sale for nearly a decade. However, the jury convicted me of a misdemeanor at this site. I had been happy to risk my life for science, but in retrospect I'm sorry I did it for less than $100.

Fossil Purchases

Collecting associate and codefendant Ed Cole was charged with stealing a large marine animal called a mosasaur, whose name was "Tiny." Since we had bought the specimen, we were accused of retaining stolen goods. Ed and his family had been camping in a Grasslands location where another fossil lay in the ground—which the Coles left there. Apparently, the government decided that had been Tiny's location, too, and they charged Ed with theft. The problem was, Ed told them he had collected the mosasaur at a town dump. The government ignored him and proceeded with prosecution. On the government's reconnaissance team for this site was Los Angeles County Museum's J.D. Stewart. He testified about his reports, from which some information seemed to be missing:

> DUFFY: Did the U.S. Attorney's office suggest
>   you remove this information from your report?
> STEWART: I think that may have been what
>   happened.

South Dakota's Hell Creek Badlands, the home of *T. rex.* Photo by Peter Larson.

Susan Hendrickson with her initial discovery: cross-sections of Sue's bones exposed by weathering of the cliff face. Photo by Peter Larson.

The beginning of Sue's excavation, with Neal Larson midway up cliff face and Susan Hendrickson at base. Exposed bones were protected from tumbling overburden by plaster and tarps. Photo by Peter Larson

Sue's skeleton exposed, thirty feet down. Photo by Peter Larson.

Mapping bones at the Stan excavation site. Photo by Ed Gerken.

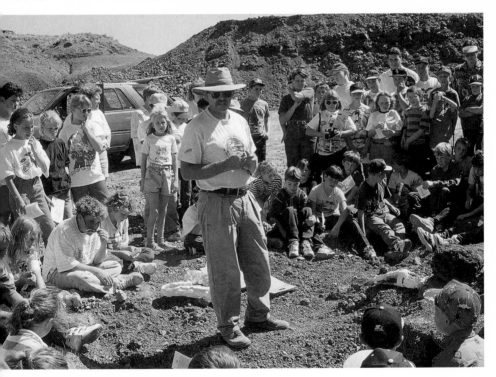

Teaching paleontology class at the Duffy site. Photo by Ed Gerken.

Cleaning Sue's skull with a miniature sand-blasting unit called an air-brade. Photo by Ed Gerken.

Fabricating steel armature to support real dinosaur bones. Photo by Ed Gerken.

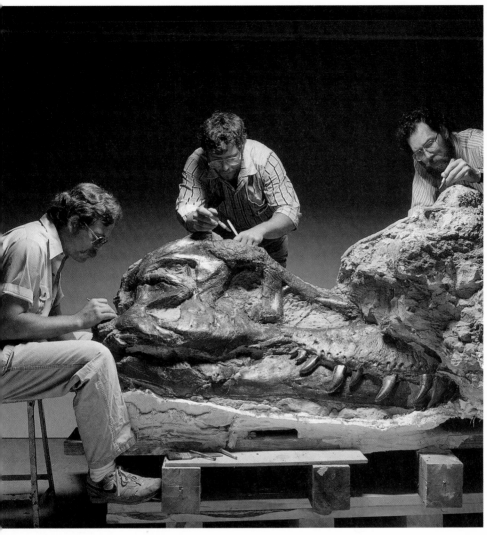

Black Hills Institute partners inspect the block containing Sue's skull. From left, Peter Larson, Neal Larson, and Bob Farrar. Photo by Louie Psihoyos.

National Guardsmen load boxes of Sue onto a truck as townsfolk protest. Photo by Louie Psihoyos.

Police escort Sue's remains from behind the institute's main building. Photo by Louie Psihoyos.

All the protests were for naught. At the end of three days, children remove signs from the walls of the institute. Sue was gone. Photo by Louie Psihoyos.

Attorney Patrick Duffy speaks to local press outside the Rapid City courthouse as defendants and supporters stand by. BHI file photo.

Scientific evidence suggests that baby *T. rex* were covered in downy feathers and received parental care, linking them to modern birds. Illustration by Michael W. Skrepnick.

"Sue's Last Day." An artist's rendition of Sue's family group based on fragmentary fossil evidence found buried with her skeleton. Illustration by Michael W. Skrepnick.

DUFFY: And what information was contained
in those paragraphs?
STEWART: Evidence that our Site 28 was wrong,
that we had misidentified one of the questioned
excavations.
DUFFY: Now how do you feel about what you
deleted—here, let me read from it: "There is a
greater likelihood that the specimen came from
the site indicated by defendants."
STEWART: That's essentially what I believe now.

"I don't think they play at all fairly," Alice began, in rather a
complaining tone, "and they all quarrel so dreadfully one can't
hear oneself speak—and they don't seem to have any rules in
particular."[6]

In another situation, we had bought a catfish fossil from an
independent dealer—who had bought it from an American Indian.
The locality information provided by the collector had been difficult for us to nail down when we sold the piece to Chicago's Field
Museum, and was even more confusing because the land fell
within the *current* boundaries of Badlands National Park. Fossil
collecting has never been allowed in a national park without a
permit; however, in this case the park had been expanded by special agreement with the Pine Ridge Indian Reservation twenty
years earlier. Not only did the Indians retain rights to harvest some
resources, but also much of the land in the newly expanded
boundaries is still privately owned. Therefore, the simple placement of a fossil within the exterior boundaries of "Badlands
National Park" does not necessarily mean the fossil came from
prohibited areas.

When presenting evidence on this count, Zuercher called to
the stand a park ranger from Badlands National Park, John
Donaldson. Donaldson's testimony was strange. He admitted that
the park had grown, and he pointed out localities on the map—
the current map—that correlated to some of our fossil records,
including the catfish. However, he did not address the existence of

private lands within the new zone, leaving the implication that the catfish had been collected from a prohibited spot.

Upon cross-examination, Donaldson admitted he had no personal knowledge as to any actual localities of any specimens on our list. Again, we attempted to introduce a different land ownership map, which highlighted the private lands within the current park borders, but were denied. Duffy also was not allowed to enter into evidence the agreement between the park and the Lakota. Nevertheless, because of the hoopla raised when Duffy made these attempts, we were sure that reasonable doubt had been proven to the jury.

Neither Ed nor any of us would be convicted in the Tiny situation, but the institute would be found guilty of a felony over the catfish retention.

The Value of a Lobster Quadrille

"You may not have lived much under the sea—" ("I haven't," said Alice) "and perhaps you were never even introduced to a lobster, so you can have no idea what a delightful thing a Lobster Quadrille is!"

"No, indeed," said Alice. "What sort of a dance is it?"[7]

As part of Count I, Conspiracy, we were accused of removing a fossil lobster from the Fort Peck Reservoir on August 15, 1988. Called a *Palaeonephrops browni*, the specimen was identified by government agents as a fossil we had sold to the Science Museum of Minnesota. Bruce Erickson, the museum's curator of paleontology, confirmed that he had indeed bought a *Palaeonephrops browni*—which he laughingly hesitated to pronounce—from Black Hills Institute. The catalog entry showed its locality as Fort Peck Reservoir.

However, apparently no one in the government noticed that Bruce Erickson had traveled to the Tucson Gem and Mineral Show, perused our collections, chosen his lobster in February

1988, and paid for it in June—finishing our transaction two full months before the lobster in the indictment supposedly had been *collected*. Our lobster had an alibi. There was no way it could have been in two places at once.

Duffy brought Erickson's attention to "that lobster that nobody can pronounce" on the indictment and pointed out that it couldn't be the same lobster. "Sir, as you sit here, you have no opinion or idea when that fossil might have been exhumed and from where, do you?"

"No." said Erickson. Zuercher leaped out of his chair.

> ZUERCHER: Has anyone ever mentioned to you that the lobster you bought is the one stated in the indictment?
> ERICKSON: No.

An incredulous silence fell over the courtroom. Bruce Erickson had been called to South Dakota for nothing. Duffy pointed to the government's magnetic board listing the counts.

> DUFFY: Your Honor, I think it's on the chart. I think he put the arrow up there.
> THE COURT: Just a minute. Do you have an objection?
> DUFFY: Well, my objection is that his redirect misstates the arrows.

At this point, for the first time in a long while, everyone but the prosecution and the judge was laughing. It was clear that a simple error had been overlooked, the indictment had charged a phantom fossil, and our lobster was in the clear.

> ZUERCHER: Might I be allowed to argue, too, Your Honor?
> THE COURT: I will let you argue, but I think the answer, pure and simple, is it might be a different lobster.

DUFFY: I didn't know that. If it's a different lobster, I don't care about it.

THE COURT: Very well.

ZUERCHER: Thank you, Your Honor.

ELLISON: Can we have a position by the government—what *is* this exhibit this witness has been
shown?

ZUERCHER: This violates the Court's order.
[What order? We never knew.]

ELLISON: It is not part of this indictment.

THE COURT: I think you two gentlemen ought to
sit down right now and be quiet. We don't want
those types of arguments before the jury.

ELLISON: First, Your Honor, what I'd like to do is
if [the lobster] is not related to anything that's in
the indictment, I would seek that it be removed
from the exhibit books and—

THE COURT: Objection overruled.

DUFFY: Your Honor, could we have limiting
instruction that instructs the jury that these
exhibits concerning this lobster are, I guess, not
"the" lobster?

After denying the motion, Battey not only excused the witness,
but also quit for the day. We were all excused, and we never heard
from the lobster again.

In a way, the whole of the indictment against us stood on the
shoulders of a few crucial words: "in excess of one hundred dollars." Stealing a fossil worth less than one hundred dollars is a
misdemeanor; over one hundred dollars and it's a felony. So the
significance of all of these alleged crimes rested on the man chosen
as the appraiser, James Madsen, a former government employee
now in the private sector.

It was perhaps the only moment in the trial that reminded me
of a courtroom drama, or a novel. Our lawyers were able to do

what lawyers always want to do, because Madsen was perhaps the least appropriate witness the government could have chosen to evaluate our fossil specimens. Mandel later would lament the difficulty of securing a star witness for this purpose, since "most anyone who knew anything about valuation of fossils was sort of philosophically in the same camp as the defendants." What Madsen must not have revealed to the prosecution team was that he had taken early retirement from his job as State Paleontologist in Utah after being accused of a conflict of interest inherent in his owning a dinosaur-casting company that copied skeletons from federal land—while paying nothing for the privilege. In his state position, he also attempted to cancel Ed Cole's (and others') commercial state trilobite-collecting leases. Ed and I were among a group of businessmen who spoke out, and there had been no love lost between Madsen and us. Once Duffy revealed the relationship as a possible source of bias against us, he then cut to the quick in how Madsen actually did the job.

Madsen contradicted himself repeatedly, waffling about the number of fossils he had closely examined before attaching values to them. He brought no comparable sales, did no adjustments for time—although he admitted fossil prices would have increased since many of the specimens had been collected. Using templates of commercial fossil catalogs—that advertised prepared specimens for sale—Madsen valued unprepared fossils at what he called "potential" values, instead of their actual, current values. Both Duffy and Ellison were able to unleash their well-honed courtroom skills, and they easily peeled away Madsen's "cloak of expertise" and revealed that he had never in his life prepared an appraisal like this.

While the big fossils—*Triceratops* skulls and the like—were obviously worth more than one hundred dollars, Madsen's inexperience threw a great question mark over the seriousness of the problem that had brought us all together. We began to see a little light in the distance, and hoped that our lawyers' cross-examinations showed there was a reasonable explanation for everything.

Take a Memo

Iirst, it was simply research for this book. I walked into court each day with my footstool, my back pillow, and a bag of steno notebooks. I kicked myself for not having learned shorthand. Having no idea what would gain importance among the hundreds of issues before the court, I tried to keep an accurate record of whatever happened, and did my best to write direct quotes whenever possible.

Second, it became a method to stay calm. If I had to focus on listening, if I had to focus on taking notes, I could not react. When people stirred and spoke under their breath at some outrageous ruling, I could not allow myself to be distracted. Either I split my personality or it was my first Zen exercise: so I could breathe and write, I pulled myself out of my body and hovered over the experience. I cut myself off from the fact that this was my husband—the one with endearingly crooked teeth who always wore white socks—and that this was our life. I had been living a dual existence as it was, interviewing people regardless of their opinions, listening openly, truly wanting to know all sides of the story. This insulation protected me from being caught unawares; without it, I felt exposed, like a creature in the forest unex-

White Collars

"Even though the image of the white collar may seem somewhat inapropos in this case," Mandel joked, "when you deal with white-collar criminals of all sorts of stripes and ilks, they invariably rationalize their behavior. Why it is okay to do what they do." Mandel meant that our explanations for our behaviors and choices should be doubted from the beginning, so we had to show the jury that, while we might not be the best managers in the world, we had integrity. That we had not even conceived of the idea to defraud by wire or launder money or transport stolen goods. Or obstruct justice.

pectedly stepping into metal jaws, snapped by the personal nature of the accusations. I had no choice but to leave the wife me at home and bring only the reporter to court.

Third, it became a tool for the defense. I don't know why we didn't get an automatic transcript, but since one would not be available until the appeal, my notes provided the only immediate record. I split into a third personality: court transcriber. Many nights after court we would stay in Duffy's office until 11:00 P.M., where I read quotes from witnesses, or rulings by the judge, which the lawyers would use in their charts, their cross-examinations, or their arguments. Witnesses like Madsen were taken apart with help from my notebooks, the legal corollary to Peter's own field notes.

From the time the case began, I started a file. After six years, the file filled three filing cabinets—volumes of legal filings, hearing and trial transcripts, press reports, interviews, notes. After eight years, there was an additional stack of boxes that didn't fit in the drawers. The courtroom notebooks still remind me of that torturous compartmentalizing I undertook to create them. They also remind me of a nagging element that pervaded the trial. Juror Richard Cordell noticed it, too. He said, "I had a hard time walking into court every day, not being able to say good morning."

Neal's box label debacle was a perfect example. Two FBI agents had watched him correcting changes he had made to boxes of fossils collected from Sharkey Williams's land. He had changed their markings to distinguish them from Sue material collected at the same time, and before knowing they also were to be seized. The agents agreed that he was writing correct data on the labels, and then handing over the boxes to Ann Elder, a government paleontologist. Both witnesses, Beverly Bates and Michelle Scott Pluta, attempted to interpret Neal's actions as surreptitious, even though he was in the middle of a busy room. In fact, on cross-examination, both women admitted that their official FBI 302 reports reflected Neal's unabashed openness.

While Pluta admitted that another agent had told her what Neal was doing, Bates was intent upon leaving the impression that she had witnessed obstruction of justice. When Ellison asked, "He was changing it to the correct date, isn't that right," Agent Bates answered, "I do not know that was the correct date." But by then, certainly, the agents did know, and there was palpable discomfort in the room. The gallery fidgeted, embarrassed. Neal made his intent vividly known later when he testified, and the jury believed him. This obstruction of justice charge wound up backfiring, making the government look petty and mean.

To be fair, however, there were plenty of uncomfortable moments for us. Especially difficult were discussions about customs, and how they were or were not impacted when we shipped fossils to or from overseas locations. How crates were labeled, and how they should have been valued, became theoretical discussions. When does a fossil gain its value? In the ground? Before it is prepared? After? Are some fossils only scientifically valuable? These were delicate issues that had never been decided in any public forum, for which there was no precedent. Lawyers from both sides relied on logic and opinions.

Specifically, in two instances when we shipped fossils to Japan, Bob Farrar filled out the customs forms. When recording the value of the materials, he had written their replacement cost instead of retail cost; in very small print, the forms had asked for retail value. Our attorneys argued that, because there is no tax when exporting fossils, he could have written $1 or $1 million and no tax, duty, or other economic difference would have resulted. The government argued that Bob intentionally undervalued the fossils for some reason that may have benefited the recipients. Although no negative financial impact could be proved in this country, the judge instructed the jury to disregard "materiality"—whether the numbers "mattered"—and simply consider if the numbers were correct.

Bob's trip to the witness stand remains one of the most intense moments of our entire legal battle. Introverted and intellectual Bob seemed to wage an internal battle between logic and second-guessing the strategy of his questioner. In the end, while attempting to defend himself, he also rightfully acknowledged that the numbers reflected replacement value. Therefore, when Mandel asked if Bob had given a false statement, he answered, simply, "Yes." Not, "*Now* I know it was false, but then I did not." Simply, Yes.

Everyone faces trauma differently. Marion, called as a government witness, was a fount of information. Despite her title of Administrative Assistant, she functioned more as our office manager, even an unwilling life manager, the hub for paperwork, correspondence, communications, travel, records, everything. Devastated by the proceedings, Marion nevertheless exuded self-confidence and professionalism—much to the chagrin of her examiner, David Zuercher. She was a diminutive, quintessential lady, who had raised a brood of children, skinned mink, earned a college degree at age forty, sold insurance, and driven a semi truck. Marion could handle this.

Zuercher asked many questions with a tone apparently intended to elicit embarrassment or chagrin. "Are these fossils and minerals *for sale?*" he asked, as if it was something dirty.

Marion didn't fall for it. Her firm and proud reply: "Absolutely."

Marion had processed innumerable overseas documents, and when faced with the same set of questions that had thrown Bob, she didn't miss a beat.

> ZUERCHER: When you give a declared value to customs, you realize you were to give the full retail price, were you not?
> MARION: In what instance?
> ZUERCHER: The instance where you [were] exporting fossils from the United States.
> MARION: To what country?
> ZUERCHER: You are suggesting there's a difference between countries as to whether you would tell United States Customs what the declared value of a fossil would be?
> MARION: United States Customs doesn't care because there is no tariff or duties on fossils. It's the customs of other countries that would be

concerned, and in the case of shipping to Japan,
it would be important that we put full value,
depending on what we were shipping and who
we were shipping to. If we were shipping retail,
we would put retail value. If we were shipping to
a wholesaler, we would put wholesale value,
because that's what we sold it at.
ZUERCHER: I am going to ask the answer be
stricken as nonresponsive and ask the question be
restated.
COURT: Answer may be stricken as nonresponsive.
. . . Ms. Zenker, if you don't understand the
question, you may ask that it [be] restated.
MARION: Thank you. Would you please restate
that, David?

In the end, while convictions resulted from Bob's two reporting
counts and another regarding a whale shipment from Peru, a new
Supreme Court ruling would require that the jury decide whether
the statements were material. Whether tariffs or retail or wholesale costs "mattered" was not up to the judge to decide. Therefore,
he was forced to "set aside" the convictions and allow for a new
trial on those issues; the government declined to retry.

I breathed a little easier when government witnesses testified
about my carrying traveler's checks from Tokyo. I had been
charged with not reporting their $31,700 value on the airplane
customs form when returning home from an annual fossil show
there. I knew, when entering the United States from another
country, one must report cash over $10,000, and I had no reason
to hide these checks—they were deposited into our business
account and reported on our taxes.

In Tokyo, I had countersigned the checks and stamped them
with our corporate "for deposit only" bank stamp, in case they
were stolen. Assuming this made them nonnegotiable, I looked
past them and counted the cash in my pocket. Banker Clinton
Walker verified that the stamps made the checks "restrictively
endorsed," which indeed made them nonnegotiable anywhere

between Tokyo and Hill City. Two Special Agents for the U.S. Customs Service, Robert Weber and Joseph Leonti, both testified unequivocally that "nonnegotiable monetary instruments" need not be declared at customs. Weber said that "restrictive endorsements are an exception" to the reporting rule, and Neal and Marion testified that we always restrictively endorsed checks we carried from shows.

The judge had two choices when selecting a jury instruction about traveler's checks. One defined "monetary instrument" as including traveler's checks only in "bearer form," which means that the carrier can cash them—which I could not. The other instruction included traveler's checks in any form; not only did the judge choose that one, but he also instructed the jury to disregard the fact that I had restrictively endorsed the checks. The jury later would say that solely because of that choice, I would be convicted of a felony.

Peter, right, collecting whales in the Atacama Desert of Peru with, from left: Swiss collector Kirby Siber; Hernando de Mecedo—director of the National Museum of Natural History and a witness who could not attend our trial—and the late Carlos Martin, caretaker of fossil whales and the museum at the site. In the foreground are the skull and vertebrae of Josephina, the first whale Peter collected in Peru. Photo by Susan Hendrickson.

Peru

I had followed my good friend Kirby Siber, an excellent fossil collector, to Peru for four of five collecting seasons. He introduced me to a new world of fossil collecting in the desert, a desert where it has not rained in recorded history, a desert where wind blows sand from incredible whale specimens that can disintegrate within days. In fact, Kirby also introduced Susan Hendrickson to Peruvian whales—and to me. After the first year, she and I traveled there together. Legal issues involving Peru fell into three categories: the legality of our collecting permits; how we managed our whale shipments; and how we arranged our finances for one season's expenses. Structuring and false declaration charges stemmed from the fact that in Hill City, I underestimated the amount of cash we would need to fund our trip. Two checks were written for a total of $15,000—but each check was under $10,000. At the time I had no idea that all checks over $10,000 require the bank to issue a standard report. "Structuring" claimed we intentionally avoided the report; "false reporting" further claimed we intentionally avoided filling out a customs form at the airport prior to departure.

Neal, Bob, and Marion testified that, per our standard practice when traveling to Peru (where I had been robbed before), Susan and I split the money between us. But no one else could testify to the fact that I did not know I was supposed to have sought out a customs form at the airport. The biggest problem here—aside from the fact that both of these charges were felonies—was that Susan apparently *did* know. On the stand she admitted she sometimes intentionally split sums over $10,000 into smaller amounts to avoid concomitant bank reports to customs.

> MANDEL: Why did you split it up to carry it out
> of the country?
> SUSAN: For safety's sake, you would each carry
> certain amounts of money. And as long as you
> are carrying less than $10,000 apiece, there's no
> need to make a declaration of it.
> MANDEL: Is it fair to say, then, that one reason
> was to avoid making a declaration?
> SUSAN: That's likely one reason, yes.

And with that, since all $15,000 was institute money, I would be convicted of one felony offense for failing to fill out the proper form, though I was not convicted of structuring.

But Peru was just getting started. A parade of Peruvian officials filed into the gallery, flown here to testify that our exporting fossils from Peru had been illegal, that our export agent was a fraud, that our permits were forged, and that we had bribed Peruvian officials to allow us to export fossils. Horrible accusations, but I felt secure within the strong relationships we had forged in Peru. I knew that Kirby and I had followed all required processes necessary to collect there. He had known the government and museum representatives for years before I first visited, and we both were well respected. Together, to support the local scientific community, and in thanks for our being able to collect there, we had built and financed a small in situ museum over a magnificent whale specimen in the desert. We also had donated other specimens and created displays for the Natural History Museum in Lima. This is the kind of thing first-world scientists are seldom able to do for their third-world colleagues. I was very proud of these accomplishments. Now, incredibly, the parade of officials called them bribery.

When we asked our Peruvian colleagues to testify, we learned that the relatively new government-affiliated National Museum had inherited permitting authority from the Natural History Museum. Also, a new regulation had been passed making any other-than-scientific fossil exports illegal; but the law had been passed *after* our last permit had been issued. Over the years, different officials had signed and sealed our permits, including various directors of the Natural History Museum and Ministers of Culture. To our disbelief, we were accused of not following a new permitting policy that *did not yet exist* when we worked in Peru.

At first I thought it would be simple to prove the facts of our permitting process. However, because of the political instability of Peru, and the intimidating lineup of government-sanctioned witnesses, our witnesses were afraid to come to my rescue. Peru can be a scary place—we had experienced gunfire from Shining Path terrorists there—and our witnesses had even been threatened with their lives. The museum staff we were familiar with had been silenced. Our export agent had fled to France. Apparently pressured by the United States, the Peruvian government couldn't let paleontology jeopardize international relations.

I saw Susan as the government's primary link between Peru and me.

I had been called the conspiracy ringleader, but Susan, according to Mandel, "certainly provided a dimension of experience that I don't believe existed at the Black Hills Institute but for her." She was the world traveler, a person who located, excavated, and dove for wonderful relics of the past. Animal, mineral, human artifacts, Susan knew them all. "She might be what you could call a bit of a global gad-about," Mandel said. When it came to how the Peruvian white-collar counts "came about," he believed Susan's presence and "much higher level of sophistication" were "very significant." Mandel believed that "at a minimum, her attitude towards things such as customs was at least cavalier. I'm referring to different things; that she was traveling back and forth, buying and selling, like conch pearls, for example. One of the things revealed through the case was that she was smuggling pre-Columbian pottery out of Peru when they were there. If you will, it's a kind of world that you don't get exposed to too much in South Dakota."

Susan was billed as the government's star witness, the one "outsider" who had visited for consecutive summers, had attended dozens of excavations and trade shows, had traveled around the world on our excursions. She had been to Lyle Heath's land, to Sharkey Williams's, had been to the site of the multiple-identity lobster, had dug ammonites and turtles and *Triceratops*. For Heaven's sake, she had discovered Sue.

Because of all of this exposure to our company, and to me, Susan was hauled in front of the grand jury on numerous occasions. An extremely independent woman, she has never liked discussing her personal arrangements with anyone, and certainly these repeated trips to South Dakota—and the associated distancing from our company—upset her tremendously. The government was so intent upon gaining evidence of our impropriety from her that they gave her extensive "transactional" immunity to testify against us, hoping she would say that we participated in a string of illegal activities.

Susan would attempt to explain and defend her own actions. For example, "Two or three times coming through customs, my luggage had been gone through and I had nuggets and pearls and amber and I had not declared them, and that was fine with them. They were not taxable items and from that I was assuming that you don't need to declare things that are nontaxable." Although her testimony was personally revealing, Duffy had no reason to object. "The judge was waiting for an objection," Duffy explained, but since Susan had not implicated me, he sat silent. Susan was not on trial, and her immunity completely protected her against criminal prosecution, so Duffy felt it was unecessary to guard her reputation.

Finally, the judge himself stopped the music. Battey called the first of two lengthy bench conferences out of the hearing of the jury. He told the attorneys that he was very concerned whether this kind of self-revelation was admissable—because what Susan was saying did not reflect upon us. Mandel argued that she and I had spent a great deal of time together, and her "knowledge will ultimately go to things that were conveyed to him."

The judge asked, "Knowledge of this witness, but how does that project knowledge of the defendant? . . . I realize she could be found by the jury to be a coconspirator, which may make her testimony admissible. [But] she hasn't been charged with an offense; she hasn't been convicted of that offense. . . . I don't see at this point in this witness's testimony how you have connected the defendant in any way. Do you have evidence that this witness will testify that she discussed with one of the defendants the fact that if fossils are duty free, you don't have to put the value on the customs form?" Mandel said no.

Later in Susan's testimony, Mandel had just begun an inquiry into a piece of pottery Susan said she had included in one of our Peruvian shipments, when Battey stopped him again. In the second bench conference, Mandel explained that he believed I knew Susan was doing something wrong—but Battey excluded the evidence, temporarily, because of a rule that says I *first* would have to deny knowing. He referred to *United States v. Jenkins,* where the prosecution was allowed to enter such evidence *after* the accused took the stand. "When the defendant took the stand in that case, the Court permitted the government to go forward in the face of his flat denial. There's been no flat denial here."

Therefore, regarding the pottery and other evidence, he told Mandel, "You may have to return to that on rebuttal."

Rebuttal comes after the prosecution and the defense have presented their cases. It is the chance for the prosecution to "answer" what the defense put forward. As I understood it, the judge's ruling meant that, after I had testified, Mandel could reintroduce the issue of Peru. Susan would be called again, even more testimony would be elicited from her, and the parade of Peruvians would take the stand.

But there was more. Near the town where we stayed in Peru, a famous pre-Incan graveyard had been looted for generations. With complete disrespect, corpses had been forcibly removed from sandy graves, their mummified limbs pulled away to free textiles—which were brazenly sold on street corners to tourists. The site was a frequent destination for visiting scientists, a site the graveyard's *commandancia* guardians invited us to tour during their nightly rounds. We went to this gruesome place with the natural history museum's director and the government escort out of scientific curiosity. Susan, as was her habit, shot a videotape of our visit. It showed broken pottery and textile remnants scattered among body parts. Human hair blew in the breeze. It was horrifying.

Despite our informal explanations about the tape, the prosecution wanted to show it to the jury—but in the bench conference, the judge specifically withheld it under the same rule as the pottery issue. I would have to testify first. The eerie tape was obviously prejudicial, because it would use the horror of the scene to imply that *we* were looting the graveyard. Despite the fact that I never removed a single artifact from either the graveyard or the country, and the tape did not show otherwise, there was no way to counteract its macabre overtones. Without witnesses to confirm that I had not participated in the desecration of graves, it would not take a rocket scientist to make a damaging link to Susan's pottery, or even worse, the possibility that I had stolen artifacts from Peru. I was devastated. I remember putting my head down in Duffy's office, crying like a baby, inconsolable. "How can I fight this?" I asked.

Duffy and I agreed that the emotion of Susan's tape was impossible to counteract with logic, facts, dates, history, common practice, or my story. That tape would be the last thing the jury would have seen before closing arguments.

We agreed that I should not testify. I simply could not provide the first link for the government's chain of implications about permits, export papers, and smuggling that would wrap itself around my neck. In my heart, I believe I could have testified anyway, if even one Peruvian supporter had come, especially the museum director who could defend my visit to the graves. But without him I could not even entertain the idea. It was a no-win situation. The tape would not be shown, but I could not testify about taking money into Peru or writing the wrong number in my field notes or conversations with Sharkey Williams or why I knew we were okay at the Funny Rock site. I could not talk about fossil regulations and invertebrate collecting practices and my intentions to forever save our crinoids. I could not even save myself.

The whole Peruvian situation blew our case into the stratosphere. We could wrap our minds around incorrect map coordinates, or missing a property boundary. We could understand how a conversation might go wrong. But when it came down to allegedly entering a foreign country after secretly sneaking money out of the United States, then tiptoeing into the wrong office to bribe someone to forge permits, then mislabeling crates of material containing hidden human artifacts ripped from the decaying bodies of Incan ancestors—*that* was somebody else's case. *That* was what Indiana Jones did while dodging boulders and poisoned darts. While being shot at by the Shining Path.

That was not my life.

(9)

The Verdict

"Let the jury consider their verdict," the King said, for about the twentieth time that day.

"No, no!" said the Queen. "Sentence first, verdict afterwards."[1]

Once the government concluded its case against us, Duffy recommended we follow the famous lead of Gerry Spence and not present a defense at all—simply declare that the government had not proved its case, dramatically proclaim, "The defense rests!" and sit down. The indictment was so far-reaching, its goal dizzyingly high—in total, the 39 counts added up to a potential of 153 convictions, if all parties were convicted on all charges. Duffy believed the government had failed to meet its burden of successfully navigating the mind-boggling number of details, and our refusal to stoop to their level would be a statement of its failure. When I contemplated the case as a whole, it felt like a shotgun blast; it was impossible to know which pellets had done damage, what witnesses to call, what misperceptions to correct.

Regardless of the case's daunting scope and my own constraints, Neal, Bob, Terry, and Ed Cole had every right to testify, every right to defend themselves. Neal in particular was inspired and impassioned. At first, the jury members' notebooks included smiley faces or jokes about Neal's love of paleontology and God, but soon they realized his exuberance and straightforwardness were for real. Ellison prepared Neal well, and Neal had taken notes on the most important things for him to remember while on the stand. After being asked each question, he referred to a small notebook he carried up to the witness stand with him. Finally,

Zuercher and the judge both asked to see what he was looking at. They made no comment as they returned the jotted lines that Neal said made all the difference:

> Slow Down
> Don't Ramble
> Focus
> Be Strong—Trust God
> Be patient and humble
> Listen to the Question
> Tell the truth
> Tell only what you know, No speculation
> Answer briefly and to the Point
> Think
> Take a breath

After we did say, "the defense rests," both sides were allowed only three hours each for closing arguments. While Mandel's task was to summarize the government's evidence supporting the 39 counts, our five lawyers had to split the same time allotment among six defendants and 153 charges. None of our lawyers was able to finish his arguments suitably within his slice of the time. Perry Mason was never asked to sit down in the middle of closing arguments.

The jury deliberated over more than two weeks of sleepless nights. They were provided with a stack of jury instructions that had been fought over by attorneys, but reflected the judge's wisdom on how to apply the law to the task of judgment. The jury's diligence in attempting to use the judge's instructions as a model for their decisions was evidenced by questions they submitted for clarification. For example, hospital employee Robert English wrote that there was confusion regarding instruction #17, and asked, "If a defendant did not know the lands they were taking fossils from were [government] owned, how could he knowingly and willfully steal?" That prevailing instruction stated that while the government had to prove beyond a reasonable doubt that we "voluntarily, intentionally, and knowingly did retain stolen property," it was "not necessary to prove that a defendant knew that the government owned the property." Battey's "clarification" to English said we were guilty if "an act [was] done knowingly," however, "the government is not required to prove that a defendant knew that his acts or omissions were unlawful." Go figure.

After the long-awaited call arrived, after I dressed in my court clothes, after we made the familiarly urgent drive to Rapid City, we defendants took our places next to our pack of lawyers at the long table for the last time. The jury filed in, studying the floor and looking as if they'd rather be anywhere but this courtroom. I stared at them, wanting reassuring nods, or maybe a secret note that read, "Everything's fine!" Instead, during the interminable moments before Judge Battey received the verdicts, I sat hardly breathing, throttled by a heart-stopping mixture of trepidation and hope. I wanted time to stop before he read one word—yet I wanted the moment to be over. The part I dreaded was living through the moment itself. When the judge finally did leaf through the multipage document—slowly, silently—a shadow passed across his face. I took one gulping breath; if he was unhappy, that looked good for us.

He began reading, not guilty, not guilty, not guilty. More breathing as I felt my stomach muscles relax. The first time he said, "guilty," my eyes shot to Duffy. "We can handle that," he whispered. And that felt right; the big charges—theft, conspiracy, money laundering—were falling away. Compared to them, the misdemeanors felt like mosquito bites, and the reporting convictions aroused incredulity more than dread. We were going to be okay.

In interviews jurors later would reveal that Duffy's "Fox" was the primary engine driving toward convictions, and that on several votes, the tally was 11–1 for acquittal; several stated they would have preferred to have convicted on nothing at all.[2] Because of this polarity, many counts were never resolved, and when the verdict form was turned in, nearly half the spaces remained unmarked. Thankfully, the list of convictions was much shorter than the list of charges.

Pat Duffy's cigar
raised many
eyebrows.

Only one "big" felony resulted from *retaining* a fossil—the purchased catfish. That conviction was not ascribed to any individual, but to our company, which also shared two other misdemeanors: Buffalo Gap National Grasslands and retaining the crinoids. This was it: one felony and two misdemeanors for the company; one misdemeanor for Neal; nothing for Bob once his reporting convictions were vacated; nothing for Terry; Ed Cole's charge would not be decided by the hung jury, and eventually would be dropped. I ended up with my two reporting felonies, and two misdemeanors. Eight convictions.

When we left the courthouse after the verdict, Pat Duffy emerged smoking a big celebratory cigar—and his picture ended up on page one in an article that hollered, "Verdict victory for fossil hunters." I have no doubt his demeanor illustrated to the newspapers that we had "won," despite our convictions. Duffy was heavily criticized for the cigar, but I loved it. We *had* won: there still was a place for us in paleontology.

Before and After

According to our lawyers, jury members are supposed to agree, but not to compromise their beliefs. The idea is for a juror to change his mind only if he has been convinced—not because he's

We the Jury

Soon after the verdict, the news cameras, and the emotional avalanche that followed, I knew it was time to talk with the jury. Its members seemed protected behind an invisible barrier, a moat that insulated them from other people associated with the case. I wondered if it was polite to intrude.

Although still raw from the trial and deliberation process, almost all the jurors were eager for conversation, some for absolution. Several seemed to take solace in the fact that they could speak their hearts to someone who was not a defendant, but still close enough to feel like one. They had seen me taking notes each day and made bets on my identity. Only three jurors were not ready to talk, and one of those was the Fox in the henhouse.

Those who were ready sounded like unsuspecting participants strapped into sparring helmets and thrown in a boxing ring. Grief, uncertainty, amazement, anger, and lots of second thoughts. As discussions progressed, many wanted to blurt out apologies to "the guys." Then they wanted to cross the moat, visit the museum, shake hands, cry—and several eventually did. It was a most unexpected response. They talked about how difficult their charge had been, how overwhelming, frustrating. They talked about arguments in the deliberation room, about their bouts with the Fox.

I learned some things I could not repeat. I learned that legal cases are not clean and orderly, that they are not dictated by the clear rules and regulations of our imaginations. Legal cases are simply escalated human interactions, fraught with all the humanity we find in a barroom brawl, airbrushed with a facade of respectability and decorum. In the deliberation room, pictures were drawn, bad jokes were made, and tempers were lost. It was the locker room, the bunker, the ring.

The jury judged the evidence and the personalities behind

it—but not just the defendants'. They found Battey "obsti-
nate,"[3] Duffy "theatrical,"[4] Ellison "smooth,"[5] and
Zuercher a "zealot."[6] "Mandel was very professional about
it," commented Richard Cordell, a sawmill supervisor. "But
he needed Zuercher's little mean streak or orneriness."
Their favorite witness was Marion Zenker, who endeared
them when she said, "I don't *do* digs"—and when she
exclaimed to Zuercher, "Oh, for heaven's sakes, David, of
course not!"[7]

"It's terrible to say someone's personality has anything
to do with it, but I really didn't like Zuercher," jury alternate Melinda Wyatt said. "He acted like he *built* the Ivory
Tower. When was that happy, happy day, when he didn't
talk at all?"

Marion Zenker, the jury's favorite witness and the woman who holds down
the institute fort. Photo by Peter Larson.

tired of arguing. It takes fortitude. In discussions following the
trial, jurors in our case shared all kinds of details about the deliberation process, including compromises on convictions they did
not want to make.[8] They said they did this not only to relieve the
pressure of the 11–1 votes,[9] but also, surprisingly, because they

thought the judge would "throw out their verdict" if it came back as a total acquittal. They believed we would be retried if the jury found us innocent on all counts.[10]

Experts on both sides of the case expressed frustration and even contempt at the jury's verdicts, but for different reasons. The prosecution wanted fewer hung counts and more convictions; our lawyers wanted jurors to stick to their guns and hold out for acquittal. For some reason, even though jurors convicted me when they didn't want to, I did not feel animosity. I empathized that there is no jury education course to explain the rules before one takes one's place in the sacred jury box. It actually made sense to me when LaNice Archer said, "I wished the guys could have come in with no lawyers and no judge. We just wanted to talk to them."[11] That seemed more immediate than the magnetic board and disjointed testimony from more than one hundred witnesses.

I also felt vindicated when jurors expressed the same frustration with the judge's instructions that we had experienced. They said the only jury "manual" they had received often clashed with logic and made their task untenable.[12] As an example, one juror said that even the Fox did not believe the conspiracy charge had been proved, but her reading of the instructions made her believe she had no choice but to convict on it.[13] "The instructions were much like reading the Bible," Archer said. "They contradicted themselves down the line."[14] Lucinda Fortin said it more forcefully: "They should have been thrown in the trash by us, those instructions that he gave us. They should have been thrown in the trash."[15]

After the verdict, Judge Battey again had the floor. The law provided him various flamingoes with which to dispatch the jurors' "hung" counts—one of which was the option to acquit us on those charges. Not surprisingly, he did not make that choice, instead allowing the government thirty days to decide whether to recharge and retry us. His ruling stated that if the government decided *not* to retry, he would make a further decision of declaring the most pro-prosecution ruling of mistrial on those counts: "without prejudice," which means that the counts would remain "available" for further legal action. In an April 25 *Rapid City Journal* article detailing the judge's decision, one of Battey's legal rules of thumb was reported from the pages of the ruling itself: "The bottom line is that a reasonable jury could have found the defendants guilty on all of those charges upon which they were unable to agree."[16]

The threat of a retrial threw juror Lucinda Fortin into a frenzy. "I have a feeling the way Battey talked to us in court, he's going to overturn this," she worried. "He said, 'You know, I can override this.'"[17] Juror LaNice Archer spoke to the newspaper, expressing her disappointment in the judge's decision, and saying, "I really had faith he would make this all go away." She also confirmed that most of the undecided charges had come down to the frustrating 11–1 vote; a few had been 10–2.[18]

Fortin, Archer, and others in the jury took personally the judge's standard for evaluating his decision—and interpreted his "bottom line" comment to mean that in his eyes the jury had been "unreasonable." Archer told the *Journal*, "'Reasonable' to me was not spending millions of dollars on a glorified trespassing case."[19]

To defend the jury's honor, intentions, and integrity—and, according to Archer, to publically apologize to us—Fortin spearheaded an unprecedented press conference which six jurors and alternate juror Melinda Wyatt attended, with the permission of two other jurors to "speak for them." The judge later accused us of staging this press event, which of course we did not. "We are the government!" Fortin said to the assembled press. "We are the ones that decide whether they are guilty or not guilty."

By then these jurors had not only read the judge's "sentence" on their sentence, but also had boned up on articles they had not read while in trial. They also had been informed that a judge's instructions are not the end-all for jurors—for example, they interpreted this to mean they did not "have to" disregard my traveler's checks stamps. In fact, in the press conference, jurors referred to what they called the jury duty pamphlet, published by the State Bar of South Dakota. "'The juror's verdict must be based only on the evidence presented in court and the individual jurors' evaluation of it,'" Wyatt read from the document. "Why aren't they told this? These people were not informed they could make decisions of conscience." When speaking out in public, these jury panelists said they had felt pushed in their verdicts—by the Fox and by the Judge. In a forum much more public than their conversations with Kristin, they admitted they had compromised.[20]

Roxanne Finck was a nursing assistant married to a farmer. "I think if we would have been better informed, I know I would have never given in on any of the counts that I gave on. I would have never, ever. I wouldn't have convicted on anything. And I've got to live with myself now, knowing that I gave."

LaNice Archer agreed: "I feel the same way, and I was one of the most skeptical." Archer was a preschool teacher, a straight-shooting woman who spoke her mind. "One person should not be able to take over a decision from eleven other people, eleven other reasonable people."

"I second that," said Jo Yates, who had taken a lead in facing down the Fox in the deliberation room, according to many jurors. "One person with a case of tunnel vision should not be able to send these people who we feel are innocent to jail, or financially bankrupt them, or cause terrible stress in their lives. Now, with a majority rule, these people would be free today. And that's the way it ought to be."

The young Cindi Fortin pulled no punches. She described that in trying to convince the Fox—who admitted to them all that her family was acquainted with the judge[21]—the other eleven jurors would search through the evidence books for something to "prove" we were innocent of an act the Fox was "assuming" we had committed. "It's not for a jury, it wasn't for us to dig through the evidence and say, 'This says [they're not guilty].' It wasn't our job; it was the government's job to prove that they *were* guilty."

"We just couldn't budge that person," lamented Richard Cordell.[22]

"Not one time did a witness say, 'These guys intentionally went on this land, knowing they weren't supposed to be there.' Not one, out of ninety-some witnesses," Archer claimed. "How could we?" Then she mentioned another juror, a rancher and the second alternate. "I don't think he'd mind, he made the comment in front of all of us here. If he would have been on the jury, he would have acquitted all the way down the line."

"It was overkill, government overkill," Archer believed. "At first, I thought this must be the biggest conspiracy since John Gotti. After the opening statement, I thought, 'My Lord, this is awful.' I thought, 'This can't be about fossils on public lands!'" After waiting for the boom to drop, hearing none, and sitting "in shock" when the prosecution rested, Archer and others believed the government had not proved its case. In attempting to execute their duty in the deliberation room, "A lot of what we were doing was damage control," Archer said.

When they were hung, they were told to continue to deliberate. Some admitted they then gave in on items they believed were minor.[23] For example, Archer and UPS employee Phyllis Parkhurst thought all the convictions had been misdemeanors, something they were not supposed to consider. "Even though we were instructed that way, if I had thought they carried heavy sentences, I wouldn't have. . . . It was wrong of us."

Afterward, some of the jurors said they were having trouble sleeping. "I feel bad about a lot of things," confessed Parkhurst. "I look back on it and I think, why, why did I do that, or why did I give up? When you know something, when you feel something, and you don't go with your instincts . . . you know afterwards you made that wrong decision . . . and you feel bad."

Enduring the waiting period—during which the government decided whether it was going to put us, our community, the jury pool, and the field of paleontology through another trial—was excruciating. On May 23, more than two months after the March

14 verdict, Mandel notified the judge that our case was over. We will never know if the press conference had an impact on the U.S. Attorney's office, but I can imagine the idea of retrying us was nearly as ghastly to them as it was to us.

We were exhausted. For the rest of 1995 we limped through our days, gradually finding our old reservoirs of strength, knowing there was more croquet in our futures. Neal and I still faced sentencing. On TV it seems a judge sentences immediately after a trial ends. Not so for us. We didn't know it then, but another year would pass while the government machine lumbered ahead with a presentencing report that took months to compile. I felt I was living on borrowed time. Except for the bags under my eyes and the permanent knot in my stomach, I suppose I seemed normal. I worked and lived as usual, although I was a felon whose case was being appealed. I hoped against hope that my convictions would be overturned before the date for sentencing was set.

Pat Duffy had lost thirty-one pounds; Neal's baby daughter Elisha had spent her first half-year in a world of emotional turmoil, angst, worry, and torment. Stan the dinosaur began his tour in Japan, to rave reviews, and we returned to the field. The next piece of science we would uncover: cannibalism at a *T. rex* site. Apparently, humans are not the only animals that turn on their own.

(10)

Time to Breathe

If anyone knew what a trilobite nose looked like, it was Leon Theisen. I guess you could say he grew up in Trilobite Country, near Sylvania, Ohio, where *Phacops rana* used to crawl in profusion at the bottom of an ancient sea. Having collected them since childhood, Leon knew every curve of the big beetles, their oval bodies striped with armored panels, their heads topped with large, multifaceted eyes and fronted by distinct noses that were textured and a little bumpy. Yes, Leon knew trilobite noses; he knew enough to tell that the tiny thing in his hand—less than a half-inch across, nearly square with angular broken edges and only about a sixteenth of an inch thick—was not one. It just looked like one.

The texture of the nose of the trilobite *Phacops* closely resembles that of theropod dinosaur eggs. Just another one of Nature's little jokes. Photo by Peter Larson.

Leon's tall frame was hunkered down on John Niemi's ranch when he brought up the issue of trilobite noses. If he had looked up, he would have been able to see both Stan's flattened hilltop and the ever-widening Duffy excavation.

"It looks sort of like a fragment of a spiny aptycus," I ventured. "But that doesn't make any sense." An aptycus is the beak of an ammonite, an extinct relative of the squid, octopus, and chambered nautilus. Since ammonites lived only in a marine environment, this fossil could not be a spiny aptycus.

The reason it took us a moment to place the fossil was that only two fragments of one had ever been found in South Dakota's Hell Creek; we simply were not used to seeing it. In fact, nearly anyone except Leon would not even have noticed it. In a sudden realization, we knew: someone had laid an *egg*. Leon had found a tiny bit of bumpy eggshell.

We scoured the area. By the time we were finished, Leon had spotted two more pieces, both in close proximity to the first. We left that spot alone for several days, hoping the wind or perhaps a rain shower would expose another fragment or two. By the time it was necessary to disturb that spot in order to excavate it, no additional eggshell fragments had been spotted. We removed the top few inches of sediment, placed the material into plastic buckets, and stored it to screen later in our laboratory.

Steven, our third *T. rex* excavation, provided welcome relief from weeks in the courtroom. Photo by Peter Larson.

Of course, since we were in the midst of a third *T. rex* excavation within a mile-long triangle, my mind automatically leaped to the possibility that this egg might have been laid by this particular dinosaur, or at least by another *T. rex*. I hoped that collecting the evidence would reveal whose egg it really was, and we dove into the matrix with a vengeance. Immediately the crew was surprised and disappointed by the quality of the bones. They were strangely broken and fragmented, and distributed among them we noticed small brown masses surrounded by perfect yellow halos—the result of the decomposition of pyrite. As we knew from Sue's saga, pyrite is no friend to *T. rex* bones. It looked as if we had found our next good mystery.

I couldn't decide what was more exciting: rare eggshell, three *T. rex*es in one area, the unique preservation of the bones, or the fact that Stan Sacrison's twin brother, Steve, had found this specimen. In the summer of 1995, he had spotted a femur weathering out; nearby were a vertebra and a rib and an unidentified bone. The specimen, which we had, predictably, named Steven, was even higher in the sediment than Duffy—perhaps within fifteen or twenty feet of the K-T Boundary. Like us, he had hovered near extinction; Steven was the perfect creature to rejuvenate us after the trial.

Evidence seemed to be piling up that *T. rex*es were relatively common in the Hell Creek Formation. Three significant specimens, Barnum Brown's, were found between 1900 and 1906. Forty years passed before the next one, then twenty years, then thirteen. In 1988 only eleven *Tyrannosaurus rex* specimens were known. But in the decade since Sue's discovery in 1990 that number tripled. Perhaps the increased frequency of specimens reflected a new interest in looking for them. Just one dinosaur takes a lot of work and money, often years of excavation and preparation; to obtain a representative sample of any species means a great commitment of time and resources. The more people are looking, the more specimens will be found, and the accuracy of paleontology's view of the ancient world will increase.

Even in an ideal habitat, *T. rex*es, as large carnivores at the top of the food chain, would have been rare compared to herding

The Shell Game

Although Leon Theisen would later be involved in the discovery of only the third *T. rex* ever found in Wyoming, his discovery of rare eggshell fragments at a *T. rex* site was potentially more scientifically important. Why were these eggshell fragments so rare? It seems unlikely that dinosaurs packed their bags and migrated hundreds of miles out of the Hell Creek Formation to lay their eggs. A more probable explanation was proposed by Denver Museum's Ken Carpenter, who theorized that any buried eggshells would be dissolved shortly after.[1] He postulated that the Hell Creek Formation's sediments contained acids derived from the decomposition of abundant plant remains. A highly acidic chemistry would spell disaster for the preservation of eggshells, since calcium carbonate is readily soluble in acid. At Steven's site, we found evidence of sulfuric acid: pyrite halos. The halos, and concomitant acid, resulted when the mineral decomposed and combined with water.

If 99 percent of the Hell Creek's eggshells have dissolved, why were these particular fragments spared? Especially considering the jumbled, crushed status of Steven's skeleton, spe-

herbivores like duckbills or *Triceratops*. At any given time during their reign, there couldn't have been more than a few thousand adults living in western North America. Finding three individuals within a hundred square miles was one thing; finding them within *one* square mile, within a few vertical feet of sediments, was another altogether. What else was at work here besides statistics?

If *Tyrannosaurus rex* was a territorial animal, perhaps what came to be the Niemi and Clanton ranches was prime hunting ground 65 million years ago. The preservation of an ancient streambed meant running water, and therefore places where animals came to drink. Fortunately the stream also carried sediments which could quickly cover and preserve carcasses, so animals dying cial factors must have contributed to their preservation. Specifically, something apparently protected the fragments until they became tightly locked in siltstone, and therefore sealed against the acid. My guess: Steven's bones had buffered the eggshell fragments. For that to happen, either his body had fallen on someone else's eggs, or (more likely) these were Steven's *own* eggs, perhaps preserved within the oviducts—in which case we'd better start calling him Stephanie.

Looking at the broken edges of Steven's eggshells, we could see waves of a radial crystalline structure known as ratite morphology—the same form found in modern bird eggs and eggshell associated with theropod embryos.[2] Because the fragments were nearly flat, it was clear they came from a large egg. Once under the microscope, the shell surfaces revealed not only raised bumps or spines, but also the perforations through which the developing embryo breathed. Following the template of both crocodilian and bird eggs, the exchange of oxygen and carbon dioxide takes place through the pores of the shell. As the embryo matures, exhaled carbon dioxide forms weak carbonic acid that slowly degrades the shell, making it progressively weaker and thinner for successful hatching.[3] I could imagine Steven's babies breaking through these thin-shelled fragments.

here had a better than average chance of being preserved as fossils. And if they were territorial, would that territory be handed down to succeeding generations? Were Stan, Duffy, and Steven *family*?

Even more pressing than questions about Steven's genealogy was something more immediate: What in the world had *happened* to him? Steven's matrix was an unusual, very loose sand, jumbled together with a friable siltstone. The whole unit seemed to have been subjected to some sort of turbulence, perhaps from a raucously flowing stream. But as we dug back into the sediment, we found that many bones were broken, some so fragmentary they could not even be identified. I love the word for the possibility this suggested: "bioturbation," the action of many large trampling

Steven's bones showed signs of cannibalism. The vertebra at lower right used to have pointy spines that held the T-bone and tenderloin steaks. Photo by Peter Larson.

feet. Did a family of *Triceratops* make *T. rex* wine with Steven's carcass, stomp, stomp, stomp? Eventually, we located one vertebra centrum (the round part) and several pieces of others, many of them extremely fragile and poorly preserved. When we got a closer look, we saw that nearly all of the vertebrae—at least six in all—were cut apart and lacked nearly *all* of their spines. The spines were not just broken off the central masses; they were gone! This helped focus the question: Who ate Steven?

The idea that someone else had stopped to dine on Steven's carcass was not new; we had found plenty of broken-off teeth from various dinosaur species in many excavations, and took it for granted that scavenging occurred. From the look of some specimens, including Sue, we also took for granted that *T. rex*es fought with one another. Perhaps territorial skirmishes resulted in injuries that left permanent scars on Sue's bones, such as the one on a partially healed rib. Although a large callus of cancellous bone had grown over the end of the fracture, the two separated ends never reconnected. In the center of this bone, almost encapsulated by the callus, was the fragment of a *T. rex* tooth. Sue had been *bitten,* and on more than one occasion. As I discussed

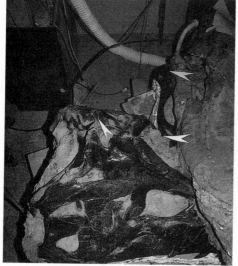

An oblique view of Sue's skull from the top right side—her nose points to the right and, at the time, still lay under her pelvis. The left arrow points to puncture wounds; the right arrows show how Sue's left lower jaw was pulled away from her face, at a right angle to her skull. Photo by Peter Larson.

Left postorbital torn and out of place

Left squamosal punctured and crushed

Left postorbital torn and out of place

How Sue's skull was positioned in the ground and reproduced on the bone map. When she fell, her jaw already had been ripped away. Illustration by Peter Larson.

before, her left postorbital "eyebrow" had been broken and left dangling below the eye. The left squamosal, the bone behind the postorbital, was also crushed, with puncture marks approximating the placement of teeth in a *T. rex* jaw. The rear of the left lower jaw was pulled out of place, while the front remained in position, causing the jaw to lay at nearly 90 degrees out of position to the skull. I believe Sue died because the left side of her face was ripped off by another *T. rex*.

Now Steven's fossil hinted that *T. rex* relations were even

When the leg of Sue's companion was snapped, his killer left tooth gouges, complete with serration marks. Photo by Ed Gerken.

darker than that. Cannibalism. I'm not talking about the "excusable" kind of cannibalism that might result when a hungry *T. rex* came upon a fallen compatriot and sneaked a quick sirloin. No, this is the kind of cannibalism that would explain the whereabouts of the missing pieces of other *T. rex* specimens found in Sue's excavation with her. Heads chopped off, legs snapped, and pass the drumstick: it was indeed a dog-eat-dog world.

> "You know," he added very gravely, "it's one of the most serious things that can possibly happen to one in a battle—to get one's head cut off."[4]

Steven's severed vertebrae appeared to provide more evidence. His vertebral spines had supported the muscles we recognize as T-bone and tenderloin steaks. In 2000 I would view another specimen that added credibility to the cannibal theory. North Dakota's first *T. rex* revealed broken and missing parts. The pattern to this specimen's damage was reminiscent of *Triceratops* skeletons we knew personally—ones that obviously had been eaten by *T. rex*. Aside from a slam-dunk clue of broken *T. rex* teeth among the *Triceratops* bones, we had identified a standard "*T. rex* dining pattern" of decimation that could be contrasted with *Nanotyrannus*'s neat-and-tidy habit of stripping meat from bones and leaving them whole. In addition, as far as we know, no other contemporaneous carnivore had the size and power to break or cut large bones besides a hungry *T. rex*.

While we all craved more of Steven's bones to prove our hypothesis, he joined the ranks of shy dinosaurs. Because of the probable cannibalism and pyrite-caused acidic environment, we found mostly scraps and a few odds and ends: the femur, vertebral chunks, some tooth fragments, what might be a skull bone, and a couple of ribs. We found less than 10 percent of Steven, a far cry from a complete dinosaur skeleton, though we had dug more than thirty feet in every direction without finding a recognizable bone. As years passed, and our crew dug further, no more of Steven appeared. Apparently he had been scattered—or swallowed—by some hungry colleagues.

In the spring of 2000 we would begin digging our most recent piece of cannibalism evidence. The same person who introduced us to Bucky, the juvenile *T. rex* with the first wishbone, also found "E.D. Cope." Bucky Derflinger—rodeo cowboy, rancher, family man, and amateur paleontologist—arrived the previous December at the institute with fragments of vertebrae and teeth, along with part of a tooth-bearing skull bone, the dentary. At first, all we could focus on was its enormous size—and how this specimen was found a mere ten miles from the mother of them all, Sue.

When we first went to visit the site, it seemed a disappointingly small outcrop, scarcely fifty feet long with only about fifteen vertical feet of exposure. One look, however, showed that the horizon was pockmarked with visible bones. When we returned in June to excavate, we quickly learned that many of them were enclosed by concretions. It was difficult to tell exactly what we had, but even so, we began to identify the telltale bitten-through vertebrae and incomplete ribs—symptoms of the Steven and North Dakota specimens. The vertebrae were cut and missing some parts, and many spines were simply gone. Hannibal Lecter had been at it again.

What he left were bones concealed within a number of punky concretions. Attempts to penetrate the masses were frustrated by the unwillingness of the rock to cleanly separate from the bone. Thus, we opted to collect the half-dozen masses, all less than three feet in greatest dimension, without knowing exactly what was inside. In mid-2001, we began the arduous task of freeing the bones from the rock—and we received a rather pleasant surprise. We had collected quite a bit of the skull, including a maxilla approximately Sue's size. Once freed completely from the matrix,

Bucky Derflinger sits next to what might be a historic find—a pile of lichen- and grass-covered vertebrae chunks that may have been placed by one of paleontology's most famous members: E.D. Cope. Photo by Peter Larson.

I'm sure Cope will have more surprises for us.

Cope's greatest surprise, however, took us a moment to understand. We had found an obvious stack of vertebral fragments beside and above the main mass. These chunks had not been washed together by water, had not fallen uphill. Instead, they had been *placed* on top of the ground millions of years after this specimen had been buried, placed carefully by someone with opposable thumbs. In human terms, the stack had been there for a long time—long enough for lichen to have covered it, which takes perhaps fifty years.

Along with many other fossil collectors, we habitually mark discoveries by piling rocks or sometimes loose bone fragments as a marker to help us relocate a site. This, I thought, must have been a previously located fossil. The moment I put two and two together—the passage of time and the location—I suddenly was struck between the eyes with a bolt of history.

In 1883 Edward Drinker Cope, the Bone War champion, had attempted to describe the first bones of *Tyrannosaurus rex.* The description focused on one of two neck vertebrae from the "south side of the Moreau River in South Dakota." This, South Dakota's *first T. rex,* was the *Manospondylus gigus* that lost its name to *Tyrannosaurus rex,* and still remains at the American Museum in New York. I held my breath. Could this pile mark the *same specimen?*

With Derflinger's blessing and a little bit of whimsy, we dubbed the new specimen E.D. Cope. To find out if there is any possibility that this dinosaur might actually be "the one," I'll need to compare trace elements from the site with Cope's original vertebra. It ranks as one of my most anticipated bits of research ever. If they match, we can be pretty sure they're the same. In that event, the rules of nomenclature may put the name *Tyrannosaurus rex* in danger. As unimaginative as *Monospondylus gigas* is, it was there first—and would take precedence. On second thought, maybe I'm not so eager to do this research.

Pronouncing Sentence

We were accustomed to the interminable drive to court. One year before, the trial had taken place in January and February, winter in South Dakota, with a late morning sun and an early moon. We had driven to and fro in the dark. In the chill of the morning, in my dented, rusty Datsun pickup, I rattled down the mountain and onto the prairie once again, feeling foreign in my professor's outfit. The half hour was at the same time unbearably long and unbearably short, with my mind racing over innumerable fragmented thoughts, but my body too exhausted to participate.

In the time that passed from our convictions to sentencing, the government laboriously prepared a lengthy report that was intended to assist the judge in choosing the correct sentence. We were asked everything from how our finances were arranged to how many dependents we had. Our children were interviewed, presumably to determine how we treated them, and how their lives were affected by our presence—and, horribly, how they might be affected by our absence. In the report, the government recommended significant jail time and fines.

Duffy's presentencing motions emphasized that even considering federal sentencing guidelines, because of my clean legal history, I should receive only probation. He listed all the figures and

translations of them, and came down to the least-offensive category: 0–6 months. I preferred zero.

Unwilling to believe that Judge Richard Battey would sentence
us fairly, we tried one last time to remove him from the case. We
had good reason to think he might step down: in our last attempt,
the appeals court had written, "precedent supports sentencing by
a different judge." In this motion, Duffy repeated his litany of
examples of Battey's perceived bias, and added, "Had Shakespeare
written the treatment for the screenplay that made up this case, he
might have titled it 'Much Ado About Nothing.'"

We lost again; Battey would preside over us twice more, at our
sentencing hearing on January 16, 1996, and at the actual sentencing a week later, on January 22. At the hearing, Mandel again
pulled Peru out of his bag of tricks. This time we were ready.

At first glace, the conviction seemed quite simple: I had not
completed a Customs form when I carried money out of the
United States in order to work in Peru. However, I also had been
accused—but not convicted—of a conspiracy, which in this
instance included forging permits and smuggling fossils. I soon
learned from Duffy if the government could convince the judge
that we had broken laws in Peru, it would provide ammunition for
a higher sentence.

Dr. Alberto Armas, an attorney who said he advised Peru's
Minister of Education, testified that Peruvian law 24047 forbade
my excavating and removing fossils from his country. Duffy cross-
examined him, asking whether this law made specific mention of
paleontological objects. Armas did not answer directly; in tangled
English, he instead mentioned a mysterious "resolution" and
Peru's constitution. In two further forays, Duffy attempted to elicit
the simple answer to his question:

> DUFFY: But my question is: the constitution does
>   not specifically mention paleontological objects,
>   does it?
> ARMAS: But it mentions public goods protected by
>   the state that also as which has been declared in
>   24047.

This apparently meant, no, it does not mention paleontological objects.

> DUFFY: 24047 makes no specific reference to pale-
> ontological objects, correct?
>
> ARMAS: When you make that question and you do
> not relate it to 24047, you could create an interpre-
> tation creating a completely different form in law.
> It would not be the truth and just because the law
> 24047 creates or speaks from posteriorly exactly to
> the obligation of Peru in reference to the conven-
> tion of in which it deals with, with very specific
> form, those that we refer to. I can read this again.

Duffy finally tried to make the point that the first specifically paleontological regulation in Peru was number 85, which post-dated our permits there.

> ARMAS: No, that is not true. In the constitution
> there has been established different levels of laws
> and determinations which is their hierarchy in
> Peru so that no disposition of this hierarchy
> could be without — could be farther than —
> could be outside the laws which are established.
> Also as well as including the patrimony of Peru.

Alice said very politely . . . "I'm afraid I can't quite follow it as you say it."

"That's nothing to what I could say if I chose," the Duchess replied, in a pleased tone.[5]

It was on Armas's testimony that the judge's determination of my behavior would hang. So far, he hadn't said anything as far as I could tell, and Duffy would write in one of our filings, "This Monty Pythonish testimony is unadulterated nonsense: no matter how many times one reads [Dr. Armas's] opinions, they remain virtually unintelligible."

Armas nonetheless soldiered on, also listing people who "fall under the category of public defamation," and who would be tried in Peruvian court. The list included those Peruvians we had worked with for so many years—especially those museum officials who had legally provided us with permits—and Kirby Siber, and me. The two of us would be tried in absentia. Although he held in his hands our eleven permits, signed and sealed by the National Institute of Culture and the director of the Museum of Natural History, Armas alleged we had in fact broken the law and that Peru's equivalent to the U.S. Attorney "has confidence they will indeed be found guilty."

Despite any personal danger he may have faced, one Peruvian witness came to our aid, Dr. Geraldo Lamas. We had no money to buy his plane ticket, but thankfully, Neal and I had frequent flier miles that he could use. While no longer director of the Museum of Natural History at Lima, Lamas was still employed there, as well as being a professor of biological science at the State University of San Marcos. Lamas also had been awarded a postdoctoral fellowship from the Smithsonian Institution.

He testified that the first permit his country had provided us was the first of its kind, and therefore it had caused quite a series of discussions among Peru's cultural ministers. At the time, the museum director—the one whose life had been threatened—had consulted with the head of the National Institute of Culture—Dr. Santisteban, "who is by Peruvian law in charge of everything related to national culture in Peru." Neither saw a problem with the permit and they cosigned it. Lamas asked a question: "If Dr. Santisteban, the head of the institution in charge of national culture in Peru, did not know the law, according to what Mr. Armas said before, how were we of the museum, how was Peter Larson going to know if there was something illegal?"

Further, not only had Lamas never received a fee for issuing permits he was "convinced . . . were legal," but also he said previous to directorate number 85, there was "absolutely no interest in protecting the paleontological remains in Peru." None of our permits postdated 85. Lamas had been director of the museum when 85 came into effect, and as the director, the government assigned him to head a committee whose intention was to create a law protecting fossils. Not only was this déjà vu for me, recalling my NAS days, but also it meant that Lamas, of anyone in the room, had been on the cutting edge of paleo law in Peru.

I wonder what the jurors would have thought if they had heard these two witnesses. This time, I hoped we had done enough—especially considering the judge's refusal to allow any character witnesses to testify on my behalf.

On January 22, I remembered dressing to go to court a year before, on the day the jury's verdict was expected. Not knowing what would happen, Kristin helped me empty my pockets. We said nothing. She put a clean handkerchief in my vest, put my wallet in her bag, and left all the usual junk that fills a man's pockets on my dresser top. Just in case I wouldn't be coming home. On this day we went through the same routine.

We all had weathered so much since the case began. I was used to my reception at the annual SVP symposia. Even though I was their standard-bearer for contention, I presented scientific papers. Outside the official talks, I spoke about the importance of com-mercialism and working together. Often I felt like a curiosity, a reluctant member of the circus. The Elephant Man. I faced hostile eyes and intrusive questions, and over those last few years of stress, I ceased to recognize myself.

In the videotapes of Sue's discovery and excavation, I saw a wiry, thin young man, with wild hair, a cowboy mustache, and vibrant energy. As time passed I remained upright through brute force of will, but my eyes were tired, my skin chalky; the weight around my middle was the bloating of tension, not the happy result of too much food. My arthritis hurt and the nerve dysfunc-tion in my right arm shook my hand more each day. Many days I could not eat. I felt that to survive, my only choice was to stare down those who judged me wrongly, to explain what I could, and to mentally, emotionally, and philosophically keep my momentum moving forward. Even if it moved in slow motion.

There were times before, during, and after the trial when I had so few emotional resources left that I simply could not utilize them to make normal daily decisions. What to choose from a menu, or to check for traffic before crossing the street. On certain days my misery dripped from my brow, and I could taste it on my tongue. I learned to settle a particular silence over my heart. I saw its equivalent in Neal's eyes, and Bob's. We all hid in one way or another.

The day I stood before Sue's hillside for the first time, looking up at the jackpot of paleontology, a big, bad diamond in the rough, I knew ecstasy. Pure exhilaration, absolute breath-stopping joy. Before that I had felt a deeper, saltier, gut-tugging thrill with the birth of my first three children—a biological exuberance that arrived stapled to sobering responsibility and a sense of belonging on the earth. These sensations expanded my experience, made me more of a man. Or, at least, more of a human.

Sadness also added its own texture as my age stacked higher. Regrets, errors of judgment, pain inflicted or sustained, the tolls of ignorance and absentmindedness and blindness. Sadness of the standard variety, the by-product of usual hard-won lessons all people add to their war chests. But this sadness was a walk in the park compared to the fear, grief, anger and anxiety that haunted us throughout the Big Mystery. Helplessness might have been the worst feeling of all. As in some science fiction film, we knew something was tracking us, but it was too big and shapeless to get a handle on. Before I understood the enormity of what the government was accusing us of doing, I was afraid. After the charges were spelled out in muddy, obfuscating language, I was terrified. I have no words for that final feeling as the red laser light stopped panning over all of us and settled onto my forehead.

With my faith trampled and my hopes tangled in crossed fingers, I climbed once again into the dented, rusty blue truck and rattled down the hill with my clean handkerchief and no money in my pocket. Once more, we faced Judge Battey. Neal, who had been convicted of only one misdemeanor, received two years' probation and a fine of $1,000. The company had to pay $10,000 and endure three years' probation.

Then it was my turn. I hoped Battey would take into account the hundreds of letters he acknowledged receiving on my behalf, letters encouraging him to sentence me lightly for personal and professional reasons. Although the judge admitted that no case in his experience had ever generated as many support letters, all my friends' best intentions would go unheeded. After I stood up on my crutches, Battey explained that I was the ringleader of our crazy circus, and he held me accountable for years of publicity, the leak to the papers about the plea bargain, and the jurors' press conference. Duffy had been right to worry: Battey used Armas's testimony to bootstrap my money-reporting conviction to conspiracy to do wrong in Peru.

I listened to the words that would decide the next years of my life. Twenty-four months in prison and a $5,000 fine, plus two years' probation. For two misdemeanors and two reporting felonies. No one put handcuffs on me and led me away. I was given a month to get my affairs in order, and I was told to "surrender myself" on February 22, 1996. I had the sensation that I had led an army into the jungle, and when I turned around . . . I was alone.

"Off with her head!" the Queen shouted, at the top of her voice. Nobody moved.[6]

The Gate

It is called "self-surrender" when a convicted felon is expected to turn himself in on a designated day. To me, self-surrender means lying awake in an ugly hotel room in Colorado Springs with a sense of dread that crushes your chest. It means driving the rest of the way from South Dakota to Florence, Colorado, a dismal, paint-chipped town. It means scouting for hotels for future family visits, and driving a test run—from town past the prison gate and back—to make sure you leave enough time in the schedule to arrive at 1:00 P.M. sharp. It means staring at the barbed-wire fence around the camp perimeter, watching inmates in green uniforms walking on the exercise track. It means looking across the field at the cluster of buildings housing prisoners at the next highest level of security, and blinking as the blinding, high-desert sun glints off razor wire coils. It means hugging your wife in the car with acute awareness of the smell of her hair, the impossibility of the task ahead.

Doing the Math

Federal Sentencing Guidelines were developed to ensure comparable sentences nationwide for comparable crimes. They are supposed to be foolproof. Presented in the form of a grid, a judge is supposed to be able to run his finger down a column until he gets to the proper cell in the grid, and then to trace over to a designated range of "point" values. The points are then translated into a sentence. That way, almost never can a judge's emotional responses impact the neutral aspect of sentencing. One loophole that does exist for a judge to escape the sentencing guidelines is called "relevant conduct." It is what Battey used to "diabolically move to the bad cell" in the grid, as Duffy put it.

I was convicted of two failure-to-report felonies, and two fossil misdemeanors. Duffy and I assumed the judge would run his finger down the grid to the sentencing range for failure-to-report felonies, consider the evidence that had to do with those felonies, and choose a number within the range. However, when utilizing the concept of relevant conduct, the law allows the judge to review and incorporate in his judgment *all* of the evidence in the case that spoke to charges "relevant to" the convictions. Therefore, Battey was allowed to take into consideration evidence for counts on which I

At about ten minutes to one in the afternoon, we drove through the gate of Florence's Federal Prison Camp, the minimum-security section of this federal penitentiary. With all the personality of a military barracks, in the dismal middle of nowhere, the FPC was neither summer camp nor country club. In my depleted state, my brain recorded only snapshots of information: an argument about keeping my cane; signing my induction papers. "You might want to leave your belt with her," somebody said.

The official reason for my incarceration was listed as "failure to fill out forms." The guard who led me through the procedure was acquitted, or on which the jury remained undecided. Specifically, he "convicted" me of conspiracy—which, in his mind, was "relevant" to my failure to report because the failure was followed by alleged illegal acts in Peru. Armas's testimony provided the other half of the equation that allowed Battey to place me into a different cell within the guideline grid. Instead of 0–6 months, I got 24–30.

We appealed my sentence, and lost on April 10, 1997. Even so, Judge Beam, one of the three judges on the panel, disagreed with his compatriots and wrote a dissenting opinion. He said that Judge Battey "seems to have generously exercised [his] discretion to enhance the penalties arising from the defendant's participation in relatively minor crimes." After stating that he believed my "weighty sentence" was "well above that called for given the minimal and uncertain nature of the offenses," Beam noted that Battey not only had "found, for sentencing purposes, that a conspiracy . . . existed," but also he had shown "some predisposition to find that a conspiracy did indeed exist."

Most important, Beam also acknowledged that Battey never should have been allowed to decide the sentence. Referring to the Eighth Circuit's failure to remove Battey in our earlier petitions, he wrote, "Denial of Larson's motion for recusal was reversible error." I would pay for their mistake.

looked down at that and said, "Wow. You must have really pissed somebody off."

It took nearly two weeks for the check-in process to be complete, for my paperwork to creep through the system, for me to turn my brain down even lower until it functioned at a low hum, for the names on my telephone list to be approved, and finally for me to be able to use the phone. I was told by seasoned inmates that this was a process intended to be slow, so as to sever my connection to family, friends, and the scaffolding that supports a life. By the time I made the first call home, my family said I sounded like someone else.

I cannot imagine a prison story to include very many happy vignettes, and I hesitate to relate mine here. I will say, however, that while I would not wish my experience on anyone, I tried to wring out of it whatever positive development I could. I was forced, for the first time in my life, to slow down. Despite the constriction, fear, and discomfort, I re-evaluated my life and my choices, the importance of my family and friends, and the value of love. While I could list many criticisms, instead I will share only an observation: while legislators and the public debate the possibilities of rehabilitation, this is not a reality of the prison system in my experience. It is punitive in nature and in reality, as other "white collar" inmates and I discovered when we started a lecture series.

The mix at a prison camp is of the least violent of convicts: lawyers, doctors, professionals, and often drug dealers or users who have notched down from higher security, on their way out of the system. One young scientist was there, taking a ten-year break in his AIDS research to serve a sentence linked to LSD. I was the only paleontologist; they called me "T. rex" and "the dinosaur man." Because of my friendship with another federal judge from our district, I was able to begin a lecture series. Those of us with experience in trades or professions composed talks and gave instructional classes intended to keep our own minds active and to help the listless and previously jobless to improve their lives. Some in the prison administration frowned on our efforts, and in more ways than one attempted to stop them. Last I heard, the program continues, and is actually passed down from short-timers to those with long sentences, or to those who have just arrived.

For 12 cents an hour, an inmate is employed in any number of jobs. Cooking, cleaning, grounds work, or, for me, the library. I took solace in my work, because I was able to help people get books and information on subjects that interested them, information often intended to help them start new lives on the outside. I helped the younger men learn to write resumes and to evaluate their skills. In my off hours I focused on writing the scientific portions of this book. Because our library consisted of dog-eared paperbacks left by inmates, and no one in the system had access to computers, my writing tasks were more difficult than usual.

Incoming scientific information arrived as photocopied articles or sections of books; I wrote longhand in pencil on ruled notepaper purchased at the commissary. To allow professional dialogue, I carefully edited the limited number of people on my telephone list to include scientists I wanted to call. Everyone was very patient with my fifteen-minute limit. Because of this support from the outside, I was also able to write new scientific papers on *T. rex* behavior and dinosaur respiration.

Back at the ranch, Neal, Bob, Marion, and Brenda had their hands full. Black Hills Institute was a small company, and each person performed specific, very important tasks. The loss of any key person could create a terrible vacuum. When I left for prison, the company was depleted after our years of legal struggles, placing even more stress on those left behind. We quickly learned that many jobs I traditionally did were, at first, unmanned. I had not sufficiently trained replacements in my specialty areas. Times were tough; the bank account was beyond empty; all of our employees, save Terry and Marion, were laid off; and it took the company quite a few months to overcome the stigma attached to my imprisonment. Our customers, along with the industry, watched with curiosity to see if, after all of this, we would survive. For a moment, Black Hills Institute went into hibernation.

Before I left, our board had agreed on an unusual arrangement: Kristin, with whom I would speak nearly every day, would attend weekly board meetings in my stead and submit suggestions on my behalf. I did not want to completely abandon my workmates, nor lose my lifeline to the business that had sustained me during my entire adulthood. My helping the company, while hopefully useful to it, was most useful in sustaining me. During the darkest days at the institute, as everyone assumed my share of the workload, Kristin and I created a workable system. The only problem was that many of our limited-time telephone calls consisted of her typing while I dictated. It was the closest I could come to being there, and it also provided a method through which I could carry at least a portion of my burden. It took two of us to make a fraction of one corporate president; it fell upon Neal and everyone else to make up the rest of me.

Teamwork

My mother bought me a cellular telephone for Christmas in 1995. Since we live in a rural area and travel frequently, she was concerned about emergencies. Midwestern snowstorms, late-night driving, flat tires. I doubt she had prison in mind.

After hugging Peter good-bye at the gate, I was forced to drive away while he was still hunched over his cane. Through tears, I watched him disappear from view. We had no idea what would happen, where he would go, how he would feel. We had no idea that he would be cold, that for the first few nights he would have to sleep with no blankets, that he would have to wear soft, water-soaked slippers in the snow until official footwear arrived for his swollen foot six weeks later. He could not even keep his own shoes.

During the first days after February 22, I thought only of the phone. The fact that prison families face a process very similar to the grief that accompanies death had not been explained. The fact that I had new responsibilities as Peter's stand-in had not yet taken hold. I just carried the cell phone, waiting for the first phone call that would explain how it all would work, what his schedule was, where he slept, what the rules were, how to visit. The phone, the phone. For eighteen months, until Peter was granted work release, people teased me about the phone. It went with me everywhere. It was one of those big, heavy, three-volt bag phones. It had great reception.

"How are you getting on?" said the Cat, as soon as there was mouth enough for it to speak with.

Alice waited till the eyes appeared, and then nodded. "It's no use speaking to it," she thought, "till its ears have come, or at least one of them."[7]

Once the phone call came and our routine was established, I invented for myself a new occupation. It hovered somewhere between assistant, transcriber, and partner. It included intervening in parenting issues, learning about business management, working tirelessly. The drive to Florence took nine hours, a little less in the summer, a little more during snowstorms. If the kids came with me and we stopped in civilization to go back-to-school shopping, the drive took two days. Literally, my bag was always packed. Inside were all those hats I wore, along with blank visiting forms.

I hadn't realized there was a culture that formed itself around visiting incarcerated people. I met many wives who had, for years, structured their holidays to include vending machine lunches and bathrooms with no locks on the doors. I became familiar with cardboard hamburgers and plastic burritos, dinosaur mounting ideas sketched on brown paper napkins. Scrabble as a backdrop to debates about high school problems; personal problems over cribbage.

Like an amoeba, life stretched to accommodate the new prison plan—in our case, dinosaur research coordination, doctors' updates, panics when phone calls didn't come on schedule, scientific events, worries about irrational behavior of guards, sorting through the personalities of a family business. Even so, Peter's children taught us that life did not revolve around prison, and people had girlfriends and parent-teacher conferences and tears and laughter. We learned that businesses go on without their presidents, food has to hit the table, and feet have to hit the floor each morning. We survived.

Slowly, thanks to the conscientious effort of everyone, a shift occurred. The bottom had been hit, and there was no place to go but up. Neal honed his sales abilities and brought in work. In addition, the "boys' club" that Neal, Bob, and I had formed pried open to include the ideas and strategies of Brenda and Marion. We were better for it, and the company's downward spiral reversed. One silver lining: because of telephone and physical constraints, our communication became more efficient. In a way life went on without me, and in a way it didn't.

We all wore green uniforms. We were counted several times a day. There were specific times when we could use the telephones—outgoing calls only, charged at 25 cents per minute. Sometimes the telephones would be turned off during lockdowns caused by a fight, or murder, at the higher-security facility across the compound. There were times I prayed that everyone would behave so that I would be able to use the phone. One of those times was to hear about a new dinosaur. I had witnessed the beginning of the story, in the field, but I was missing the good stuff.

Before the trial, before prison, Stan Sacrison had walked right into Rex Hall with a bone in his hand and that look in his eye. It was the fall of 1994, and, at first, I thought he'd done it yet again. But no, this was Lloyd Fox's bone. Sort of.

The Fox family, a father-and-son ranching outfit, lived on the edge of East Short Pine Hills near Redig, South Dakota. Population 5, Redig is located about thirty miles south of Buffalo and consists of a post office, a couple of trailer houses, and a few abandoned buildings. The ranch, which they were then converting from cattle to bison, contained some Hell Creek Formation—and an unfenced twenty-acre plot of Harding County land. It also contained a dinosaur. Once we drove to the site, I immediately spotted a cross-section of a vertebra, and numerous fragments that scattered down the slope; we had to step carefully. At the bottom of a wash, some relatively large fragments had accumulated. Their preservation was exquisite, and there seemed to be very little, if any, iron oxide coating or permineralization of the cell spaces. The bone itself was very sturdy, with wonderful surface texture.

Lloyd's son, Russell, pointed out a large, complete bone poking out of the embankment: a neck vertebra. A huge neck vertebra. A Sue-like neck vertebra.

I pulled from the truck our new GPS unit and recorded the position data. Russell Fox showed us the property boundaries, which I checked against our maps. The county parcel was completely surrounded by Fox territory, but indeed it appeared as if this new specimen was on that parcel. Later, the courthouse would confirm our assessment, and both Lloyd and Russell agreed to accompany me to the county commissioners in order to gain permission for an excavation. The good news: *this* was how citizens and their government were meant to interact. The bad news: this fossil didn't have several years to wait for the red tape to clear. It was critical to act as soon as possible; already I had counted more than half a dozen exposed bones, in various stages of erosion and decomposition. The vertebra was in particular danger, coming out on the edge of a small gully. We pulled out our superglue to protect what we could not yet dig.

This time, we were patient. We wanted to deliver another *T. rex,* but this dinosaur would remain nameless until it was born.

The Foxes, true to their word, kindly assisted in obtaining permission to salvage, collect and stabilize what was exposed on the surface. The commissioners left the question of final disposition of the fossil until later, but we were grateful for their willingness to work with us. Even under the cloud of indictments, landowners, our neighbors, and the local South Dakota governmental entities never withdrew their support. I'll never forget how, less than a month after the seizure, our local Pennington County Commissioners had voted to "do anything possible to help the owners of the Black Hills Institute of Geological Research . . . return the skeleton" to Hill City.[8]

To prepare this new Harding County fossil to weather the upcoming winter, we underwent an abbreviated standard procedure, mapped what was exposed, removed the vertebra—and another endangered bone from the skull—and glued and covered the rest with flat rocks. We even located tooth fragments before covering them for their winter slumber. By the fall of 1995, after the conclusion of our trial, the commissioners were still considering our proposal. We checked our patient and kissed her goodnight for another season. In the summer of 1996, our plan for removal and disposition of the specimen was approved. On August 13—six years and a day since Susan Hendrickson found Sue—our crew was on the site ready to begin the true excavation.

I stood in prison in my green uniform, making repeated phone calls, waiting impatiently for news from the dig.

The usual surface collecting, gluing, and mapping was completed quickly, but at this site, the material that had washed into the gullies had to be churned and screened—revealing a number of pieces of a large femur. The matrix was a sandy siltstone without much structure, but plenty of extra residents: a lot of freshwater gastropods and pelecypods were mixed in with turtle and crocodile bones, *Sequoia datototensis* cones, and plant debris. It appeared that the "County Rex," as we referred to the specimen, could have fallen into an oxbow lake, a water body cut off from the main stream channel. The specimen was preserved by sand and silt dumped during a flood, perhaps when a levy burst. The deposit was also markedly different from that entombing any of our other specimens: preservation was so excellent, the crew fantasized that fragments of DNA might be retrievable. At the very least, internal details would be preserved.

Excitement peaks at the Foxy Lady dig when teeth and parts of her skull start to emerge. In the foreground is her left dentary, part of the lower jaw.
Photo by Ed Gerken.

Now experts at scattered dig sites, the crew was undaunted when bones and teeth began appearing sporadically. Bones from the lower jaw, a couple of ribs, some vertebrae. Plenty of teeth. A little here, a little there. Then, on August 20 and 21, the left dentary appeared, which is the tooth-bearing element of the lower jaw, followed by a palate bone, and then the right dentary. After twenty days and six hundred square feet of excavation, twenty-five *T. rex* bones were recovered, along with a dozen shed *Nanotyrannus* teeth. Since the *T. rex* was so beautifully preserved, the idea that the well-mannered *Nanotyrannus* had fed upon this carcass was supported. Had I been present, I would have kept my eye peeled for a remnant of an ancient napkin, a petrified tooth-pick, perhaps a wine glass.

On almost the last day of the dig, Neal found the left postor-bital—the eyebrow bone that is more lumpy in a female than a male. This one was upside-down in the ground, with its telltale lump out of sight. Everyone waited with baited breath as Neal carefully turned the bone over and began cleaning the underside. Suddenly, he announced, "It's a girl!" We couldn't call her Lloyd, and we couldn't call her The Fox—we already had one of those in our lives. Thus, the name "Foxy Lady" was born.

As had become our new "standard procedure," this dig would not be completed in one season. However, even on our first pass, the crew could tell that Foxy Lady was found at the bottom of the sedimentary section, in some of the oldest Hell Creek Formation on Earth. She is the oldest-yet discovered *Tyrannosaurus rex,* per-haps a million years older than Sue, and may help show us how the species changed through time. Hers also is the first good, dis-articulated female skull. We all have our fingers crossed for Foxy Lady; earthmovers are in order before we can take our next peek at what else she may hold in store.

The Breath of Life

The world is full of synchronicities. The prison stood on marine sediments, and sometimes concretions with ammonites would weather out after a rain. A few of the inmates would catch me poking at them with my cane, or would bring me something to look at. I laughed at the implications: did this count as retention of fossils from public lands? Just to be sure, I always put them back after I had a look.

As I walked, and later ran, around our exercise track, I could see out across the rolling hills. The fences that marked my boundaries could contain my thoughts no more than the birds that flew freely in and out. I thought about Foxy Lady, about Sue and Stan and Duffy, and their relationships to these robins and turkey vultures and hawks and jays. I wondered what links in the chain had led from a creature with no wings to one that could fly. After a little research, I realized it started not with wings, and not even with feathers—but with breathing. So, while I was catching my own breath in prison, after weathering the worst period of my life, I undertook a research project focusing on dinosaur respiration.

I started with the honeycombs within *T. rex* vertebrae, which have been noted by every scientist who has written about the beast. These honeycombs are wonderfully diagnostic. It started with Osborn's illustration of Cope's original specimen and then his subsequent papers on *T. rex,* which described "deep pits," and noted that "lateral cavities (pleurocoelia) appear[ed] at the *sides* of the centra." Barnum Brown's field report on his first find read, "[The] vertebrae of lumbar-dorsal region are deeply excavated . . . [and] extremely hollow."[9]

What were these hollow spaces for? Why had they evolved? As usual, I turned to *T. rex*'s relatives. We see similar patterns in the bones of birds. Interestingly, they have been identified as part of an advanced breathing system—a system shared by no other living animals. Therefore, more than just an interesting link, perhaps this is definitive evidence of the ancestral relationship between dinosaurs and birds. If so, *T. rex*'s reputation as a cold-blooded reptile is over, once and for all.

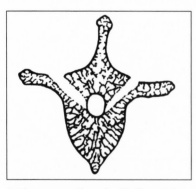

In the cross-section of a bird's vertebra, the honeycombed structure is clearly visible. It is a result of the respiratory air sacs invading the bone. Illustration by Dorothy Sigler Norton.

Birds' unique breathing system includes lungs and air sacs. Air sacs that lie next to bones may change bone shape—and at times actually invade bones like the roots of a tree penetrating a rock. Air sac tissue appears to "need" more real estate; bones give up what they don't need, leaving only a structural trestle-work of bone for support. That is why bird bones are hollow, and that is also why *T. rex* bones are hollow: they had an avian respiratory system. The "fingerprints" of this system are clear on the ribs and vertebrae of the body and neck, where surfaces are punctured by large airway openings, called

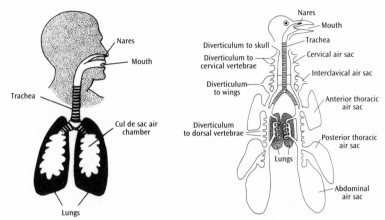

A comparison of the relatively simple mammalian breathing system (left) and the much more complex avian one (right). Illustration by Dorothy Sigler Norton.

pneumatic foramina. Inside the vertebrae are either open chambers, called camerae, or divided chambers, known as camellae, that form the familiar honeycomb structure. And on vertebral and rib surfaces, contact points are marked with walled, cuplike depressions, called fossae. In the most evolved bird species, bone invasion becomes even more extreme. The upper arm's humerus and other limb bones of many modern birds have pneumatic foramina, and thus have actually become part of the respiratory system. Remarkably, this is dramatically demonstrated by the fact that some birds can breathe through a compound fracture of the humerus if their mouth and nares (nose) are closed off.[10]

But *how* do birds breathe through their bones? And how is the avian respiratory system different from everyone else's? All mammals, reptiles, and amphibians breathe by means of a simple "cul-de-sac" respiratory system. That is to say, each of our lungs is like a balloon, open at one end. As we inhale, our chest cavities expand, allowing air to enter our lungs; carbon dioxide is exchanged for oxygen as blood passes through the lungs' capillaries. When we exhale, a portion of the spent air is forced back out through the mouth and nose. While simple, this system has one problem: we never completely empty our lungs when we exhale. Therefore, each time we inhale, oxygen-rich fresh air is mixed with the remaining carbon dioxide–laden air. In essence, we

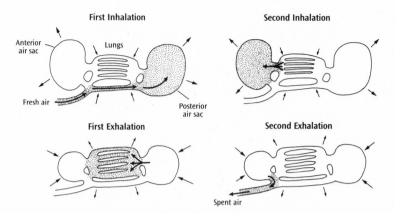

First Inhalation   Second Inhalation

Anterior
air sac   Lungs

Fresh air

Posterior
air sac

First Exhalation   Second Exhalation

Spent air

A simplified view of how air moves through a bird's air sacs and lungs. Illustration by Dorothy Sigler Norton.

are constantly "rebreathing" a portion of the spent air. We could never fly with this inefficient arrangement.

Birds improved the whole respiration idea, or, perhaps more correctly, they enjoy an improvement that was passed down to them. The hollowed-out regions of bones are not actually used to breathe, but are simply side-effects of the air-sac pumps. I think of this system like a two-cycle pump. If there were a moment when a bird could be considered to take a "first" breath, the air's passage could be traced. 1. On the way in, air flows through the mouth and nares into the first of two sets of air sacs, positioned behind the lungs. 2. On the first exhalation, that air is forced into highly vascularized lungs from the rear. While passing through the lungs, the air achieves its oxygen hand-off via blood within the lungs' capillaries—in a more efficient manner than ours, because the blood flows in the opposite direction as the air flow. 3. Then, on the second inhalation, that same air is forced out the front of the lungs and into the second set of air sacs. 4. During the second exhalation, that air, now carrying carbon dioxide, is breathed out the nares and mouth.

In this process, each time the bird inhales or exhales, fresh air passes through the lungs. This one-way track not only acts as a system of bellows continuously bathing the lungs in fresh air, but also the new air and used air don't mix with each other. The continuous supply of fresh air and oxygen, both on inhalation and exhalation, makes the avian respiratory system so efficient that birds actually have smaller lungs than comparably sized mammals.[11] But that's not all. Blood, which delivers oxygen through the body, plays a part, as well.

Reptiles are still primitive when it comes to circulation. As cold-blooded creatures, their priorities do not include maintainable speed and endurance; therefore, their equipment can support only a slow metabolic rate. The combination of a three-chambered heart and a shared system of blood vessels means that oxygen mixes with carbon dioxide in the blood. Birds' warm-bloodedness already improves circulatory efficiency thanks to their mammal-like set-up: four-chambered hearts and a double circulatory system including veins and arteries that keep oxygen and waste products separate. However, birds blow mammals out of the water with a final piece of equipment: for their size, bird hearts are one-and-a-half to two times as large as mammalian hearts.[12] They pump a relatively greater volume of blood per stroke at a higher pressure with fewer beats per minute. And if that weren't enough, their blood actually surrenders oxygen into the system more easily than mammals'. This means that a pigeon can utilize about 60 percent of its arterial oxygen, while a human can utilize only about 27 percent.[13] Avian blood is also more nutrient rich than mammalian blood. You could say that birds run on high octane fuel.

Because of the remarkable combination of respiration and circulation, birds can efficiently expend incredible amounts of energy for a prolonged period—using nearly every available molecule of oxygen. They are uniquely designed to fly, some as high as 30,000 feet,[14] an altitude at which mammals are not just comatose, but dead.

Did *T. rex* need to fly? No. But it needed to run faster than anyone else if it wanted to wear the crown of King of the Food Chain. And what did its ancestors offer as basic equipment? Probably reptilian systems—which would have *T. rex* offering its kingdom for a horse after only a few steps. As dinosaurs evolved from their reptilian ancestors, they needed more efficient biology. But did *all* dinosaurs do it? The presence of hollow spaces in some

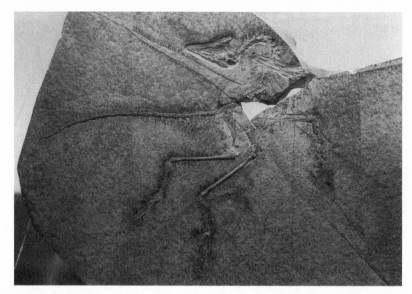

The fifth known specimen of *Archaeopteryx*, collected in the 1970s and displayed at the Jura-Museum in Eichstätt, Germany, was preserved without feathers. Had we not seen earlier feathered specimens, this creature may never have been classified as a bird. Photo by Peter Larson.

dinosaur bones indicates they had air sacs, and presumably bird-like respiratory and circulatory systems. At the very least, these dinosaurs had a high metabolic rate, which would mean they were warm-blooded.

But when we report "similarities," just how close are they? The fossil record shows the earliest known "bird" as a little fellow we call *Archaeopteryx,* whose first full skeleton was discovered in 1861. Like today's birds, *Archaeopteryx*'s ribs and body vertebrae had large pneumatic foramina and/or open chambers.[15] However, at only a little over a foot long, *Archaeopteryx* also possessed a classic theropod chassis; in fact, if the specimen had not been preserved with beautiful impressions of long, functional flight feathers on its "arms" and tail, we never would have suspected it was a bird! It would have been ranked as a meat-eating dinosaur, period.

Does *Archaeopteryx* indicate that *all* dinosaurs were giant birds without wings? Did they all have air sacs and hollow spaces in their bones? The simple answer is no.

Coelophysis, an upper Triassic New Mexico theropod from

220 million years ago, is the earliest meat-eater whose skeleton clearly shows the birds' respiratory system fingerprints—70 million years before *Archaeopteryx* took its first breath. In his 1989 monograph on *Coelophysis,* former curator at the American Museum of Natural History, Edwin H. Colbert, stated, "the parallelisms in structure between the skeleton in the coelurosaurs and the skeleton in birds are numerous and striking. . . . [The] possibility at once is raised that the highly pneumatic vertebrae of *Coelophysis* and *Coelurus* indicate the development of air sacs similar to the air sacs of modern birds." After *Coelophysis,* all theropods—and then birds—inherited the most efficient breathing system known to biology. *Tyrannosaurus rex,* the king of theropods, is no exception. Nearly every neck and body vertebra, as well as ribs attached to the neck and the spine, is perforated with numerous large pneumatic foramina, and most also have cuplike fossae. The famous honeycomb structure inside the neck and body vertebrae were multichambered pockets formed from the invasion of the respiratory system.

Predators were not the only heavy breathers. We see these same skeletal fingerprints in sauropods, long-necked dinosaurs. Some researchers have interpreted this as a means to lighten their huge skeletons.[16] While that would be a useful side-effect, might it just be that these creatures, also, needed to breathe more efficiently? For many sauropods, the volume in their lungs was less than the volume in their enormous tracheae. If they had a reptile's respiratory system, fresh air would only make it part-way down their necks. Sauropods solved this problem with a one-way avian respiratory system.

In addition, the inflation and deflation of air sacs could have acted as a pumping mechanism to regulate blood pressure. Bob Bakker has said that without respiratory and circulatory efficiency, long-necks would have suffered from blood pressure regulation problems. "Brontosaurus's spine is so full of holes and indentations that the actual bony tissue is reduced to thin partitions," he said. "There can be little doubt that an avian-style system of air sacs was at work in these Mesozoic animals."[17]

Finally, pterosaurs, sometimes called flying reptiles, certainly share obvious similarities to birds. Although their wings are formed in an entirely different way, they are easy to identify in the field because their bones are hollow, extremely thin-walled, and usually crushed flat from extended burial under tons of sediment. Their skeletons have been so invaded by their respiratory system that the entire skeleton, all the way out to the claws, bears pneumatic foramina.[18]

Science would be simple if the same pieces of evidence could be observed in all dinosaurs. If hip formation and wrist position and eyebrow bumps and pneumatic foramina all were standard. If the family tree marched neatly along its limbs, dividing and subdividing into logical groups.

But science is not simple.

Shortly after Sir Richard Owen coined the term "Dinosauria" in 1842, dinosaurs were divided into two subgroups based on the configuration of the pelvis. "Lizard-hipped" dinosaurs, called saurischians, included theropods, sauropods, and prosauropods, a group thought to be ancestors of sauropods. All of these—including at least one prosauropod, *Platyosaurus*—had the advanced respiratory system. "Basal" dinosaurs—groups probably ancestral to dinosaurs, such as *Staurikasaurus* or *Herrerasaurus*—show no evidence of air sacs or the advanced breathing system.

"Bird-hipped" dinosaurs, called ornithischians, included the herbivorous duckbills, ceratopsians like *Triceratops,* nodosaurs, stegosaurs, and all other "beaked" dinosaurs. Their skeletons do *not* show pneumatic invasions; they apparently did not evolve this avian system, which probably made it much more fun for *T. rex* to chase them, and certainly easier to catch them.

Interestingly, pterosaurs, which have been thought to be closely related to dinosaurs for many years, have never been united formally with "dinosaurs." They emerged some 220 million years ago, at about the same time as the Triassic *Coelophysis,* the first theropod with the advanced system. This seems to indicate that the evolution of this efficient breathing system probably arose from a common ancestor sometime before the late Triassic. Perhaps breathing systems would make a better and clearer dividing line than hips.

This means the air-sac subgroup, like birds, must have possessed a large four-chambered heart, a double circulatory system, high arterial blood pressure, high levels of blood nutrients, and the ability to tolerate high levels of exercise without hyperventilation. *T. rex*'s honeycombed vertebrae imply warm-bloodedness; the king of carnivores had a metabolism that matched a Golden Eagle's. This gigantic, unwinged bird was likely more closely related to *Diplodocus,* pterodactyls, and hummingbirds than it was to *Triceratops* and *Stegosaurus.* This implies that the term "Dinosauria" may soon become extinct. More important, this means dinosaurs didn't die out at the end of the Cretaceous—they just downsized. As Bob Bakker so poetically put it, "When Canada geese honk their way northward, we can say, 'The dinosaurs are migrating—it must be spring!'"[19]

(11)

Family Values

Jane Goodall, Joy Adamson, and Diane Fossey lived with their animal subjects, watching their movements and habits, studying the looks in their eyes and the grooming of their young, hearing their screams. In the minds of the scientists, these creatures became family members, clan members. Paleontologists should be so lucky. No wonder *Jurassic Park* was so compelling. It held the promise of standing next to the flesh-and-blood incarnation of bones we have looked at from every possible angle; the intrigue of witnessing the moment of decision, fight or flight; the completion of the autopsy.

But then, perhaps, that would take the fun out of it.

In 1991 Phil Currie and Ken Carpenter came to see us at the institute. More exactly, I suppose, they came to see Sue. Everyone had been focusing on her enormity, her robust bones, her huge, nearly perfect skull. Accordingly, I had not had a chance to see most of the smaller bones we collected with Sue since they had been mapped, labeled, wrapped in foil and removed from the quarry. Currie, Carpenter, and I would see the newly cleaned bones at the same time—and some of them did not belong to Sue.

Terry pulled out crocodile vertebrae and teeth; a *Thescelosaurus* pelvis and vertebrae; *Nanotyrannus, Dromaeosaurus,* and Coelurosaur teeth; and a huge oviraptorid lower jaw. A few isolated braincase fragments. One was a tiny exoccipital, a bone from the back of the head containing part of the ball-like articulation for the neck vertebrae. *Thescelosaurus?* we wondered at first. Another was a frontal, but initially all we could tell was that it came from a tyrannosaur of some sort. A left lachrymal—much too small to be Sue's—

was definitely *T. rex*. Then there was a broken *T. rex* tibia and fibula from the same lower leg, bitten in half.

These were the leftovers of other animals found with Sue. The small skull bones we eventually agreed were *T. rex*, and their skulls would have been ten and eighteen inches long. Sue's was more than sixty. The leg was from a near-adult, but one much smaller and more gracile than Sue. Youngsters, perhaps a boyfriend, and Sue had spent their last day together.

Other excavations also have shown multiple specimens caught forever, united in time: the LACM *T. rex* pair, where the baby had been misidentified as *Gorgosaurus,* and a new multiple in Montana that is still unfinished. Excavations of some of the earliest theropods revealed adults and young trapped together. Triassic Aged sediment at Ghost Ranch, New Mexico, preserved articulated adult *Coelophysis* skeletons with partially grown juveniles.[1] Disarticulated remains of a closely related form, *Syntarsus*, of the Jurassic of South Africa, were found in a bonebed of adults and juveniles.[2]

Found with Sue was an extra lachrymal, a bone in front of the eye, from a much smaller *T. rex*, whose skull would have been only eighteen inches long. Photo by Ed Gerken.

We were very familiar with duck-bill dinosaur bonebeds like Ruth Mason's and the implications of finding tens of thousands of specimens all mixed up together. Understanding their herbivorous natures, and the tendency of modern herding animals to travel in great numbers, paleontologists have long interpreted these bonebeds as evidence of ancient herding behavior. However, today's theropod equivalents, land-dwelling meat-eaters such as big cats and bears, wolves and coyotes, generally do not travel in herds; they live in packs, extended families, or sometimes are solitary. While standing there gazing at the collection of remnants of Sue's grave-mates, I could not help but put the pieces together. I could not help but wonder if Sue's *family* had perished with her.

I knew this evidence might turn out to be history in the making. And *T. rex,* the famous "solitary hunter," might be in danger of losing its reputation. I started imagining *T. rex* pups gamboling around the nest, perhaps bedtime stories of murder and mayhem. But that was my dilemma: I never could actually witness *T. rex* pups interacting with their mom. After uncovering identifiable skeletal characters that help distinguish males from females, after documenting the avian respiratory system, I had a solid idea of what bones could tell us about *T. rex.* I also knew what the bones could *not* tell us—about someone's eye color, pulse rate, mating rituals, or family dynamics. To project what *T. rex* family life might have been like, I'd have to go out on a scientific limb.

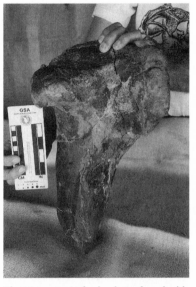

The upper part of a leg bone found with Sue belonging to a smaller male *T. rex.* About two-thirds of it were bitten off and perhaps swallowed. Photo by Ed Gerken.

Because I was still incarcerated, however, I would not be logging any physical miles to root out their habits. For this expedition, I needed neither plane ticket nor Land Rover. I stuffed my virtual backpack with field glasses, notebooks, video camera, sleeping bag, and time machine. I was ready to begin my next field trip: "watching" *T. rex* in the wild.

For the Record

The first stop on my safari was dinosaur nesting sites, one of the most basic sources of family evidence. When Roy Chapman Andrews discovered the first complete dinosaur eggs and nest in Mongolia in 1923 near the remains of numerous adult and juvenile ceratopsian *Protoceratops,* he quite naturally assumed they belonged to that beast. Andrews's subsequent discovery of a toothless, ostrichlike theropod on top of one of the nests led to the assumption that this new dinosaur was stealing eggs for a tasty and nutritious meal. Hence, this second specimen was dubbed *Oviraptor*, which means "egg thief."[3]

Since these early discoveries, plenty of solitary, circular nests had been discovered—many of them filled with, on average, one or two dozen elongated eggs believed to be theropods'. Nests also have been found in clusters, sometimes several clusters sprinkled through different sedimentary horizons.

While acting as a senior member of a joint Canadian-Chinese Dinosaur Project in outer Mongolia in 1994, Phil Currie dropped a dinosaur family bombshell. He announced the second dis-

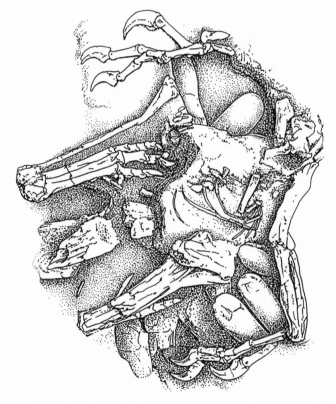

A drawing of the American Museum's Mongolian *Oviraptor* nest found with a sitting adult in incubation position. Surrounding the eggs are the adult's arms; toward the middle of the diagram can be seen the legs and remnants of the pelvis and rib cage.
Illustration by Dorothy Sigler Norton.

covery of a skeleton of the dastardly *Oviraptor* lurking on a clutch of *"Protoceratops"* eggs.[4] Soon after, in 1995, the American Museum of Natural History's Mark Norell, working in Mongolia proper, also uncovered two more specimens of *Oviraptor* sitting upon separate clutches of eggs. Norell's team also found an *Oviraptor* embryo still *within* the egg. And with these new discoveries, Andrews's seventy-year-old conclusions were disproved. The *"Protoceratops"* eggs were really *Oviraptor* eggs all along.[5] For all those years *Oviraptor* endured an undeserved rap as an egg stealer instead of an egg incubator, and forever must live with that slanderous name.

Subsequent discoveries simply provided more evidence. In Montana in 1997, Jack Horner's students also found a similar specimen, this time a *Troodon* nest with an incomplete but articulated adult *Troodon* in contact with the eggs.[6] These theropods were relatively small, measuring at most forty inches tall at the hips, and this one, like the *Oviraptors,* was incubating its eggs! These theropod dinosaurs had been caught dead to rights using body heat—in a manner seen only in modern birds. Not only was this yet more unequivocal proof of theropods' warm-bloodedness, but also of their nesting habits.

The Montana *Troodon* nesting locality also provided the best-recorded theropod nest construction ever. A clutch of twenty-four eggs had been laid within a shallow bowl-shaped depression with a distinctive rim. The rim measures four inches high and eight inches wide, and encircles a depression forty inches in diameter. The egg clutch itself is about twenty inches across and slightly off-center from the rim.[7] As the eggs were laid, they were forced into the loose sediment at the bottom of the nest—just as the enormous *Macroelongatoolithus* eggs had been. After the embryos had hatched, the bottom halves of the eggs remained implanted and undisturbed; the hatchlings climbed out the tops.

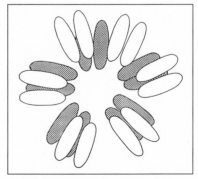

A typical theropod nest as seen from above. Note the circular, double-tiered arrangement of the eggs. Illustration by Dorothy Sigler Norton.

The same nest viewed from the side, showing the nest's pushed-up rim and how the eggs were implanted in loose sediment. Illustration by Dorothy Sigler Norton.

My first hypotheses seemed self-evident. The world's most famous nesters today are crocodiles and birds; if those nests are similar to dinosaur nests found in the fossil record, perhaps living nest builders can provide insight into the probable behavior of dinosaur nest builders. Beginning with the striking structure of the *Troodon* nest, I recognized a similarity to crocodile nests that are formed by a kicking motion of the rear feet, while bracing with the breast and forearms.[8] Plus, modern ground-nesting birds, who produce a cuplike depression for their nests, create a circular rim by rising and turning thirty degrees or so, repeating similar excavation movements until they turn in a circle several times.[9]

Dinosaurs may be extinct, but their behaviors are not. Let's look at some more examples.

Nesting

There is more to nesting than simply building nests. There is also being a good parent. Mammal chauvinism might tend to project that the only warm and fuzzy parent-child relationships occur when everybody has fur. Or at least eyebrows. However, although extended parental care is "almost universal among warm-blooded organisms,"[10] even the Amazon's spotted poison frogs, *Dendrobates vanzolinii,* sometimes exhibit complex care and feeding of their young.[11] *T. rex* relatives also care for their young in varying degrees, and, therefore, presumably so did *T. rex.* As nesting creatures, they would have begun by building nests.

Modern crocodile and bird nests range from holes dug in sand or depressions in grass to elaborate, reusable, branch-and-twig bunkers perched near the top of a tree. From the equator to the poles, nests become the center of the universe for countless embryos who benefit from various levels of parental attention. On one end of the scale are some crocodilians, and even some birds, who cover their eggs in sand or with plant material, quit the nest, and rely on the environment to incubate their eggs. For example, a family of birds called the Megapodiidae of Australia bury their eggs in black sand, near volcanic steam fissures or within piles of rotting vegetation. Most Megapod species go on with their business, although in some the males tend the mounds, removing vegetation to let the noonday sun warm the eggs, and replacing rotting and heat-providing vegetation as night draws near. Once hatched, the young are completely on their own.[12] Likewise, while crocodiles sometimes abandon their nests, and certainly do not actively tend them, in most species females can be found guarding against predators. To remain close to their nests, some crocodiles even fast for the entire incubation period of sixty-five to ninety days[13]—and therefore likely become very crabby toward unwelcome visitors.

Even in these "minimalist" societies, some sort of parental care often occurs, and the results are crucial. Especially in covered ground nests, nest construction and temperature regulation are vastly important, because sustained temperatures that are too cold or too hot will kill the embryos. Whereas bird embryo gender is determined by sex chromosomes, in crocodiles the temperature of egg incubation is the key to gender. If eggs develop in temperatures of 28–30°C (82–86°F), they produce females; temperatures of 32–34°C (90–93°F) produce males. With intermediate temperatures, both sexes are produced.[14]

Nearly all birds care for their eggs in some fashion—even if it is through sending their children off for foster care. The European Cuckoo, *Cuculus canorus*, avoids getting its hands dirty by laying an egg in the nest of another species. The host parents usually accept the egg, incubating it and feeding the hatchling as their own, even to the detriment of their true offspring who are usually kicked from the nest by the cuckoo chick.[15] Most birds, however, sit on their own nests, actively incubating their eggs, warming or cooling them, depending on the environment. In fact, most even rotate their eggs on a regular basis by drawing and rolling each egg backward with their beaks. Turning eggs prevents the embryos from adhering to the inner surface of the shell.

In many crocodile and bird species, nests, or at least nesting sites, are sometimes used repeatedly for many years.[16] Some crocodiles and about 13 percent of birds—including 93 percent of seabirds—nest in colonies.[17] Sometimes the colonies consist of only a few individuals, such as the barn swallows I watched as a child, who hung their mud nests from the eaves of my father's barn. But colonies also may be huge, containing hundreds of thousands of individual nests clustered over vast areas, as is exemplified by the rookeries of penguins, pelicans, flamingos, petrels, gannets, gulls, terns, and auks.[18] "Safety in numbers" provides the best protection against predators for Guanay Cormorants of Peru, who have reached colony sizes of 4 to 5 million birds.[19] In cases like these, it behooves a predator bird to locate its nest near a prey animal's rookery, offering a ready food supply to incubating parents and new hatchlings. For example, out of thirteen Eastern European heron colonies, eleven included a nest of a peregrine falcon.[20]

Bird incubation periods vary from as little as ten days in some woodpeckers and songbirds to as much as ninety days in the albatross and kiwi.[21] Ninety percent of birds have monogamous relationships,[22] with nest duty likely being a primary reason.[23] Sometimes both partners take turns incubating the nest and feeding hatchlings; other times, only one of the partners incubates, while the other may bring food to its partner.

Hatching

From a mammal's perspective, egg hatching is magic. Baby alligators grunt from within their eggs when it is time to see the world. Mother, by then undoubtedly hallucinating from lack of food, hears them, joyfully tears open the nest, and picks up each egg. Ever so gently, she rolls it against the roof of her mouth with her tongue, cracking it and freeing the young. With a ravenous mother gator, this might seem like a case of "out of the frying pan and into the fire." But no, the hatchlings are usually carried to the water in the mouth of their nurturing mother and released, never to return to the nest.[24]

Birds, who process only one egg at a time in the oviduct, need up to twenty-four hours for it to travel from ovary to delivery. That means days elapse from the time the first egg hits the nest until the last one is laid. Therefore, in some bird species, incubation is postponed until the whole clutch of time-delayed capsules is laid. The equivalent of tiny radio transmitters exist in each egg. The chicks are, strictly speaking, all of different ages, because of the laying delay. Incredibly, the older chick embryos vocalize in a slower series of "clicks," while younger ones click rapidly. Using these vocalizations, individuals either speed up or slow down their hatching process, so that the entire clutch may hatch synchronously, within a matter of minutes.[25] Magic. Even though all this excitement is going on, parents rarely assist chicks in their struggle to free themselves from their eggs.[26]

Along with the synchronized radios provided upon fertilization, a bird also is issued two other specialized tools: a small, calcified egg tooth near the top of the upper bill, and a "hatchling muscle" in its neck. Using the tooth, and powered by the muscle, the chick breaks through and rhythmically strikes at its calcium carbonate shell, at the same time thrusting with its left leg—thereby slightly rotating its body for each successive strike, and eventually cutting off the top of the shell and crawling out.[27]

After surviving these alarming rigors of birth, hatchlings emerge in various states of development. Crocodiles are precocial, which means they are born able to move about under their own power, locate food, and run away from predators. They are alert and able to learn.[28] Birds, however, vary by species. Some are precocial, and hatch as down-covered, well-developed birds. Within a week, they have achieved 90 percent of their adult temperature-regulatory ability, developed as their downy covering improves and their skeletal muscle, the main source of heat production, grows in mass.[29] The pelves of precocial hatchlings are also more ossified—made of bone instead of cartilage—than those of less developed birds, so their little legs are stronger and they can run earlier.[30] With their own internal engines, and the ability to feed themselves right out of the gate, most precocial chicks abandon the nest shortly after emerging from the egg.

Other bird species are altricial—born naked, blind, and nearly immobile. Altricial birds cannot regulate their body temperature and are completely dependent upon their parents for their warmth, care, and feeding. The young altricial birds remain in the nest and are fed and brooded by the parents. With this arrangement, parents want to avoid the attention of predators, and therefore either eat discarded shells and feces or carry them away from the nest.[31]

Toddlers

As independent as they would like to see themselves, precocial toddlers still need their parents. For the first few weeks of life, young crocodiles stay close to their mother, who provides vicious protection from predators. Cayman young spend their entire, inactive daytimes resting on or near their mother. At night they scatter looking for insects, while she stands guard at the entrance of the inlet or lake that is their territory. In the morning, the young cry out and regroup for their rest period. In all crocodiles, if a hatchling should stray too far, or when danger threatens, it will utter a loud distress call. If the baby is simply lost, the mother will immediately respond, locate the youngster, and carry it in her mouth back to the fold. If the more serious "threatened" call is given, however, more than one parent may come to the rescue. Even adults who are not the parents may defend hatchlings. Some crocodilian mothers remain with their young for up to seven months, and siblings usually remain together in a group for up to eighteen months. Even with this level of earnest attention, only about two percent of all crocodile eggs survive to reach maturity. Most babies succumb to accident, disease, or predators—including other crocodiles.[32]

In precocial species of birds, the female usually, but not always, takes charge of the hatchlings. The array of parental duties varies by species, but certainly it begins with a few basics. Until their chicks have revved their internal heating systems to full power, parents brood them at night or on cold, damp days. They also have to feed them, in one way or another—usually by letting them experiment. For example, the chicks of domestic birds and water-fowl are led to food, but are not fed directly, perhaps because their diets sometimes differ from their parents'; for example, even if their parents' diet is plant-based, chicks instinctually eat a diet high in protein, usually insects, which promotes rapid growth.[33]

Protection from predators is probably the most demanding aspect of parental care. This often involves the attention of both parents, who may alternate in watching over the young and later feeding themselves. When threatened, rails may pick up their chicks, using their bills. Grebes and some species of ducks have been known to carry their young upon their backs.[34] Young ratites, large flightless birds such as the ostrich and emu, will form tight clusters, while the attending adult challenges the intruder. The adult may then attempt to lead the intruder away from the brood by fleeing, perhaps feigning a broken wing.[35]

Even after young birds have reached adult size, many stay with their parents for an extended period of time. Young boobies and terns remain for up to six months after they fledge, to learn the art of fishing. Swans, precocial birds, stay with their parents for one to two years, following them through long migrations.[36] Birds, who lay fewer eggs than crocodiles, have better survival rates. In part this is due to the rapid growth rate of birds; it takes crocodiles from seven to eighteen years to reach adult size, whereas most bird species get there within three months. Only the largest albatrosses, condors, and some penguins take up to one year to be full-grown. Parental care in birds also is generally more advanced than in crocodiles, and they have fewer young to keep track of. But still, the mortality rate for young birds is greater than 50 percent and up to as much as 90 percent during the first year.[37]

The Biggest Bird of Them All

So, armed with my evidence from birds and crocodiles, and my time machine, I can now go back and do some field observations of a mother *T. rex* and her young.

We have a good idea of the shape of *T. rex*'s nest and eggs, based on the nests of other theropods. The excavated *Troodon* lipped nest helps us guess about how the nests were made, probably through kicking a hollow into the earth. As is evidenced by the *Oviraptor, Troodon,* and giant *Macroelongatoolithus* nests, we can assume that *T. rex* eggs were pushed into the soil and that hatchlings popped the tops off their eggs and climbed out—possibly with help from parents.

As for size, since *T. rex* was the largest known meat-eater on the planet at the end of the Cretaceous, most likely its eggs were closer in size to footballs than golfballs. *How* close? A developing embryo must breathe through its eggshell. As it grows, this shell's surface area increases at a slower rate than its internal volume, which means there is a maximum egg volume—approximately two gallons—that an embryo could occupy before the shell surface area would be unable to provide enough air for the embryo's survival. A two-gallon egg is about the size of those *Macroelongatoolithus* theropod eggs, approximately 20 inches long by 5 inches in diameter.

Before the revolutionary theropod nests had been found, researchers assumed that most, if not all, dinosaur eggs were buried after they were laid. The expanded fossil record points away from this—not only with the *Troodon*s and *Oviraptor*s caught incubating, but also with a lack of evidence of incubation-enhancing nest coverings.

So here I sit, perched in my imaginary tree in my camouflage outfit, binoculars to my eyes. Not all scientists agree on what I see, but from here it looks like the nest has been dug, enormous eggs

Size comparison of a chicken, ostrich, and large theropod egg. Photo by Ed Gerken.

have been laid in pairs, and they are lodged in the sediment in a circle. As Mother *T. rex* steps one of her huge feet into the center, I cringe at the thought that she might just smash the eggs to bits. But she settles nicely on them, and physics calms my nerves, reminding me that because the eggs are planted firmly, as her body presses against their exposed ends the remaining stress from her weight is distributed over their entire surfaces.

Although from my vantage point in the tree I cannot see her belly, she must have the equivalent of a brood patch. In a bird, this is an exposed abdominal area where warm skin rich in blood vessels directly contacts the eggs, providing increased heat transfer.[38] Since she is warm-blooded, she could not fast for anywhere near ninety days, nor would she be able to live alone and leave her nest unprotected for the length of time it would take to track, stalk, kill, and eat a meal. Even if no predator found the eggs, they would cool down or heat up to a deadly temperature. Therefore, I see her gracile husband occasionally bringing her a bloody steak, or even spelling her on the nest so she can stretch her legs.

The fact that hatched theropod nests show the intact bottoms of eggshells suggests that precocial young popped out of them and went exploring—no extended stays for the kids, who would have crunched the shells. Additional evidence of ossified pelvic girdles and advanced development of the femur in theropod embryos supports this: these hatchlings were born ready to scamper. And look at those big snouts and oversized teeth—they also are ready to kill. They start small, on big insects, but during the summer I watch them pantomime hunting. Small mammals, crocodiles, and, in the fall, the little ones help Mom and Dad take down a *Triceratops*.

The Nail in the Coffin

If, as the evidence strongly indicates, *T. rex* and other theropods hatched precocial young and were endothermic, the next question is what the hatchlings looked like. Were they covered with fuzzy, insulating, downy feathers to help preserve body heat and regulate temperature? Fiction writers and dinosaur illustrators have

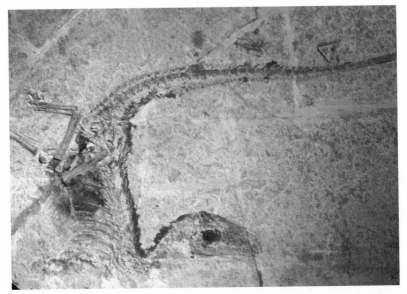

The "feathered" compsignathid dinosaur, *Sinosauropteryx*, that rocked the 1996 SVP conference. Photo by Phil Currie.

guessed so, but it wasn't until 1996 that Phil Currie announced the first hard evidence to support this hypothesis.

He first brought the news to the 1996 SVP annual meeting in his shirt pocket. It was a single photograph shot at the Institute of Paleontology and Paleoanthropology in Beijing, China. It was a photograph of a little compsignathid dinosaur, a small theropod related to *T. rex*, 120 million years old and only about three feet long from the tip of its nose to the tip of its tail. The skeleton was beautifully articulated and marvelously preserved on a thin slab of freshwater limestone. This fine-grained sediment captured more than just the bones of this predator.

Along the neck, back, tail, and sides of the animal, retained in microscopic detail, was an array of what appeared to be small, downy feathers, called protofeathers.[39]

In July 2001, the American Museum's Mark Norell made news again with his Chinese colleague, Ji Qiang. A Chinese farmer had unearthed a 130-million-year-old creature that had more than just protofeathers. This one, a three-foot-long dromaeosaur, was "the specimen we've been waiting for," Norell told *Popular Science*.

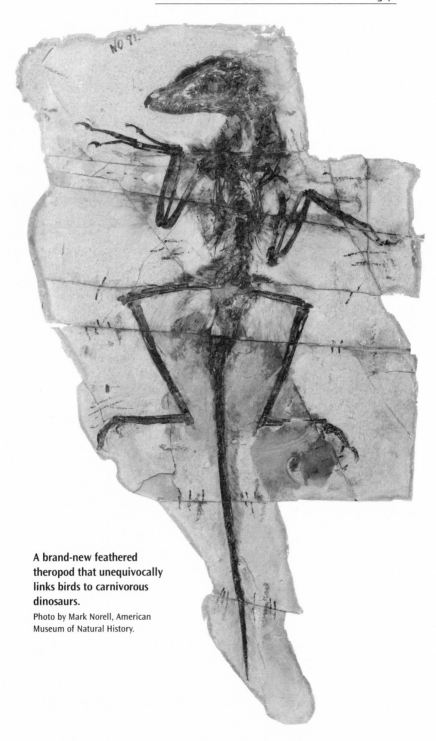

A brand-new feathered theropod that unequivocally links birds to carnivorous dinosaurs.
Photo by Mark Norell, American Museum of Natural History.

Covered with both true feathers and protofeathers, from head to tail, this specimen seemed to prove that feathers *predated* birds.

Feathers were made for insulating warm-blooded creatures, and certainly these feathered creatures' offspring—and presumably *T. rex*'s—would have possessed downy feathers to keep their tiny bodies warm. Like birds, complete endothermy was probably not developed until after a few days or weeks. Thus, *T. rex* parents probably brooded their young for that period during the night and, perhaps, even provided shade for them during the heat of the day. We presume they did not play cards during these lazy afternoons, because their arms simply were too short.

Probably a low percentage of *T. rex* hatchlings survived their childhoods. Predation by other theropods, crocodiles, or even rival siblings probably took its toll on the hatchlings. From my tree blind, I cringe again. Mom is 41 feet long and 13 feet tall at the hip. The hatchlings are only a yard long and a foot tall. A misstep here or there would spell catastrophe. While they grew quickly to maturity, I wonder how many *T. rex*es were accidentally smushed by those who loved them most?

Sue's site suggests that from two successive hatchings, only one individual survived from each. Considering that theropod nests contained from twelve to twenty-four or more eggs, on average a much greater number than the clutches of birds, it seems unlikely that even 10 percent of *T. rex* eggs ever reached maturity.

The ones who lived, however, had to eat. In fact, that probably was their most time-consuming and invigorating pastime. As they grew, stalking the forest in deadly family groups, probably young theropods stayed close to home. The fossil record revealed a Jurassic South African *Syntarsus* bonebed that contained juveniles with a majority of robust females.[40] In that species, perhaps fathers hunted for their families. The Ghost Ranch, New Mexico, *Coelophysis* skeletons revealed adults of both genders with partially grown junveniles.[41] A migration, or a picnic? Of the two LACM *T. rex* specimens found together, the larger is a gracile adult, a male.[42] Perhaps it was Daddy's day out with the kid.

An artist's rendition of a happy *T. rex* parent and feathered child. Illustration by Todd Marshall.

The more I "watch" these families, the more my imagination fills in. I hear a young *T. rex* squeak a crocodile-like alarm call; its mother runs to its aid. I see gawky, molting teenagers and a sleek adult male practicing hunting techniques. And in this scenario, I cannot help but envision Sue's last day—the one that ripped her face to shreds, sliced her mate in two, and all but consumed her progeny.

Family values did not end with parental care. Once a *T. rex* survived childhood, it faced a lifetime of challenge. How long a lifetime? Crocodiles grow slowly throughout their lives, living

Adding Insult to Injury

On July 9th, 1996, four and a half months after I began serving my sentence, we received good news from Peru. Criminal judge Pilar Carbonel Vilches ruled in our in absentia trial. Official court documents said that our "penal responsibility" had "not been proven in these proceedings." We had not violated Peruvian law! There was no conspiracy. I was no ringleader after all.

The day Duffy received a translation of the Peruvian decision, he hastily amended our pending Eighth Circuit appeal. "I am placing what I know before this Court as quickly as I can because of the grave nature of the injustice which has taken place in this case," he wrote. "The entire basis for the enhancement of my client's sentence for criminal wrongdoing in Peru is a farce. What my client did in Peru cannot be judged criminal activity in this country when Peru says it is no crime in Peru." In addition, Duffy accused, "The government knew or should have known of this Peruvian decision, and simply never informed anyone of its existence. This is wrong. The government's attorneys have a higher duty to the system and to my client than to behave in this fashion."

Mandel countered. "I saw those documents. I saw those and I said [then] I had no knowledge as to the authenticity of any of this stuff." When asked whether it was incumbent upon him to investigate the documents' authenticity, he replied, "No, it was incumbent upon defense counsel to

more than fifty years.[43] Small birds live only two to five years, but larger ones live twenty to thirty years or more. One female royal albatross from New Zealand was banded in 1937 and observed on her nest forty-eight years later at an estimated age of fifty-eight. Parrots have lived in captivity for eighty years.[44] Larger animals tend to have longer lifetimes; elephants, although unrelated to dinosaurs, are a similar size to *T. rex* and live sixty or seventy obtain that stuff through some kind of proper channels, to have a certified interpreter look at it." I could imagine only one interpretation of Mandel's statement: if *anyone* in the U.S. Attorney's office really did know about my Peruvian acquittal, they feigned ignorance about it so as not to upset their legal apple cart.

I waited for a decision for nearly another year. Four months before I was to be released to the halfway house, my "emergency appeal" was decided. The appeals court wrote that evidentiary issues had to be viewed "in the light most favorable to the prosecution," and it upheld my convictions. Regarding exportation of Peruvian fossils, it wrote that because Judge Battey had found that I had intended to promote a conspiracy—regardless of the jury's decision—"we need not reach the question of whether Larson's exportation of fossils from Peru was unlawful under Peruvian law."

Judge Beam, again the appeals court's dissenter, wrote that my convictions were "based upon hotly disputed, barely viable and generally unenforced legal theories. Indeed, as correctly pointed out in Larson's brief, good faith disagreement exists as to the proper interpretation of both the foreign law involved and the federal statutes and rules enforced in this prosecution." The Eighth Circuit also ruled against an adjustment in my sentence, although Beam said the "weighty sentence was, in my view, inappropriate given the questionable presentations at trial concerning the existence of and the substance of the Peruvian law at issue."

years.[45] These templates, coupled with Sue's numerous healed injuries, suggest she lived a long and adventurous life, probably between fifty and one hundred years. During that time, it appeared that Sue took several convalescences, not the least of which resulted from the leg break—an incapacitation that would have necessitated breakfast in bed for weeks. My guess is that it took teamwork to survive in the Cretaceous.

Homo sapien Family Values

My prison sentence was two years, but with adjustments for good behavior I spent eighteen months at the prison camp, one month in a halfway house, and two months in home confinement, followed by twenty-four months of probation. I received about thirty visits from my family and numerous stopovers from friends. Colleagues even came to discuss science, and I was able to contribute to the institute's business with dinosaur mount diagrams and project ideas.

In 1997 a *T. rex* even was named after me. My longtime friend and colleague Kraig Derstler, from the University of New Orleans, led a crew into the Lance Creek badlands of Wyoming. One of his students, Rob Patchus, came upon some unusually large theropod bone fragments eroding from a grassy hillside. Subsequent excavation yielded well-preserved stomach gastralia, ribs, and body and neck vertebrae. Derstler and Patchus named it "Pete."[46] It was a good omen, and it really warmed my heart.

Compared to prison, the halfway house was paradise. A little floor scrubbing, a little clock watching, some missing shampoo, clean socks that came from my very own dresser at home. Kristin picked me up at the first possible moment each morning, 6:00 A.M., drove me up into the Black Hills for work, and either she or Marion, who lived in the same town, drove me back in the evenings. My mind was so full with the idea of living life again, of working in my laboratory again, of seeing my children again every day. What I didn't anticipate was that my heart was several steps ahead of my mind.

My first challenge: Sue went on the auction block. Ironically, Kevin Schieffer's first comments after the seizure were that he had saved Sue from being sold to the highest bidder. Now, apparently with the government's blessing, Maurice Williams had officially handed over Sue to Sotheby's in New York. Even considering all that had happened between us, I still had hope. Call me crazy.

Rumors were flying all over paleontology. This university teamed with that sugar daddy, more than one museum canvassed its board, and *this* man hoped against hope. As one of the world's

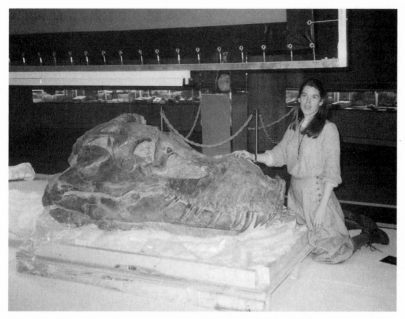

Since Peter, still on home confinement, was unable to leave Hill City for the auction, Kristin went to New York to visit Sue on his behalf. Photo by Terry Wentz.

ranking fossil assessors, I did the math. Our duckbilled Ruth Mason Quarry dinosaurs were among the most expensive fossils ever sold. They went for a price of $350,000. But Sue was famous. She was the best. Even so, I could not imagine a fossil, even this fossil, being worth more than $1 million. Our bank accounts could not support a used car, let alone a million-dollar dinosaur. We talked about partnering with other museums, we talked about funding Sue's purchase with tours, perhaps even advertising. It was too late to form a contract with a big company; there was only one white horse on our horizon. A very successful local businessman, philanthropist, and family friend, Stanford Adelstein, responded to a plea for help—not only from us, but also from Sue. He could see the future of a South Dakota venture, the most famous South Dakota dinosaur staying in her home state. He saw participation in worldwide tours, merchandising, the works.

I could see it, too. But we would be bidding against the big dogs.

Stanford Adelstein generously attempted to save Sue for South Dakota. Photo by Terry Wentz.

Adelstein leveraged $1.5 million. It was only October, and I was still tethered by home confinement and could not yet leave South Dakota. I attended the auction via telephone, where a most amazing thing happened. In only a matter of moments, it was over. My jaw was on the floor. Adelstein—who bid beyond his budget—had to put his paddle away after thirty seconds. In fewer than eight minutes, Maurice Williams received $7.6 million, tax free, "the proceeds of a trust." Ronald McDonald House and Disney footed the bill for the Chicago Field Museum.

I never would have guessed it, neither the participants nor the amount. After Sotheby's added its commission, the total price was $8.36 million.

"One can't believe impossible things."

"I dare say you haven't had much practice," said the Queen. "When I was your age, I always did it for half an hour a day. Why, sometimes I've believed as many as six impossible things before breakfast."[47]

By then, our lien action long ago had been lost, and Maurice Williams did not reimburse our excavation or preparation expenses. In fact, the following spring, I was in the town of Faith, a few miles from Sue's grave, talking on the telephone. Williams came up behind me, punched me, and threatened to kill me. Because I was still on probation, it was necessary that I file a police report corroborated by witnesses, which I did immediately. I filed no charges. My probation officer suggested that instead of assaulting me, Williams might have said thank you.

The auction added only one notch of disappointment to my generally shell-shocked demeanor, and it fit perfectly with the outrageous and unbelievable dimensions of our entire case. I would have been no more surprised to see a unicorn walk by, arm-in-arm with a jabberwock. With Sue's final disposition settled for good, and my prison sentence over, I was supposedly free to reclaim my life. But I was still in another reality. When I ventured into the nearest city for shopping, I was afraid to leave the car in the parking lot for fear I would be unable to find it again—even when my family was with me. The mall was too much for my senses; too many people, too many things, too many options. At work, I would pick up an air-scribe and try to focus on a fossil, but within a couple of minutes the telephone would ring or people would stop by or my mind would drift. It took a good six months for my brain to orient itself and for my comfort in public places to return.

While I was busy looking for my car, the Bone Wars continued. Keith Rigby, a professor at the University of Notre Dame, was the next target.

In the summer of 1997, Rigby and his crew of volunteers from Earth Watch, an organization that provides support to a variety of conservation projects, were prospecting outcrops for new sites on both sides of the K-T Boundary. They were working on the Walton ranch south of the town of Fort Peck, Montana. Midway in the season, one of these volunteers, Louis Trembley, came upon some large bone fragments, weathering from what appeared to be a small bonebed on the edge of a low butte. Although Rigby had concentrated his studies on small mammals, when Trembley and another volunteer brought in fragments of a huge rib and large theropod claw, Rigby knew this could mean only one thing: *T. rex*. Excited by the discovery, Rigby moved his team to the new site. Weeks of work produced the bones of a number of different types of dinosaurs, but mostly *T. rex*. These included parts of the pelvis, limbs, vertebrae, ribs, and skull bones. At the end of August, Rigby and his crew closed the quarry and went home, eager to return the following summer.[48]

However, in September, landowner Fred Walton called Nate Murphy, a freelance paleontologist from Malta, Montana. According to Murphy, Walton was eager to finish the collection and did not relish the prospect of waiting another year. He asked for excavation help. Murphy was aware of Rigby's previous work at the site, but he was unable to contact him. Reluctantly, he consented to help with the excavation, hoping to protect the specimen from damage that could occur without trained hands at work. He was told that Walton needed money from the specimen, and that Walton was aware of Sue's well-advertised and impending auction. Sensing something amiss in Walton's approach, and concerned that there was a problem with the site's land designation, Murphy quickly left.[49]

What followed seems almost a replay of the Sue saga. Rigby was alerted to the activities of the Waltons and asked the sheriff's office to check on the site. After a title search, it was determined that the Waltons no longer owned the land on which the new *T. rex* had been discovered. Instead, title had been lost three years earlier to the federal government for failure to pay an FSA loan. Neither the Waltons nor Rigby had permission to work the site.[50] Enter the FBI.

Murphy and later Rigby returned to the site, now guarded day and night by FBI agents. Emergency permits were issued to collect and protect the specimen. To add to the problems of this 65-million-year-old casualty, the jaws had been removed hurriedly by the Waltons (who had continued without Murphy's assistance) and were feared damaged. They were later located in Great Falls, Montana, and safely reunited with the rest of the specimen.[51]

Despite an intensive investigation and tons of trepidation, no one was charged with wrongdoing. Fortunately, most of the site now has been excavated and the specimen saved. No indictments, no auction; just an informal agreement among the state, the feds, and a number of museums who wanted the specimen. Their solution: the *T. rex* will be the centerpiece of a new museum near its discovery site at Fort Peck, a happy ending to what could have been a tragic story.

The "Peck's *rex*," as it is now called, is still under preparation and rather tight security. Rigby and Murphy continue to work on the specimen. Although Rigby is convinced that this *T. rex* is huge, Murphy believes it comparable to Stan in size. It has a disarticulated skull and quite a bit of the rest of the skeleton. Both men tell me there are parts of two or perhaps three individual *T. rex* from the same deposit!

While this story had a happy ending for both the dinosaur and the humans, the politics of it could have escalated into something quite awful. This was the paleo-equivalent of Ruby Ridge; there were lots of guns. While the standoff was happening, I could not help but feel empathy for Keith Rigby. The fact that he had no permit and had believed the rancher when he said he owned the land sent chills of déjà vu down my spine. Both Rigby and this new specimen were in great danger, and I am glad Rigby's credentials saved him from a fate similar to mine. Paleontology will not be safe until people put their guns away. We are all on the same side: we want these fossils safe and preserved from the violence of nature *and* politics. Those are our family values.

(12)

Life after Death

In an "instant" of geologic time about 65 million years ago, life as dinosaurs knew it ceased to exist. We know this by looking at the K-T Boundary, a finite "line in the sand," a thin layer of evidence of what happened to the planet to cause the extinction of perhaps 75 percent of all its species.[1] The mass extinctions associated with this boundary between the Cretaceous and Tertiary time periods have come to be known as the "K-T Boundary Extinction Event." Above the line we find no more fossils of any sort of dinosaurs, pterosaurs, or any land vertebrate whose body mass was greater than sixty pounds.[2] We find that plants also perished, with many forms of evergreens not making it past the boundary. Underwater life was decimated. Large sea-going reptiles, including an entire family of huge sea turtles typified by the fourteen-foot giant *Archelon*, disappeared. Mosasaurs, a group of monstrous sea lizards, vanished, along with icthyosaurs, a reptile version of the dolphin, and both long- and short-necked plesiosaurs. Also killed were ammonites and their cephalopod cousins, the belemnites, and many species of mollusk.

The massacre continued even on the microscopic level. Tiny animals and plants, called forminifera and plankton, were ravaged from the upper reaches of the ocean all the way down to the deep-sea floor. Of the thirty-six species of these groups present before the boundary, only one survived.[3]

The Tyrant Lizard ruled North America for more than a million years, generation after generation walking the earth stalking, terrorizing, and murdering the other inhabitants. Neither before nor after was there a beast to equal the power, mass, or engineering sophistication of this terrestrial killing machine we call *Tyrannosaurus rex.*

And then one day they were gone. Every last one of them. This magnificent species had become extinct.

We know when, but scientists are still arguing over why. And how. Speculation has spanned more than one hundred years, and today there are probably that many extinction theories. Truly spanning the scope of human imagination, theories propose everything from alien intervention to mammals eating all the dinosaur eggs. But a scientific theory, in order to be viable, must be *verifiable;* it must hold up to scientific scrutiny. For example, while it is true that certain mammals of today, particularly skunks, minks, weasels, polecats, and the like, do enjoy feasting upon bird and reptile eggs, they do not *subsist* on them. It would be a far stretch that in the terminal Cretaceous, typical mammalian egg-eating behavior would have brought about the extinction of at least two orders of animals. Plus, the proponents of this argument have failed to explain how mammals coexisted with theropods, sauropods, and ornithischians for 150 million years and then suddenly changed their eating habits. Even so, testing the viability of a theory does not end with logic.

Evidence is found at the crime scene. The fossil record shows no general increase in mammal population, nor general decrease in dinosaur population, and instead shows a sudden loss of particular segments of the population. In addition, although paleontologists have identified scores of nesting dinosaur sites around the world, not once has a fossil mammal been found with a nest, "caught in the act" of destroying the eggs. Nor have any fossil nests or individual eggs been found that apparently were ravaged by mammals. There simply is no physical evidence for mammalian ovicide. The last straw: this extinction was not just limited to egg-laying dinosaurs.

Theories are much more likely to be proven if they *begin* from observations of the evidence. For example, the fossil record does show a general lowering of sea levels toward the end of the Cretaceous. This caused the shrinkage and eventual disappearance of warm, shallow inland seas over the continental landmasses. For most of the Cretaceous, one of several such inland seaways covered a large portion of the ancestral continent of North America, stretching from the Gulf of Mexico to the Arctic Ocean. This body of water did three important things: it bisected the continent into two landmasses; it provided a special habitat for billions of organisms; and, along with others like it on other continents, it influenced the climate of the entire planet.

Bob Bakker theorizes that as these inland seaways dried up, habitat was lost to vast numbers of marine organisms. Ocean currents and passages changed, ultimately causing the extinction of many marine species. Concurrently, on land, huge new areas were opened up to colonization, and previously unconnected landmasses linked for the first time—causing animals to mix. Diseases found new, unresistant hosts and caused unchecked waves of epidemics. Predators found new defenseless prey. Further complicating this were the changes in climate affected by the same lowering of sea levels: the world changed, but many of its occupants could not, and they expired. Bakker also points out that at least some of the K-T Boundary extinctions appear to have happened *before* the boundary, coinciding with the changing environment.[4] Certainly this is a well thought-out theory based upon observations of real changes taking place on Earth.

The most convincing theory for Mother Nature's coup de grâce, however, came about by accident. In June 1980, researchers Luis and Walter Alvarez, Frank Asero, and Helen Michel published their version of the origins of the K-T Boundary Extinction Event.[5] Their study had started with a different goal in mind: to determine how long the extinction event's "geologic instant" really took. They focused on a section of rock in the Umbrian Apennines of northern Italy. Here lies a sequence of deep marine sediments which were deposited across the K-T Boundary in an uninterrupted fashion. Terrestrial environments, which are susceptible after deposition to erosion, have preserved the K-T Boundary only under special circumstances, but marine sediments maintained their integrity and today provide a more continuous record.

In Italy the last typical Upper Cretaceous forminifera were preserved, and they abruptly disappeared to be replaced by much smaller, Lower Tertiary forms. The change is "instantaneous": the two zones are separated by only a half-inch clay layer which has become known as the "Boundary clay." Alvarez and his group were not trying to speculate on *why* the clay was deposited, just in *how long* it took.

To calculate this time period, they began with some basic assumptions. First, because of their density, platinum group elements—platinum, iridium, osmium, and rhodium—are concentrated at the earth's core. They are not very abundant in the earth's crust. Second, these elements occur more abundantly in stony, or "chondritic," meteorites, which erode and filter to earth as they constantly pass through the atmosphere. Therefore, meteorite-caused low concentrations of platinum group elements are found in sedimentary rock in relatively constant concentrations. The Alvarez group thought that measuring the rate of change in concentration of these elements would determine the length of time it took to accumulate the layer of clay.

Iridium was the easiest to measure. The group began measuring iridium concentrations in the sediments below the clay, and found they remained consistent throughout the entire Upper Cretaceous of the Italian section. Above the clay, the Tertiary readings were the same. The iridium "background" reading was 0.3 parts per billion. In the Boundary clay itself, however, something unexpected occurred: iridium was concentrated at 9.1 parts per billion! The half-inch boundary clay had accumulated *thirty times* the iridium concentration of the normal section. Although there were other clays in the section, this was the only one with this abnormally high reading, so the reading could not be blamed on the presence of clays. Was it possible that the sedimentation rate for this clay slowed to one-thirtieth of the normal sedimentation rate for this deep ocean sediment? If so, it would have to be a strictly local feature, perhaps produced by hydrothermal vents; the Alvarez group moved to Denmark to compare readings.

Here, too, the K-T Boundary is marked by a clay. Repeating their experiment, they found a background iridium level of 0.26 parts per billion, and a clay reading of 29 parts per billion, more than *one hundred times* the normal amount of iridium expected.

Other sites around the world showed this same high amount of iridium, exactly at the K-T Boundary. Clearly, something out of the ordinary had happened at that instant. And it happened worldwide.

The Alvarez team looked to the skies for a solution. They considered the supernova hypothesis: did a star explode in the near vicinity of the sun, bombarding the earth and its inhabitants with cosmic rays and particles, wiping out many forms of life? This theory could be tested: if a star 0.1 light years from Earth were to release the sudden and huge burst of energy of a supernova, neutron capture and beta decay could have produced and deposited iridium in the quantities the team had discovered. However, if such an event had occurred, the iridium would have been accompanied by a lesser, but detectable, quantity of Plutonium 244. No Plutonium 244 was detected in any of the samples.

The team went back to the original proposed source of sedimentary iridium: chondritic meteorites. Could it be that they had found a twist on the "alien" theory—the record of the impact of an object from space? If so, there was one problem—*corpus delicti*. The "body" was missing. In order to account for such an anomalous amount of iridium, Earth would have to have collided with and vaporized an object approximately six miles in diameter! Such a collision would have left a crater 113 miles wide.

Could this have happened? Certainly it has on the surfaces of our close neighbors, Venus, Mars, and the moon. Researchers began to search the globe. With such a specific question in mind, they began locating all sorts of clues. First, there was "shocked quartz," an impact side effect occurring in some of the North American sections, where the K-T Boundary clay preserved fractured quartz grains. Shocked quartz also was found in oil well core samples in the Pacific, but not on land in the European, African, or Asian sections.[6]

Second, coarse, rocky detritus from the late Cretaceous was found on the gulf coasts of Haiti, Cuba, Mexico, and Texas. It was theorized that these were the end result of huge tsunamis caused by the impact of a large meteorite in the nearby sea. Third, in Haiti researchers discovered an eighteen-inch layer of fallout debris with pea-size claylike teardrops whose unaltered glassy interiors were identified as tektites.[7] Tektites are formed when, thanks to an impact, molten rock is torn from Earth's crust and thrown high into the atmosphere. As the drops fall back to Earth, they harden into glassy, aerodynamic globules. With these convincing pieces of evidence, the search concentrated on the Caribbean Sea and the Gulf of Mexico.

But it wasn't until 1991 that the investigators finally hit upon the object of their search. Hidden beneath accumulated sediments just over a half mile thick were the remains of an impact crater nearly 110 miles in diameter—the perfect size and age for the proposed K-T Boundary collision.[8] Half in and half out of the Gulf of Mexico, this buried crater is located on the northern edge of the Yucatan Peninsula. At its center lies the Mexican village of Chicxulub (pronounced *CHICK-sha-lube*), which in Mayan means, very fittingly, "tail of the devil." Oddly enough, this particular crater's discovery actually had been announced in 1981, only a year after Alvarez and his group put forward their theory, but the information had circled the scientific community like a game of telephone that never reached its destination.

Research at and around this site since 1991 has yielded even more startling evidence. Up to one hundred feet of *mega breccia,* irregularly broken and recemented rock, has been found around the Chicxulub crater. It consists of striated pebbles, cobbles, and boulders up to thirty feet in diameter.[9] These broken rocks are in a matrix of fine material that includes green glass tektites. When the six-mile asteroid struck the earth, the released kinetic energy caused an impact "melt sheet," a planar pool of liquid rock now solidified into glass. Its thickness has been calculated at two to five miles in the center of the crater, and samples have been recovered from half-mile bore holes near the center. Since this recrystallized material is composed only of sediments found in the earth's crust, it appears that the object did not penetrate to the mantle.[10] Had it done so, its effects might have been even worse, including huge upwellings of lava. In the meantime, scientists around the world were scouring sites that preserved the sedimentary sequence crossing the K-T Boundary. They found iridium anomalies, shocked quartz, and tektites. Carbon particles also showed up, both in the form of soot and in an unusual carbon isotope, suggesting that tremendous fires on land coincided with the impact.[11]

The evidence is overwhelming. About 65 million years ago, synchronized with the extinction of three-quarters of all species of plants and animals on the lands and in the waters, an asteroid, or a dried-out comet, crashed into our planet. It would have been traveling at perhaps 36,000 miles per hour. It would have exploded with a force equal to one billion megatons of TNT[12]— 50 *billion* times the power of the atom bomb that destroyed Hiroshima in 1945. Earth experienced an explosion equivalent to a million times the total nuclear arsenal of humankind, detonated simultaneously, at one location. It is possible that ejecta from the blast actually reached the moon.

In July 1994, fragments of the Levy-Shoemaker comet crashed into the far side of Jupiter. Using the Hubbell space telescope, we were able to see on television the effects of the impacts upon the atmosphere of Jupiter, a planet more than eleven times the diameter of Earth—1,300 Earths would fit inside it. The largest fragment of this comet was only three to four kilometers in diameter, and it alone created a fireball "at least 3,000 kilometers high and left a multi-ringed 'black eye' in the Jovian stratosphere twice the diameter of Earth."[13]

Sodom and Gomorrah

Imagine the effect of a six-mile cannonball smashing into Earth: the shock of the Chicxulub impact vaporized 700 cubic kilometers of material—the entire asteroid—in less than half a second. In that same time period, a hole 110 miles across and 7 to 8 miles deep was blasted into the face of Earth. This material was either ejected or vaporized, like the asteroid itself. Richard Norton, an astronomer friend of mine, has imagined what it was like on Earth that fateful day.

> Earth trembled as the shock wave spread outward from ground zero. Instantaneously, energy equivalent to that of a billion-megaton nuclear bomb was

An artist's rendition of the six-mile-diameter Chicxulub asteroid that smashed into the earth 65 million years ago, wiping out 75 percent of all life forms. Illustration by Dorothy Sigler Norton.

released, blowing away part of the atmosphere above ground zero and sending hundreds of cubic miles of dust and water vapor into and above the stratosphere. . . .

The expanding shock wave created enormous tidal waves several thousand feet high, which roared across the ocean at hundreds of miles per hour, carrying with them great masses of oceanic crust displaced by the explosion. . . . Accompanying these waves were winds that reached speeds of hundreds of miles per hour, blowing away from the impact point.[14]

Near the blast site the atmosphere would become superheated, to tens of thousands of degrees Celsius. The intensely hot and violent winds brought instantaneous fiery death to every living thing within hundreds of miles of the site. Violent earthquakes shook the earth as new fractures and faults ripped through the earth's crust, radiating outward from the center of the impact. Farther from the blast, instantaneous incineration did not take place; however, the blasting winds were still hot enough to start forest fires, perhaps more than a thousand miles from the crater's edge. The larger fragments of the earth's crust, blasted into space, began their fall back to earth. Not only did they reheat as they reentered the atmosphere, but also some pieces were caught in decaying orbits that caused them to land far afield. No place on Earth was safe from these new balls of fire falling from the sky.

Fires started over the face of Earth until it seemed as if the entire world would be consumed. Smoke and ash from burning vegetation joined perhaps four hundred billion metric tons of dust-size particles from the impact, which were already spreading out in the upper atmosphere and blanketing the planet. This blanket of ash and dust was so thick that sunshine could not penetrate it,[15] and within days the entire surface of Earth was plunged into utter darkness. Earth experienced night, a night without stars, for several *years,* a night that caused photosynthesis to stop in the plants lucky enough to have survived the initial blast and firestorm. *All* green plants died or became dormant, unable to use the energy from the sun, unable to grow, unable to reproduce, unable to provide food to consumers. The ecosystem of Earth collapsed.

In the oceans, all microscopic floating plants died. Most of the species became extinct, but a few survived by lying dormant, waiting. The food web of the oceans was decimated. Primary consumers fell next, followed shortly by higher orders. Scavengers made out well, at least for a while, feeding casually upon the growing pile of dying and rotting organisms. On land the story was much the same. If you weren't small enough to subsist on dried foliage, buried roots, or small herbivores, you were history. First the plants, then the large plant eaters, and finally the large carnivores breathed their last.

"What does it live on?" Alice asked, with great curiosity.
"Sap and sawdust," said the gnat.[16]

During the darkness, rampant thunderstorms, electrically charged by a massive infusion of dust, brought lightning and more fires. But even worse, these thunderstorms brought back to Earth the sulfur dioxide and nitrous oxides generated by the explosion—the gasses combined with water and formed sulfuric and nitric acids.[17] The ensuing thunderstorms brought down an acid rain from hell, further shredding the web of life.

As the months wore on, the airborne dust and ash slowly settled to earth. Little by little, the light of the sun was able to penetrate more deeply into the choked atmosphere until the blackness on the ground gave way to shades of gray, then brown. Eventually, the sun could be seen as a haloed orange orb, and young shoots unrolled from fern rhizomes, reaching for the light. They had been rooted beneath the surface of the fire-blackened soil, waiting. (Millions of years later, we would witness this same process when seeds salvaged from Incan tombs were exposed to sun and water—and sprouted corn, four hundred years after they had been buried.) The tenacity of life was not thwarted because of an asteroid, devastating fires, and acid rain. It would take more than that to prevent all evergreen cones and deciduous tree seeds from opening to the welcome hazy light of the long-absent sun, sending out feelers, drawing water up their roots and through the stems to the green cells within the tiny, growing plants. Chlorophyll combined with water and carbon dioxide, forming glucose, food for the growing plant. The miracle of photosynthesis had begun anew, even in the seas, where phytoplankton also awoke.

Insects reemerged from underground safe havens; frogs and toads crawled up out of the mud where they had lain dormant; turtles popped to the surface of ponds; crocodiles crawled from their banishment in dark swamps; birds took flight from sheltering crevices; and a few primitive, small-bodied mammals poked their tiny, pointed, hairy noses from their protective caves. These mammals diversified so rapidly that, within 30 million years, they split into all the basic forms we see today. They even invaded the seas, replacing their lost reptilian predecessors. They inherited a world previously ruled by *T. rex* and its kin. The terminal Cretaceous extinction, exacerbated by decreasing sea levels and sealed with the kiss of a visitor from outer space, had destroyed all large-bodied land animals. Suddenly, new real estate was open, and a vast array of biological niches was available for those left alive—the *K-T Times* headlines proclaimed, "Jobs Available!" The meek had indeed inherited the Earth.

From their weasel-like beginnings, one group of mammals developed larger and larger brains. They needed to hold their altricial young with one arm, which made it more difficult to dangle about in trees; our ancestors left the forests and walked out onto the plains—on two legs.[18] They picked up tree limbs and rocks as tools, and further developed gregarious relationships with individuals of the same species. Culture, eventually, was born.

Today, humans have the ability and the power to cause the extinction of other species. We also have developed weapons capable of wiping out our own species. Even so, we are not yet able to create the kind of explosion that echoed around the world 65 million years ago. We do not have the power to destroy life on this planet.

On Sunday, April 28, 1996, Malcolm Browne of the *New York Times* released a story on the wire. Mathematician Dr. Andrea Milani and his group at the University of Pisa, Italy, had just published a paper in *Nature*—about the changing orbital path of an asteroid known as 433 Eros. This is a large asteroid, fourteen miles in diameter, larger even than Chicxulub's. Its destructive force and resulting dust cloud would be twelve times as great if it collided with Earth. The team plotted the successive orbits of the asteroid, taking into account the effects of the larger planets in the solar system. The good news: 433 Eros is not plotted to intersect with Earth's orbit for some 1.14 million years.

The bad news: scientists have not been able to track and project the flight plans of all the *other* asteroids that might have an "impact" on us. If humans exist to witness a collision like 433 Eros's, it seems unlikely we would survive much longer. However, because they are small, birds just might carry the *Tyrannosaurus rex* torch into eternity.

Let There Be Light

When I think of surviving extinction, I think of *The Empire Strikes Back*. Remember that scene when Han Solo rushed out on the frozen planet to rescue Luke Skywalker? Han was riding a weird camel–*T. rex* thing that galloped along on its two hind legs. Once the creature succumbed to cold—and, possibly, hyperventilation, since it had an antiquated respiratory system—Han did what any good friend and future Indiana Jones would do. He used a light saber to slice open the belly of the beast and pulled the nearly frozen Luke up inside its steaming viscera. He saved both their lives even though the environment was, shall we say, unpleasant.

I imagine that is how birds survived their extinction event. At the end of the Cretaceous, a large number of bird species already had developed from their feathered *Archaeopteryx* and compsignathid ancestors. I imagine that survivors of the Chicxulub blast holed up in safe havens, protected from fires and acid rain in nooks and crannies of whatever was handy, including, possibly, a former *T. rex*. A dessicated carcass would have provided everything a growing family needed in the way of dried meat and insulation from the hostile environment. And when the sun emerged again, these brave birds hopped out of the remains of their cousin, eager for something other than jerky as a main course. Surviving birds rapidly would diversify in the new world at nearly the same rate as mammals, taking over a large number of the niches for medium- and small-bodied animals. As the air cleared, I imagine they took to the tortured sky with great relief and anticipation.

When they did so, they carried with them some of the very same genetic material that powered *T. rex*'s cells. Today, birds are more than an echo of the world's bloodiest royal dynasty. They are more than templates of *T. rex*. Birds are blood brothers to extinct theropods, descended from the very same ancestors. They are gatekeepers to a time lost forever—keeping *T. rex* alive not only in rocks and in our imaginations, but in their very DNA.

I wrote this chapter about dinosaur extinction while in prison. One of my greatest daily pleasures there was watching today's dinosaurs, who, aside from some small rabbits, were the only source of wildlife accessible to me. Thankfully, these birds nested in our rafters and yanked insects from the air. In more ways than one, they helped me survive my own extinction event. They fed my science and my spirit. When the sun came out, and my gates opened, I followed their lead into a new world. I took to the sky with great relief and anticipation.

EPILOGUE

Thus grew the tale of Wonderland:
Thus slowly, one by one,
Its quaint events were hammered out
And now the tale is done,
And home we steer, a merry crew,
Beneath the setting sun.[1]

Dinosaurs, as we commonly think of them, are extinct—but our challenge of knowing them is alive and well. In some ways, since BHI's croquet game with the U.S. government, that challenge has increased exponentially. Some people who followed our case have postulated that while interest in paleontology is higher than ever, willingness of people to stick their necks out to find new dinosaurs has diminished. Time will tell. Meanwhile, new specimens are being found each year, with *T. rex* still the headliner. In fact, during the summer of 2001, Jack Horner's MOR crew began excavating five—yes, five!—new *T. rex* specimens. In a single season.[2] If these dinosaurs prove to be scientifically significant, and not just fragmentary, they will raise our total number of *Tyrannosaurus rex* specimens to thirty-six!

Other fresh finds have not even been announced officially. Two were made by a rancher friend from the heart of *T. rex* country in South Dakota. He is working slowly on them, and one specimen in particular has a very interesting skull, including a disarticulated braincase potentially of great scientific value. A former University of Wisconsin paleontology student has been excavating another nicely preserved Montana skeleton for the past three seasons, and a Wyoming rancher discovered a specimen which has given up ribs, vertebrae, gastralia, and quite a bit of a skull.

While the beat goes on in the field, it is true that land policy issues and legislation are no clearer than when we slogged through them in court. For example, about fifty years ago, a *T. rex* specimen was found in Wyoming, but it remained unrecognized until 1994. Then, Leonard Zerbst, an avid amateur paleontologist-rancher and friend of mine (who tragically passed away in the spring of 2000), led the University of New Orleans's Kraig Derstler to the site.[3] Zerbst and his wife, Arlene, previously had made a number of important *Triceratops* discoveries over the years, but Derstler immediately recognized this specimen as *Tyrannosaurus rex*. The rub: it lay on a small parcel of Bureau of Land Management land within the Zerbst ranch.

Derstler previously had requested approval to conduct paleontological resource surveys on BLM lands, and had been denied. More exactly, BLM agent Laurie Bryant—the same person who headed up a reconnaissance team in our trial—claimed Derstler's paperwork had been lost in the system. We wondered if this was a dodge, a reaction partially generated due to Derstler's vocal support of us, and of other collectors, throughout our legal drama. When considering submitting future applications, Derstler was convinced his institution would not qualify in Bryant's mind as "a suitable repository" for public fossils—despite its thousands of specimens in residence. Assuming that he would be rejected, Derstler did not bother to apply for a permit to collect this new *T. rex*.[4]

In the summer of 2000, Rob Patchus, Derstler's former student and now a doctoral candidate at North Carolina University, took me to see the specimen. The occasion was a visit from Paul Sereno of the University of Chicago, an acclaimed paleontologist whose work on African dinosaurs has made a significant impact on the field. Sereno, a group of his students, and I saw the specimen together for the first time, and I instantly agreed with Derstler's identification. Broken edges of a somewhat large concretion exposed the cross-sections of large vertebrae riddled with honeycomb structure.

After careful examination, we identified the first-ever articulated *T. rex* thorax—where the entire upper body's vertebrae, ribs, and gastralia remained in place. We also saw the cross-section of part of a shoulder blade, an eroded but articulated leg and partial pelvis, perhaps even an articulated arm and furcula within the concretion. Not much chance of a head, but still a very, very important specimen. Then we looked more closely. "What's this?" I asked.

Amazingly, what appeared to be a string of articulated duck-bill tail vertebrae seemed to be jutting out of the dinosaur's throat. *This T. rex may have choked on its dinner!* Such an important moment in time was enough to send Sereno immediately to the telephone, and he applied to the BLM for permission to excavate. What happened next I chalk up to an irresistible impulse of sexual dimorphism.

Ironically, Laurie Bryant took Sereno's call, and responded immediately. She could not follow some orderly, national legislation outlining permitting procedures for fossil excavations on public lands, because none exists. My guess is she followed the laws of biology. Despite what males would like to believe, these laws dictate that while males strut their stuff, the *female* of a species always chooses her mate. Bryant's office had processed

Once Sue moved to the Chicago Field Museum, her banner was draped across the museum's facade until her debut in May 2000. Photo by Peter Larson.

Sue's coming out party. She is shrouded behind the curtain at back. Photo by Peter Larson.

requests from two scientists: Derstler, a robust specimen with graying plumage and a nest mid-tree; and Sereno, whose immediate and insistent call she may have interpreted as virility. He was gracile, younger, darker, and perched on a higher limb. Fame had dusted him with especially long and luminous tail feathers.

Sereno got the permit, and the dinosaur. Once preparation is complete, maybe he will tell us if this particular *T. rex* became extinct because it didn't chew its food. Hopefully, sometime soon, Bryant's mysterious method of selection also will become extinct. Paleontology is not well served as long as land managers arbitrarily decide who is qualified to collect fossils.

In May 2000, after the most tumultuous adolescence of any piece of paleontology, Sue finally walked down the debutante runway. I had discussed her bones with her new preparators and donated all of my research on her excavation and study to her new home. I still had not seen the X-ray of her leg, nor hashed out the details of all her pathologies, nor settled a scientific debate with one Field scientist about whether Sue's face actually was ripped off. But that was okay. Complete scientific agreement would take the fun out of it.

Sue with her new entourage. Photo by Peter Larson.

At the Chicago Field Museum, we attended a ball to end all balls, a cotillion fancier than Alice's Lobster Quadrille, covered by worldwide media and punctuated by a symphony. It was a four-star event anticipated not only by everyone in paleontology, not only by many a child in grade school, but also by an entire population of people who had fallen in love with Sue. Even considering the excitement of everyone else collected in the great hall, I knew this moment was special for the two of us. No one thought about Sue exactly as I did. I had waited a long time to see her.

She was backlit, behind an enormous curtain, her stark shadow racing along the fabric. There were speeches and questions and answers and applause—and then the curtain came down.

> "The Queen! The Queen!" and the three gardeners instantly threw themselves flat upon their faces.[5]

She stood there completely exposed for the first time.

An interminable, agonizing, slow-motion period elapsed during which photographs and autographs and interviews took place. Finally, I sneaked away for the moment I had been waiting for. I

Sue's first chevron, center, is "girl-shaped," and her healed tail injury, top right, probably occurred during copulation. Photo by Peter Larson.

sneaked a peek under Sue's tail. Although some of her primary chevrons were out of place when she was collected, the preparators had carefully replaced them in their original order. I was not surprised to note that Sue's first chevron was only two-thirds the size of the second. Definitely a girl.

I saw something else. The fourth through seventh tail vertebrae, close to the top of her tail, showed a unique healed injury. The dorsal spines had grown unusual fingers of bone reaching from spine to spine, nearly fusing them. This type of modification is the result of extreme stress upon the ligaments that unite the bones. Usually, these ligaments act like the cables of a suspension bridge, uniting them into one flexible, but strong, structure. What could have caused such a pathology? I propose that the extra weight of a copulating male is the simplest explanation—yet another indicator of gender.

John McCarter, president of the Field Museum, has invited me to spend more time with my oldest girlfriend, and she and I have much to discuss. Her pathologies were the subject of my submission to the 2001 SVP conference, and maybe she will have something to say about my next topic: the last word on sex.

It starts like this. Laying birds store calcium for production of eggshell inside the bones of their skeletons.[6] The demand for calcium is extreme. A laying hen will mobilize 8 to 10 percent of the total calcium in her bones in fifteen to sixteen hours to produce the two grams of calcium necessary for the creation of the hard covering on a single egg. Laying birds are able to accomplish this because they possess a special system of secondary bone in the marrow cavities of most of their skeleton. This unique tissue is called "medullary bone," and it resembles the cancellous, spongy bone found at the growing ends of bird bones.[7]

Medullary bone *only* occurs in female birds and *only* during the period of reproduction. It first appears with ovulation. The amount of medullary bone present at any time during the reproductive period depends upon the sequence of the egg production cycle. The most medullary bone is present right before the beginning of the laying down of eggshell; the last medullary bone disappears about a week after the laying of the last egg.[8]

If theropods also possessed this same system of calcium storage and retrieval for the production of eggshell, we should be able to find medullary bone within the skeletons of laying females. The absence of medullary bone would be inconclusive, because it could point either to a male or to a nonlaying female. However, its presence would absolutely guarantee that the bones belonged to a female, and a female who died during the period of producing eggs. Since Steven was found with fragments of theropod eggshell, "he" is a prime candidate to test for the presence of medullary bone.

Ultimately, I hope that we will be able to derive sexual identification even more directly. A team of scientists has found a way to determine gender from fragments of two-thousand-year-old bone. The Israeli-based team extracted DNA from the skeletal remains of ancient Roman babies found buried on the southern coast of Israel. After copying fragments of the gene for sex determination, the scientists were able to identify the sex of each individual.[9] Hopefully, this will work for extinct creatures as well.

Thanks to Sue, and everything she stands for—good and bad— paleontology has entered a new age. In the Dinosaur Naissance, bold adventurers cut fresh paths into the *Maco Sika* to find bones of ancient, unbelievable monsters. As these fossils poured into museums, they sliced open the belief systems of the public and blew away theories of a young planet described in Genesis. Decades later, with a makeover featuring warm blood, bird brains, and fleet feet, dinosaurs blasted into their Renaissance. It was a time of political confusion, unresolved policies, and caste-system condescension. The shadow cast by the debate over money was large and intimidating, but when the spotlight turned off, the beast itself was smaller than it had seemed.

Today, the playing field is much more level. No longer is the issue *whether* finance should impact science, but how it should be managed. The truth is, government cannot provide all the necessary funding for science in general, let alone paleontology. Nowadays, Sue holds hands with Ronald McDonald in the same way that the Giants play baseball at PacBell Park. The objects of our desire are at once nature, science, art, and commodity, and our objective is to distill them from politics as much as possible.

How does science avoid politics? That has been our question from the beginning, and we have navigated it with more or less success. I believe private money, freely given, provides the fewest strings. The best way I can think to accomplish that is through sales. When our paychecks are written, they are tied to no one else's agendas, bottom line, or sponsorship.

I have great hope that paleontology will find peace with its relationship to money, and with the politics of opening a purse. Let's face it: it takes money to prove our theories. We need star power: new fossils, research funding, increased expeditions, energy to catalogue past discoveries, and—more than anything—encouraged, enthusiastic, and skilled hands in the field. Perhaps this will be the age of the well-financed Dinosaur Diva. It will take Sue a little more time to hush the crowds and assign tasks to her assistants. I've seen the list:

1. Deal with that bad blood between paleo-people.
2. Find out whom to talk to about these silly arms.
3. Pass some sane laws.

The current attitude of the managers of our public lands each year makes it increasingly difficult for fossils to be collected and

Neal and youngest son Lief doing what they love best. Photo by Layne Kennedy.

preserved. The science of paleontology needs rational laws and regulations that will encourage the collection and curation of as many fossils as possible. The collectors' affiliations or degrees should not matter; their knowledge, experience and how much they care should. My fingers are crossed that the legislation submitted in the 2001–2002 congressional session gets lost in the shuffle in favor of more collector-friendly options.

When Duffy looks back at our dinosaur case, he isn't thinking of laws and governments and policies, or even dinosaurs. He's thinking of people, and he has one reflection. "If I had been older, if I had had more maturity, then . . . I was a young giant in a china closet." Yes he was. Although he wasn't even thirty-five years old, the young giant bravely and innovatively led the defense in the most dangerous game of my life.

Duffy remarried and started a new family. He is calmer, healthier, and more at peace than I have ever seen him. And he's not alone; everyone's life is different now. Neal's work with ammonites has steadily climbed into making history. He tirelessly sorts through the uncharted territory of the Great Plains sediments, discovering new species along the way. Especially important, Neal has brought to this research a unique, hands-on

Matthew, now 22, directs the excavation of Black Hills Institute's seventh *T. rex,* Bucky. The pelvic bone being removed is the left ilium. Photo by Henry Rust.

approach, and fresh ideas about the behavior of these long-dead cephalopods. His wife Brenda has turned our retail store into an enterprise none of us men could have conceived; their "baby" Elisha is now seven. My musician son Matthew currently manages some of our dig sites, a grown man who, like me, refuses to wear a hat most of the time in the field. Sarah is diving into studies in biology, while Tim is slated to be the next Tim Burton.

Bob still roams the catacombs of the institute, tracking our exponentially growing collection. Terry Wentz, still perhaps the best preparator on the planet, has moved to Seattle, where he conducts lecture series on paleontology—and still lends a hand on our toughest preparation projects. Marion Zenker still rules our family business with a firm hand, and our crew is busier than ever. Stan and Steve Sacrison are still kicking around for fossils.

Kevin Schieffer, the makeup-wearing Acting U.S. Attorney who seized Sue, remains embroiled in controversy. This time, as the president of Dakota, Montana & Eastern Railroad, Schieffer is in the midst of attempting to utilize government powers of eminent domain to condemn private lands for his company's new rail line.

A recent news article reported that the proposed route also would "disturb" land "known to hold fossils." Apparently he sends his hedgehogs through both sides of the croquet wicket.[10] Pat Duffy, Bruce Ellison, Bob Mandel, and David Zuercher still practice law, but rarely in front of Judge Battey, who is now semi-retired. And Susan Hendrickson? Disgusted with the American legal system, she is now a citizen of France who continues her underwater archaeological expeditions, including Cleopatra's celebrated palace in the sunken city of Alexandria. Susan also remains a loyal friend, and a spokesperson for Sue.

Kristin's and my marriage did not survive our harrowing trip to Wonderland, although our friendship remains unscathed. We had some of our best times while smoothing this text and recalling a shared experience that will bind us together forever. She still marches across the earth's crust to her own drummer, living a creative life as out-of-the-ordinary as my own. I got luckier than I could have imagined by marrying Naidine—and now we share baby Ella. It's true what they say: time heals, life goes on, silver linings. Stuff like that.

Black Hills Institute is different now, too. No rancher ever will wonder who we are when we knock on their doors. With the bottom falling out of agronomy, fossils have become a cash crop, and our record has played in jukeboxes in every diner in the Midwest. While we receive even more phone calls from ranch houses dotted across the plains, times have changed since we pounded the prairie virtually alone, mapping uncharted territory in our field notebooks, shaking hands and sweating in the hot sun, collecting bones for months on end. Now we have bent to common wisdom, which whispers that Dinosaur Divas demand a little civilization even in the middle of nowhere. They like contracts before they appear on stage. And Porta-Potties. Don't forget the limo.

Black Hills Institute was conceived as a commercial fossil and mineral supply house simply because I didn't want to draw a paycheck as a geologist at an oil company, or as someone's field collector. My partners and I just wanted to play in the dirt and get paid for it, and one day I woke up as the poster child for private enterprise. I didn't see myself making a statement; I was just doing my thing. People, including Kristin, have said that because of the prominence of my company, because of what we do, and because of what we experienced, it is incumbent upon me to have opinions about how to pave the way for constructive fossil legislation, to reach out to those of polar philosophical views, to stand firmly with one foot in science and one foot in private enterprise. Today I paced around, waving my arms, telling her I don't know all the answers. "I'm just a guy!" I replied. She said I sounded a little like Rodney King, wishing everyone could just get along.

This is what I know: what we are doing is meant to be. As our trial and my prison sentence faded into history, business in Hill City picked up more than tenfold. As of this writing, we are starting the largest project of our careers: The Children's Museum of Indianapolis has ordered a new dinosaur hall, filled with original skeletons. Perhaps our survival sent a biological message out into the field: "What didn't kill us made us stronger." Our company's genes will carry on.

I'm still thinking about sex, and remain on the trail of DNA and gender-typing *T. rex* skeletons, along with extrapolating ancient behavior. My experiences have led to some interesting and diverse speaking invitations, sometimes well out of the realm of paleontology. For example, standing at Sue's feet in the Field Museum, I told medical doctors about the evidence in that gnarly skeleton of her array of medical problems. My most recent engagement: I shared what I had learned about wrestling with the law, at none other than the annual gathering of the National Association of Court Reporters.

I wore a collecting vest and blue jeans.

Extinction Timeline

Extinctions appear to coincide with large impact events and may be one of the driving forces of evolution.

Illustration by Paul R. Janke.

Key Events Timeline

1842 Owens coins the name "Dinosauria"

1861 First full skeleton of *Archaeopteryx* is discovered

1883 Cope describes *Monospondylus gigas,* which will turn out to be the first *T. rex* bone on record—although of a different name

1900–1906 Barnum Brown discovers the first three recognized *Tyrannosaurus rex* skeletons, BM-R7995, CM-9380, and AMNH-5027

1906 The Antiquities Act is passed to protect human artifacts

1915 Osborn unveils the first mounted *T. rex* skeleton at the American Museum of Natural History

1923 Andrews finds first complete dinosaur eggs and nests in Mongolia

1969 Williams places some of his land in trust with the U.S. government

1974 Black Hills Institute is founded

1979 BHI opens Ruth Mason Duckbill Dinosaur Quarry

June 1980 Alvarez team postulates asteroid theory of dinosaur extinction

1982 BLM publishes proposed rules for collecting fossils, kick-starting a legislative battle

1984–1986 NAS Committee on Paleontological Collecting convened to make Congressional recommendations; its report is ignored

Winters 1985, 1987–1990 Peter works in Peru

1989 SVP issues position statement against commercial collecting

August 12, 1990 Susan Hendrickson discovers Sue

August 14–September 1, 1990 Sue excavation; on August 27, BHI pays Maurice Williams $5,000

October 1990 Cheyenne River Sioux Tribe passes a resolution claiming ownership of Sue

March 13, 1992 Sue donated to the newly incorporated Black Hills Museum of Natural History (on Friday the 13th)

April 14, 1992 Stan excavation begins

May 14–16, 1992 FBI and National Guard seize Sue from BHI

May 22, 1992 Legal A: BHI files suit for return of Sue, which Judge Battey denies on May 28

June 1, 1992 Re A: BHI appeals to Eighth Circuit; on June 26, a custody hearing is ordered

July 9–13, 1992 Re A: BHI loses custody hearing

July 20, 1992 Re A: BHI files custody appeal to Eighth Circuit

July 31, 1992 Legal B: BHI files another complaint, this time asking for "superior possessory interest" of Sue—the closest they can get to ownership

August 28, 1992 Re B: Judge Battey converts the argument into a motion for "summary judgment"

November 2, 1992 Re A: Eighth Circuit upholds custody decision

January 28, 1993 The U.S. government serves an enormous subpoena on BHI, wherein the company is ordered to turn over voluminous files within twenty-four hours

February 3, 1993 Re B: BHI loses "summary judgment" and its legal interest in Sue—Battey calls Sue "real estate"

April 13, 1993 Cheyenne River Sioux Tribe files suit in tribal court, requesting forfeiture of Sue based on business license law

April 19, 1993 Re B: BHI appeals real estate decision to the Eighth Circuit

July 5, 1994 In its own tribal court, Cheyenne River Sioux Tribe is denied forfeiture of Sue

1993 First recognized theropod embryo, discovered in China, goes public

June 4, 1993 FBI conducts Seizure II at BHI

July 12, 1993 Duffy excavation begins

November 19, 1993 BHI and principals indicted

November 21, 1993 Tokyo Broadcasting commits to BHI's *T. rex* world tour

December 15, 1993 Arraignment; on the same day, Eighth Circuit affirms real estate decision

January 6, 1994 Recusal 1: BHI files for the judge to step down based on allowing a wrongful seizure; Battey refuses on January 19

February 15, 1994 Legal C: BHI files lien against Williams to recoup its more than $200,000 expenses if/when Sue is sold

February 18, 1994 Re Recusal 1: BHI appeals to Eighth Circuit; on March 24, appeals court upholds Battey's decision to stay on the bench

May 2, 1994 Re B: BHI files certiorari with the Supreme Court, appealing the Sue-as-real-estate decision

July 23, 1994 In criminal case, BHI files for suppression of evidence based on an illegal seizure of Sue and illegal use of the military

July–September 1994 Plea bargaining nearly ends the legal nightmare

September 20–22, 1994 Plea bargain news article appears, revealing the secret negotiations; Judge Battey admits violating Rule 11(e) during subsequent talks

September 29, 1994 Recusal 2: BHI asks Battey to step down again, this time based on Rule 11(e) violation; he refuses on October 6

Fall 1994 BHI first visits the Foxy Lady site; excavation must await approval of the Harding County commissioners

October 3, 1994 Re B: Supreme Court refuses to hear Sue case

October 10, 1994 Re Recusal 2: BHI appeals to Eighth Circuit; BHI loses on December 29

January 10–February 24, 1995 Trial; verdict is delivered March 14 after nearly three weeks of deliberation

April 25, 1995 Recusal 3: BHI asks Battey to step down so another judge can decide sentencing; Battey refuses on May 23

April 27, 1995 Jurors call a press conference criticizing the judge and how the case was handled

May 23, 1995 U.S. Attorney's office decides not to retry "hung" counts

Summer 1995 Stan headlines the *T. rex* World Exposition in Japan; at home, Steven's excavation begins

August 11, 1995 Re C: Battey denies BHI's lien against Williams

September 8, 1995 Re C: BHI appeals lien decision to Eighth Circuit

January 16, 1996 Presentencing hearing, with Peruvian testimony; sentencing occurs on January 22

February 22, 1996 Peter surrenders to the Federal Prison Camp

Summer 1996 Excavation of Foxy Lady begins

July 5, 1996 Re C: Eighth Circuit upholds lien decision

July 9, 1996 In Peruvian court, Peter is acquitted of wrongdoing in Peru, but will not see the decision until December

July 10, 1996 Legal D: BHI appeals convictions and sentence to Eighth Circuit

October 1996 Chinese compsignathid is revealed to have had protofeathers, removing any doubt that dinosaurs and birds are related

December 19, 1996 Re D: Pat Duffy files an emergency amendment to the appeal of convictions—this document includes the vital Peruvian decision

April 10, 1997 Re D: Eighth Circuit upholds convictions and sentencing

September 18, 1997 Peter released from prison into home confinement

October 27, 1997 Sue auctioned at Sotheby's for $8.36 million

November 18, 1997 Peter released from home confinement and begins two years of probation

May 2000 Sue is debuted at the Chicago Field Museum

June 6, 2000 E.D. Cope excavation begins

2001 Announcement of a feathered Chinese dromaeosaur, 130 million years old, proves that feathers predated the advent of birds

April 18, 2002 Bucky excavation begins

The Modern Bone War

	Establishment view	Independent view
National Treasures	Fossils are the heritage of the state or country where they are found, and should be reposited and curated only by state-sanctioned facilities. (Some countries retain state ownership of all fossils.)	Fossils are part of the history of the planet. As such, they should be allowed to travel freely across human borders. Everyone should be able to own a fossil.
Renewable and Nonrenewable Resources	The number of fossils imbedded in the earth is finite and, theoretically, each one should be protected.	Fossils occur abundantly wherever there is sedimentary rock. Weathering constantly exposes and destroys them, literally by the billions each day. They should be harvested.
Morality	It is immoral to sell national treasures or cultural heritage because the process puts a price tag on priceless items of antiquity.	The great majority of fossils can be thought of like art, gravel, oil, minerals, or grazing rights—which are commonly sold or leased. Morality is not a factor.
Public Resources	When fossil specimens are sold to private collectors, these limited, valuable scientific materials are lost to the public. When sold out of the United States, they are lost to Americans.	Scientifically important specimens should be sold or donated to museums. However, common fossils are so abundant that it doesn't matter who owns them.

	Establishment view	Independent view
Fossil Sales	Skyrocketing fossil prices prevent public institutions from competing for fossils in an open marketplace because they cannot match funds with private enterprise.	Buying fossils provides a cost-effective method by which institutions can increase their number of display or research specimens. It is often cheaper than the alternative: combined costs of discovery, excavation, preparation, mounting, and staff salaries.
Land Fees	Independents pollute the process of land access by offering to pay private landowners either for access to their land or for the fossils discovered there. Today many landowners expect payments that exceed typical museum or university budgets.	A landowner should not be expected to give something of value for free, although many do. Private and government concerns routinely pay for hunting or grazing rights, oil exploration, or the quarrying of sand, gravel, or limestone.
Qualified Personnel	Only government-affiliated paleontologists should have access to public lands and fossil resources. This ensures the safety of public resources.	The government does not have enough resources or personnel to collect and curate all fossils on the half-billion acres of public land. The participation of commercial and amateur collectors allows more fossils to be saved from the effects of weathering.
Expertise	Commercial collectors sometimes destroy important scientific finds—and accompanying data—due to their inexperience or attitude.	Legitimate independent collectors, who typically spend each season in the field, are as trained, careful, and thorough as academic crews—often more so.

	Establishment view	Independent view
Efficiency vs. Careless Collecting	Digging fossils correctly and carefully takes time. Sometimes budgetary or other constraints determine excavation choices or length, but it is not unusual for the removal of one large, significant fossil to span one or more entire collecting season(s). Quicker schedules can result in damaged bones, and are often undertaken by commercial entities most concerned with production, not science.	Independent collectors are not bound by committee grants or institutional demands, and they pay all excavation bills themselves. Thus, they often are motivated to create more efficient (and equally careful) techniques of removing the fossils from the ground or preparing them in the laboratory. Even so, these collectors also often spend several seasons digging one single specimen.
Ethics	Because of fossils' increased economic value, they are at the mercy of unscrupulous commercial collectors who will sell anything to the highest bidder. To procure and successfully market valuable specimens, these people might even collect in off-limits areas or intentionally misstate localities.	Legitimate independent companies are bound by the same ethics as museums and universities. Marketing fossils does not by definition indicate unethical behavior. Instead, a unified front among all professional paleontologists will help to identify and curb those who do the most harm to fossil resources.
Regulation & Legislation	At present, public land management agencies independently regulate fossil collection on their own lands. Ideally, new, more far-reaching laws should provide stiffer penalties for the unauthorized collection of fossils from public lands.	Nationwide, consistent regulation of fossil collecting on public lands is the best plan. Sharing the collecting and custodial responsibilities among all professional and amateur collectors will cause the most fossils to be saved for posterity.

APPENDIX D

Tyrannosaurus rex Specimen Timeline

October 2001

SPECIMEN	DISCOVERER*	YEAR	LOCALE	SKELETON	DISPLAY	SEX	LOCATION	SKULL >10%
1. AMNH-5866	Cope-P	1892	SD	<1%	No	?	AMNH, New York, NY	no
2. BM-R7995	Brown-P	1900	WY	13%	No	?	British Museum, London	no
3. CM-9380	Brown-P	1902	MT	10%	Yes	F	CMNH, Pittsburgh, PA	yes
4. AMNH-5027	Brown-P	1906	MT	45%	Yes	?M	AMNH, New York, NY	yes
5. TMP.81.12.1	Sternberg-P	1946	Alb	20%	Yes	M	RTMP, Drumheller, Alberta	no
6. LACM-23844	Garbani-A	1966	MT	25%	Yes	M	LACM, Los Angeles, CA	yes
7. LACM-23845	Garbani-A	1966	MT	12%	No	?	LACM, Los Angeles, CA	yes
8. MOR-008	MacMannis-A	1967	MT	40% of skull	No	F	MOR, Bozeman, MT	yes
9. SDSM-12047	Floden-A	1980	SD	25%	Yes	?	SDSMT Museum, Rapid City, SD	yes
10. TMP.81.6.1	Student-A	1981	Alb	25%	Yes	F	RTMP, Drumheller, Alberta	yes
11. MOR-009	Hager-P	1981	MT	15%	No	?	MOR, Bozeman, MT	no
12. MOR-555	Wankel-A	1988	MT	46%	No	M	MOR, Bozeman, MT	yes
13. SUE-BHI2033	Hendrickson-A	1990	SD	80%	Yes	F	FMNH-PR2081, Chicago IL	yes
14. STAN-BHI3033	Sacrison-A	1992	SD	66%	Yes	M	BH Institute, Hill City, SD	yes
15. DMNH-2827	Fickle-A	1992	CO	2%	Yes	?	DMNH, Denver, CO	no
16. Z-rex	Zimmerscheid-A	1992	SD	42%	No	?	Private - Kansas	yes
17. Bowman	Pearson-A	1993	ND	10%	Yes	?	Bowman, ND	no
18. DUFFY-BHI4100	Sacrison-A	1993	SD	25% to date	Yes	?	BH Institute, Hill City, SD	yes
19. "Scottie"	Gebhardt-A	1994	Sask	50%?	No	?M	RSM, Regina, Saskatchewan	?
20. U of Wisconsin	Pfister-A	1994	MT	<10%	No	?	U of WI @ Madison Museum	?
21. FOX 8-12-96	L. Fox-A	1994	SD	10% to date	No	?F	BH Institute, Hill City, SD	?
22. STEVEN 9-14-95	Sacrison-A	1995	SD	?	No	?	BH Institute, Hill City, SD	no
23. Pete	Patchus-A	1995	WY	approx. 10%	?	?	UNO, New Orleans, LA	no
24. RJB	Theisen-P	1995	WY	20%	No	?	South Dakota	?
25. Peck's rex	Tremblay-A	1997	MT	?	Yes	?	Ft Peck Visitor's Center, MT	yes
26. Tinker-juvenile	Eatman-P	1997	SD	20% to date	No	?	Private, TX	yes
27. Rex A	P	1998	MT	20% to date	No	?	Private, MT	?
28. Rex B	A	1998	SD	>10% to date	No	?	Private SD	?
29. Rex C	A	1999	SD	>10% to date	No	?	Private, SD	yes
30. E.D. Cope	Derflinger-A	1999	SD	>10% to date	Yes	?	BH Institute, Hill City, SD	?
31. Monty	A	2000	WY	?	No	?	Private, WY	yes
32. Bucky	Derflinger-A	2001	SD	>30% to date	No	F	The Children's Museum, Indpls, IN	?

Table compiled by Black Hills Institute paleo staff

* P = Professional collector and A = Amateur collector

* % = calculation = number of bones represented divided by bone count in complete skeleton.

Note: There are two skeletal morphotypes: a robust form we believe is female and a gracile form we believe is male.

Carnivorous Dinosaur Family Tree

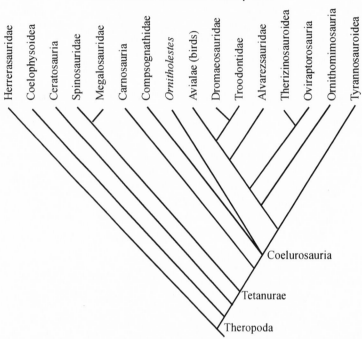

Tyrannosaurus and Its Closest Cousins

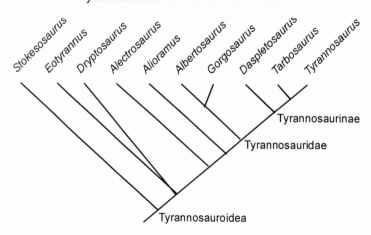

APPENDIX F

Tyrannosaurus rex Bone Diagrams

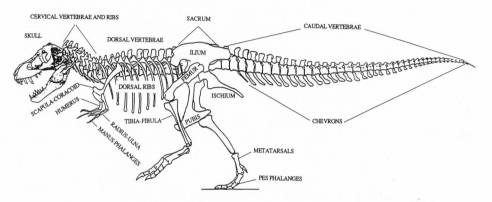

Bone diagram of the skeleton of *Tyrannosaurus rex*.

Illustration by Peter Larson, modified from Dorothy Sigler Norton and Ken Carpenter.

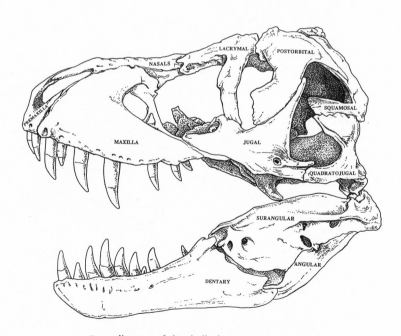

Bone diagram of the skull of *Tyrannosaurus rex*.

Illustration by Dorothy Sigler Norton.

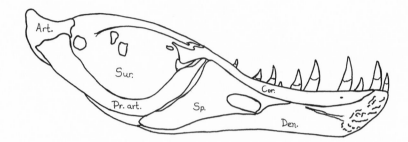

Bone diagram of *T. rex* lower jaw, medial (inside the mouth) view. From left: Art. = Articular; Sur. = Surangular; Pr. art. = Prearticular; Sp. = Splenial; Cor. = Coronoid; Den. = Dentary. Illustration by Peter Larson.

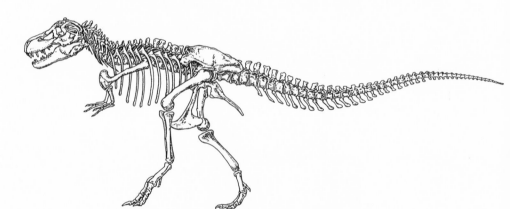

Scientific illustration of Sue's skeleton.
Illustration by Dorothy Sigler Norton.

Artist's rendition of Sue's skull and neck vertebrae.
Illustration by Vera Krejsa.

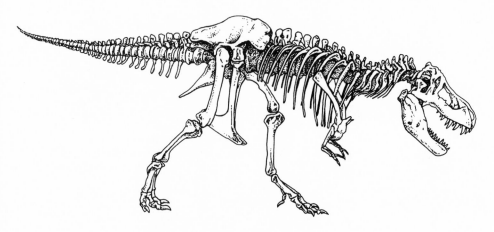

Scientific illustration of Stan's skeleton.
Illustration by Dorothy Sigler Norton.

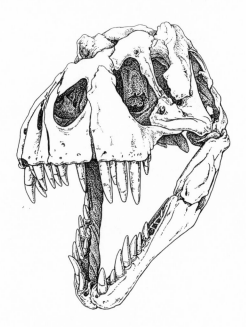

Scientific illustration of Stan's skull after cleaning and assembly.
Illustration by Dorothy Sigler Norton.

Protest poster circulated around the world.

Illustration by Dorothy Sigler Norton, Marion Zenker, and Terry Wentz.

Free at Last.

Illustration by Dorothy Sigler Norton.

Glossary

AAPS: American Association of Paleontological Suppliers, a group of independent fossil collectors and vendors.

Acetabulum: The socket of the hip joint created by the junction of the ilium, ischium, and the pubis.

Albertosaurus: An extinct genus of theropod belonging to a group called tyrannosaurids. *Albertosaurus* has been found in Western North America in sediments around 75 million years old.

Ammonite: Belonging to the extinct order Ammonoidea, class Cephalopoda. Its nearest living relatives are octopus, squid, and the chambered nautilus.

Anatotitan: An extinct genus of hadrosaurian (duckbill) ornithischian dinosaur that lived contemporaneously with *Tyrannosaurus rex.*

Anorbital fenestra: An opening, or window, in the skull located just in front of the orbit (eye). This character (along with a trend toward bipedalism) unites dinosaurs with crocodiles, pterosaurs, and a few other forms into a larger group called archosauria.

Appeal: A legal request that a higher court review a decision of a lower court.

Archaeology: The study of ancient humans and their culture.

Archaeopteryx: The earliest recognized genus of fossil bird. The few known specimens all come from the Jurassic age (150 million years ago) Solnhoffen Limestone of Germany. The extremely well preserved specimens combine many typical theropod features with modern bird asymmetrical flight feathers.

Arraignment: To enter pleas in court, answering the charges of an indictment.

Articulated: Skeletal elements preserved in life position.

Asteroid: A planetoid body that orbits the sun. Most are found in the asteroid belt between Mars and Jupiter, however the gravity of Jupiter occasionally forces asteroids into erratic orbits, some of which intersect Earth's.

Aves: A phylogenetic group containing all birds and confined within the larger group called theropoda.

Avian respiratory system: A two-cycle, one-way, efficient breathing system found today only in birds. The fossil record gives us evidence that it also occurred in other theropods, pterosaurs, and sauropods.

Badlands: Land cut by erosion, devoid of plants, and often fossiliferous.

BIA: Bureau of Indian Affairs, a branch of the Department of the Interior developed to oversee American Indian issues such as the administration of trust lands.

BLM: Bureau of Land Management, a branch of the Department of the Interior currently charged with managing excess public land holdings.

Bone Wars: Begun in the late 1800s by feuding paleontologists, the Bone Wars continue today as a battle between independent and establishment paleontologists over who should collect fossils.

Butte: A flat-topped hill.

Camellate: A texture or structure found within the vertebrae of animals possessing an avian respiratory system. It consists of connecting air chambers divided by thin walls of bone called trabeculae.

Camera: A large air-filled space within a vertebra, connected to the respiratory system by way of a diverticula.

CAT scan: Also known as CT Scan, this technique uses computerized tomography to produce sectional X-ray views through an object. These images can be viewed either as slices or compiled into a three-dimensional array.

Caudal: Of, or pertaining to, the tail.

Centrum: The main body of a vertebra.

Ceratopsian: An extinct group of horned ornithischian dinosaurs characterized by an extension of the rear of the skull, creating a protective frill over the neck. Ceratopsians are found only in Cretaceous-aged sediments.

Certiorari: A writ to a superior court intending to correct errors of a lower court.

Cervical: Of, or pertaining to, the neck.

Character: A term used in the cladistics classification system that aids in uniting like organisms on the basis of physiological similarities. For example, all members of the genus *Homo* have characters of upright stature, large brains, and highly derived voice boxes.

Chevron: Also haemal arch, this bony spine attaches to the underside of the tail vertebrae.

Cladogram: A phylogenetic (family) tree linking organisms based on shared characters.

Cladistics: A system of classifying animals based upon shared derived or primitive characters.

Cloaca: The single opening in reptiles, amphibians, birds, and dinosaurs used for sexual reproduction and the removal of liquid and solid waste.

Coelophysis: An extinct genus of theropod from the Late Triassic (210 million years ago) of North America.

Coelurosauria: A group of mostly small theropod dinosaurs including velociraptors, oviraptors, ornithomimids, birds, and tyrannosaurs.

Coprolite: Fossilized excrement.

Cranial kinesis: The ability of the skull bones to move relative to one another.

Cretaceous: A geologic period at the end of the Mesozoic Era, the age of dinosaurs, from 144 to 65 million years ago.

Cross-bedding: A diagnostic pattern of sediment deposition that allows researchers to determine the flow direction of wind or water.

Dentary: The tooth-bearing element of the lower jaw.

Desplatosaurus: An extinct genus of Upper Cretaceous theropod belonging to the group tyrannosauridae.

Dinosauria: A group of animals including sauropods, theropods, and ornithischians. The only living representatives are birds.

Disarticulated: Skeletal elements preserved randomly, out of their life positions.

Diverticulum: An outgrowth of the respiratory system that presses against and eventually invades bones of the skeleton, especially the vertebrae.

DNA: Deoxyribonucleic acid, a self-replicating, complex, organic molecule. The definitive building blocks of earthly life.

Dorsal: Of, or pertaining to, the back.

Dorsal vertebrae: Vertebrae between sacrum and neck.

Dromaeosaurus: An Upper Cretaceous extinct genus of theropod often called "raptors."

Ectotherm: An animal that is dependent upon the environment to regulate its body temperature. Cold-blooded.

Edmontosaurus: An extinct genus of hadrosaurian (duckbill) ornithischian dinosaurs. These very common herbivores were contemporaries (and dinner!) of *T. rex.*

Endotherm: An animal that maintains a relative constant body temperature through internal processes. Warm-blooded.

Eoraptor: An extinct genus of primitive theropod from the Triassic of Argentina. At 225 million years old, it is currently the oldest member of the group.

Eotyrannus: A recently discovered genus of extinct theropod, perhaps a direct ancestor of *Tyrannosaurus rex.* At 140 million years old, it is one of the earliest tyrannosaurids.

Femur: Upper leg bone.

Fenestra: Windowlike opening in bone.

Fibula: Smaller of two lower leg bones in the shin. Its companion is the tibia.

Foramen: Small opening in bone for the passage of nerves, arteries, or veins.

Fossa: A pit or depression in bone.

Fossil: Evidence of ancient life, including bones, leaves, impressions, and trackways.

Furcula: The "wishbone" created from the fusion of the right and left clavicles, or collar bones.

Gastralia: Abdominal ribs or riblike structures protecting the belly. Gastralia are found in dinosaurs and in living reptiles.

Geologic section: A measurement of a rock face to record changes in lithology, allowing the study of environmental changes through time.

Gorgosaurus: An extinct genus of the group tyrannosauridae which lived approximately 75 million years ago.

GPR: Ground Probing Radar, a technique used to locate buried gas tanks and lost graves.

GPS: Global Positioning System, a method of using satellites to locate precise coordinates on the surface of the earth.

Hadrosaur: A group of ornithischian dinosaurs characterized by a broad, toothless beak fronting a complex and highly derived cheek tooth battery used to grind plants. Species of this diverse group of Upper Cretaceous herbivores are often preserved in large bonebeds, indicating they travelled in herds.

Humerus: Upper arm bone.

Ilium: The dorsal-most pelvic bone; its partners are the ischium and pubis.

Indictment: A formal statement of criminal charges presented by a prosecuting attorney with the approval of a grand jury.

Intromittent organ: A primitive, retractable penis found in some birds and reptiles.

Invertebrate: In simple terms, an animal without a backbone.

Ischium: The pelvic bone lying below the ilium and behind the pubis.

Jurassic: A geologic period in the middle of the Mesozoic (the age of dinosaurs), from 206 to 144 million years ago.

K-T Boundary: A horizontal line separating the Cretaceous from the Tertiary Periods, deposited approximately 65 million years ago, sometimes marked by a thin layer of clay. This boundary delineates a mass global extinction which included all dinosaurs except birds.

Lateral: Located on the side.

Lithology: The character of a rock formation, including structure, composition, color, and texture.

Maastrichtian stage: The uppermost Cretaceous, from 71 to 65 million years ago. *T. rex* lived in the latter half of this stage.

Manus: The hand.

Maxilla: The larger tooth-bearing element of the upper jaw. Its smaller counterpart is the premaxilla.

Medial: Relating to the middle.

Mesozoic: A geologic era from 250 to 65 million years ago. Literally, "middle life," the Mesozoic era is sandwiched between the Paleozoic ("ancient life") and Cenozoic ("new life").

Metacarpals: The long bones of the hand, between the wrist (carpals) and the phalanges.

Metatarsals: The long bones of the foot, between the ankle (tarsals) and the phalanges.

Nanotyrannus: An extinct genus of theropod closely related to and contemporaneous with *Tyrannosaurus rex.* Also called "pigmy tyrannus."

NAS: National Academy of Sciences, a federal advisory board concerned particularly with scientific research and funding.

Nodosaurs: An extinct group of ornithischian dinosaurs characterized by heavily armoured skin. Nodosaurs lived from the Late Jurassic to the K-T Boundary.

Occipital condyle: On dinosaurs, the ball on the back of the head which articulates with the first vertebra of the neck, also called the atlas.

Olfactory: Pertaining to the sense of smell.

Ornithischian: Literally "bird-hipped," this extinct herbivorous group is one of two major divisions of Dinosauria; the other is Saurischian. Named because the shape of the pelvis is superficially reminiscent of a bird's, ornithischians' chief defining characters include the presence of a predentary bone at the front of the lower jaw. This group lived from 220 to 65 million years ago.

Ornithomimus: Literally "bird mimic," this extinct genus was contemporaneous to and a close relative of *T. rex.* These toothless coelurosaurs resembled an ostrich with a long tail.

Ovary: One of the paired female gonads. This reproductive organ produces eggs and female hormones.

Oviduct: The passage through which the egg travels from the ovary to the cloaca.

Oviraptor: An extinct genus of toothless theropod belonging to the group Coelurosauria. Literally "egg thief," *Oviraptor* was found in Asia in sediments approximately 80 million years old.

Oviraptorid: An extinct group of toothless coelurosaurs found in North America and Asia in Cretaceous-aged sediments.

Pachycephalosaurus: Literally "thick-headed lizard," this extinct genus belongs to a primitive group of ornithischian dinosaurs with a thick layer of bone protecting its tiny brain, giving it the superficial appearance of intelligence.

Paleontology: The study of ancient animal and plant life.

Pathology: Physiological evidence of injury or disease.

Pes: The foot.

Phalange: Finger or toe bone.

Plaster of paris: Powdered calcium sulfate. When mixed with water, it crystallizes into a hard shell that protects fossils and aids in their safe collection.

Pleurocoels: Depressions in bone caused by the attempted invasion of the respiratory system.

Pneumatic: Air-filled.

Pneumatic foramina: Openings in bone caused by the invasion of the respiratory system.

Pneumatic tools: Tools whose power source is compressed air.

Posse comitatus: Illegal use of the military in actions against citizens of the United States.

Premaxilla: One of a pair of tooth-bearing bones in the front of the upper jaw.

Private land: Land whose title is held by private individuals, groups, or corporations. This is the only land subject to property taxes.

Probation: A sentence imposed by a court during which a person must report regularly to a probation officer and remain within a specified area except under special permission.

Prosauropods: A group of primitive saurischian dinosaurs that is thought to have given rise to long-necked sauropods. They lived from 215 to 200 million years ago.

Pterosaur: "Flying reptiles," this extinct group includes the robin-sized *Pterodactylus* and the giant *Quetzalcoatlus,* whose wing span reached forty feet. Pterosaurs have been found in sediments 230 to 65 million years old.

Pubis: The pelvic bone lying below and forward of the ilium.

Pubic boot: A ventral expansion of the pubis that would have allowed nesting and sleeping dinosaurs to roost without putting undue pressure on their internal organs.

Public land: Land whose title is held by the federal government for the benefit of its citizens. These lands are managed by agencies including the Bureau of Land Management and the Forest Service. In most western states there is more public land than private.

PVA: Polyvinyl acetate, a hardener and consolidant used in the conservation of fossils.

Radius: The smaller of the two lower arm bones; its partner is the ulna.

Recusal motion: A legal filing requesting a judge to step down from presiding over a case.

Sacrum: The fused vertebrae located within the pelvis.

Saurischian: Literally "lizard-hipped," this group is one of two major divisions of Dinosauria; the other is Ornithischian. Saurischians include extinct sauropods, prosauropods, and theropods, as well as today's birds. This group arose 225 million years ago.

Sauropods: An extinct group of herbivorous saurischian dinosaurs, these animals are characterized by elongated necks and elephantine proportions. They lived from 200 to 65 million years ago.

Struthiomimus: Literally "ostrich mimic," this extinct genus of ornithomimid dinosaurs is characterized by a small, toothless skull with a surprisingly large brain, and legs built for speed. This North American genus was contemporaneous with *T. rex.*

Syntarsus: An extinct genus of primitive theropod from the Lower Jurassic of southern Africa, it is closely related to the Triassic *Coelophysis.*

Subpoena: A summons signed by a judge ordering the appearance in court of a defendant or witness, and/or ordering the surrender of documents or possessions.

Superglue: Cyanoacrylate. Strong, multiple-viscosity liquids used to glue fossil fragments. Superglues are indispensable in the field and lab.

SVP: Society of Vertebrate Paleontology, a group founded for the promotion of the science of vertebrate paleontology.

Lateral: Located on the side.

Taphonomy: The study of the series of events that led to a fossil deposit.

Thescelosaurus: An extinct genus of primitive Ornithischian dinosaur that lived at the close of the Cretaceous in North America.

Three-Piece-Suitification: Coined by Bob Bakker, this term attempts to explain the division between groups in paleontology, which was initiated by a lack of scientific funding.

Torosaurus: A close and contemporaneous relative of *Triceratops,* this extinct genus possessed the largest skull of any land animal ever—nine feet in length.

Trabecula: Thin bony walls separating air chambers within vertebrae invaded by the respiratory system. See *camellate.*

Triassic: A geologic period at the beginning of the Mesozoic era (the age of the dinosaurs) from 250 to 206 million years ago.

Tribal land: See Trust Land.

Triceratops: Literally "three-horned face," this large-bodied extinct genus of ceratopsian dinosaurs was contemporaneous with *T. rex*. Although protected by a massive bony frill and three substantial horns, it was still one of *T. rex*'s favorite meals.

Trilobite: An extinct group of marine arthropods characterized by a three-lobed body, trilobites lived from 540 to 250 million years ago. Often called "bugs," many species possessed large, compound, insectlike eyes.

Trust land: Untaxed land owned by an individual American Indian, an Indian group, or a tribe, the title of which is held by the U.S. government for the benefit of the owner.

Turbinates: Thin, coiled sinus bones used by some endotherms to manage respiratory moisture. Turbinates are also the site for olfactory sensors.

Tyrannosaur: See *Tyrannosaurid.*

Tyrannosaurid: An Upper Cretaceous group of relatively large theropods including *Tyrannosaurus rex*. Among the defining characters of this group are large skulls, an S-shaped neck, and tiny arms with only two fingers.

Tyrannosaurus bataar: Also known as *Tarbosaurus bataar.* At 70 million years old, this Asian tyrannosaur is probably the direct ancestor of *T. rex.*

Tyrannosaurus rex: My favorite dinosaur.

Tyrannosaurus X: Potentially a new and undescribed species of *Tyrannosaurus,* this animal is found in the same sediments as *T. rex.* Its skull is different from *T. rex*'s in both proportion and morphology.

Ulna: One of the two bones of the lower arm; its partner is the radius.

U.S. Forest Service: A branch of the Department of Agriculture whose duties are to manage public forest and grasslands.

Ventral: Of, or pertaining to, the underside or belly.

Vertebrate: In simple terms, an animal with a backbone.

Acknowledgments

A life's work is never done alone. This particular project claims its shape thanks to a day of used-bookstore hopping with the inspiring Robert Bakker and Constance Clark. Thanks for your vision. Throughout years of drafts, meat was added to this story's bones because one small group never said no to research inquiries. In alphabetical order: Patrick Duffy, Debbie Erickson, Bob Farrar, Neal Larson, and Marion Zenker.

When a life's work is challenged by circumstances calling for extraordinary sacrifices, the contributions made by family, friends, and workmates increase exponentially. In our work with dinosaurs and the court system, assistance fell into very different categories, each of extreme importance.

The Community

Families and workmates, dear friends, townsfolk and public servants supported us for months and years on end. Now, especially, our own personal friendship—and our ability to complete this project—exists thanks to the encouragement of Peter's wife, Naidine Adams Larson. To our parents—Gert and Neal; Marcia, Tom, and Jack; and "adopted" mother June Zeitner—thank you for your undying strength. Sarah, Matthew, and Timothy—along with your mother, Deni—thanks for staying true through a rocky ride; baby Ella, fasten your seatbelt. The world would be different without Neal and Brenda Larson, Peter's ballast, and their business partner Bob Farrar.

To Black Hills Institute staff, present and past, you never wavered. Especially those who lived through the blackest nights, your hearts and hands made all the difference: Barry Brown, Dave Burnham, Shirley Duwenhoegger, Denise Etzkorn, Kathy

Farrar, Dorothy Fischer, Ed Gerken, Bruce and Nel Hatcher, Lynn Hochstafl, Larry Shaffer, Casey Smith, Diana Theisen, Terry Wentz, and the unequaled Marion Zenker.

Political representatives bolstered their constituents at possible risk to their own careers: former Hill City Mayor and current State Senator Drue Vitter, Governor Bill Janklow, and U.S. Senators Tom Daschle and Tim Johnson.

Our knight in shining armor: Stanford Adelstein. Thank you for trying to bring Sue back.

A tip of the hat to Dan Counter for tirelessly documenting our work on video, and to Lloyd Dobyns and Dan for volunteering their time and media expertise when we needed it most. Love to Kristin's stalwart writing cheerleaders, who never let her quit, despite the odds: Marcia, Tina, Kat, Ellise, Sara and Greg, Bonnie, Jack, Marcy, Ricci, Ariadne, Janet, Kevin, Lloyd, Freddie, Gail and Jon, Viki and Louie, Constance and Bob, and the Bush Artists Fellowship.

Special thanks to Mark Harlow, Terri Stuck, Geri Konenkamp, and Gus Hercules for keeping us upright. And to those who supported us but whom we lost before the story's end, we miss you: Kristin's father Jack Donnan, Peter's grandma Cora Larson, Pauline Adams, Ray Boyce, Charlotte Brenner, Earl Brockelsby, Bonnie Clanton, Debbie and Lloyd Fox, Glen Crossman, Maryann Licking, Ruth Mason, Governor George Mickelson, Wayne Olson, Erwin Ploetz, Bill and Jean Roberts, Jack Sacrison, Mel Spencer, Sharkey Williams, Albert Zeitner, and Leonard Zerbst.

The Science

It all started with *T. rex* discoveries, and especially helpful to Peter's research were those made by Susan Hendrickson, Stan and Steven Sacrison, Lloyd and Russell Fox, Bill Alley, Bucky Derflinger, Kathy Wankel, and Barnum Brown. Thanks for looking!

Black Hills Institute has explored for and excavated fossils over the years thanks to the openhearted generosity of private landowners of the Northern Plains. We celebrate each and every one, and for this project we especially acknowledge those families and individuals whose land produced fossils that furthered our understanding of *T. rex* and its environment: the Niemis, Bill Alley, the Clantons, Dahls, Derflingers, Fordyces, Foxes, Hamiltons, Hausers, Heairets, Lickings, Monnens, Prices, Mel Spencer, the Tumblins, Weicherts, Williamses, Zerbsts, the Standing Rock Sioux Indian Tribe, and our dear departed Ruth Mason.

Friends and colleagues provided essential scientific and technical information for the text, along with heartwarming comraderie. Bob Bakker, David Berman, Brooks Brett, Chris Brochu, Orville Bonner, Lisa Buckley, Alan Charig, David Burnham, Ken Carpenter, Tom Carr, Karen Chin, Bill Clemens, Bill Cobban, Phil Currie, Kraig Derstler, Peter Dodson, Greg Erickson, Richard Estes, Andy Farke, Bob Farrar, Jim Grier, Eberhard Frey, Mark Harlow, Yoshikazu Hasagawa, the late Karl Hirsch, Tom Holtz, Jack Horner, Yoshio Ito, Paul Janke, Farish Jenkins, Kirk Johnson, Neil Landman, Neal Larson, Andrew Leitch, Alvis Lisenbee, Martin Lockley, Larry Martin, Joe Martinetti, Ralph Molnar, Nate Murphy, Gayle Nelms, Mark Norrell, John Ostrom, Chris Ott, Rob Patchus, Elizabeth Rega, Greg Retallack, Keith Rigby, Bill Roggenthen, Bruce Rothschild, Dale Russell, John Scandizzo, Mary Schweitzer, Paul Sereno, Larry Shaffer, Bill Simpson, Darren Tanke, Leon Theisen, Klaus Westphal, Rupert Wild, Tom Williamson, Don Wolberg, and Dave Varricchio.

Additional scientific information was collected thanks to curators, preparators, and private collectors who provided access to specimens: Larry Barnes, Phil Bjork, Mike Brett-Surman, Japh Boyce, David Burman, Ken Carpenter, Zhu Chunlin, Phil Currie, Ron Dahlquist, Alan Detrich, Ron Frihof, Warren Getler, Mike Greenwald, Rick Hebdon, Kim Hollrah, John McCarter, Sam McCloud, Andy Newman, Mark Norrell, Fred and Candy Nuss, Ken Olson, Chris Ott, Altangerel Perle, Dean Pearson, Craig Pfister, Bill Simpson, Gael Summers, Craig Sundell, Klaus Westphal, and Guo Zhouping

For diehard service in the field, and endless weeks of labor and friendship, our hat is off to Black Hills Institute's annual volunteers, especially those who helped excavate the *T. rex*es profiled in this project: Casey Carmody, John Carter, Bob Cassaday, Dan Counter, Susan Hendrickson, John Larson, Dan Lien, Victor and

Dee Ann Porter, Robert Tate, Stan, Steve and Ginger Sacrison, Leon Theisen, and everybody's kids.

The Legal Crusade

To Peter's codefendants, words are inadequate to describe your fortitude and bravery while under fire: Neal Larson, Robert Farrar, Terry Wentz, the Ed Cole family, Jun Shimizu, and your loved ones, who stood firm with you. Deepest gratitude to business associates, friends, and employees who were questioned by government officials, who testified before the grand jury, and/or who appeared in trial.

We trusted our lives to the legal team: Patrick Duffy, Bruce Ellison, Ron Banks, Randy Connelly, George Grassby, Joe Butler, Dan Duffy, Bruce Peterson, Clifford Gardener, Richard Kleindeinst, the late Gary Colbath, and other attorneys, particularly from Bangs, McCullen law firm, who assisted on our cases. Thank you for steering, for fighting, for caring, and for believing in us. In addition, appreciation to Greg and Sara Bernstein for introducing us to the invaluable Gardener; to the Mitchells for the connection to Harvey Cohen, and to Mr. Cohen for pointing us to Bruce Peterson; and to Hugh and Mary Rose for sending Kleindeinst our way.

The prison-sentence support group consisted of those who wrote the two thousand letters that made Peter's stay less foreign (Roy Young, thanks for all those books!), and to the visitors who brightened his weekends (especially the Bogues for their timely trek). Thanks also to his fellow inmates, who made the experience tolerable and even interesting. On the home and away fronts, a team provided Kristin sustenance, a roof, hot tea, a warm bath, and an ear: Marcia and Tom Mitchell, Tina Ball, Freddie Eason, Janet Vogenthaler, Louie and Viki Psihoyos, and Bob Bakker and Constance Clark.

The Manuscript

Thanks to each and every interviewee who sat for questions or told stories over the years, including the jurors, who faced an unequaled task. Our special acknowledgment also goes to representatives of "the other sides" for their willingness to be interviewed, particularly Assistant U.S. Attorney Bob Mandel. Access to the trial transcript was greatly facilitated by the efforts of court reporter Judy Thompson.

Our gratitude goes to Invisible Cities Press for believing in us, and especially to Rowan Jacobsen for gracefully melding two books into one. Through endless drafts of this manuscript, our most fierce editor, advisor, and champion was Marcia Mitchell: transcriber of raw, bleeding, handwritten text directly from within prison walls. Lloyd Dobyns also lent his skilled hand from the beginning—thank you always. Other editors and readers added unique and crucial perspectives: Pat Duffy for legal accuracy; Neal Larson for details and historical accuracy; Jack Batsel for scientific clarity and gnarly line editing; June Zeitner for the big picture; Naidine Adams Larson, Sara Bernstein, and Janet Vogenthaler for fresh eyes; and our reviewers. A special nod to Joel Bernstein for unfailing enthusiasm while searching for the finest story.

Illustrations and art appear courtesy of Dorothy Norton, Ken Carpenter, Paul Janke, Todd Marshall, Michael Skrepnick, and Terry Wentz. Thanks to them, and also to John Lanzendorf for his great illustration ideas. Photographers included David Burnham, Dan Counter, Ed Gerken, Susan Hendrickson, Layne Kennedy, Neal Larson, Marcia Mitchell, Mark Norell, and Louie Psihoyos. Larry Hutson, Neal Andrew Larson, and Sarah Ness helped us with photo technology. Peter Holm wrapped everything together in ICP's design department, and agent Shawna McCarthy tied the bow.

And an unusual thanks to Judge Richard Battey, who gave Pete the "time" to write his portion of this project.

The Dinosaurs

We offer our gratitude to the ancient creatures who crawled out from Mother Earth to live with us again. Sue, Queen of the Tyrants, you are forever in our hearts. Thanks for blowing our minds. And Stan, thanks for sticking with us, and having such a good head on your shoulders.

Notes

Authors' Note
1. Carroll, 1961.

1. A Dinosaur Named Sue
1. Carroll, 1961.
2. Dodson, 1996.
3. Carroll, 1962.

2. Past Finders and Three-Piece Suits
1. Osborn, 1905.
2. Ibid.
3. Osborn, 1912, 1916.
4. Brown, L., 1950.
5. Osborn, 1906.
6. Berman, D., Carnegie Museum of Natural History, personal communication.
7. Charig, A., British Museum of Natural History, personal communication.
8. Cope, 1892.
9. Osborn, 1906, 1912.
10. Marsh, 1892.
11. Sternberg, 1917.
12. Howard, 1975.
13. Howard, 1975, p. 219.
14. MacDonald, 1965.
15. Horner and Lessem, 1993.
16. MacDonald, 1966, and personal communication.
17. Harris, 1996.
18. Hager, M., San Diego Museum of Nature and Science, personal communication; Larson and Burnham, 1993.
19. Floden, J., Leona, S.D., personal communication.
20. Currie, 1993.
21. Ibid.
22. Ibid.
23. Gillette, Wolberg, and Hunt, 1986.
24. Carpenter, K., Denver Museum of Nature and Science, personal communication.
25. Osborn, 1905.
26. Carroll, 1961.
27. NAS, 1987.
28. Horner and Lessem, 1993.
29. Ibid.
30. Makovicky and Currie, 1996.
31. Carpenter and Smith, 2001.
32. Carpenter and Smith, 1995.
33. Ibid.; Larson, 1991, 1994, 1996.
34. Osborn, 1906.
35. Newman, 1970.
36. Carpenter and Smith, 1995, 2001.

3. Free at Last
1. Carroll, 1961.
2. Bakker, 1986.
3. Larson, 1991, 1997b, 1998.

4. Sex and the Single Rex
1. Abel, 1924.
2. Dodson, 1976.
3. Grier, J., North Dakota State University, personal communication.
4. Larson, 1995.
5. Welty and Baptista, 1988.
6. Larson, 1995.
7. Raath, 1990.
8. Carptenter, 1990.
9. Bakker, Boulder, CO, personal communication.
10. Sacrison, Steve, Buffalo, SD, personal communication.
11. Molnar, 1991.
12. Carpenter, 1990.
13. Whitmer, 1995.
14. Bellairs, 1970.
15. Gill, 1995.
16. Larson and Frey, 1992; Larson, 1995.
17. Holtz, 1996.
18. Currie, Royal Tyrrell Museum, Drumheller, Alberta, personal communication.
19. Moratella and Powell, 1995.
20. Carpenter and Alf, 1995.
21. Currie, 1996.
22. Welty, 1990.
23. Varricchio et al., 1997.
24. Bellairs, 1970.
25. Magnusson et al., 1989.
26. Gill, 1995; Welty and Baptista, 1988.
27. Horner, 1987.

5. A Body of Evidence
1. Carroll, 1962.
2. Timber Lake Topic, "Will Hill City Sue become Cheyenne River Sue?" May 7, 1992.
3. Stanley Robins affidavit, 1992.
4. Ibid.
5. Robert Hunt, University of Nebraska, Lincoln, Letter to Sen. Exon, 1991.
6. Schweitzer and Cano, 1994.
7. Johnson, 1993.
8. Johnson, 1996.
9. Carroll, 1961.
10. Psihoyos, 1994.
11. *Rapid City Journal,* "Feds seize *T. rex* fossil," May 15, 1992.
12. Carroll, 1961.
13. *Capital Journal,* "FBI agents return to Hill City fossil firm," Jan. 29, 1993.
14. Carroll, 1961.
15. Getches et al., 1979.
16. *Rapid City Journal,* "Feds seize *T. rex* fossil," May 15, 1992; "Rancher stakes his claim to Sue," December 3, 1992.
17. Duffy and Lofgren, 1994.
18. *The New York Times,* "F.B.I. seizes Tyrannosaur in fight on fossil custody," May 19, 1992.
19. Carroll, 1961.

6. The Young and the Restless

1. Letter to Ed Gerken, July 9, 1993, Exhibit E of *posse comitatus* filing.
2. *Rapid City Journal,* "Duffy calls fossil memo 'a wicked fabrication,'" Oct. 9, 1993.
3. *Rapid City Journal,* "Sue unnamed in *T. rex* indictment," Nov. 24, 1993.
4. *Rapid City Journal,* "Black Hills Institute loses claim to Sue," Dec. 16, 1993.
5. Gillette, 1994.
6. *The Denver Post,* "Dowsing rod finds dinos," Aug. 11, 1996.
7. Chinsamy, 1994; Chinsamy and Dodson, 1995; Chinsamy, Chiappe, and Dodson, 1995.
8. Bakker, 1996.
9. Chinsamy, 1994.
10. Chinsamy and Dodson, 1995.
11. Russell, 1970.

7. Worlds Apart

1. Letter to Ed Gerken, June 15, 1992, Exhibit B of *posse comitatus* motion.
2. *Rapid City Journal,* "*T. rex* fossil finders say government lied," Dec. 19, 1992.
3. Tokaryk and Currie, East End Fossil Research Station, SK, personal communications.
4. Westphall and Ott, Geology Museum, University of Wisconsin, Madison, personal communications.
5. Johnson, 1997.
6. Retallack, 1994.
7. Johnson, 1997.
8. Estes, 1964; Estes and Berberian, 1970.
9. Ibid.
10. Estes, 1964.
11. Bellairs, 1970.
12. Welty and Baptista, 1988.
13. Molnar, 1991.
14. Bakker, 1986.
15. Molnar, 1991.
16. Bakker, 1986.
17. Erickson et al., 1996.
18. Osborn, 1912.
19. Ibid.
20. Currie, 1993.
21. Bakker, 1992.
22. Brochu, 2000.
23. Bellairs, 1970.
24. Ibid.
25. Ibid.
26. Gill, 1995.
27. Osborn, 1912.
28. Gill, 1995.
29. Welty and Baptista, 1988.
30. Welty and Baptista, 1988; Molnar, 1991.
31. Currie, 1985.
32. Bellairs, 1970; Mazzotti, 1989.
33. Welty and Baptista, 1988.
34. Erickson, 1996.
35. Horner, 1994.
36. Carroll, 1961.
37. Larson, 1991.

38. Paul, 1988.
39. "Vultures: The Carrion Gang," Discovery Channel, *Nigel's Wild, Wild World,* broadcast November 12, 2001.
40. Estes, 1991.
41. Mills, 1989.
42. Chinsamy, 1994.
43. Thulborn, 1982; Bakker, 1986; Paul, 1988.
44. Farlow et al., 1995.
45. Mazzotti, 1989.
46. Horner, 1994.
47. Horner and Lessem, 1993.
48. Carpenter and Smith, 2001.
49. Carroll, 1961.
50. Carpenter, 1998.
51. Horner and Lessem, 1993.

8. A Mad Tea Party

1. *Rapid City Journal,* "Fossil case won't go to trial," Sept. 20, 1994.
2. Transcript, judge's chambers, Sept. 21, 1994.
3. Carroll, 1961.
4. Lucinda Fortin, press conference, April, 27, 1995.
5. Carroll, 1961.
6. Ibid.
7. Ibid.

9. The Verdict

1. Carroll, 1961.
2. LaNice Archer, Roxanne Finck, Lucinda Fortin, Jo Yates, personal communications; *Rapid City Journal,* "Juror angry about fossil decision," April 27, 1995.
3. Jo Yates, personal communication.
4. LaNice Archer, Phyllis Parkhurst, Melinda Wyatt, personal communications.
5. Robert English, personal communication.
6. Jo Yates, personal communication.
7. LaNice Archer, Wilbur Bachand, Robert English, Lucinda Fortin, Phyllis Parkhurst, Melinda Wyatt, personal communications.
8. LaNice Archer, Phyllis Parkhurst, press conference.
9. Lucinda Fortin, press conference; personal communication.
10. LaNice Archer, Robert English, personal communications.
11. LaNice Archer, personal communication.
12. Richard Cordell, Robert English, Phyllis Parkhurst, Patty Sharp, personal communications.
13. Patty Sharp, personal communication.
14. LaNice Archer, personal communication.
15. Lucinda Fortin, press conference.
16. *Rapid City Journal,* "Battey denies acquittals on undecided charges," April 25, 1995.
17. Lucinda Fortin, personal communication.
18. *Rapid City Journal,* "Juror angry about fossil decision," April 27, 1995.
19. Ibid.
20. LaNice Archer, Roxanne Finck, Phyllis Parkhurst, press conference.
21. Phyllis Parkhurst, personal communication.
22. Richard Cordell, personal communication.
23. LaNice Archer, Phyllis Parkhurst, press conference.

10. Time to Breathe

1. Carpenter, Denver Museum of Nature and Science, personal communication.
2. Hirsch and Zelenitsky, 1996.
3. Magnusson et al., 1989.
4. Carroll, 1962.
5. Carroll, 1961.
6. Ibid.
7. Ibid.
8. *Rapid City Journal,* "More money sought to renovate courthouse," June 3, 1992.
9. Osborn, 1905, 1906, 1916.
10. Welty and Baptista, 1988.
11. Ibid.
12. Gill, 1995; Welty and Baptista, 1988.
13. Welty and Baptista, 1988.
14. Ibid.
15. deBeer, 1954; Ostrom, 1976.
16. Carroll, 1988; MacIntosh, 1990.
17. Bakker, 1986.
18. Eaton, 1910; Carroll, 1988; Brett, 1993.
19. Bakker, 1986.

11. Family Values

1. Colbert, 1989.
2. Raath, 1990.
3. Webster, 1996.
4. Currie, 1996.
5. Webster, 1996.
6. Varricchio et al., 1997.
7. Ibid.
8. Magnusson et al., 1989.
9. Gill, 1995.
10. Coombs, 1990.
11. Caldwell, 1997.
12. Welty and Baptista, 1988.
13. Magnusson et al., 1989.
14. Ibid.
15. Attenborough, 1998.
16. Gill, 1995; Magnusson, 1988.
17. Welty and Baptista, 1988.
18. Ibid.
19. Gill, 1995.
20. Welty and Baptista, 1988.
21. Gill, 1995.
22. Ibid.
23. Welty and Baptista, 1988.
24. Magnusson et al., 1989.
25. Gill, 1995.
26. Welty and Baptista, 1988.
27. Ibid.
28. Magnusson et al., 1989.
29. Gill, 1995.
30. Horner and Weishampel, 1988.

31. Welty and Baptista, 1988.
32. Magnusson et al., 1989.
33. Welty and Baptista, 1988.
34. Ibid.
35. Coombs, 1989.
36. Gill, 1995.
37. Welty and Baptista, 1988.
38. Gill, 1995; Welty and Baptista, 1988.
39. Morrell, 1997.
40. Raath, 1990.
41. Colbert, 1989.
42. Larson, 1997.
43. Pope, 1990.
44. Gill, 1995.
45. Sanderson, 1990.
46. Derstler and Patches, personal communications.
47. Carroll, 1961.
48. Roberts, 1998.
49. Murphy, personal communication.
50. Roberts, 1998.
51. Ibid.

12. Life after Death

1. Cocciori and Galeotti, 1994.
2. Dodson and Tatarinov, 1990.
3. Padian et al., 1984.
4. Bakker, 1986.
5. Alvarez et al., 1980.
6. Alvarez et al., 1995.
7. Dietz, 1991.
8. Penfield and Camargo, 1981.
9. King, personal communication, 1996.
10. Kring, 1995.
11. Ivany and Salawitch, 1993.
12. Alvarez et al., 1995.
13. Beaty and Goldman, 1994.
14. Norton, 1995.
15. Alvarez et al., 1980.
16. Carroll, 1962.
17. D'Hondt et al., 1994.
18. Johanson and Edey, 1981.

Epilogue

1. Carroll, 1961.
2. *Discover,* "Bargain hunting for fossils," Jan. 2001.
3. Zerbst, Derstler, personal communications.
4. Derstler, personal communication.
5. Carroll, 1961.
6. Welty and Baptista, 1988.
7. Taylor, 1970.
8. Ibid.
9. Faerman et al., 1997.
10. *Rapid City Journal,* "Route to disturb fossils, not ferrets," Jan. 31, 2002, p. A8.

Bibliography

Abel, O. "Die neuen Dinosaurienfunde in der Oberkreide Canadas." Berlin: *Naturwiss* 12 (1924): 709–716.

Alvarez, L., Alvarez, W., Asero, F., and Michel, H. "Extraterrestrial Cause for the Cretaceous-Tertiary Extinction: Experimental Results and Theoretical Interpretation." *Science* 208, 6 June 1980:1095–1107.

Alvarez, W., Claeys, P., Kieffer, S. "Emplacement of Cretaceous-Tertiary Boundary Shocked Quartz from Chicxulub Crater." *Science* 269, 18 August 1996: 930–935.

Attenborough, D. *The Life of Birds.* Princeton, NJ: Princeton University Press, 1998.

Bakker, R.T. *The Dinosaur Heresies.* New York: Zebra Books, 1986.

———. "Inside the Head of a Tiny *T. Rex.*" *Discover,* March 1992: 58–69.

Beaty, J. and Goldman, S. "The Great Crash of 1994: A First Report." *Sky and Telescope,* October 1994: 18–23.

Bellairs, A. *The Life of Reptiles,* Vol. 2. New York: Universe Books, 1970.

Britt, B.B. "Pneumatic Postcranial Bones in Dinosaurs and Other Archosaurs." Alberta: University of Calgary, Department of Geology and Geophysics Dissertation, 1993.

Brochu, C.A. "A Digitally Rendered Endocast for *Tyrannosaurus rex.*" *Journal of Vertebrate Paleontology* 20, March 2000: 1–6.

Brown, L. *I Married a Dinosaur.* New York: Dodd Mead and Company, 1950.

Caldwell, J.P. "Pair Bonding in Spotted Poison Frogs." *Nature* 365, 16 January 1997: 211.

Carpenter, K. "Variations in *Tyrannosaurus rex.*" In *Dinosaur Systematics,* K. Carpenter and P. Currie (eds.): 141–145. Cambridge, MA: Cambridge University Press, 1990.

———. "Evidence of Predatory Behavior by Carnivorous Dinosaurs." In *Gaia (Aspects of Theropod Paleobiology),* B.P. Perez, T. Holtz, Jr., J.L. Sanz, and J. Moratalla (eds.): 135–144. Lisbon, Portugal: Museu de Historia Natural, 1998.

Carpenter, K. and Alf, K. "Global Distribution of Dinosaur Eggs, Nests and Babies." In *Dinosaur Eggs and Babies,* K. Carpenter, K.F. Hirsch, and J.R. Horner (eds.): 15–30. Cambridge, MA: Cambridge University Press, 1995.

Carpenter, K. and Smith, M. "Osteology and Functional Morphology of the

Forelimbs in Tyrannosaurids as Compared with Other Theropods (Dinosauria)." *Journal of Vertebrate Paleontology* 15 (3), 1995: 21A.

———. "Forelimb Osteology and Biomechanics of *Tyrannosaurus rex*." In *Mesozoic Vertebrate Life: New Research Inspired by the Paleontology of Philip J. Currie*, D. Tanke and K. Carpenter (eds.): 90–116. Bloomington, IN: Indiana University Press, 2001.

Carroll, L. *Alice's Adventures in Wonderland*. London: The Folio Society, 1961.

———. *Through the Looking Glass*. London: The Folio Society, 1962.

Carroll, R.L. *Vertebrate Paleontology and Evolution*. New York: W.H. Freeman and Company, 1988.

Chinsamy, A. "Dinosaur Bone Histology: Implications and Inferences." In *Dinofest: Proceedings of a Conference for the General Public*, G. Rosenberg and D. Wolberg (eds.): 213–227. Knoxville, TN: Department of Geological Sciences, The University of Tennessee, 1994.

Chinsamy, A., Chiappe, L.M., and Dodson, P. "Mesozoic Avian Bore Microstructure: Physiological Implications." *Paleobiology* 21 (4), 1995: 561–574.

Chinsamy, A. and Dodson, P. "Inside a Dinosaur Bone." *American Scientist* 83, 1995: 174–180.

Coccioni, R. and Galeotti, S. "K-T Boundary Extinction: Geologically Instantaneous or Gradual Event? Evidence from Deep-Sea Benthic Foraminifera." *Geology*, September 1994: 779–782.

Colbert, E.H. "The Triassic Dinosaur *Coelophysis*." *Museum of Northern Arizona Bulletin 5*, 1989: 71–174.

Coombs, W.P. "Modern Analogs for Dinosaur Nesting and Parental Behavior." In *Paleobiology of the Dinosaurs*, J. Farlow (ed.). Boulder, CO: Geological Society of America Special Paper No. 238, 1989: 21–53.

Coombs, W.P. "Behavior Patterns of Dinosaurs." In *The Dinosauria*, D.B. Weishampel, P. Dodson, and H. Osmolska (eds.): 32–42. Berkeley, CA: University of California Press, 1990.

Cope, E.D. "Fourth Note on the Dinosauria of the Laramie." *American Naturalist* 26, September 1892: 756–758.

Currie, P.J. "Cranial Anatomy of *Stenonychosaurus inequalis* (Saurischia, Theropoda) and Its Bearing on the Origin of Birds." *Canadian Journal of Earth Science* 22, 1985: 1643–1658.

Currie, P.J. "Black Beauty." Tokyo: Gakken Mook, *Dino Frontline* 4, 1993: 22–36.

Currie, P.J. "The Great Dinosaur Egg Hunt." *National Geographic* 189 (5), 1996: 96–111.

de Beer, G. Archaeopteryx Lithographica: *A Study Based on the Bristish Museum Specimen*. London: British Museum of Natural History Publication No. 224, 1954.

D'Hondt, S., et al. "Surface-Water Acidification and Extinction at the Cretaceous-Tertiary Boundary." *Geology*, November 1994: 983–986.

Dietz, R. "Demise of the Dinosaurs: Mystery Solved?" *Astronomy* 19 (97), July 1991: 30–37.

Dodson, P. "Quantitative Aspects of Relative Growth and Sexual Dimorphism in *Protoceratops*." *Journal of Paleontology* 50, 1976: 929–940.

———. *The Horned Dinosaurs*. Princeton, NJ: Princeton University Press, 1996.

Dodson, P. and Tatautrov, L. "Dinosaur Extinction." In *The Dinosauria*, D.B. Weishampel, P. Dodson, and H. Osmolska (eds.): 55–62. Berkeley,CA: University of California Press, 1990.

Duffy, P.K. and Lofgren, L.A. "Jurassic Farce: A Critical Analysis of the Government's Seizure of 'Sue,' a Sixty-Five-Million-Year-Old Tyrannosaurus Rex Fossil." *South Dakota Law Review* 39 (3), 1994: 478–528.

Eaton, G.F. "Osteology of *Pteranodon*." New Haven, CT: *Connecticut Academy of Science Memoir* 2, 1910: 1–38.

Erickson, G.M. "Incremental Lines of von Ebner in Dinosaurs and the Assessment of Tooth Replacement Rates Using Growth Line Counts." Washington, DC: *National Academy of Sciences Proceedings* 93 (1996): 14623–14627.

Estes, R.D. "Fossil Vertebrates from the Late Cretaceous Lance Formation, Eastern Wyoming." *Geological Science* 49, 1964: 1–180.

———. *The Behavioral Guide to African Mammals*. Berkeley, CA: University of California Press, 1991.

Estes, R.D. and Berberian, P. "Paleoecology of a Late Cretaceous Vertebrate Community from Montana." *Breviona* 343, 1970: 1–35.

Faerman, M., et al. "DNA Analysis Reveals the Sex of Infanticide Victims." *Nature* 385, 16 January 1997: 221–223.

Farlow, J.O., Smith, M.B., and Robinson, J.M. "Body Mass, Bone 'Strength Indicator,' and Cursorial Potential of *Tyrannosaurus rex*." *Journal of Vertebrate Paleontology* 15 (4), 1995: 713–725.

Farrar, R.A. "*Tyrannosaurus rex* Walking and Running Speed." Black Hills Institute publication (1995): 1.

Getches, D.H., Rosenfelt, D.M., Wilkinson, C.F. *Cases and Materials on Federal Indian Law*. St. Paul, MN: West Publishing Co.,1979.

Gill, F.B. *Ornithology*, Second Edition. New York: W.H. Freeman and Company, 1995.

Gillette, D.D. Seismosaurus: *the earth shaker*. New York: Columbia University Press, 1994.

Gillette, D.D., Wolberg, D.L., and Hunt, A.P. "*Tyrannosaurus rex* from the McRae Formation (Lancian, Upper Cretaceous), Elephant Butte Reservoir, Sierra County, New Mexico." In *New Mexico Geological Society Guidebook, 37th Annual Field Conference*: 235–238. Truth or Consequences, NM: New Mexico Geological Society, 1986.

Harris, J.M. "Dueling Dinosaurs." *Terra* 33 (5), Sept./Oct. 1996: 2–5.

Hirsch, K.F. and Zelenitsky, D.K. "Dinosaur Eggs: Identification and Classification." In *Dinofest International: Proceedings of a Symposium Held at Arizona State University*, D. Wolberg, E. Stump, and G. Rosenberg (eds.): 279–286. Philadelphia: The Academy of Natural Sciences, 1997.

Holtz, T.R., Jr. "Phylogenetic Taxonomy of the Coelurosauria (Dinosauria: Theropoda)." *Journal of Paleontology* 70 (3), 1996: 536–538.

Horner, J.R. "Ecological and Behavioral Implications Derived from a Dinosaur Nesting Site." In *Dinosaurs Past and Present,* Vol. 2, S. Czerkas and E. Olson (eds.): 51–63. Seattle: University of Washington Press, 1987.

———. "Steak Knives, Beady Eyes and Tiny Little Arms (A Portrait of *T. rex* as a Scavenger)." In *Dinofest: Proceedings of a Conference for the General Public,* G. Rosenberg and D. Wolberg (eds.): 157–164. Knoxville, TN: Department of Geological Sciences, The University of Tennessee, 1994.

Horner, J.R., and Lessem, D. *The Complete T. rex.* New York: Touchstone, Simon and Schuster, 1993.

Horner, J.R. and Weishampel, D.B. "A Comparative Embryological Study of Two Ornithischian Dinosaurs." *Nature* 332, 1988: 256–7.

Howard, R.W. *The Dawnseekers: The First History of American Paleontology.* New York: Harcourt, Brace and Jovanovich, 1975.

Ivany, L.C. and Salawitch, R.J. "Carbon Isotopic Evidence for Biomass Burning at the K-T Boundary." *Geology,* June 1993: 487–490.

Johanson, D. and Edey, M. *Lucy: The Beginnings of Human Kind.* New York: Simon and Schuster, 1981.

Johnson, K.R. "The Geology and Paleobotany of the Hell Creek and Fort Union Formations in Slope and Bowman Counties, North Dakota." Bowman, North Dakota: *Contributions to the Marshall Lambert Symposium* 1993: 56–65.

Johnson, K.R. "Description of Seven Common Fossil Leaf Species from the Hell Creek Formation (Upper Cretaceous: Upper Maastrichtian), North Dakota, South Dakota, and Montana." *Denver Museum of Natural History Proceedings,* Series 3 (12), 1 April 1996: 47.

Johnson, K.R. "Hell Creek Flora." In *The Encyclopedia of Dinosaurs,* P.J. Currie and K. Padian (eds.): 300–302. San Diego: Academic Press, 1997.

Kring, D. "The Dimensions of the Chicxulub Impact Crater and Impact Melt Sheet." *Journal of Geophysical Research* 108 (E8), 1995: 16976–16986.

Larson, P.L. "The Black Hills Institute *Tyrannosaurus rex* —A Preliminary Report." *Journal of Vertebrate Paleontology* Abstract II (3), September 1991: 41A–42A.

———. "*Tyrannosaurus sex.*" In *Dinofest: Proceedings of a Conference for the General Public,* G. Rosenberg and D. Wolberg (eds.): 139–155. Knoxville, TN: Department of Geological Sciences, The University of Tennessee, 1994.

———. "To Sex a Rex." *Nature Australia,* Spring 1995: 45–53.

———. "Do Dinosaurs Have Class: The Implications of the Avian Respiratory System." In *Dinofest International: Proceedings of a Symposium Held at Arizona State University,* D. Wolberg, E. Stump, and G. Rosenberg (eds.): 105–111. Philadelphia: The Academy of Natural Sciences, 1997.

————. "The King's New Clothes: A Fress Look at *Tyrannosaurus rex*." In *Dinofest International: Proceedings of a Symposium Held at Arizona State University,* D. Wolberg, E. Stump, and G. Rosenberg (eds.): 65–71. Philadelphia: The Academy of Natural Sciences, 1997.

Larson, P.L. and Frey, E. "Sexual Dimorphism in the Abundant Upper Cretaceous Theropod, *Tyrannosaurus rex.*" *Journal of Vertebrate Paleontology* 12, Abstract 96 (Supplement to No. 3), 3 September 1992: 38a.

MacDonald, J.R. "The Search for the King of the Tyrant Lizards." *Terra* 4, 1965: 18–22.

————. "The *Tyrannosaurus* Search Goes On." *Terra* 5, 1966: 12–14.

MacIntosh, J.S. "Sauropoda."In *The Dinosauria,* D.B. Weishampel, P. Dodson, and H. Osmolska (eds.): 345–401. Berkeley, CA: University of California Press, 1990.

Magnussen, W.E., Vlict, K.A., Pooley, A.C., and Whitaker, R. "Reproduction." In *Crocodiles and Alligators,* C.A.Ross, S. Garrett, and T. Pyrzakowski(eds.): 118–135. New York: Facts on File, 1989.

Makovicky, P. and Currie, P.J. "The Presence of a Furcula in Tyrannosaurid Theropods, and Its Phylogenetic and Functional Implications." *Journal of Vertebrate Paleontology* 18 (1), March 1998: 143–149.

Marsh, Othniel C. "Notice of New Reptiles from the Laramie Formation." *American Journal of Science* 43, 1892: 449–453.

Mazzotti, F. "Structure and Function." In *Crocodiles and Alligators,* C.A.Ross, S. Garrett, and T. Pyrzakowski(eds.): 43–57. New York: Facts on File, 1989.

Mikhailov, K., Sabath, K., and Kurzanov, S. "Eggs and Nests from the Cretaceous of Mongolia." In *Dinosaur Eggs and Babies,* K. Carpenter, K.F. Hirsch, and J.R. Horner (eds.): 88–115. Cambridge, MA: Cambridge University Press, 1994.

Mills, M.G.L. "The Comparative Behavioral Ecology of Hyenas: The Importance of Diet and Food Dispersion." In *Carnivore Behavior: Ecology and Evolution,* J.L. Gittleman (ed.): 25–142. Ithaca, NY: Cornell University Press, 1989.

Molnar, R.E. "The Cranial Morphology of *Tyrannosaurus rex.*" Stuttgart: *Palaeontographica* 217 (1991): 137–176 and 15 plates.

Moratella, J.J. and Powell, J.E. "Dinosaur Nesting Patterns." In *Dinosaur Eggs and Babies,* K. Carpenter, K.F. Hirsch, and J.R. Horner (eds.): 37–46. Cambridge, MA: Cambridge University Press, 1994.

Morrell, V. "The Origin of Birds: The Dinosaur Debate." *Audubon,* March/April 1997: 36–45.

Newman, B.H. "Stance and Gait in the Flesh-Eating Dinosaur, *Tyrannosaurus.*" *Biological Journal of the Linnaean Society* 2 (2), 1970: 119–123.

Norton, O.R. *Rocks from Space: Meteorites and Meteorite Hunters.* Missoula, MT: Mountain Press Publishing Co., 1994.

Osborn, H.F. "*Tyrannosaurus* and Other Cretaceous Carnivorous Dinosaurs." New York: American Museum of Natural History Bulletin XXI, 1905: 259–265.

————. "*Tyrannosaurus,* Upper Cretaceous Carnivorous Dinosaur (Second Communication)." New York: American Museum of Natural History Bulletin XXII, 1906: 281–296.

————. "The Crania of *Tyrannosaurus* and *Allosaurus.*" New York: American Museum of Natural History Memoirs, New Series No. 1 (1), 1912: 1–30.

————. "The skeleton of *Tyrannosaurus rex.*" New York: American Museum of Natural History Bulletin 35, 1916: 762–771.

Ostrom, J.H. 1976. "*Archaeopteryx* and the Origin of Birds." London: *Biological Journal of the Linnaean Society* 8, 1976: 91–182.

Padian, K., et al. "The Possible Influences of Sudden Events on Biological Radiations and Extinctions, Group Report." In *Patterns of Change in Earth Evolution,* H. Holland and A. Trendall (eds.): 77–102. New York: Springer Verlag, 1984.

Paleontological Collecting. Washington, DC: National Academy Press, 1987.

Paul, G.S. *Predatory Dinosaurs of the World: A Complete Illustrated Guide.* New York: Simon and Schuster, 1988.

Penfield, G.T. and Camargo, A. Definition of a Major Igneous Zone in the Central Yucatan Platform with Aeromagnetics and Gravity." *Society of Exploratoration Geophysicists,* Technical Program Abstract 51, 1981: 37.

Pope, C.H. "Crocodilian." In *The Encyclopedia Americana,* Vol. 8: 232–233. Danbury, CT: Grolier Inc., 1990.

Psihoyos, L. *Hunting Dinosaurs.* New York: Random House, 1994.

Raath, M.A. "Morphological Variation in Small Theropods." In *Dinosaur Systematics,* K. Carpenter and P.J. Currie (eds.): 91–105. Cambridge, MA: Cambridge University Press, 1990.

Retallack, G.J. "A Pedotype Approach to Latest Cretaceous and Earliest Tertiary Paleosols in Eastern Montana." *Geological Society of America Bulletin* 106, 1994: 1377–1397.

Rigby, J.K., Jr. "Paleocene Dinosaurs—The Reworked Smple Qestion." Boulder, CO: Rocky Mountain Section, Geological Society of America 38th Annual Meeting Abstract, 1985: 262.

Roberts, D. "Digging for Dinosaur Gold." *Smithsonian Magazine,* March 1998: 141–153.

Russell, D.A. "Tyrannosaurs from the Late Cretaceous of Western Canada." *Paleontology* 1, 1970: 1–34.

Sanderson, I.T. "Elephant." In *The Encyclopedia Americana,* Vol. 10: 210–213. Danbury, CT: Grolier Inc., 1990.

Schweitzer, M.H. and Cano, R.J. "Will Dinosaurs Rise Again?" In *Dinofest: Proceedings of a Conference for the General Public,* D. Wolberg and G. Rosenberg (eds.): 309–326. Knoxville, TN: Department of Geological Sciences, The University of Tennessee, 1994.

Sloan, R.E., Rigby, J.K., Jr., Van Valen, L., and Gabriel, D. "Gradual Dinosaur Extinction and Simultaneous Ungulate Radiation in the Hell Creek Formation." *Science* 232 (4750), 1986: 629–633.

Sternberg, C.M. *Hunting Dinosaurs in the Badlands of the Red Deer River, Alberta, Canada.* Lawrence, KS: World Company Press, 1917.

Taylor, T.G. "How an Egg Shell Is Made." *Scientific American* 222 (3), 1970: 88–95.

Thulborn, R.A. "Speeds and Gaits of Dinosaurs." *Palaeogeography, Palaeoclimatology, Palaeoecology* 38, 1982: 227–256.

Verricchio, D.J., Jackson, F., Borkowsk, J.J., and Horner J.R. "Nest and Egg Clutches of the Dinosaur *Troodon formosus* and the Evolution of Avian Reproductive Tracts." *Nature* 385, 1997: 247–250.

"Vultures: The Carrion Gang." In *Nigel's Wild, Wild World,* Discovery Channel, November 12, 2001.

Webster, D. "Dinosaurs of the Gobi: Unearthing a Fossil Trove." *National Geographic* 190 (1), 1996: 70–89.

Welty, J.C. "Elephant Bird." In *Encyclopedia Americana,* Vol. 10: 214. Danbury, CT: Grolier, Inc., 1990.

Welty, J.C. and Baptista, L. *The Life of Birds,* Fourth Edition. Fort Worth: Saunders College Publishing, 1988.

Whitmer, L.M. "The Extant Phylogenetic Bracket and the Importance of Reconstructing Soft Tissues in Fossils." In *Functional Morphology in Vertebrate Paleontology.* J. Thomason (ed.). Cambridge, MA: Cambridge University Press, 1995: 19–33.

Index